A COUNTRY UNMASKED

'Are you not aware that there comes a midnight hour when everyone must unmask; do you believe that one can sneak away just before midnight in order to avoid it? Are you not dismayed by it?'

SØREN KIERKEGAARD

Alex Boraine

A COUNTRY
UNMASKED

OXFORD
UNIVERSITY PRESS

OXFORD
UNIVERSITY PRESS

Great Clarendon Street, Oxford OX2 6DP

Oxford University Press is a department of the University of Oxford.
It furthers the University's objective of excellence in research, scholarship,
and education by publishing worldwide in

Oxford New York

Athens Auckland Bangkok Bogotá Buenos Aires Calcutta
Cape Town Chennai Dar es Salaam Delhi Florence Hong Kong
Istanbul Karachi Kuala Lumpur Madrid Melbourne Mexico City
Mumbai Nairobi Paris São Paulo Shanghai Singapore Taipei Tokyo
Toronto Warsaw

with associated companies in Berlin Ibadan

Oxford is a registered trade mark of Oxford University Press
in the UK and certain other countries

Published in South Africa
by Oxford University Press Southern Africa, Cape Town

A COUNTRY UNMASKED: INSIDE SOUTH AFRICA'S TRUTH AND
RECONCILIATION COMMISSION
ISBN 0 19 571805 4

DESIGNER: Peter Burgess
INDEXER: Mary Lennox

Published by Oxford University Press Southern Africa
PO Box 12119, N1 City, 7463, Cape Town, South Africa

Set in 9.5/13 pt Trump Medieval by PeterMac
Reproduction by PeterMac
Cover reproduction by The Image Bureau
Printed and bound by CTP Book Printers

EPIGRAPH   *Neither/Or: Part II*
(edited by Howard V Hong and Edna H Hong).
Princeton, New Jersey:
Princeton University Press, 1967, page 160.

Advance praise for

A COUNTRY UNMASKED

'Of the many efforts that have been made in recent years to confront the crimes of the past, the South African Truth and Reconciliation Commission was unique in putting both the victims and the perpetrators in the spotlight. Alex Boraine was one of the main architects of the Commission and, together with Archbishop Desmond Tutu, he led its work ... *A Country Unmasked* is a powerful book. It deserves to be read by anyone concerned about contemporary South Africa or about how to reveal truth and do justice in a turbulent political context.'

ARYEH NEIER,
co-founder of Human Rights Watch and President of the Open Society Institute, New York

'This is a very good book ... and will be around for a long while to come ... The chapter on reconciliation is quite superb and the best thing I have read on the subject.'

DESMOND TUTU,
former Archbishop of Cape Town and chairperson of the TRC

'This is a compelling and frank inside account of the Truth and Reconciliation Commission by one of its chief architects. It will substantially advance the debate on transitional justice. It is essential reading for everyone interested in the subject.'

RICHARD GOLDSTONE,
Justice of the Constitutional Court of South Africa and former Chief Prosecutor of the International War Crimes Tribunal for the Former Yugoslavia in The Hague

'This is the kind of book that should come out of every Truth Commission ... It deals thoroughly with historical contexts, exposes the wrestling within the commission with these issues and finally links the South African attempts to international thinking ... [A]lways relevant, always with understanding but never vindictive.'

ANTJIE KROG,
poet, journalist, and award-winning author of
Country of my Skull

'Of the growing number of works appearing in the aftermath of the South African TRC process this is bound to be one of the few really indispensable texts. Alex Boraine took the lead in launching the idea of a truth commission in South Africa; as Deputy Chair of the Commission he was also responsible for making it actually work. *A Country Unmasked* is his uniquely authoritative account of this profound and contested national experiment in truth, justice and reconciliation which might now serve as a model from the Balkans and Northern Ireland to Indonesia and Rwanda/Burundi. It ... provides his interpretations of (and justifications for) key controversial issues and crucial decisions and incidents which in one way or another go to the heart of the Commission's work ... [T]he chapters on exchanging amnesty for truth and on the problems of reconciliation will stand as authoritative assessments of the special contributions of the South African TRC to the international field of comparative transitional justice. No doubt not everyone will agree with Boraine's version of the TRC's significance, but no serious analyst will be able to ignore it.'

ANDRÉ DU TOIT,
Professor of Political Studies, University of Cape Town

'In the edifice of everything that has already been written, and is still bound to be written, about South Africa's Truth and Reconciliation Commission, *A Country Unmasked* is the missing cornerstone. Written with controlled passion, both brilliant and moving, it offers not only an indispensable inside view but places the entire exercise of the Commission from its inception to its possible consequences within a broad historical, political and philosophical framework. Straddling the divide between personal experience and broad perspective, it impresses the reader not only with its incisiveness and perception but with its acute sense of balance and fairness. For anyone interested in South Africa today, and in the larger human and social problem of dealing with the past in order to face the future, Alex Boraine's book is required reading.'

ANDRÉ BRINK,
award-winning South African author

'Boraine writes, not from the ringside, as it were, but from the ring itself; ... not as a participant in the conflict itself, but more as a referee from a position of deep involvement in the exercise which the country was going through. His vantage position lends a special quality to the intensely emotional story he tells; the manner in which he articulates that time in our history makes this an enormously valuable contribution in the account of our nation in travail.'

Pius Langa,
deputy president of the Constitutional Court

'Boraine ... combines dispassionate analysis with passionate involvement, in trying to develop an analytical framework that can be applied, on a comparative basis, to other countries struggling to come to terms with the past. Essential reading for those who grapple with this problem.'

Frederik Van Zyl Slabbert,
political consultant

'At the end of an incredible journey of recollection, analysis and insight, we are left deeply affected.'

Njabulo Ndebele,
Vice Chancellor of the University of Cape Town

'With wide exposure to conflicts elsewhere and steeped in the international human rights literature, Boraine evokes the rich texture of the South African transition that elevated its victim affirmation and qualified amnesty to a global model ... The portrayal of P.W. Botha and Winnie Madikizela-Mandela as two extremes of a brutalising polarisation perceptively illustrates that atrocities recognise no colour line.'

Heribert Adam,
Simon Fraser University, Vancouver, Canada

'Boraine has written a powerful, insightful account of the political turbulence, the social ramifications and the profound moral dilemmas that accompanied the birth, practice and completion of the work of the Commission. With considerable deftness and commendable honesty, combining the literary skills of the essayist with the analytical mind of a social scientist, he records a deeply personal narrative of the experiences of the Commission and the intense and unpredictable journey covered by its members as they heard the heart-wrenching stories of brutality and oppression.'

Rajeev Bhargava,
Centre for Political Studies, Jawaharlal Nehru University, New Delhi

To Jenny

Contents

Abbreviations

ANC   African National Congress
Apla   Azanian People's Liberation Army
Armscor   Armaments Development Corporation
Azapo   Azanian People's Organisation
Cosas   Congress of South African Students
Cosatu   Congress of South African Trade Unions
DP   Democratic Party
FF   Freedom Front
IDASA   Institute for a Democratic Alternative for South Africa
IFP   Inkatha Freedom Party
IRA   Irish Republican Army
KZP   KwaZulu Police
MDM   Mass Democratic Movement
MK   Umkhonto weSizwe
MP   member of Parliament
NEC   National Executive Committee
NGO   non-governmental organisation
NIACRO   Northern Ireland Association for the Care and
    Resettlement of Offenders
NP   National Party
OSCE   Organisation for Security and Cooperation in Europe
PAC   Pan African Congress
SAAF   South African Air Force
SABC   South African Broadcasting Corporation
SACP   South African Communist Party
SADF   South African Defence Force
SAP   South African Police
SASO   South African Students' Organisation
SSC   State Security Council
SDU   self-defence unit
TRC   Truth and Reconciliation Commission
UDF   United Democratic Front
USIP   United States Institute for Peace

Acknowledgements

It all started when Kate McCallum suggested to me that I should write a book on the Truth and Reconciliation Commission and said that Oxford University Press would like to publish it. Thus began a very enjoyable and creative relationship with the publishing house. I have been wonderfully assisted by an excellent team and in particular Mary Reynolds and Robert Plummer who were quite invaluable in their work on the project. The book owes a great deal to their many suggestions, and Robert's tough and erudite editing deserves the highest praise.

It is impossible to do justice to all who have assisted me over the last year or more but I must at least try to record my appreciation and thanks to some key people. Dullah Omar, Kader Asmal, and Albie Sachs were among those who inspired many of the thoughts and ideas which I jotted down in my diary in the earliest days of the lead-up to the Commission. Some very good friends were a constant source of inspiration and encouragement. They include André du Toit, Charles Villa-Vicencio, John de Gruchy, Mike Savage, Richard Goldstone, Heribert Adam, and Kogila Moodley. In the midst of a very difficult time, Van Zyl and Jane Slabbert opened their hearts and home to me, providing a bed, good food, and good wine, which enabled me to keep going.

Those who read the manuscript and sent invaluable comments and suggestions included Albie Sachs, André

Brink, André du Toit, Antjie Krog, Desmond Tutu, Leon Wessels, Njabulo Ndebele, Pius Langa, Richard Goldstone, and Van Zyl Slabbert, as well as Aryeh Neier and George Mitchell in the USA, Heribert Adam and Kogila Moodley in Canada, and Rajeev Bhargava in India.

After I completed my work on the Commission I was offered a Visiting Fellowship to the School of Law at New York University and I was immediately made to feel at home and was offered the assistance of an outstanding library. I also made a number of new friends. John Sexton, Norman Dorsen, Debra la Morte, and Harvey Dale were among those who offered guidance and warm hospitality. My colleagues at NYU were unfailingly generous in their friendship and advice. I later taught at the School of Law and I want to pay tribute to the class of 2000, who challenged and inspired me in so many different ways. Cathy Amirfar was especially helpful.

Jenny and I also spent time with people in New York who provided friendship and assistance. They included Bob and Helen Bernstein, Dawn and Bert Horwitz, Vincent Mai, Don and Peggy Shriver, Sandy and Cynthia Levinson, Aryeh Neier, Paul and Jo van Zyl, Priscilla Hayner, and so many more.

In the course of writing this book I visited a number of countries which were experiencing similar transitions to South Africa's. In responding to their requests for assistance and advice, I was in turn assisted by their commitment and courage. I think especially of David Wall, Oliver Wilkinson, and Harold Good in Belfast, John Healy in Dublin, Sonya Licht in Belgrade, and many, too numerous to mention, in Bosnia and Indonesia.

I also want to acknowledge financial assistance received from the Carnegie Corporation of New York and the Andrew W. Mellon Foundation.

Those who know me best will not be surprised when I say that without the assistance, encouragement, and criticism of Paddy Clark the book would never have been written. She has been a secretary, an assistant, a researcher, and a marvellous friend who made the project her very own and without whom I could never have completed the manuscript.

I have dedicated this book to my wife, Jenny. She has been constant in her loyalty and solidarity throughout our life together, a lover and friend who endured the many absences, the fixation with research and writing for so long, with understanding and support. Our home was a refuge of peace and serenity in the demanding world of the Commission and the writing of the book. This book would never have seen the light of day without her remarkable commitment to me and to our family. We are lucky not only in our life together but in our common commitment to justice and reconciliation. My children and their children brought great joy at times when the going was rough, and they never complained about my inability to give them the time and attention which they so richly deserve. I have been greatly blessed in my family and in my friends.

ALEX BORAINE
Cape Town
August 2000

Introduction

WHAT FOLLOWS IS a story. It is my account of the genesis, establishment, and life of South Africa's Truth and Reconciliation Commission. The official account is contained in the five-volume report published in October 1998. My account is seen from my own vantage point and therefore is influenced by my own experiences, observations, participation, feelings, prejudices, biases, and the like. It is a different story from that told, and still to be told, by other commissioners, committee members, and staff. It is a different story from that told by observers, onlookers, academics, and critics. It is an insider's story which arises out of the white heat of traumatic and often heart-wrenching disclosures from victims, survivors, and perpetrators alike. At times it is a careful attempt to deal with the facts – dates, times, events. At others it is my personal interpretation of those events, so it is often descriptive, controversial, and anecdotal, as well as reflective and analytical. Without claiming too much, my story, which relies on public documents but also on my personal diary, is a many-faceted truth-telling which attempts to share the journey we undertook to come to terms with our past.

In the official report we describe our wrestling with truth-seeking in a fourfold manner. There we distinguish between factual or forensic truth, personal or narrative truth, social truth, and healing or restorative truth. My story attempts to reflect all four of these, but I readily acknowledge that this is not the whole truth of the

Commission's work. Nor indeed did the Commission itself find the whole truth. Truth requires a perpetual search and many others have contributed and will contribute to the overall truth of what has made South Africa what it is today.

In telling the story of the TRC, I have leant heavily on the stories told to us by victims and survivors of apartheid, as well as by the perpetrators. This book, therefore, is all about stories as seen through my eyes and heard through my ears, and should therefore be weighed up in the context of wider accounts that others have offered and accounts yet to be written. I stand by my story but acknowledge that it is only a fragment of the overall experience of so many. I have tried to enter into a dialogue with those who came to the Commission.

The ugliness of many of the stories which assaulted our ears and our imaginations can only be described as evil, so abnormal and inexplicable were they. Yet, despite the weariness of the constant pressure, despite the tawdriness and horror of the unfolding drama, I have come through the experience with hope and confidence in the future of humankind and South Africa in particular. I share the vision of Vaclav Havel, who, when he was President of the Czech and Slovak Federal Republic, offered these words at the Oslo conference 'The Anatomy of Hate' in 1990:

> I am not an optimist because I am not sure that every-
> thing ends well, nor am I a pessimist because I am not
> sure that everything ends badly. I just carry hope in
> my heart. Hope is not a feeling of certainty that every-
> thing ends well. Hope is just a feeling that life and
> work have a meaning. It is not an estimate of the state
> of the world. It is something that you either have
> or you don't, regardless of the state of the world that
> surrounds you. It is a dimension of human existence.[1]

I would go a little further than Havel, however, and say that the hope that I have is not 'just a feeling that life and work have a meaning'. My hope and my optimism stem not from my feelings about the world, nor indeed from a conviction that things will get better, that wars will cease,

[2]

that we will come to our senses and live on earth as brothers and sisters instead of enemies at each other's throats. On the contrary, I agree with sentiments expressed by Albert Einstein. His photographer, Philippe Halsman, who took the legendary photograph of the scientist in 1947 which was featured on the cover of *Time* magazine, asked Einstein, 'So you don't believe there will ever be peace?' He asked this as he released the camera's shutter. 'Einstein's eyes had a look of immense sadness', Halsman recalled, 'a question and a reproach in them. He answered, "No, as long as there will be man there will be war."'[2]

Nevertheless, I still believe that goodness and beauty, compassion and new beginnings, can triumph over the evil which seems to be all-pervasive. The 'nevertheless' arises not from my own feelings but from the courage and the generosity of spirit of those South Africans who had been hurt the most and who had been regarded and treated as less than human. I listened in awe as many of the tortured, the mourning, the insulted, the damaged, and the poor shared with us not only their experiences as victims but their triumph as survivors. More than that, many expressed their willingness to forsake revenge and commit themselves to forgiveness and reconciliation. It is this truth which gives me hope for the future.

The 'nevertheless' stems also from watching Desmond Tutu and my fellow commissioners agonising over and rising above the sordid history of our country, and, as wounded people themselves, offering healing and comfort to those who came to us with their dark and painful stories. I also witnessed the courage of a commission which despite all its weaknesses and shortcomings dared to stand up to the former regime and the powerful ANC government.

The story I have tried to tell, therefore, is a personal account of hope breaking the bonds of hopelessness and goodness triumphing over evil, through truth-telling and accountability.

South Africa, like so many other countries, was faced with a past blighted by gross human rights violations which had occurred during centuries of colonialism, racism, and repression. Like many other countries, South Africa also debated how to deal with the past. Timothy Garton Ash reminds us that 'There is the old wisdom of the Jewish tradition: to remember is the secret of redemption.'[3] George Santayana, so often quoted in relation to Nazism and the Holocaust, said, 'Those who forget the past are condemned to repeat it.'[4] Cathleen Smith, in her book *Remembering Stalin's Victims*, quotes Lev Tolstoy along the same lines:

> People say why recall the past? What is the good of remembering what has been swept away? What is the good of irritating the nation? How can one ask such questions? If I suffered from a serious and dangerous disease and recovered or was cured from it, I would recollect the fact with joy. I would be disturbed by it only if I was still ill or if I'd taken a turn for the worse and wanted to deceive myself.[5]

On the other hand, there are powerful voices that urge that the way to deal with the past is to forget and to move on. To be fair to those who argue this way, for many of them it is not a question of ignoring the atrocities that have been committed so much as a concern to consolidate and protect our newly emerging democracy. Of course there are some who simply wish to ignore the past because of their own involvement in it. But there is a defensible position which calls for moving on into the new future and not allowing the past to destroy or inhibit the new democracy. Garton Ash refers to this school of thought:

> There is the profound insight of the historian Ernest Renan that every nation is a community both of shared memory and shared forgetting. 'Forgetting', writes Renan, 'and I would say even historical error, is an essential factor in the history of a nation.' Historically, the advocates of forgetting are many and impressive. They range from Cicero in 44 BC, demanding just two days after Caesar's murder that the memory of past discord be consigned to 'eternal oblivion', to

[4]

Winston Churchill in his Zurich speech two thousand years later, recalling Gladstone's appeal for a 'blessed act of oblivion' between former enemies.[6]

Professor Bruce Ackerman of Yale University has strongly criticised those who 'squander moral capital in an ineffective effort to right past wrongs – creating martyrs and fostering political alienation, rather than contributing to a genuine sense of vindication'. Indeed, he says, 'moral capital' is better spent in educating the population in the limits of the law rather than in engaging in a 'quixotic quest after the mirage of corrective justice'. He cautions that any attempts to engage in corrective justice will generate 'the perpetuation of moral arbitrariness and the creation of a new generation of victims because of the inevitable deviations from due process that would attach to trials'.[7]

Some South Africans argued very strenuously for amnesia, but the overwhelming majority were anxious to come to terms with our past and then to move on. We accepted that it was necessary to turn the page of history but first we needed to read that page. As a fellow commissioner, Mary Burton, put it, 'We must wipe the slate clean but we haven't even written on the slate yet!'[8]

The prevailing view was that, even if we wanted to, we could not ignore the past. Shari Motro, one of my students at the New York University School of Law, makes this point very powerfully when she quotes Uri Savir, an Israeli negotiator, who refers to the peace talks with the Palestinians. The first important watershed in the talks, recounts Savir, came on the day when he and Palestinian negotiator Abu Ala arrived at their first understanding – never to argue about the past:

> I ... told him: 'You are a threat, because you want to live in my home. In my house.'
> 'Where are you from?' he asked.
> 'Jerusalem,' I replied.
> 'So am I,' he continued, somberly. 'Where is your father from?'

'He was born in Germany.'

'Mine was born in Jerusalem and still lives there.'

'Why don't you ask about my grandfathers and their forebears? We could go back to King David,' I said, making no effort to hide my anger. 'I'm sure we can debate the past for years and never agree. Let's see if we can agree about the future.'

'Fine,' he said, barely above a mumble.

We had arrived at our first understanding. Never again would we argue about the past. This was an important step, for it moved us beyond an endless wrangle over right and wrong. Discussing the future would mean reconciling two rights, not readdressing ancient wrongs.[9]

Further on in her essay, however, Motro quotes Uri Savir again:

Most surprising to me were the many defenses we shared: suspicion, cynicism, defensive humor, deep feelings of historical deprivation.

'You know why we don't like you?' I asked Abu Ala one evening. 'It's because you remind us of ourselves.'

'Really!' he replied. 'That's also my problem with you!'

'Perhaps it's because we're the sons of suffering peoples.'

'And perhaps it's because we're from the same place,' he said, never forgetting – or letting me forget – that we both came from Jerusalem.[10]

For the Israelis, for the Palestinians, and for South Africans, dealing with the past is inescapable if we are working towards a peaceful future.

Very early on in the reform process in South Africa, the ANC and civil society stressed that the past could not be ignored and that accountability was a prerequisite for a human rights culture. To ignore the past is to perpetuate victimhood. We were aware that many countries continue to be haunted by their past. Contemporary examples are the culpability of Switzerland and the Swiss bank in the Holocaust, and Japan's use of 'comfort women' during the Second World War. For the sake of justice, for stability and the restoration of dignity to victims, there must be accountability for the past. And as an added benefit, such accountability could be a deterrent to those who might be tempted in the future to engage in gross human rights violations.

A more pointed question with which South Africa wrestled, however, was what form that accountability should take. There were many who supported the international demand for the punishment of the perpetrators. Others argued as strongly that to go this route would be impossible and even dangerous for the country. The establishment of the Truth and Reconciliation Commission in South Africa, while not a direct product of the negotiating process which led to a new, democratic dispensation, was certainly very deeply influenced by that process. In particular, the postamble of the Interim Constitution, which made provision for a limited form of amnesty, was a powerful impetus towards the establishment of the Commission. One alternative would have been blanket amnesty, which was unacceptable. Another would have been criminal trials, which would have been unworkable. Simply put, it was impossible for the ANC in particular to accept the protection of the security services throughout the negotiating process and then to say to them, 'Once the election is over we are going to prosecute you.' If they had done so there would have been no peaceful election. It is as simple as that. The generals of the old regime had made that abundantly clear. It follows that there would have been no democratic constitution and the country would have deteriorated into a state of siege with many more deaths and further destruction of property. We really had no choice but to look for another way of coming to terms with the past. We decided on a truth and reconciliation commission which would hold in tension truth-telling, limited amnesty, and reparation. It was on this basis that the Commission was established, and the fact that its

[7]

hearings were held in public was a challenge to denial and the beginning of an acceptance of accountability and a commitment that what we had experienced must never happen again.

Because of the intensity of our experience as commissioners and the never-ending demands on our time and energy, closure was always going to be difficult. It was made all the more so because the Amnesty Committee had not completed its work and still needed to hear a large number of applications for amnesty long after the Commission had to finalise and hand in its report. Over and above this practical problem, closure of the TRC's work brought with it particular and peculiar problems. How does one end the process of seeking the truth? Yet we had to draw a line and accept that truth-telling and truth-seeking cannot be confined to a particular commission. The search for truth and a commitment to truth must be undertaken by the entire nation: ordinary people, government agencies, poets, writers, historians, academics, and whoever cares about the future. The Commission has given a focus to what must now become a common endeavour. Transparency, accountability, and truth are essential ingredients in any nation which seeks integrity, the consolidation of democracy, and a culture of human rights. So the search hasn't ended; it has simply deepened and broadened to include all concerned South African citizens.

How do we end the elusive search for reconciliation? Of course it must never stop, but a single commission made up of a handful of commissioners and a dedicated staff cannot on its own achieve the reconciliation that is so desperately needed in South Africa's deeply divided society. Perhaps the TRC's greatest contribution in this regard has been its strong emphasis that reconciliation is never easy, is never cheap, and remains a constant challenge. In our work we have discovered a few building blocks on which many other institutions, structures, and individuals will be able to build. Reconciliation is a process which engaged the energy of the Commission but will always remain the responsibility of the entire nation.

[8]

Closure has taken place for many of the people who appeared before us. Many of the victims and survivors expressed in dramatic language their longing to put the past behind them and to regain control over their lives. Many publicly testified that appearing before the Commission put an end to 'the nightmares of isolation' that had haunted them. Many others told us that for the first time since losing their loved ones they could sleep at night. Yet others told of a 'broken heart which had been healed'. Some specifically expressed relief at knowing the truth, even though it was so painful for them. For others, closure did not come and will not come until they know the truth of their loss and their own bitter experiences. And for others, closure did not come even when they did discover the truth. The Commission tried very hard to meet the requests and demands of all of those who came to us, but it was impossible to tell the entire story.

In some instances the Commission provided an opportunity for perpetrators to find closure as well. Memories locked in frozen minds were unlocked, bringing a measure of relief and the possibility of fresh beginnings. Many of those who told their stories at the Amnesty Committee hearings expressed their relief at 'coming clean', and expressed their gratitude for the opportunity to show their remorse for past actions.

However, the process will not be completed until all South Africans who benefited from apartheid confront the reality of the past, accept the uncomfortable truth of complicity, give practical expression to remorse, and commit themselves to a way of life which accepts and offers the dignity of humanness.

Yes, closure is decidedly messy and agonising, but it was necessary. Dealing with the past is essential, but our focus must be on building a new future. Our journey together as a Commission was demanding, traumatic, and often painful, but I know I would not have missed being a part of it for all the world.

Closure is a little bit like dying to the old in order for a new life to begin. Those who served on the Commission

[9]

have moved on to new opportunities and challenges, deeply enriched by our common search for truth and healing. We will never be the same again. My heartfelt thanks go to Desmond Tutu and all my colleagues for a very special time in our lives. Above all, I want to thank those brave people who told their stories and made this story possible.

1

The road to reconciliation: The genesis of the TRC

THE IDEA OF a truth commission for South Africa came first from the African National Congress. No sooner was the ANC unbanned and operating freely, and working towards the negotiation of a new dispensation, than accusations were levelled against the party that it had perpetrated human rights violations in some of its training camps in Tanzania and other parts of southern Africa. The response of the ANC was to set up its own internal inquiries. These included the Stuart, the Skweyiya, and the Motsuenyane Commissions, the last of which had the greatest credibility and independence.[1] The Motsuenyane Commission confirmed that gross human rights violations had taken place in the camps during the time of exile. Its report was placed before the National Executive Committee (NEC) of the ANC, which accepted the findings.

The NEC decided, however, that these violations should be seen against the overall human rights violations which had gripped South Africa over a very long period. The way to tackle the party's own violations and those of the state and other organisations was to appoint a truth commission. It is surely a matter of supreme irony that the ANC was accused of human rights violations during the course of negotiations with a state which had been responsible for state crimes and persecution of the majority of its people. It must be the first time in history that a liberation movement, rather than seeking general amnesty,

[11]

called for an independent truth commission so that everyone could be accountable for the past:

> It is because we believe that there must be full disclosure and accountability that the NEC has proposed that a truth commission be set up to investigate all abuses that have flowed from the policy of apartheid. Instead of self-indemnity, we need the whole truth, so that all the victims of disappearances, murder, torture and dirty tricks or their families know what happened.[2]

The NEC outlined the benefits of a truth commission:

> The most important reason for the establishment of such a commission is to get to the truth. The experience of Chile, Argentina and El Salvador keenly reflects the cleaning power of the truth. Thousands of people who gave evidence rarely, if ever, showed a desire for vengeance. What mattered to most was that the memory of their loved ones would not be denigrated or forgotten and that such terrible things never happen again.[3]

The NEC concluded its response to the Motsuenyane Commission's report in 1993 by calling on the government 'to agree, following discussions with the ANC and other political and non-governmental organisations, to set up, without delay, a Commission of Inquiry or Truth Commission into all violations of human rights since 1948'.[4]

There is no doubt that the person who deserves the highest commendation for fleshing out this proposal is Professor Kader Asmal. Asmal grew up in South Africa in a small town called Stanger. He recalls that if he saw a white man walking in the street he was expected to step off the pavement to make way for him.[5] He was strongly influenced by Chief Albert Luthuli, South Africa's first Nobel Peace Prize laureate and then president of the African National Congress. Asmal's early awareness of the atrocities of Nazi Germany internationalised his human rights perspective, and his later life as an academic lawyer informed his view that apartheid was a crime against humanity. As he states in the book *Dealing with the Past*, a major influence on his life was a conference held in Harare in 1987 which focused on children, repression, and apartheid. He describes it in this way: 'It was a moving experience in which about 300 South Africans took part. Some of them recounted a catalogue of violence, torture and obscene ill-treatment of the 15 000 to 16 000 children detained during the state of emergency and from 1984 onwards.'[6] He continues: 'This horrific description of organised torture, ill-treatment and disappearances led to a suggestion that I prepare an indictment against apartheid. I spent two and a half years working on it in the context of an attempt by the United Nations to stage a tribunal on apartheid, similar to that on the issue of war crimes in Bosnia-Herzegovina.'[7]

Asmal adds, however, that the events of 2 February 1990, when President F.W. de Klerk unbanned the liberation movements and freed Nelson Mandela and other political prisoners, put an end to his proposed indictment, because South Africa was now entering the politics of negotiation: 'As a result of these historic developments my work towards the indictment became a matter for the record only and not for consummation.'[8]

In his inaugural lecture at the University of the Western Cape on 25 May 1992 Asmal gave form and content to the ANC's proposal to establish a truth commission once a political settlement had been reached.[9]

It is common knowledge that Kader Asmal, together with many of his colleagues, campaigned for a South African equivalent of the Nuremberg trials. It was only his experiences as a key member of the ANC constitutional panel during the negotiated transition that changed his mind and made him a strong advocate for a South African commission on truth and reconciliation. Thabo Mbeki explains this shift in thinking:

> Within the ANC the cry was 'to catch the bastards and hang them'. But we realised that you could not

[13]

simultaneously prepare for a peaceful transition. If we had not taken this route I don't know where the country would be today. Had there been a threat of Nuremberg-style trials for the members of the apartheid state security establishment we would never have undergone a peaceful change.[10]

IT WAS ALSO in 1992 that others, quite independently of the decision taken by the ANC and the strong lead given by Asmal, began to think for the first time how to deal with South Africa's past. Very few of us had even considered this matter before 1990. Up to that time none of us, inside or outside the country, had the luxury of considering seriously an imminent alternative and therefore the need to address the past. The past was all too present with us, and our major focus was on how to confront the present and transform it rather than to look back to the past. In 1992 a small group of South Africans, travelling under the auspices of the Institute for a Democratic Alternative for South Africa (IDASA), of which I was the executive director, visited several countries in Eastern Europe. The objective was straightforward, namely to witness at first hand societies in transition from totalitarianism to democracy. We visited Germany, the former Czechoslovakia, and Hungary.[11]

This trip made us aware of the devastation in those and other Eastern European countries resulting from fascism and communism, from extreme authoritarianism and the denial of fundamental human rights. But for the first time we began to be aware that there was a new problem in the field of human rights, which had emerged as a consequence of the transition to democracy. Each country was unique, but the new leaders in the three countries we visited were wrestling with the same questions: how do emerging democracies deal with past violations of human rights? In particular, how do new democratic governments deal with leaders and individuals who were responsible for disappearances, death squads, psychological and physical

[14]

torture, and other human rights violations? This last question was made even more complex by the fact that some of the perpetrators were part of the new government or security forces or held important positions in public life.[12]

One memorable evening, several of the South African group sat in a pub in East Berlin and listened for some hours to a senior official telling us about the so-called Stasi files (Stasi is short for the East German State Security, which kept extensive files on almost every citizen within that state). With teutonic thoroughness a mountain of files had been created, and it would seem that almost everyone in East Germany had informed on his or her fellow citizens. Some were officials, others business leaders, labour representatives, members of the clergy, academics, even family members. Everyone, it seemed, had either volunteered to inform for the state or had been pressured into doing so. Late that night the South Africans began to look away from Eastern Europe to the transition taking place in our country with its long history of gross violations of fundamental human rights. There were serious differences between us. Some believed that the only way forward was to hold trials and prosecutions, some felt that we should forget the past and focus on building a new South Africa, while others felt very strongly that on our return we should immediately try to ensure that existing files were safeguarded and made available so we could have a fuller picture of what had really happened in South Africa.

Later that year I visited the same countries, as well as Poland and the Ukraine, under the auspices of the Open Society Institute. Here again, I met many people and attended several conferences and debates on what course of action, if any, should be followed in coming to terms with the past in various parts of Eastern and Central Europe.

At a breakfast at the Taverna Hotel in Budapest with Aryeh Neier, president of the Open Society Institute in New York, my own thoughts began to crystallise. I thought IDASA would be an ideal vehicle for preparing the ground in relation to South Africa's past so that an informed decision could be taken as to what, if anything, we should do

[15]

about the conflicts of the past. Aryeh Neier, who has a formidable and distinguished record as a human rights advocate, urged me not only to consider the examples in Eastern and Central Europe but also to look at the literature of recent transitions in Latin America and in particular in Argentina and Chile. He was then, and remains, my mentor in transitional justice.

I began to do what he had suggested and soon realised that there were a number of instances where the experiences of other countries could be of assistance to South Africa.

With the help of people such as Wendy Luers, Tim Phillips, and Eric Nonacs of the Project for Justice in Times of Transition I decided to plan towards a conference in South Africa on this theme. Another person who assisted me enormously in my initial thinking was a writer for *The New Yorker*, Lawrence Weschler. I read his book entitled *A Miracle, A Universe: Settling Accounts with Torturers*,[13] which focuses on the situation in Brazil and Uruguay. His insights and sensitive spirit helped to shape my own approach.

When I returned to South Africa I discussed my ideas with some close colleagues and friends and with the senior staff of IDASA. There was some initial resistance because of the proximity of South Africa's first-ever democratic election, which was to be held on 27 April 1994. But despite this, and perhaps because of the importance of the times in which we were living and the decisions which would have to be taken after the election, it was decided to proceed with two conferences. The first would be a preparatory conference focusing on the experiences of Eastern Europe and Latin America in order to assist South Africans towards a better appreciation of the complexity and extent of the problem and to narrow the options which might be open to us. The conference was held in Somerset West in the Western Cape in February 1994. Looking back now at the participants from abroad, it reads almost like a Who's Who of human rights and transitional justice. The names are familiar to many who work in this field and included

Aryeh Neier, Pepe Zalaquett from Chile, Adam Michnik from Poland, Juan Mendez from Argentina, Lawrence Weschler, Roberto Canas from El Salvador, Andras Sajo from Hungary, Tina Rosenberg, the author of two excellent books, one focusing on South America and the other on Eastern Europe, Joachim Gauck from Germany, Dimitrina Petrova from Bulgaria, and Karel Schwarzenberg from the Czech Republic. There were also rich contributions from some who had been in the forefront of the struggle against apartheid and some who had experienced severe repression themselves, people such as Albie Sachs, Paizoah Gcina, Michael Lapsley, and Nomonde Calata. Other prominent human rights practitioners and activists included Mary Burton, Van Zyl Slabbert, and Dumisa Ntsebeza. Academics such as Heribert Adam, John de Gruchy, André du Toit, Wilmot James, and of course Kader Asmal were also present.

The contribution made by this astonishingly knowledgeable and experienced group cannot be overestimated. Anyone who reads the Promotion of National Unity and Reconciliation Act which was written months later will detect their influence. I will have occasion to refer back to some of their writings, but let me emphasise how fortunate South Africa has been in receiving guidance from people who have had particular experience in their own countries or in international human rights, which gave us a road map with which to pursue our own quest. In considering models from other parts of the world we took into account both their failures and successes when working out our own approach, which has considerably enriched the concept of a truth and reconciliation commission.

Pepe Zalaquett of Chile summed it up in one of his addresses to the conference when he said,

> A pool of world experiences is contributing to an understanding of the lessons to be learnt about justice in times of transition. For those grappling with these problems such an understanding can point to possible solutions. More importantly, it can help shape the

[**17**]

correct attitude both ethically and politically among all participants.[14]

At the request of the conference delegates it was decided that IDASA would publish the proceedings of the conference and we did this in record time. I was assisted in this task by my two co-editors, Janet Levy and Ronel Scheffer. The book was entitled *Dealing with the Past* and is in its second edition. As we worked through the various contributions I could not help but think again how astonishing it was to be focusing on 'the past' when so much of our energy up to that time had been directed at fighting the present scourge of apartheid. I thought again, as we put together the book, how wonderful it was that we were poised on the very brink of our first-ever democratic election when it had never ever occurred to me prior to 1990 that I would see the end of apartheid in my own lifetime. Some may claim that they knew it was only a matter of time, but for the overwhelming majority of those who opposed apartheid, very few of us ever imagined that there would come a time when we would be considering the problem of how to deal with the past rather than actively considering strategies and options to defeat and overthrow apartheid.

I LOOK BACK in my own life to my work in the church, in business, in politics, and in civil society, and everywhere there is evidence of a wrestling with what seemed to be an insoluble problem. The stubborn mindset of the National Party and its leadership seemed destined to take us not to the brink of a democratic election but to the edge of a precipice. In 1970 I delivered a series of addresses when I was elected President of the Methodist Church of Southern Africa. In one of those addresses I made the point that God's word is never only in the past tense or futuristic, but is always contemporary, timely, for the now. Outlining the many challenges facing the church in the 1970s, I urged the Methodist Church to select its priorities in relation to the major problems facing our own country: 'There is one concern which faces the South African Church with an urgency unlike any other. I refer to the naked and aggressive sin of racism. Racism which is fundamentally a denial of personhood to another human being and is seen in all its monstrous inhumanity of white superiority and imposed black inferiority in South Africa.' I added that apartheid was like a runaway veld fire destroying everything in its path. I urged the church to accept that it couldn't ignore this voracious fire, otherwise we ourselves would become victims of this marauding, invading force. The only solution, it seemed to me at the time, was that the fire of racism had to be countered and overcome with another fire – a blazing love which had at its heart justice and reconciliation. But nowhere in my address did I suggest that we would be able to overthrow the policies of the National Party government. It was almost as if I was suggesting that the church had to be an ambulance, dealing with the victims of apartheid, but never having the power or the ability to stop those who were victimising so many. Indeed, it would seem that my main task at that time was to convince the majority of members of the church that apartheid was a false gospel. Their major complaint was, 'too many of our preachers are preaching politics instead of the gospel'. What they really meant was 'too many of our preachers will persist in urging reconciliation between black and white in South Africa', or, more starkly, 'too many of our church leaders are too critical of the government and should leave politics to the politicians'.

I tried to say then that the South African government in the 1970s had in many ways and at many times declared that its policies rested on Western civilisation and Christian principles. It followed that the government had to expect its policies to be subject to the scrutiny of the faith which it professed. The hallmarks of the Christian faith are love and justice and truth, and these had to be the measure by which we judged the policies of our land. When we looked at policies such as the Group Areas Act, the forced removals of millions of people, migratory labour, bannings and detentions, the suffering which came in the wake of

pass laws, the desperate situations created by race classifi-
cation, the inequity of land distribution, discrimination in
education allowances, and so many others, it was impossible to conclude that these policies characterised love of
God and love of neighbour. Apartheid was exploitation and
therefore had to be challenged and opposed by all who were
committed to justice and truth.

In the early 1970s I moved out of the church briefly
into the world of business, primarily because it seemed
that the church was unwilling or unable to take its task of
combating apartheid seriously enough. There were all
sorts of contradictions in the life of the church itself, and
many were embarrassed when this was pointed out and became extremely defensive. These double standards made it
difficult to confront, for example, as some of us did, Prime
Minister John Vorster when he knew full well that many
church members were either supporters of apartheid or had
decided 'to look the other way'.

While working for the Anglo American Corporation
for a brief two years, my major task was to address the
labour policies of the corporation in relation to its vast
black labour force. This involved proposing reform measures relating to housing and accommodation, wage structures, training, and other personnel considerations. Here
again, I was confronted immediately by an implacable
government which refused to entertain even the modest
proposals put forward to bring about a better deal for black
workers and migrant labourers in particular. To obtain permission to provide additional family housing was impossible. Even then it was a case of having to try to ameliorate
conditions, to make some improvements inch by inch
against laws and regulations which frustrated us at every
turn. There was no thought, certainly in my own mind,
that there would come a time when we would no longer
have to deal with apartheid legislation, when we could
introduce any or all of the changes that we envisaged. The
present was so much with us that our strategies, understandably at that time, were geared towards trying to find
the gaps in apartheid policy rather than considering any

strategy to put the government out of office. It seemed to be entrenched forever.

One of the major reasons why I moved out of the corporate world directly into politics was that I wanted to 'look the beast in the eye'. I wanted to look particularly at the top leadership of the National Party and tell them what their policies were doing, not only in the church and in business, but in every section of the community. I suppose it gave me some satisfaction to speak directly in Parliament, and therefore in the public arena, to John Vorster, P.W. Botha, F.W. de Klerk, and so many other government leaders and describe to them what was really happening as a result of their policies and the implementation of those policies by the security forces. It is for this reason that I was aghast when De Klerk told us over and over again at Commission hearings that he hadn't known what had been happening. As an educated, discerning, intelligent man he must have known. But even if ideology clouded his judgement, he was told not only by me but many of my colleagues within the hallowed halls of Parliament what the true situation was. He was certainly told, I am sure, by many delegations from churches and non-governmental organisations in private discussions and conversations.

But again, in the speeches I made in Parliament during those twelve years, the emphasis was on trying to confront the government with the bankruptcy and the horror of its policies; I little anticipated that transformation would come on a voluntary basis and that the government would move away from the heart of its policies, which saw black South Africans as a major threat to white aspirations and therefore kept blacks where they were very largely so that the white culture and white languages, mainly Afrikaans, would remain pre-eminent.

In 1974 I was elected as the seventh member of the Progressive Party, which was the liberal opposition party in Parliament. We were a very small group which included the indefatigable member for Houghton, Helen Suzman. We probably exercised an influence way beyond our size. The major thrust of our debates was to indicate the bankruptcy, the cruelty, and the dangers of the policies of the government. From time to time we tried to offer alternatives, but they were never seriously considered, and our own response was to focus mainly on trying to tear down this edifice of white power. At the same time, black resistance was growing.

Ironically, the black consciousness movement, led by the articulate and intelligent Steve Biko, was publicly very critical of any so-called opposition in what they saw as an illegitimate parliament. I got to know Biko when he was a medical student in Durban and he often visited our home. We spoke at a number of youth conferences on the same platform. One day he came to our home and as he sipped a beer on the verandah he said that this was the last time he would be there. I didn't initially understand him, but he made it very clear that the time had come for a period of withdrawal between black and white so that we could eventually come together as equal partners. I was sorry about that decision, but understood what he was saying, and later when he and other black students broke with the National Union of South African Students, a liberal, multi-racial student body, to form the blacks-only South African Students' Organisation, I realised that he was committed to carrying out what he had talked about fairly casually.

Public contact between us was now denied, but Biko and I continued to communicate by telephone and by letter, even when he was banned in King William's Town. I saw him then and talked with him about his philosophy and ideas and shared some of mine with him. He suggested only a few months before he was killed that we, as a white opposition party in Parliament, and he as head of the black consciousness movement, together with his colleagues, should meet to talk about what kind of political future we saw for South Africa. Tragically, he was arrested, interrogated, and killed before this could happen.

In a speech I made on 21 June 1977, in debate with the then Minister of Justice, Jimmy Kruger, I traced the rise of black power in response to the abuse of white power. I quoted an African leader by the name of Selope Thema, who said in 1922,

> Today the African is being rendered landless and homeless, taxed heavily and cruelly exploited because he has no voice in the making of laws. Daily he is coming more and more to look upon the laws of the country not as protecting safeguards but as sources of humiliation and oppression. There can be no doubt that the perpetuation of this system will only serve to aggravate the race prejudice which now exists...
> What is wanted is a policy which will permit mutual understanding and cooperation between the races. The policy of 'white South Africa' has naturally given rise on this side of the colour line to a cry of 'Africa for the Africans' and as a result the two races are drifting apart.

And then he gave this warning and prophecy: 'Unless a change is made now, the coming generation will be separated by active hatred and hostility.'[15]

My own comment was, 'How true that prophecy has come since 1922... It didn't start in 1948, the 1960s or the early 70s. This is the conflict which is inherent in the South African situation and with which we have to come to terms if we are going to have any kind of development in the future at all.'[16]

Calling attention to the basic problem of white power, I added,

> What I am saying is that the Government has actually encouraged what it calls 'pride of identity' and it is significant that in many of the SASO and BPC documents, this need to have an identity and pride in one's language, culture and race is prominently featured.
> What I am saying is that the Government has actually encouraged the emergence of Black consciousness and should not be surprised when finally it is actually thwarted in its expression so that it leads to something worse. The thesis is White power, the antithesis

[23]

is Black power, and what we have to struggle together for in this country is a synthesis which will resolve the basic conflict between White and Black power.[17]

In the mid 1980s there was a general state of emergency in South Africa; thousands of people were imprisoned, almost every opposition grouping was banned, and the country was in practice governed not by Parliament but by the State President, P.W. Botha, and the South African Defence Force. Frederik van Zyl Slabbert, then leader of the opposition in Parliament, and I were very uncomfortable at being in Parliament, an illegitimate institution that had no answers for the crisis facing the country.

We had grown tired of being associated with an all-white National Party–controlled Parliament. I had no doubt in my mind that the Progressive Federal Party had played a resistant role when so many other voices had been silenced by the state. But again the extra-parliamentary movement had an ambivalent relationship with the parliamentary opposition. On the one hand they were understandably very critical of an exclusive Parliament, but on the other hand they often used us when they needed us. For example, they asked us to raise questions in Parliament, which we did. They asked us to visit areas which had suffered particular oppression and where massacres had taken place and to raise these issues in Parliament. They called on us when people went missing, to assist them to locate their whereabouts. They often summoned us, sometimes in the middle of the night, when forced removals were taking place. It was an uncomfortable relationship, but I expected nothing different. Of course they could not identify with what we were trying to do; we were white and they were excluded. Nevertheless, there was a measure of cooperation which I certainly welcomed. At that stage our links with the African National Congress were nil. The movement was banned inside South Africa, its leaders were in jail, and it was only later that we attempted to make direct contact with the ANC leadership in exile. Obviously I was aware that there were many people within South Africa, almost entirely black but with some exceptions, who secretly belonged to the ANC but dared not announce this fact for fear of prosecution and worse.

Slabbert decided to announce his resignation from Parliament at the end of the no confidence debate in February 1986. We had discussed this prior to the announcement, and, although I was anxious to leave at the same time, he asked me, as chairperson of the party, to stay on and help deal with the fallout flowing from his resignation. I tried to do this but it soon became clear that I had either to distance myself completely from Slabbert's resignation and the reasons he offered or to announce my own departure from Parliament. This I did a week later.

We had no real plans for an alternative course of action, simply an awareness that genuine negotiation politics could not emerge from a Parliament dominated by whites, and we wanted to make that point as starkly as we could. Our first objective, therefore, was to make contact with the extra-parliamentary movement. We were encouraged by the warmth with which we were accepted.

After several months of consultation with black people in leadership both inside and outside the country, including the ANC, we decided to form a new non-governmental organisation. We called it the Institute for a Democratic Alternative for South Africa. Our major aim was to work towards negotiation politics.

In May 1987, at the first conference held by IDASA in Port Elizabeth, the major theme was a democratic alternative to apartheid, and we looked at the implications of democracy in seven major areas of society: government, labour, business, education, law, media, and the church. This was a recognition that apartheid was not merely a government policy but that it had impacted on every area of life. Therefore the task before us was not only to change laws but also to transform an unnatural society.

It has to be said, however, that even at this time, while we were committed to negotiation politics, we did not believe that the conditions were right for negotiations, but thought that that much preparation was needed if

[25]

meaningful negotiations, involving all constituencies, were to take place. It was for this reason that we decided to meet face to face with the ANC in exile in Dakar, Senegal. Negotiations could not begin until genuine partners were welcome at the table. Our aim was to try to make this happen.

In the very first issue of IDASA's news bulletin, *Democracy in Action*, published in August 1987, I wrote:

> I am writing this message on the eve of our departure for West Africa. I want to stress that our decision to take a group of South Africans to meet with representatives of the ANC falls squarely within the objectives of IDASA. We have already been meeting a wide cross-section of people but there are South Africans outside of our country who are not able to return. We believe it is important to meet with them as well, particularly as these same people have considerable support inside South Africa. If IDASA can make a contribution towards the resolution of our present conflict our efforts will have been worthwhile. Negotiation is always preferable to violence and confrontation.[18]

In October that year, when I was asked why I had met with the ANC in Dakar, I replied,

> The answer is twofold. Firstly, our initiative arose out of a deep concern for our country which is so hopelessly divided and a victim of escalating violence. At present there exists a stalemate. The state cannot govern without a state of emergency and all the state apparatus which is so visible in the total society and in the townships in particular. On the other hand, the black majority cannot overthrow the state by force.
>
> The second reason why we went to Dakar arises from our experience in talking with leaders of the black community and with organisations in those communities. It is quite clear that the ANC is the largest single political party in South Africa, but they are banned. We are committed to the politics

of negotiation and as the ANC are forbidden from returning to South Africa, we arranged to meet with them in Senegal.

We have been criticised that in meeting with them we have given the ANC credibility. The simple answer is, of course, that we met with them because they have credibility, have been in existence for 75 years and their real base of support is not in Lusaka or in London but in South Africa.[19]

We appreciated then that we had no authority and no power to negotiate with the ANC. What we were trying to do was to display symbolically to white South Africans and to the government in particular that the only way forward was for the legitimate structures of authority, namely government and those in resistance to it, to meet around a table and negotiate a completely new blueprint for the future.

However, there is very little indication in our statements at that time that we were hopeful that the government would respond positively. In fact, the response by State President P.W. Botha in particular, Defence Minister Magnus Malan, and other senior members of the Cabinet was to criticise and threaten us, and to accuse us of being disloyal and unpatriotic. Because we had experienced for so long their unwillingness to face up to the realities of their policies, we never imagined that meeting with the ANC and all the encounters that followed would become reasons for a major shift in National Party thinking which led ultimately to F.W. de Klerk's speech of 2 February 1990. Two years before that speech Van Zyl Slabbert had written,

> In politics a mood of cynical resignation seems to prevail; things may not be good but they are better than they would be if things were different. And of course the tricameral Parliament begins another session infusing its annual ritualistic urgency into public affairs; parliamentary debates, votes, columns and reviews reassure us that the democratic tradition is being honoured in some form, even in the absence of any substance. If only the state could succeed in

getting a few 'heavyweight', 'credible', 'good' blacks
to come and sit on the national statutory council, the
picture would be complete and 'the real negotiation'
could begin.

   Nothing is further from the truth. As far as the
politics of negotiation is concerned we live in highly
abnormal circumstances and we are not even in
the proper pre-negotiation phase of politics.[20]

He concluded,

> Those of us who take democracy seriously must re-
> double our efforts to encourage a mood conducive to
> negotiations and to bring about pressure to establish
> the practical conditions which make negotiations
> possible. One way of doing so is to expose the fallacy at
> every opportunity that this government is ready and
> willing to negotiate under the present circumstances.[21]

This certainly was our view of the government at the time
and I suggest that it was the mood of most political commentators who were opposed to it. We imagined that the
fundamental change towards negotiation politics was a
long, long way away.

   In the meantime, in 1983, a major development took
place with the formation of the United Democratic Front
(UDF). Under the inspirational leadership of Allan Boesak
this movement gave new vigour and virility to the opposition to the status quo. However, the UDF soon attracted
the attention of the security police and after its banning it
was replaced with the Mass Democratic Movement
(MDM). Every week, new banning orders were issued
and new names had to be found for virtually the same
institutions.

   In 1989 we began to get a whiff of the possibilities of
what was to transpire in 1990. In May 1989 IDASA held
a conference entitled 'Options for the Future'. We were
beginning to look beyond apartheid, but we still remained cautious. However, Van Zyl Slabbert reminded
the conference,

Once we have knocked the shifts in NP policy as cosmetic, we mustn't under-estimate the influence of these shifts on the political process. The NP is on a slippery slide towards accepting the idea of one nation. The debate about negotiation has now shifted and we are now talking about the kind of society we want to live in and this has placed the Mass Democratic Movement in a very powerful position to influence the debate.[22]

In an editorial in *Democracy in Action* in the same month, commenting on Constitutional Affairs Minister Chris Heunis's superficial commitment to negotiation and his call that all South Africans should participate in negotiations towards a new constitution, I wrote, 'Negotiation politics has become a buzz word in government circles and therefore it is important for us to understand what negotiation really means.' But again the emphasis was on how we could persuade the government that negotiations could work only if they were open-ended and took place on the basis that apartheid could not be reformed but had to be completely abandoned. In the same editorial I stressed that

legitimate leaders have to be part of the negotiation process. In other words, our responsibility should be to work out strategies which would compel the government to move away from mere rhetoric to a commitment in word and deed to genuine negotiation so that a non-racial, democratic South Africa can become a reality. This is the urgent challenge facing all of us.[23]

An honest and probably healthy scepticism still existed among many of us as to whether the government was really committed to open and genuine negotiation. Therefore the last thing in our minds was to talk about the legacy of the past and how we would have to come to terms with that heavy baggage.

Then in 1990 came a momentous change that was to revolutionise South African history: F.W. de Klerk

[29]

announced that the ANC was unbanned and political prisoners, including Nelson Mandela, were to be released. The shift to negotiation politics was heady stuff, and I had to pinch myself to believe that reversing the policy of oppression was a real possibility. Many of us were on a high, although every hiccup in the process brought us down with a thump.

Thus it was that a conference entitled 'Dealing with the Past' was an entirely new initiative, made possible by the successful negotiations conducted at Kempton Park between the key political actors.

SOON AFTER THE conference, held in February 1994 in Cape Town, I was approached by Kader Asmal and Albie Sachs to talk about steps that needed to be taken to translate a conference of ideas into a practical plan of action. The critical question was, how could we put flesh on the decision taken by the ANC NEC in 1993 to set up a truth commission? At the conclusion of the meeting they asked me if I would draft a short proposal for the president of the ANC, Nelson Mandela, with some options which he might wish to consider in relation to dealing with the past. I agreed to do this, and after consulting a number of close colleagues I wrote to Mandela:

19 April 1994

Dear Mr President

RE: Commission on Truth and Reconciliation

It is public knowledge that the African National Congress has called for a truth commission to be appointed as soon as possible after the installation of the new government. However, there has been very little debate on this issue and Kader Asmal and Albie Sachs asked me whether I would put a small group together in order to let you have a possible mandate for the appointment of such a commission, should you decide to go ahead.

I have done this against the background of a very important and useful conference which we held under the auspices of IDASA. It included speakers from Eastern Europe and Latin America who shared with us their experiences of 'dealing with the past' as fledgling democracies replacing totalitarian governments. We are publishing the proceedings of the conference and the book will be available approximately the third week of May. I have written the introduction and the conclusion and I attach copies of these for your information.

I am also attaching for your information and interest a short memorandum on a Commission of Truth and Reconciliation. In this I have dealt very briefly with the motivation, the objectives and the terms of reference which may be of some assistance to you in considering the appointment of such a Commission.

With respect, it seems to me that you have three alternatives: Firstly, for whatever reason, you can decide not to proceed with the appointment of a Commission. Secondly, you can announce at your inauguration the appointment of such a Commission, spelling out its objectives and terms of reference and the reason why you think this is important. Thirdly, you may wish to announce your intention to appoint such a Commission but that your first step will be the appointment of a small task force to investigate thoroughly and sensitively the downside and upside of appointing such a Commission. This task force to report to you by not later than 1 September 1994. The advantage of the third alternative is that it gives you more time to encourage and persuade a cabinet of national unity that such a Commission is in the best interests of all South Africans.

Finally, if I can be of any further assistance to you, please don't hesitate to call on me. As I told you some months ago, I am leaving IDASA and am devoting all my time to a consideration of how South Africa can work effectively for reconciliation and peace through dealing with its past honestly and fearlessly.

On the eve of the election, I wish you and your colleagues every success and express my hope, with you, for a peaceful and just society at last.

The draft proposal which I attached to the letter was as follows:

South Africa is a deeply divided society and a major aim for the new Government of National Unity will be to work urgently towards national reconciliation. It is with this central aim in mind that it is proposed that a Commission of Truth and Reconciliation be appointed as a matter of urgency.

Its major purpose will be to give effect to reconciliation by seeking the truth and reality of South Africa's past.

If it is decided to proceed with such a Commission, it will not be without risk. These risks include at least the following:

1 There is a natural tendency amongst the current regime and ordinary people to avoid dealing with the past and a desire to turn the page and focus on a new future;

2 The energy and resources required to adequately fulfil the mandate of such a Commission could take away from the energy and dynamism required to build a new democratic order;

3 Even an honest attempt to deal with the past could deteriorate into a search for revenge and become a witch-hunt;

4 The focus on past violations of human rights runs the risk of being counter-productive and, instead of bringing about healing to the nation, could actually cause fresh wounds and cleavages;

5 If prosecutions were to follow from the Commission's inquiry, it could tie up the courts for many years to come;

6 It must be conceded that although access to security files would have to be assured, these files could
in turn be violated;

7 Unless precautions are taken, due process could be
ignored and the human rights of the violators could
in turn be violated;

8 Apartheid as a political, social and economic
system has been in existence for a very long time.
This raises the problem as to how to limit the
inquiry because the system was so all-pervasive
and to determine where the cut-off point should
be.

On the other hand, there are compelling reasons why
a Commission of Truth and Reconciliation could
actually assist the healing process:

1 The past cannot be avoided and if attempts
are made to conceal or ignore past violations of
human rights it could make reconciliation even
more difficult;

2 If there is to be a readiness to forgive, it is
important to know what evil is being forgiven
and who caused it;

3 If dignity is to be restored to the thousands of
victims who have suffered under the apartheid
system, then these violations have to be known
and acceptance of this has to be public rather
than private;

4 It follows that if the truth is known about the
victims' plight, then a further question has to
be raised about compensation. It is impossible
to do this adequately without knowledge and
detail of the violations;

5 As others have found to their cost, the worst alternative would be to try to ignore the past, because
the costs of such a cover-up are simply too big;

6 Amnesty is part and parcel of the new constitutional proposal but it would be dangerous to confuse amnesty with amnesia;

7 It is important not only to secure knowledge of the truth, but this must also be acknowledged by the state and by the people of South Africa;

8 There is no guarantee that gross violations of the past will not reoccur;

9 If victims do not believe that their violations have been acknowledged, and if they do not feel that justice will ever be done, then the door is open to private acts of vengeance and retribution.

Whilst it is impossible to ensure that this doesn't happen again, the knowledge and awareness of these violations, the dealing with them in terms of acknowledgement and compensation to victims and possible prosecutions of some of the perpetrators could well assist in ensuring that the long years of apartheid will never occur again in South Africa.

Soon after I wrote the letter I was asked to meet with Mandela in his offices in Johannesburg. It should be borne in mind that this was only a couple of days before the election and Mandela was extremely busy, rushing around the country attending one political rally after another. The meeting was fairly brief, lasting only about twenty minutes. Mandela expressed great interest in the letter and proposal and asked me to make sure that the proposal was seen by Thabo Mbeki, ANC chief constitutional negotiator Cyril Ramaphosa, and Communist Party leader Joe Slovo. In fact, he called Joe Slovo in and left us talking about the issue. I sensed that Slovo's mind was anywhere but on this particular subject because of the political events at that time, but he said he would study the draft proposal and discuss it further with some of his senior colleagues.

I heard nothing more about the proposal, and the election duly took place and resulted in South Africa's first-ever democratic Parliament. Mandela was busy appointing his Cabinet. Two of those appointed were Thabo Mbeki as one of two Deputy Presidents and Dullah Omar as Minister of Justice.

I had come to know Thabo Mbeki very well when he was in exile and found him a man of enormous charm and ability. He is a supreme strategist who chooses his words very carefully, and I thought that I should write to him to ensure that he had seen the draft document. If the ANC were not ready to follow it through, then at least I would know where I stood in relation to my own objectives and ideals. The letter to Thabo Mbeki was as follows:

5 May 1994

My dear Thabo

I am not sure whether the President has shared with you a copy of a letter I wrote to him on 19 April, together with an outline of a proposal for a Commission on Truth and Reconciliation. In case he hasn't, I am attaching a copy of the proposal and the covering letter.

This all arose out of a major conference that we held in February of this year involving a number of leading actors from Eastern Europe and Latin America, focusing on their experiences on 'dealing with the past'. Following that, Kader Asmal and Albie Sachs asked me if I would put together a motivation, objectives and terms of reference, should the President wish to appoint such a Commission. I have also had numerous discussions with Richard Goldstone on this matter.

It is a very tricky situation I know, but I think it is extremely important that we treat this matter with the utmost seriousness and make absolutely sure that we are following the correct procedures in terms of truth, reconciliation and healing. I am particularly concerned that the untold and unsung victims throughout the country believe that a Commission could do them a great service, let alone upholding human rights and assisting South Africa towards a new and better security system.

As I mentioned to the President, if there is any way in which I can be of assistance in this matter, please don't hesitate to contact me.

[35]

I also wrote to Dullah Omar, the newly appointed Minister of Justice, who would, I imagined, have major responsibility for initiatives dealing with the past. I was hesitant to write because I remembered vividly my first meeting with him, in 1984. I was still in Parliament; he was in jail. I had been approached by the families of several people in detention who were extremely worried about their welfare because there had been reports of assault and torture, and even of deaths in detention. Among those who spoke to me was Farieda Omar, Dullah's wife. I requested permission from the then Minister of Justice to visit detainees in prison. At first the Minister was adamant that I could see only white prisoners. I refused and said that as far as I was concerned a prisoner was a prisoner, and race had nothing to do with it. He eventually relented, on condition that I would see some white, some 'coloured', and some black prisoners. I was quite happy to do that because my concerns were with the welfare of prisoners, not with one particular race group.

When I saw some of the prisoners, I was welcomed with an immediate sense of relief to have somebody from the outside bringing messages of love and support, and some material assistance as well. When I went to see Dullah Omar, however, the situation was very different. Dullah Omar is a man of considerable principle, with hooded eyes and a solemn countenance, a formidable opponent who is not easy to get close to. He as a lawyer was deeply angered at what he regarded, rightly, as a transgression of the rule of law and wanted to take the government to court for his loss of liberty. He was not prepared to suffer in silence. It was a very difficult meeting because we had to meet in the company of the prison commander and several of the prison warders. Omar clearly also saw me as a white liberal in an illegitimate Parliament and therefore was not terribly keen to receive a visit giving me, as it were, a certain amount of legitimacy. I gave him a message from Farieda which I think took away a little of the hostility, but he told me quite bluntly that he wasn't keen to talk because it might affect his court case against the state. He was released soon after, so I never had occasion to visit him in prison again.

[36]

Nevertheless, in 1994 I went ahead and wrote to him:

20 May 1994

Dear Dullah

I am very anxious for a discussion with you about your own views regarding the possibility of the appointment of a Truth and Reconciliation Commission. I appreciate that this is a very controversial and sensitive matter and therefore would be grateful for your advice at your earliest opportunity.

As you know, there have been programmes on TV and a number of articles in newspapers. Some while back, Albie Sachs and Kader Asmal asked me to send a motivation for the President's consideration. I did this before the election but so far have not had any response. Thabo, Cyril and Joe Slovo have seen copies of this. For your information and interest, I am attaching a copy of same and perhaps we could discuss this when we meet.

I was gratified to receive a phone call from Omar almost immediately, offering to come and see me to discuss the draft proposal which I had given to Mandela and which Mandela had passed on to him. My response was that he was the Minister and I would go and see him! We met the following day and he made it very clear that he was totally committed to a truth commission. He reminded me that the ANC NEC had made that decision in 1993 and that he was anxious that amnesty, which was allowed for in the postamble of the Interim Constitution, should not be the dominant theme in dealing with the past but that we should be concerned always with victims, with reparation, and with truth. I was delighted to hear his response because it coincided very much with my own views, and from that day on we had a quite remarkable partnership which contributed towards an Act of Parliament creating the Truth and Reconciliation Commission.

At that very first meeting, when we talked about the possibility of a commission, I urged Omar not to call it simply a truth commission, because of the Orwellian overtones of the term, but rather to talk in terms of truth and reconciliation, in the hope that the uncovering of the truth, which could lead to acknowledgement of that truth and accountability, would assist us in bringing about the elusive prize of peace and reconciliation. He agreed almost immediately but said that obviously the final decision about the title would have to be made in consultation with his own colleagues and with Parliament. It may well be that the title promised more than we could ever hope to deliver.

———————

IN ANOTHER chapter I will deal extensively with the question of the amnesty law. But an important point which needs to be made at this stage is that were it not for the initiative of people like Kader Asmal, Albie Sachs, and Dullah Omar, as well as my own contribution, we could have landed up with a general amnesty similar to that granted by General Pinochet in Chile. That would have been a disaster, for it would have encouraged impunity and may even have led to acts of personal revenge. A more qualified form of amnesty had been inserted as a postamble to the Interim Constitution at the last moment. The postamble reads as follows:

> This Constitution provides a historic bridge between the past of a deeply divided society characterised by strife, conflict, untold suffering and injustice, and a future founded on the recognition of human rights, democracy and peaceful co-existence and development opportunities for all South Africans, irrespective of colour, race, class, belief or sex.
> The pursuit of national unity, the well-being of all South African citizens and peace require reconciliation between the people of South Africa and the reconstruction of society.
> The adoption of this Constitution lays the secure foundation for the people of South Africa to transcend the divisions and strife of the past, which generated gross violations of human rights, the transgression of

humanitarian principles in violent conflicts and a legacy of hatred, fear, guilt and revenge.

These can now be addressed on the basis that there is a need for understanding but not for vengeance, a need for reparation but not for retaliation, a need for ubuntu but not for victimisation.

In order to advance such reconciliation and reconstruction, amnesty shall be granted in respect of acts, omissions and offences associated with political objectives and committed in the course of the conflicts of the past. To this end, Parliament under this Constitution shall adopt a law determining a firm cut-off date, which shall be a date after 8 October 1990 and before 6 December 1993, and providing for the mechanisms, criteria and procedures, including tribunals, if any, through which such amnesty shall be dealt with at any time after the law has been passed.

With this new Constitution and these commitments we, the people of South Africa, open a new chapter in the history of our country.

Nkosi sikelel' iAfrika. God seën Suid-Afrika
Morena boloka sechaba sa heso. May God bless
our country
Mudzimu fhatutshedza Afrika. Hosi katekisa Afrika.

In his lecture at the conference 'Dealing with the Past', Lourens du Plessis traced the development of the postamble. He reminded the conference that the negotiating parties realised that something relating to amnesty had to be included in the Interim Constitution, but that they found it extraordinarily difficult to agree on the 'nature, content and status of possible provisions to this effect'.

It is his view, and I think there is considerable substance to this, that because of time constraints the technical committee responsible for drafting the text had to be bypassed and the final postamble was not couched in legal or technical language. 'The central theme of the post-script', he argues, 'appears to be this: for the sake of reconciliation we must forgive but for the sake of reconstruction we dare not forget.'[24]

F.W. de Klerk and his colleagues insisted that the implication of the postamble was that everyone involved in the political conflicts of the past was eligible for amnesty. What I think made all the difference was the emphasis that some of us placed on the need not only to look at perpetrators but to consider as a priority the fate and the suffering of victims during the period of conflict. It was as a result of this conviction that the South African Truth and Reconciliation Commission became something totally unique. We managed to combine a limited form of amnesty, setting out clear criteria, and with no guarantee that amnesty would be granted, with a very strong emphasis on truth-telling by victims, a reparation policy, and an attempt to reach consensus on what really happened during the period under review, namely between 1960 and 1994. This determination, and here considerable credit must be given to Dullah Omar in particular, ensured that the South African model would not only include specific reference to and concern for victims, but would hold in tension both truth-telling by perpetrators and victims and a commitment to restorative justice. In a later chapter we will consider in some detail the matter of retributive justice and restorative justice.

In my first meeting with Dullah Omar in 1994 I brought him up to date with the conference that had been held in February, told him that there was a second conference planned for June, and asked him if he would give the keynote address. He agreed immediately; the idea was that he would spell out in some detail, at a public conference, the intentions of the government in relation to a truth and reconciliation commission.

ON 27 MAY 1994 Dullah Omar announced to Parliament the decision of the government to set up a commission of truth and reconciliation to enable South Africa to come to terms with its past.

He emphasised that reconciliation was not simply
a question of indemnity through amnesty and letting
bygones be bygones:

> If the wounds of the past are to be healed, if a multi-
> plicity of legal actions are to be avoided, if future
> human rights violations are to be avoided and indeed,
> if we are to successfully initiate the building of a
> human rights culture, then disclosure of the truth and
> its acknowledgement are essential. We cannot forgive
> on behalf of victims, nor do we have the moral right
> to do so. It is the victims themselves who must speak.
> Their voices need to be heard. The fundamental issue
> for all South Africans is therefore to come to terms
> with our past on the only moral basis possible,
> namely that the truth be told and that the truth
> be acknowledged.[25]

We see here the immediate priority given to victims by
Omar, and he was consistent in putting the stress on the
need for victims to be heard and for the truth to be acknowledged.

In that first announcement to Parliament and to the
country, the Minister presented the proposals that the
government was considering. They included (1) the composition of the Commission; (2) its terms of reference, which
would include investigating and establishing the truth
about human rights violations and their acknowledgement; (3) fair procedures and adherence to international
law relating to human rights. He said (4) that in terms of
reparation a framework needed to be created to deal with all
claims, especially those based on gross violations of human
rights, with the power to bring finality to such matters.
Even at this very early stage he warned that the democratic
government would have to bear the financial burden. In
addition, he indicated (5) that the Commission would be
appointed for a period of eighteen months to two years; and
(6) that there would have to be a final and complete report
which would be presented to the President by the

Commission, and that this would be a report to the nation which would close the chapter on South Africa's past.

It was against this background that the question of amnesty would be considered. Here the Minister made five brief points: firstly, that the Commission would set up a specialised structure to deal with applications and make recommendations; secondly, that the cut-off date in respect of offences committed would be no later than 5 December 1993; thirdly, that the offences in respect of which amnesty could be applied for would be defined strictly within the framework of the constitutional provision on national unity and reconciliation; fourthly, that the recommendations of the Commission should be referred to the President, whose decision would be final (this was changed later in the final Act, which gave complete autonomy to the Amnesty Committee to make a final decision); and, fifthly, that there would be a fixed cut-off date for applications and that date would be determined later.

Finally, the Minister made a very important point regarding participation in the process of setting up the Commission. He stressed that while his statements represented the thinking within government, individuals, organisations, religious bodies, and members of the general public were invited to submit their comments and proposals by 30 June 1994, before the legislation was finalised. Such responses would receive careful consideration before legislative proposals were placed before the Cabinet.

THE SECOND conference in preparation for the Commission was held under the auspices of Justice in Transition, a free-standing NGO. I had felt that the issue of the Commission was of such importance that I should leave IDASA and give all my energy to assisting in the democratisation of the process and of the debate so that government would have, as it expressly asked for, the best possible advice before embarking upon the legislation itself. This I did in March 1994, and through the good offices of Aryeh Neier the Open Society Institute, based in New York, funded my appointment as executive director and Paddy Clark as my assistant.

The conference was held in Cape Town in July 1994 and was entitled simply 'Truth and Reconciliation'. In this instance the focus was more on South African participation than international attendance, although we were extremely fortunate in securing the presence of Patricio Aylwin, the former President of Chile, who had appointed that country's Truth and Reconciliation Commission earlier in the 1990s. Pepe Zalaquett accompanied him, and, as always, his contribution was invaluable. But the major speakers were drawn from a wide spectrum of organisations and institutions within South Africa itself, and the keynote speech was delivered by Dullah Omar. In a very real sense, the public debate had now begun. When we had met in February many expressed doubt as to whether the new government would have the political will to appoint a commission. Now there was no longer any doubt; the government had declared its intentions clearly and publicly, and the responsibility of all of us now was to ensure that the very best efforts were made towards truth and reconciliation in South Africa.

As with the first conference, the papers delivered, together with an introduction and conclusion, were published. The title of the book was *The Healing of a Nation?* It was edited by Janet Levy and me and published in 1995 by Justice in Transition.

As I explained in my introduction to the book, there were several reasons why there was a question mark in the title. Firstly, I explained that

> there is no quick-fix for the healing of a nation; there are no magic formulae which will instantaneously remedy the sickness that reached epidemic proportions over many years and left thousands of victims in its wake. The healing of a nation cannot be achieved merely by holding a conference or several conferences. Nor can genuine relief be obtained by the

writing of books or even through the appointment of a Truth and Reconciliation Commission! Discussion, debate, analysis and the recording of the truth can be a significant part of the healing process, but only that. Much more will need to take place over many years. The wounds incurred in the long and bitter period of repression and resistance are too deep to be trivialised by imagining that a single initiative can bring about a peaceful, stable and restored society.[26]

In particular I stressed that

the legacy of apartheid includes a badly skewed economy which has left in its wake socio-economic problems of such magnitude that it will take not just decades but at least a generation for any kind of equilibrium to be reached in South Africa. The healing of a nation will thus require disciplined commitment to economic growth so that the alleviation of poverty can begin in earnest. Healing of persons and communities should include, for example, a clinic within walking distance, clean water, housing, schools and economic opportunities for all.[27]

In other words, the restoration of the moral order and economic justice are two sides of a single coin.

A further reason for the question mark in the title is linked to the controversy that surrounded the Truth and Reconciliation Commission from the very first time it was mooted. Despite many reassurances given, a strong stream of criticism came in particular from the National Party, the Freedom Front, the Inkatha Freedom Party, and the security forces. F.W. de Klerk declared that the TRC 'could undermine the goodwill and sense of national unity that has begun to take root since Mandela's inauguration'. In the same speech he warned that South Africa would be foolish if it 'precipitately tore out the stitches from wounds that are only now beginning to heal'.[28] The right-wing Freedom Front expressed similar views, with Constand Viljoen, the leader of the party, warning that the

Commission could become 'a witch hunt against the Afrikaner'.

In reply to such criticism, Omar stated in his address to the 'Truth and Reconciliation' conference, 'I wish to stress that the objective of the exercise is not to conduct a witch hunt or to haul violators of human rights before court to face charges. It is a necessary exercise to enable South Africans to come to terms with their past on a morally acceptable basis and to advance the cause of reconciliation.'[29]

The Minister made a number of other points in his keynote address. Firstly, he paid tribute to President Mandela as a leader who was committed to genuine reconciliation and the transformation of South Africa into a non-racial, non-sexist democracy based on the recognition of universally accepted human rights. He very clearly indicated that this was not a commission he was pushing himself but that 'the President supports the setting up of a Commission of Truth and Reconciliation. The democratic government is committed to the building up of a human rights culture in our land.' It was important that he should make that point, because there were those who argued then and still do that the ANC was divided and that Mandela, in his commitment to reconciliation, had not been keen on the TRC. Clearly this was not Omar's view, and it certainly wasn't my experience when we met with the President on a number of occasions during the life of the Commission. He was remarkably supportive, and determined that the Commission would stick to its task and remain independent of himself, of the government, and of the ANC. He was quick to defend the Commission on a number of occasions. Omar always believed that the TRC was in tune with the new Constitution, which emphasised unity and peace. He stressed the positive character of the Commission: 'There is a commitment to break from the past, to heal the wounds of the past, to forgive but not to forget and to build a future based on respect for human rights.' He also stressed that the Commission and those who would serve on it could not be charged alone

[45]

with the responsibility of achieving the objectives of truth and of reconciliation. He urged all the participants and, through the media, all South Africans to pledge themselves to this commitment to a future based on respect for human rights.

The stage was set. We had learnt from other countries, we had consulted widely, the commitment of the government was clear. Now the hard and detailed work of drafting the Bill had to be tackled.

2

Consultation and legislation: The Promotion of National Unity and Reconciliation Act

VERY EARLY ON it was decided to involve as many individuals and organisations as possible in the framing of the Bill that would give substance to the idea of a truth and reconciliation commission. This decision to democratise the process paid rich dividends. The response was encouraging and swift, and from the plethora of comments and responses a structure began to take shape. Obviously the broad outline would change many times in the following months.

In particular, the Portfolio Committee on Justice spent many hours receiving evidence and debating among themselves the finer points of the structure. This committee consists of members of all political parties represented in the South African Parliament. It was their task to take the draft Bill as proposed by the Department of Justice, and on which many of us had worked, and present it finally to Parliament for debate and decision.

But in July 1994 the Justice Minister was able to indicate that the Commission would consist of eight to ten persons, appointed by the President on the recommendation of a joint committee of Parliament. He also announced that there would be three specialised committees, one dealing with amnesty, one with violations of human rights, and one with the issue of reparation for victims. At this time the cut-off date for offences was 5 December 1993 and a precondition for amnesty was 'full disclosure'. In the constitution of the draft Act the

Commission's independence was made very clear: 'The Commission shall function without political bias and interference and shall be independent and separate from any party, government and its administration or any other functionary or body, whether directly or indirectly representing the interests of any such entity.' The period suggested for the life of the Commission was twelve months, with a possible extension of a further six months.

It was now possible to set out the objectives of the Commission:

1 To establish in accordance with the principles of international law and the Constitution as complete a picture as possible of gross human rights violations that occurred during the conflicts of the past, which took place inside and outside South Africa between 1 March 1960 and 5 December 1993, as well as their antecedents and circumstances, in order to achieve national reconciliation.

2 To gather information and evidence that would make it possible to identify the victims by name and determine their fate or whereabouts.

3 To recommend measures of reparation that would lead to the restoration of the human and civil dignity of the victims of human rights violations.

4 To receive applications for amnesty and indemnity in terms of disclosure, and at any time to make recommendations to the President.

5 To prepare a report that would contain the findings of the investigations conducted and offer objective information about what transpired during this period.

6 To recommend legal and administrative measures to prevent future gross human rights violations.

In summary form, the aims of the proposed Truth and Reconciliation Commission were:

1 To return to victims their civil and human rights.
2 To restore the moral order.
3 To record the truth.
4 To grant amnesty to those who qualified.

5 To create a culture of human rights and respect for the rule of law.
6 To prevent the violations of human rights of the past from ever happening again.

In the meantime the Minister of Justice called together a group of people to assist in the drafting of the Bill which would be distributed, and, after organisations and individuals had had an opportunity to make representation, to put it before the Portfolio Committee on Justice for further debate. The group, which was very small initially, consisted of Medard Rwelamira, a Tanzanian academic lawyer teaching at the University of the Western Cape, Johnny de Lange MP, chairperson of the Portfolio Committee on Justice, Willie Hofmeyr MP, Enver Daniels, Dullah Omar, and me. While the group continued to meet over many months and often long into the night, many others were drawn into the process, including representatives of the Black Lawyers' Association, Lawyers for Human Rights, the Legal Resources Centre, the National Association of Democratic Lawyers, and other human rights organisations. Prominent individuals who also assisted with early drafts of the Bill included George Bizos, Mohammed Navsa, and Richard Goldstone. Albie Sachs wrote a very insightful and wise commentary on one of the earlier drafts.

Important international contributions came from Professor Carl Norgaard, at the time president of the European Human Rights Commission, Helle Norgaard his wife, and Pepe Zalaquett, who was a member of Chile's Truth and Reconciliation Commission.

Throughout this process the Minister kept stressing that it was important to democratise the debate and to include as many people as possible in the process. Media reports showed that there was considerable confusion and controversy surrounding the very idea of a truth commission, and he felt that the more people who participated, the better the end product would be.

To that end, the draft Bill was circulated to leading non-governmental organisations throughout South Africa.

[49]

In addition, the Minister approached me in my capacity as executive director of Justice in Transition and asked if I would coordinate a campaign to reach as many people as possible. Justice in Transition therefore undertook a number of initiatives. More than thirty seminars were held nationwide giving a very wide cross-section of people an opportunity to understand the philosophy behind the Commission, and also to make their own contributions to its establishment. Workshops were held on several occasions, drawing together professionals, lawyers, psychologists, academics, church leaders, and others to consider the full implications of the proposed Commission. In each instance the findings of the seminars and workshops were made available to the small group working on the draft Bill as well as, at a later stage, the Portfolio Committee on Justice. In addition, as was mentioned in the last chapter, a national conference on 'Truth and Reconciliation' was held in Cape Town, which was attended by key leaders from throughout South Africa.

Justice in Transition printed 150 000 booklets entitled *The Truth and Reconciliation Commission*, which dealt with the main ideas of the Commission. The booklet was printed in six languages and distributed throughout South Africa. Four radio programmes were prepared and broadcast on national radio in six languages, and made available to NGOs, churches, and other organisations throughout the country. A history workshop was held which brought together twenty-four leading historians to consider the challenge that would face the Commission in trying to record as objectively as possible what actually happened in the period between 1960 and 1993.

Finally, a project dealing with the documentation of human rights violations was established. The objective was to provide an accurate and professional record of human rights violations which had already been documented, by gathering together records held by various organisations throughout South Africa and in the international community. These records had to be checked, cross-referenced, completed in some cases, stored on a database, and prepared so that when the Commission began its work it would have a very large body of material to process from day one. This project continued until the Commission was appointed.

All this preparatory work undertaken by Justice in Transition would not have been possible without the co-operation of several organisations and above all the remarkable efficiency and commitment of my assistant Paddy Clark.

The Portfolio Committee on Justice, to whom the final draft Bill was given, invited representations from individuals and organisations. After a two-day workshop, organised by Justice in Transition, representations were made to the committee on behalf of twenty-one human rights organisations, indicating their support for the Truth and Reconciliation Commission and suggesting a number of amendments to the draft Bill. A little later, when we consider the evidence put before the Portfolio Committee, reference will be made to this initiative.

Medard Rwelamira and I drew up an administrative structure to serve the Commission. This was discussed at some length with the director-general of the Department of Justice, who in turn made the Department's views known to the Minister. I arranged a further workshop on the administration of the Commission, and a more developed administrative structure was submitted to the Minister for his consideration.

In the meantime, technical workshops, under the auspices of Justice in Transition, were held and discussions took place within the Department of Justice concerning logistics, infrastructure, staffing, and other administrative matters.

In keeping with the general spirit of openness, the Portfolio Committee publicly debated the issues for many, many weeks and these discussions were attended by interested parties. In addition, institutions, organisations, and individuals were invited to submit evidence for consideration by the Portfolio Committee before the penultimate draft was completed. This drew an enormous response, with many leading organisations sending in evidence. Among these were the twenty-one non-governmental organisations that had attended the two-day workshop organised by Justice in Transition earlier in the year. Others included major churches, in particular the Southern African Catholic Bishops' Conference, well-known organisations such as the Black Sash, Amnesty International, the Chief State Law Advisor, the Council of the Bar of South Africa, Lawyers for Human Rights, the World Conference on Religion and Peace, and a host of others. These representations all make very interesting reading and it is clear that the Committee took the evidence of those who appeared before them very seriously, although in the end there were too many questions for the time allowed.

I WANT TO consider three of the documents submitted to the Portfolio Committee on Justice, from the Inkatha Freedom Party, the Freedom Front, and the South African Police, as well as the presentation that I made on behalf of the twenty-one NGOs.

The reason why I have selected these submissions is that the first three had principled objections to the establishment of a truth commission and their main thrust was not a question of detail or an attempt to improve the Bill; it is clear that their preference was that the very idea of a truth commission should be scrapped. The reason for focusing on the recommendations of the NGOs is that without the contribution of civil society the Promotion of National Unity and Reconciliation Act would have been considerably the poorer. It would be an injustice to overlook the extraordinary contribution by representatives of a wide variety of human rights organisations who gave of their time, energy, and expertise to ensure that the Commission would meet the demands, as they saw it, of adequately dealing with South Africa's past.

The Inkatha Freedom Party had expressed its strong opposition to the notion of a truth commission from the very beginning, even before the first draft appeared. In their memorandum they explained that because their opposition was an opposition in principle, they reserved the right to make specific comment on various chapters and sections of the proposed legislation at a later stage. Ironically, the IFP argued that there had not been sufficient debate in the country on whether the truth commission as proposed was the best vehicle for achieving national reconciliation and granting amnesty. This despite the background of wide debate, of many, many months of workshops, conferences, seminars, publications – all of which had been available to individual members and leaders of the IFP, including the president, Chief Mangosuthu Buthelezi. The National Council of the IFP had met in Ulundi on 22 October 1994 and had adopted a resolution which expressed the party's views on the Commission. Firstly, the party argued that it is not the business of government to

> guide the manufacturing of historical truths and that unified government-produced historical truths are often not accepted by the people and open much greater conflicts and wounds than those they are purported to heal... [T]he multifaced soul of our country contains a polarity of truths which no government may express in a unified report.

What this criticism seems to have overlooked is the fact that the Commission's findings would not be a government report as such, but a report of Parliament, representing all political parties, that the Commission would not consist of government members but a nominated group of South Africans from a cross-section of society who would submit their report to Parliament, and that it was only Parliament itself which could accept or reject that report.

The IFP's second major point was that the resources that would be 'wasted on a truth commission' could be used to promote a nationwide debate, an information-seeking exercise in schools and communities, 'so that from this grass root process a real and multifaceted plurality of historical truths emerges which would be the truth of the people rather than the truth of the government'. Here again it would appear that the draft legislation had not been carefully considered, otherwise it would have been very clear that one of the major objectives of the Commission would be to seek grass-root information from across the land, and, indeed, that is exactly what did take place.

More seriously, possibly, the IFP expressed its deep concern about the 'ill-conceived idea of having a truth-finding exercise driven by the confession of those who are in jail and seek amnesty by rendering statements under the spotlight of the press'. This was a very real concern expressed not only by the IFP but by many other parties. Certainly, the enormous media coverage was a double-edged sword; I will return to the role of the media in a later chapter.

A further difference between the IFP's view and the draft legislation was their argument that amnesty should be administered on a judicial rather than a political basis, and, surprisingly, they demanded that amnesty should be granted by courts of law 'on the basis of clearly defined legal parameters rather than on the basis of broad political parameters set out in the truth commission legislation'. I say 'surprisingly' because the IFP refused to participate in the amnesty process and never indicated that they would support such a process even if it took place in a court of law. It was my impression, after many meetings with IFP leaders, that they would have given far more support to the drawing of a veil over the past in the form of general amnesty. This was borne out towards the end of the life of the Commission and since then, in the IFP's argument that a new form of 'general amnesty' should be administered at least in KwaZulu-Natal.

Finally, the IFP was disturbed that the Commission would be provided with powers of search and seizure and powers of subpoena.

While it is true that Buthelezi and other IFP members eventually appeared before the Commission, their general attitude towards it was negative and destructive. In one meeting with Buthelezi, Desmond Tutu and I appealed to him to cooperate with the Commission's work. He was adamant that his party had resolved not to do so and that he was unable to change that. My own view was, and remains, that he was one of the key architects of opposition to the Commission and that if he had made a statement of support this would have been followed by the leadership and the rank and file of the IFP. I pointed out to him in that particular meeting that his refusal to cooperate would have the effect of denying his members the right to any reparation which might be proposed by the Commission and accepted by Parliament. The Act made it very clear that only those who actually applied, either in writing or in a public statement before the Commission, would qualify as 'victims'. He admitted that he hadn't realised that this was so and said that he would look into the matter and report back to his National Council.

Subsequent to that, despite a great deal of correspondence, we never had a satisfactory reply, although it was reported to us that a number of IFP supporters did begin to make application to the Human Rights Violations Committee once the hearings were under way, in order to be considered as victims and thereby qualify for reparation.

In a live television debate with the then secretary-general of the IFP, Dr Z.B. Jiyane, I challenged the criticisms raised by his party. At the end of the interview, the secretary-general said that, having heard my responses to the IFP's criticisms and questions, he would ask their Federal Council to reconsider their position on the Commission. Unfortunately this never happened and very soon thereafter Dr Jiyane was given his marching orders. I have no doubt that part of the reason for his dismissal was the fact that his sympathetic attitude towards the Commission was not tolerated by Buthelezi and his senior colleagues.

It is also interesting to bear in mind that despite the IFP's objection to the Commission in principle and its considerable objections to a number of the chapters and clauses in the Act, the party participated in the selection committee which provided President Mandela with a

[55]

shortlist of names of people to serve on the Commission. The IFP member of Parliament who participated, and who did so very actively, was Dr Harriet Ngubane. This fascinated me because Buthelezi on so many occasions was extremely hostile towards many of us who served on the Commission and argued that it was an ANC committee. Nevertheless, when President Mandela presented the final seventeen names, together with his appointment of Archbishop Tutu as chairperson and me as deputy chairperson, to F.W. de Klerk and Buthelezi, the IFP leader said that this was the President's decision and therefore he accepted it.

I think the attitude of the IFP was a serious setback to the Commission and in particular denied many of their own members the right and the opportunity to appear before the Commission and to share in the story-telling and the search for reconciliation. I shall return to the relationship between the IFP and the Commission in a later chapter.

General Constand Viljoen, representing the Freedom Front, gave evidence before the Portfolio Committee on Justice on 6 February 1995. In his opening statement he urged the committee to move away from the wording contained in the draft Bill as it related to amnesty, and to retain that of the Interim Constitution, which, he argued, called for a general amnesty.

Secondly, he indicated his uneasiness about a lack of 'even-handedness' and urged that the legislation be tightened up to ensure that the commissioners were not given too much leeway, which might result in biased assessments.

General Viljoen expressed considerable concern about the cut-off date for the period to which amnesty would apply. The original cut-off date was 5 December 1993, the date on which agreement was reached on the postamble. This was perhaps an arbitrary decision, but in order to encourage peaceful opposition in the lead-up to the election, due in April 1994, and to avoid impunity, this particular date was chosen. The valid point made by the general was that at the time that the postamble was drawn up, the Free-dom Front, the IFP, and the PAC were not party to that agreement: 'For them the conflicts of the past did not come to an end on Friday 5 December 1993, because the aspira-tions and demands of those parties were not met. In fact, the final accord between my party and the ANC was only completed on 23 April 1994.'

The general linked his concerns about the cut-off date with an argument that the legislation should not be based on the perpetrators of gross violations of human rights alone, but also on the victims thereof: 'If the cut-off date remains 5 December 1993 it will mean all victims of gross violations of human rights after that date will be excluded from the provisions of reparation and rehabilitation.' This would certainly be no fault of the victims and therefore the general urged that the date be changed, either to 27 April or 11 May 1994, the day after the inauguration of President Mandela.

A major concern for General Viljoen was the emphasis on the pursuit of truth and the revelation of the names of the perpetrators. He stressed that he had no objections to seeking truth and reconciliation, but he criticised very severely the NGO contribution to the debate. His view was that many of the people in the NGOs who had played a role in the formulation of the Commission were 'invariably moralists and some even sentimentalists and whilst they were good people their judgement in the field of public life is based on prejudice and they ought not be trusted because of their high ideals and their frustration'. He went even further to suggest that holding these ideals could result in 'some form of fanaticism'. The implication was that such people couldn't be pragmatic and that this was why they had emphasised the need for full exposure of the names of the perpetrators as a precondition for national reconciliation. It is quite clear that General Viljoen had no idea that the emphasis on exposure did not originate from the NGOs but came from the leadership of the ANC as well as some members of civil society. What may have confused him was the very strong emphasis by NGOs in particular on transparency and the need for the amnesty hearings to be held in public.

I have no doubt that General Viljoen is a sincere man, informed by his experiences when head of the South African Defence Force, and a man very close to his Afrikaner roots. He often struck me, when he appeared before the Commission and when we talked privately and in open debate, as a tortured soul. He had taken an enormous risk in leading the Afrikaner right wing away from all-out violence in 1994 to participate in the election. He was still in touch with former generals, and was very sympathetic towards them, and he had total loyalty to the commanders and members who had served in the army when he was its chief. I think he believed that he could speak on their behalf: that it was not necessary for them to appear before any commission, but that he could assume collective responsibility and that would be the end of it. I think he was also out of touch with the political history of the opposition to apartheid. I remember on one occasion describing to him some of the non-violent resistance against racism in South Africa, particularly from the early twentieth century to the late 1950s. He acknowledged that he knew nothing about this history and said that he would go back and study it because it was important for him to know about it. It was astonishing to note the blind obedience of those who had commanded the Defence Force (and indeed the police force) and the ease with which they had swallowed, it would appear, hook, line, and sinker the propaganda of the politicians. I have no doubt that Viljoen had believed that he was fighting against communism and terrorism and would have used any means at his disposal as a soldier to destroy the ANC. There was no appreciation and no understanding – at least this is what I gathered from him – that there might be another side to the story, that people were being dehumanised, discriminated against, and oppressed, and therefore were bound to resist.

We talked many times about his concerns, and about his commitment to reconciliation. What annoyed me and bothered me was that we would – I thought – reach a consensus in our discussion and then he would walk from my office to Parliament and attack the Commission at the earliest opportunity in a debate, accusing it of being biased, of conducting a witch hunt, and in particular a witch hunt against the Afrikaner. When I challenged him in a subsequent discussion he told me that he had a constituency 'out there' and that he had to keep faith with those who supported him. I challenged him to do what he said he had always done, to give leadership rather than to allow himself to be led by the prejudices and ignorance of so many of his supporters. It was clear then, and it is clear now, that he could not follow that suggestion.

The South African Police at its highest level had from the very first opposed the establishment of a truth commission. Like the IFP and the Freedom Front, the SAP were opposed to the Commission on principle, but they also included a number of suggested amendments and improvements to the draft legislation relating to matters of pivotal and substantive importance.

A major thrust of their argument was similar to that of General Viljoen, namely that there ought to be collective responsibility for acts of violence committed during the past political conflict rather than a focus on individuals. They argued that the political leadership of the National Party and the African National Congress were primarily and collectively responsible for creating a climate conducive to furthering their political objectives. Both parties were on record (in ANC publications such as *Sechaba* and *Mayibuye* and in the records of the State Security Council of the National Party government) for making statements to the effect that the power struggle had resulted in a state of war, and 'the National Party even created and actively implemented the doctrine of "total onslaught"'.

Commands given by the political leadership of both parties had been ambivalent. This was a position taken over and over again by members of the security forces when they appeared before the Commission. According to the SAP's submission to the Portfolio Committee on Justice,

[59]

Although direct instructions were sometimes given, the normal practice was that subordinates would act upon the implied authority which stemmed from such ambivalent commands. This included the actions of the Civil Cooperation Bureau and the implementation of strategic communications projects under the State Security Council as well as the activities of Umkhonto we Sizwe Special Operations.

The point they made was that, in their judgement and experience, 'individuals entrusted with carrying out the orders of the national government were left to their own initiative and devices in order to carry them out and were personally commended on an individual and group basis by members of the cabinet'.

In the view of the SAP, the chief culprits, and those who had to accept major responsibility, were not the policemen and the soldiers who carried out the orders but the political leaders who were the originators and planners of the very actions which were now going to be investigated by the proposed Truth and Reconciliation Commission.

It is clear, then, that even before the Commission was formed, the leadership of the SAP pointed a finger at the politicians. In their memorandum they referred to the so-called Simonstown deliberations of 1979, which gave specific orders concerning information gathering and cross-border operations: 'This included the utilisation of the South African Police where the emphasis was placed on abnormal intelligence-gathering methodology and not according to international norms and practices.' A number of structures were put in place in order to implement the new strategies. These included the Counter-Revolutionary Information Target Centre (Trewits), which was responsible for identifying organisational structures and individuals involved in the armed struggle of the liberation movements, and the Division for Strategic Communications. The point the SAP made in their memorandum was that 'these structures were fully sanctioned by the Nationalist government and senior members of the cabinet were briefed on a continuous and structured basis'. In addition, the government 'used members of the public, academics, senior personnel in the public service, informers, agents and members of the security forces in a covert manner'.

In summary, the SAP argued that before any legislation could be promulgated and before any truth commission could start its work, it was imperative for the Government of National Unity to 'come clean' on the following:

> firstly, acknowledgement of principal and collective responsibility and liability for actions aimed at the achievement and furtherance of political aims and objectives of the past; secondly, acceptance of principal and collective liability for crimes and acts committed by individuals which must fall within the ambit of 'acts associated with a political objective', in furtherance of the above, for which amnesty shall be granted; thirdly, full public disclosure by political leaders of all means employed towards the furtherance of political aims and objectives including structures, strategies, elements of propaganda, deeds of terror and destruction, the use of state machinery and its apparatus, covert projects, etc. Finally, public acknowledgement of the fact that ambivalent orders and commands over a long period of time created a situation in which the execution of such orders was left to the discretion of individuals who were forced to operate under a system of implied authority.

This submission by the SAP at such an early stage indicates that the conflict was not so much between the Commission and the National Party leadership, but between political leaders and the forces that they used to implement their strategy against apartheid's opponents. Tragically, the political leaders refused to accept the responsibility that was urged on them by the very people who had carried out their dirty deeds. In the light of these powerful and direct charges by senior members of the police force, it was difficult then, and remains difficult today, to accept the claims by senior politicians that they 'hadn't known' what was happening.

On 30 January 1995 I wrote to the Portfolio Committee on Justice informing them of a planning workshop which had been held on 16 and 17 January, attended by a large number of non-governmental organisations. I included a number of proposed amendments and outlined the reservations that had been raised during the course of the workshop. The NGOs included the South African Council of Churches, the Black Sash, the Trauma Centre for Victims of Violence and Torture, and the Legal Resources Centre.[1] Advocate George Bizos and then Acting Judge Mohammed Navsa were given a mandate by the twenty-one NGOs to record the general consensus which arose during the two-day debate.

In my letter to the Portfolio Committee I wrote that we would appreciate an opportunity to appear before them to answer any questions which might arise from the suggested amendments set out in the memorandum attached to the letter. The committee agreed to the request, and early in February 1995 I appeared before them. I pointed out that I was there in my capacity as executive director of Justice in Transition and stressed that this institute had no political affiliation. I also took the opportunity to mention to the committee that I was no longer a member of any political party. Some people still linked me with the political party that I had formerly represented and I wanted to make it clear from the start that I was not a member of any political party, and had not been so for the past ten years. I stated that the only reason for my being before the committee was my deep concern that South Africa should find ways and means to deal with its past in such a way that we could move on to the challenge of the future. I also stressed that the Truth and Reconciliation Commission should not be seen in isolation but as only one of the several interventions that would be necessary if we were to achieve the stability and peace which could flow from the election and the Interim Constitution.

In reminding the committee that I was not there merely in my personal capacity but had been given a mandate by twenty-one NGOs to report on their behalf, I took the opportunity to pay tribute to the role that NGOs had played in the struggle for human rights in South Africa, a role that they could continue playing by supplementing and complementing the work of the Truth and Reconciliation Commission. I added, 'It is my view that if there is no warm and strong cooperation from NGOs the Commission will not be able to reach its objectives and will be a poorer Commission as a result of that.'

I tried to make a number of points before the committee. Firstly, referring to Chapter 2 and Clause 2 of the Objectives in the draft legislation, I stressed that there should be a clear understanding that the Commission's work was not merely to investigate isolated events which took place in South Africa over the period under consideration, but rather an attempt to paint, as it were, the big picture. To deal with this honestly and historically would require advice from and consultation with historians so that the Commission could come up with the most accurate and objective picture possible, even though it could never, ever be a complete picture. Secondly, I stressed that there ought to be more rather than fewer commissioners, bearing in mind the nature and demand of the work as outlined in the Objectives. The draft legislation proposed that there should be between eleven and fifteen commissioners, and I emphasised that we ought to have the maximum possible. In the end, of course, that number was increased to seventeen, and I think this was a wise decision.

The third point I made was that commissioners ought to be appointed on a full-time basis. It would be extraordinarily difficult to achieve continuity in a commission where some were full-time and others were part-time. Furthermore, our aim and objective ought to be to get the work done as soon as possible, to deal with the past and not to dwell in it.

My fourth point was that the legislation allowed a period of twelve months for the Commission to complete its work, with the possibility of an additional six months. I argued that if one looked at the length of time between 1960 and 1993 and the enormous amount of research, interviewing, and other work that would have to be done, we should think in terms of eighteen months with the possibility of an additional six months, so that the job could be done thoroughly. This was agreed to and, indeed, the Commission was forced to ask for a further extension because of the enormity of the task.

The major point I made, however, was in relation to Clause 15, which made provision for the Amnesty Committee to meet behind closed doors. This was a cause of great concern to the NGO representatives with whom I had met in January. I felt very strongly that all the committees of the Commission should be open, and that it should be left to the discretion of the Commission itself whether or not there would be circumstances which would make it wise for one or other hearing to be closed. The circumstances I had in mind were if someone's life might be endangered if they testified, or if a request came from the person concerned; consideration could then be given to holding the hearing in camera and the decision would be at the discretion of the committee. Our view was that if the Amnesty Committee were to do its work behind closed doors, it could be subject to a constitutional challenge. Certainly, closed hearings flew in the face of the commitment to transparency, openness, and accountability required by the Constitution. A further argument was that victims or other parties who might have a very real interest in contesting or supporting amnesty applications, and who might wish to lead evidence at such hearings, would, in effect, be precluded from doing so. It might also hamper the efficient working of the other committees, as it might not be clear to them what had transpired 'behind closed doors'.

I concluded my argument by pointing out that the Truth and Reconciliation Commission as envisaged was already compromised: 'There are many, many South Africans who would want the state to go much further, who would opt for a Nuremberg court style approach and would want trials and prosecutions.' For that reason, openness was essential:

> In our wisdom we have opted for amnesty and recon-
> ciliation, but if we attempt to work behind closed
> doors we are saying to victims who have suffered
> enormously and to the survivors of gross violations of
> human rights that not only will justice be limited but
> even that limited justice will not be seen to be done.
> There is enormous suspicion in South Africa because
> of the cover-ups of the past, and the very least we can
> do is that the Commission must hold in tension on
> the one hand a fragile democracy and on the other a
> commitment to a human rights culture, and therefore
> there is an irreducible minimum and that is the
> search for truth. We will never be able to achieve that
> entirely but the search remains paramount. There is
> incentive for people to come and receive pardon. The
> fact of the matter is that those who have perpetrated
> gross human rights violations should at least be asked
> to tell the truth as they have experienced it. That is
> the very least of the demands that can be made of
> them. But that ought to be seen to be done. The
> Commission can be a torch for healing and reconcilia-
> tion, it can restore dignity to survivors, it can be a
> catharsis for South Africa. It can contribute towards
> respect for the rule of law and a human rights culture
> in our country. We should therefore not spoil it by
> cloaking the Amnesty Committee with secrecy. Let
> the Commission do its work in the light.

Interestingly, the Minister of Justice had considered closed hearings earlier that month: 'I do not think that the idea of hearings in camera should be simply dismissed. There is a need to look at the provisions afresh to strike a proper balance. There will, in my view, be a need to make provision for hearings in camera to encourage those who appear before the Committee to disclose the full truth.' Never-theless, he did add, 'At the same time I do think that the public debate is useful. Ultimately I am confident that the

Standing Committees of Parliament will come up with a formula which will take all factors into account.'² In discussion with the Minister I pointed out that, in any event, applicants would have to 'disclose the full truth' whether in private or in public, or they would not receive amnesty.

During question time I was asked by Priscilla Jana (ANC MP) to say something about the demand by other people who had appeared before the Portfolio Committee for 'collective responsibility'. In my reply I stressed that in the end the buck has to stop somewhere and the critical question was, who takes final responsibility? Is it the politician who told the generals what to do, is it the generals who told the foot soldiers, or is the foot soldiers themselves who carried out the orders?

> I think to give people the opportunity to come clean is something that we should not withhold from them. It may be noble for a former head of the Defence Force to accept collective responsibility but I don't think it is good enough. I think we need to know the chain of command, but we need to know the whole story rather than have one person simply saying, I will take responsibility and that is it.

Another important question was put to me by Dene Smuts (DP MP). She argued that what was needed to give effect to the postamble was an Amnesty Act: 'the simple fact of the matter is that you could shorten the whole exercise by granting amnesty and working out a reparation package'. Her main point of departure was that the Commission was taking on too much and that its task would be impossible.

In many ways she was right. Certainly, in terms of the postamble all that was needed was to set up the necessary mechanism to grant amnesty to those who had committed violations as a part of the political conflict. Her point about reparation was also correct, for without it I think those who opposed the amnesty provision would have had a good case in law. But I felt that the postamble gave South Africa an opportunity to come to terms with the past, as it involved victims and perpetrators and impacted on the whole of society.

In developing my argument I emphasised the uniqueness of the South African model. We had not simply succumbed to the idea of granting blanket amnesty, but were insisting on personal applications and full disclosure of the acts which had taken place. Furthermore, because of our commitment to victims, we had proposed that there should be truth-telling so that the focus would be very much on victims at last being able to tell their stories and get a decent hearing, at last being able to regain something of their social and individual human dignity. This process would take a great deal more time, energy, and resources, but, in my own judgement, truth was the one part of the equation that we could not sacrifice. It was not good enough to listen only to the perpetrators; victims should take centre stage.

THE PROMOTION of National Unity and Reconciliation Bill was published by the newly appointed government in November 1994. This Bill was the subject of examination, scrutiny, additions, deletions, and amendments by the Portfolio Committee on Justice. After hearing the evidence and finalising the Bill for debate, the Minister of Justice, Dullah Omar, introduced it in Parliament on 17 May 1995. In his introductory speech the Minister focused on many of the important issues that had been in dispute during the short life of the draft Bill. He stressed, however, that the Bill

> provides a pathway, a stepping stone, towards that
> 'historic bridge' of which the Constitution speaks
> whereby our society can leave behind the past of a
> deeply divided society, characterised by strife, con-
> flict, untold suffering and injustice and commence the
> journey towards a future founded on the recognition of
> human rights, democracy and peaceful coexistence
> and development opportunities for all South Africans,
> irrespective of colour, race, class, belief or sex.[3]

[67]

It was important that the Minister linked the Bill with the Interim Constitution, because the Interim Constitution had secured the support of all parties in Parliament. What he was emphasising was that the Bill was not a new intervention, it was not a departure from the past; it was simply implementing something which had already received support from all concerned.

In the second place, he stressed that the Bill was to provide that 'secure foundation' which the Constitution enjoins, 'for the people of South Africa to transcend the divisions and strife of the past which generated gross violations of human rights, transgression of humanitarian principles in conflict and a legacy of hatred, fear, guilt and revenge'. This was a salutary reminder to South Africa that the Commission was set up not only to achieve truth and reconciliation but also to lay a foundation to fulfil the commitment by all parties who were signatories to the Interim Constitution to create the possibility of a new, more decent, more fair, more just society.

In the third place, the Minister stressed that it would be easy to publish a Bill which would grant amnesty to applicants under certain conditions. It was much more difficult to respond to the terrible suffering that countless people inside and outside South Africa had endured under the apartheid system. It is not surprising, he continued, that these victims demanded that justice be done. An attempt, therefore, had to be made to address the injustices of the past, and, more importantly, to

> take such steps as are necessary to heal the wounds of the past. To do anything less would be to ignore the sufferings of countless victims… Merely granting amnesty to perpetrators without addressing our international obligations, dealing with wounds of the past and our duty to victims will undermine the process of reconciliation. It is necessary, therefore, to deal with South Africa's past, including the question of amnesty, on a morally acceptable basis.

Omar emphasised that the Commission would not be a court of law and would not conduct trials. The role of the criminal justice system was to remain unaffected by the Bill. In other words, the Commission was not to take the place of the normal process of criminal justice, nor was criminal justice to be suspended during the life of the Commission. The two would operate side by side. The aim of the Bill was to re-establish the rule of law and the principle of accountability: 'This is our one hope of turning South Africa around from the path of violence and intolerance.'

The Minister made an important point about the liberation movements: 'The Bill before Parliament applies equally to all and therefore any human rights violation, no matter from which quarter, is within the terms of reference of the Commission. We would never want to see ourselves condoning human rights violations simply because they were committed by freedom fighters.' He also stated that 'Whilst the number of persons who were victims of the ANC are very few, they should none the less not be glossed over, nor swept under the carpet. They, too, should be subject to inquiry by the Truth and Reconciliation Commission.'

He did qualify this point, however, by adding that

It is morally and legally wrong to equate the anti-apartheid struggle for liberation and democracy with the apartheid state, its agents and operatives whose motivation was to maintain apartheid and suppress democracy. The struggle for liberation was rooted in principles of human dignity and human rights. The apartheid state and its quest to sustain itself through repression was an affront to humanity itself.

Nevertheless, he emphasised once again that 'this does not mean that there were not excesses committed by the liberation movements. There were such excesses and the ANC declared itself in favour of a truth commission which would, in a transparent manner, investigate all human rights violations.'

[69]

The Minister also raised the issue of the appointment of the people who would serve on the Commission. The legislation, he said, allowed for between eleven and seventeen commissioners, and for the President to 'appoint persons who are impartial, respected and have no high political profile'. He added that 'Such appointments are to be made in consultation with the cabinet but the views of all political parties not represented in the cabinet will also be considered.'

The question of whether the Amnesty Committee would meet behind closed doors was also raised by the Minister. This proposal had finally been rejected, and the Bill called for the proceedings of all committees to be open to the public. Nevertheless, the committee was given the discretion to hold proceedings or parts thereof in camera 'where there is a likelihood of harm... or where the interests of justice otherwise require that the proceedings be held in camera'. This was a major victory for civil society, which from the very beginning had urged that transparency should prevail and that the people of South Africa, through the media, should be able to participate in the life and work of the Commission.

The final issue dealt with by the Minister was the cut-off date for amnesty applications. As indicated earlier, General Viljoen of the Freedom Front and some other parties and organisations had urged that the cut-off date should be changed from 5 December 1993 to 10 May 1994. This proposal was resisted, however, and the original cut-off date was retained. The reason given was that 'Perpetrators of violence or potential perpetrators must be under no illusion that action will not be taken against anyone responsible for such violence. Changing the cut-off date sends the wrong signal, namely, "you can commit crime and sometime or other you will be forgiven." We cannot afford such a situation.' The Minister left the door slightly ajar, however, when he stated that 'This matter could be reviewed when peace has been sufficiently restored in affected areas.' In the end the cut-off date was changed in order to meet the requests and needs of right-wing parties and the Pan African Congress, whose members and followers were responsible for violence immediately prior to the April 1994 election.

The Minister concluded his speech with the following words:

> I would like to reiterate what the Commission's main objective is: to facilitate the healing of our deeply divided society on a morally acceptable basis. Unless we are bold enough to deal with the past we shall never be able to face the challenges of the future. It is not a witch hunt exercise, but one based on the need to restore a national moral conscience. The future will remain elusive unless we start seriously to work towards a society based on respect for human rights and human dignity.

All the party leaders and members participated vigorously in the debate that followed. It was, in fact, the longest debate of the newly elected democratic Parliament. Objections to certain clauses were raised and thoroughly debated, but no significant changes were made to the Bill, particularly because party representatives had had opportunity to put their case while the draft Bill was still before the Portfolio Committee on Justice. In the final vote all the parties voted for the Bill, with the exception of the Freedom Front, which voted against it mainly because the cut-off date had not been altered, and the Inkatha Freedom Party, which abstained because they were not convinced that 'even-handedness' would prevail.

The Bill was signed into law on 19 July 1995, and came into effect on 15 December 1995 when the commissioners were appointed.

THE APPOINTMENT of the commissioners followed a similar democratic pattern. President Mandela decided that he would not nominate members and appoint the Commission, but instead would ask a specially appointed committee to draw up a shortlist before he made the final

[71]

decision in consultation with his Cabinet. The committee consisted of the following members of Parliament: Harriet Ngubane (IFP), Ray Radue (NP), Rosier de Ville (FF), and Baleka Kgositsile (ANC). It also included four members of the NGO community, Bishop Peter Storey, Jayendra Naidoo, Jody Kollapen, and Brigalia Bam, and was chaired by Professor Nicholas Haysom, legal advisor to the President.

This decision was widely advertised and all organisations, political parties, churches, agents of civil society, and individuals were invited to nominate people who they thought would be suitable to serve on the Commission. In the end, 299 nominations were received. This list was whittled down by the committee to a more manageable size. There followed public hearings which once again enabled the people of South Africa, who could attend the public hearings or follow them on television or radio, to participate in the TRC process. All this took a considerable time.

Much earlier Dullah Omar had asked me what I thought about the process that should be adopted in the appointment of the commissioners. In a letter to him dated 12 April 1995 I replied,

> The more I think about it the more I am convinced that hearings would be preferable. In the first instance, it would meet the demand for transparency; secondly, it would enable anyone to apply so that we can never be accused of turning away from anyone without a hearing; thirdly, it would sort out a lot of people whose record relating to human rights is either neutral or worse. Finally, it would I think give greater confidence to the final selection and enable Commissioners to defend their position much more effectively.

I did, however, add that 'There is, of course, a downside and that is a further delay. However, when one bears in mind the importance of the Commission and the fact that it will be meeting probably for two years, then a delay of a few weeks is worth the advantages which would accrue.'

[72]

Inevitably, the process took much longer than a few weeks, but I am still convinced that the procedures that were followed were the right ones. Following the public hearings, the specially appointed committee sent twenty-five names to the President. Mandela selected fifteen of those twenty-five and added two new names. In addition he appointed Archbishop Tutu as the chairperson and me as deputy chairperson of the Commission. This was gazetted on 15 December 1995, and the Commission held its first meeting on 16 December, appropriately the Day of Reconciliation.

Earlier in the month I had been on my way to attend a conference in Bad Boll in Germany. When I was checking in at the Cape Town airport I was told to go to the first-class lounge. I was delighted: I thought that in some miraculous way I had been upgraded! When I glanced at my ticket, however, it was clear that this was not so. When I inquired why I should go to the lounge I was told that that was where the journalists and cameras were. I had no idea what this was about and imagined it might have something to do with the German conference. I went into the first-class lounge and was faced with a large crowd of journalists. Immediately the cameras began rolling and I was asked what I thought about the names that had been announced of those who would be serving on the Commission. I told them that I hadn't the slightest idea about the final list of names. The journalists told me that I was on the Commission and had been appointed by President Mandela as deputy chairperson. I was bowled over. I said to them that the road ahead of us would be an extremely tough one, deeply emotional, highly charged, and always controversial. I didn't realise how true that forecast would prove to be.

I had had no doubt that Archbishop Tutu would be the first choice for chairperson and certainly that was my own choice as well. However, I imagined that because of the strong gender emphasis within the ANC the President would appoint a woman as deputy chairperson. That was not to be and I was grateful for the opportunity to serve

[73]

together with Desmond Tutu and my fellow commissioners in the capacity of deputy chairperson.

The final list of commissioners contained a number of surprises. One was the omission of Stanley Mogoba, Presiding Bishop of the Methodist Church of Southern Africa and later president of the Pan African Congress. He had been on the list of twenty-five and it was generally agreed that his name would be high on the list of the final seventeen. There was an outcry, particularly from people within the Methodist Church, the PAC, and the general public, because his name was omitted. Rumours circulated that the ANC distrusted him, but nothing was ever confirmed or established. I am not sure whether the matter was discussed between the President and Mogoba. Another controversial omission was that of André du Toit. Du Toit was an experienced academic, with impeccable Afrikaner credentials, who had been very involved in the lead-up to the Commission. The fact that he was not appointed caused me personal disappointment because I knew how much he wanted to serve and also knew the considerable moral integrity that he would bring to the Commission.

Another surprise was the appointment of two commissioners whose names had not been on the original list of twenty-five and who had not appeared in public to be questioned as the other nominees had. The first was Khoza Mgojo, a prominent Methodist leader from KwaZulu-Natal. The second was Denzil Potgieter, an advocate who had been in charge of the organisation of the selection procedures. There were many who could not understand how, at this late stage in the selection process, his name came to be considered and indeed confirmed by President Mandela. Both these people had obvious gifts and graces, but because their appointment departed so strikingly from the procedures it caused some comment. Another appointment that surprised many was that of Mapule Ramashala, although her name had been on the shortlist. She had spent more than two decades outside South Africa, studying and teaching in the United States, and no one seemed to know much about her. She had not appeared in public, and her name had been proposed by the committee only on the basis of a telephone interview and her impressive curriculum vitae.

The final list of commissioners didn't please everyone. F.W. de Klerk was not happy with the list and in particular was not pleased with the appointment of Tutu and me at the head. The same was true of Mangosuthu Buthelezi, who said that he agreed with the list, but that it would not be his choice. His antipathy towards Tutu was well known and the friendship which we had once enjoyed had unfortunately fallen by the way in the heat of political debate. I think the appointment of human rights activists, human rights lawyers, and church persons confirmed his view that even-handedness would be impossible.

Among the seventeen commissioners there were seven women, ten men, seven Africans, two 'coloureds', two Indians, and six whites. It was, therefore, a fairly representative group that had been appointed by President Mandela. However, as the Commission started its work and began to make a number of decisions and statements, the criticisms from some quarters in relation to balance and impartiality were to become more and more pronounced.

3

Getting under way:
The Commission at work

THE ANNOUNCEMENT of the appointment of commissioners appeared in the *Government Gazette* on 15 December 1995. Remarkably, we were able to assemble sixteen of the seventeen on 16 December; only Khoza Mgojo was unable to be present. We met at Bishopscourt in Cape Town, at the official residence of Archbishop Tutu. We had barely begun to make arrangements for the meeting when we were contacted by the head of the National Protection Services, who proposed that we ought to have full security for the meeting. Clearly our lives were going to be drastically different from the past. When I arrived at Bishopscourt that morning there were security guards at the gate and everyone was thoroughly searched before they were allowed in.

While the names of the commissioners were published in the *Government Gazette*, we had received no official notification of our appointment from President Mandela or anyone in government. Several of the commissioners urged me to obtain a letter of appointment, and it took about six months to accomplish this. Eventually I drafted the letter myself and sent it to Jakes Gerwel, the director-general in the President's office; I suggested that it might be a suitable letter of appointment but that the President, or anyone else, should change it in any way he saw fit. The letter duly arrived, and it is a treasured possession in the files of each of the commissioners.

Despite the fact that there was no contract, regulations were published a little later which outlined salaries and allowances. The salary in my view, and in the view of most of my colleagues, was extraordinarily generous. Some of us felt it was too high, others felt it was too low. Dumisa Ntsebeza, in his inimitable way, stated in the press that he would first see what they were going to pay before he accepted his appointment as a commissioner! I think some of the lawyers in particular, who normally enjoyed high incomes, felt that we were underpaid, but the rest of us believed the salary was embarrassingly high. Mary Burton decided not to take an official car and she was highly commended by many, particularly in the press, which showed a photograph of her with her fairly old car and made the rest of us feel rather bad. Some of us decided to give a percentage of our income away, in particular to education for black children.

The December meeting was an exciting and intriguing experience: I was meeting all my colleagues with whom I would work for the next two or three years. I knew a number of them already. I had known Desmond Tutu for more than thirty years but hadn't worked with him very closely. He is a man of many gifts and graces, and with his genial, embracing manner he quickly put all of us at ease. I will have occasion to say more about Tutu and his special qualities later on. As the meeting began, however, there was strong evidence of his episcopal authority, which was very quickly challenged. It didn't take him too long to realise that he wasn't dealing with a group of priests or even bishops, but some independent-minded and quite often difficult people.

Dumisa Ntsebeza I had met at various conferences and had always liked. Nothing changed in the next two or three years, although inevitably there were at times differences of opinion. He is a very fine lawyer, who had been active in politics, particularly in supporting people who were detained under the former government's emergency regulations, and had himself spent several years in prison.

Mary Burton is an old friend whom I had come to know very well through her work in the Black Sash. (I also play tennis with her husband!) Mary is a person of great integrity, strong and relatively unflappable, and at the same time sensitive and caring. Her courageous stand as a prominent leader of the Black Sash had earned her deep respect from black and white alike. Wendy Orr I had known for quite a while: I met her first when she was a youngster, and had known her father, who was a distinguished leader in the Presbyterian Church. Wendy came to fame, as it were, when she was working for the District Surgeon's office in Port Elizabeth and brought a successful application to the Supreme Court to prevent the police from assaulting detainees. This was in 1985 when she was only twenty-five years old.

Wynand Malan was another commissioner whom I had known for a number of years. We had been in Parliament together, he representing the National Party and I the Progressive Federal Party, which at the time was the only party in Parliament which unambiguously opposed apartheid. After the meeting, I wrote a few comments in my diary about my impressions: 'Wynand Malan is clearly determined to play an active role and is certainly no pushover! It is early days, but I have no doubt that he is going to be heard as a very dominant voice in the Commission's proceedings.' It seemed that he had a watching brief, either on his own behalf or that of the Afrikaner community or his former party. I was never sure. An excitable man, he often appeared to be a deeply troubled spirit. He was very much a De Klerk man who felt that P.W. Botha was the devil incarnate, and I think he sought to put most of the blame for apartheid on Botha rather than accepting the overall responsibility of the National Party, which of course would include himself. We had had many clashes in Parliament before, but I have to say I saw him then as an ally rather than an enemy because I knew that he had been uncomfortable with the apartheid policies and had had the very difficult job of trying to defend the indefensible. At the first Commission meeting we greeted each other very warmly and there was a meeting of minds and even hearts, but over the months I think he came to see me as a kind of stormy petrel; we drifted apart and became antagonists in the Commission.

As I looked around me at the faces of those I didn't know personally, I wondered how we were going to fit into a cohesive whole. It has been quite a revelation getting to know some of these people who were strangers to me, and I to them, on that very first day.

Bongani Finca, a minister of religion, is a man of absolute integrity. From early on, whenever he spoke at a meeting I listened carefully. He is a wise man and deeply respected by the Eastern Cape community in particular. We all soon discovered that he also possessed a wonderful sense of humour, and he often eased a tense situation with a quip or two.

Yasmin Sooka, a human rights lawyer of note, was a major asset, not only in the Commission but also on the Human Rights Violations Committee, of which she was co-deputy chair, and in the Gauteng region. She had many a run-in with Wynand Malan and always gave as good as she got. Yasmin is a Hindu and I don't think she enjoyed the strong religious and largely Christian emphasis in the Commission. Although she was tough she was sensitive to the racial climate which intruded into our work from time to time, and more than once was moved to tears. She saw herself as black but, like so many Indian and 'coloured' people, I think found herself stranded between the black/white divide in the country as well as in the Commission.

Richard Lyster, also a lawyer, was one of the hardest-working members of the team. Thoroughly disliked and often vilified by the Inkatha Freedom Party, he was like a rock in his determination to get to the truth about covert operations in KwaZulu-Natal. In his heart of hearts I think he favoured prosecutions, but having joined the Commission he put all his energies and talent into making the process work. He and Yasmin Sooka were indispensable in working on the early drafts of the Commission's findings in relation to gross human rights violations.

Sisi Khampepe, a tough no-nonsense lawyer, has very close links with the trade union movement. She always spoke her mind and one knew exactly where she stood. Her presence on the Amnesty Committee was particularly helpful.

Glenda Wildschut started in the Commission almost like a little mouse! She appeared shy and retiring, seldom saying very much. But that soon changed. I watched her grow in confidence and become an outstanding commissioner. A psychiatric nurse by profession, she used all her skills in helping all of us to reach sensitive decisions. She cared deeply for commissioners and staff alike.

Fazel Randera, a medical doctor, had helped many who were on the run from the security police during the apartheid era, often at great personal risk. He is warm and engaging but was better at process than getting the job done. He is a very committed member of the ANC and sometimes battled to put party loyalty to one side. This was especially evident as we made our findings on the ANC and human rights violations.

Another commissioner I had not met before was Chris de Jager, who had been a member of Parliament for the right-wing Conservative Party. In my diary I noted, 'Chris looks subdued, wary, almost as though he is out of place and is nervous about the thought of working with his fellow Commissioners!' As the months passed I came to admire Chris very much. He was honest, and stated his position clearly and carefully. He also revealed an impish sense of humour, which was all the more delightful because of his serious appearance. This assisted his acceptance by a group of people who were largely of a very different political persuasion.

One person who intrigued me very much was Mapule Ramashala. She had spent more than twenty-five years in the United States and dressed like an American and spoke with a pronounced American accent. I found it difficult to accept her as a South African, and this influenced my approach to her from day one. She is a powerful figure, a brooding presence, with considerable abilities, and I think that almost from the beginning she was frustrated, and felt that her talents were not recognised; she perhaps resented having no executive position. This despite the fact that she had exercised considerable leadership in her work in the United States.

Hlengiwe Mkhize was an enigma not only to me but I think to many of us. By all accounts she did very well in her public interview during the selection process, and possessed a good academic and service record, but I felt she seldom revealed this in her work on the Commission. As chairperson of the Reparation and Rehabilitation Committee she held a key position, but she seemed unable to get on top of that job and was often confused and insecure in her reports to the Commission. Unfortunately she was overly sensitive, and when she was criticised (as we all were from time to time) I felt she took refuge in playing the race card.

Denzil Potgieter, a lawyer, started off very quietly, perhaps because he was conscious of not having gone through the same process of selection as the other commissioners but had been appointed by President Mandela at the last minute. But he soon revealed his considerable legal skills and helped the Commission through many a sticky patch. He was very correct and very determined. I liked him very much but didn't find it easy to get close to him.

Khoza Mgojo, who like Denzil Potgieter had been appointed at the last minute, didn't attend that first meeting. He is someone I have known for many years, through my work in the Methodist Church. He is a distinguished, upright, careful ecclesiastic who stood very firm on ceremony and correct procedures.

One of the decisions we took at the initial meeting of the Commission was to go on a retreat together in order to consider the enormous challenges awaiting us, and to begin welding together disparate people into a workable and flexible team.

We met at the Anglican Centre at Faure, in the Western Cape; it was secluded and very peaceful, an ideal place to be quiet and to prepare for further, very intensive,

Commission meetings. It certainly brought back memories for me of my days in the Methodist Church. There was a sense of *déjà vu*; nothing had really changed, certainly not the religious in-jokes! It seems that most of them are eternal and are recycled for every occasion.

We all assembled on a Sunday evening and met at 8.30 the following morning. Father Francis Cull, a small, eighty-one-year-old, white-haired, white-bearded priest, led the retreat. He was a lovely man, deeply spiritual, with a wonderful fund of stories and a wise, mature mixture of spirituality and common sense. What I liked particularly about him was his sensitivity to members of the Commission who represented different faiths and those who were agnostic. He spoke briefly and very much to the point. Some of his notes were helpful and constantly emphasised the need for roots, for introspection, for self-love and affirmation, for humility and fidelity. He referred to an old rabbi who is reported to have said, 'An angel walks before every human being saying "make way, make way for the image of God".' For me this summed up the goal of the Commission. During the apartheid years the basic humanity of millions of people had been denied. Our task was to restore the human dignity which had been trampled upon. Father Cull also helped us to distinguish between grievances and grief and to hold together a passion for justice and a compassion for the perpetrators. His reminder of Kierkegaard's telling phrase, 'At midnight the masks must be taken off', was especially challenging: a real need to understand who we are as we face an unpredictable and challenging future.

Most of the time was spent in silence, even when we broke for tea and meals. This was quite a tough assignment for usually busy and wordy people. In one session Father Cull suggested to us that in our living together we would need to remember faithfulness, forbearance, and forgiveness. One scriptural reference he mentioned was Isaiah 43, verses 2 and 3, and this was a constant reminder and comfort to me during the life of the Commission: 'When you pass through the water I will be with you; in the rivers you shall not drown. When you walk through fire you shall not be burned; flames will not consume you. For I am the Lord your God, the holy one of Israel, your Saviour.' That certainly had to be remembered through many deep waters and fiery encounters, particularly within the Commission and with its opponents.

In very strange contrast to the days of solitude and affirmation, there followed four days of exacting, frustrating, and demanding meetings. All of us had strong egos and had been leaders in our fields, and it was clear that there was a great deal of suspicion, some fear, a sense of vulnerability, and often simple bloody-mindedness.

PARLIAMENT HAD voted to establish a Commission, the President had announced the names of the commissioners, but that was where it stopped. As yet we had no budget, no offices, no staff, not even a paper clip. We had nothing. It was decided at the first meetings that I would be charged with the responsibility of getting the logistics in place, drawing up a staff complement, and initiating a search for key staff members. This was an extraordinarily difficult task. January is very much a holiday month in South Africa and as I moved around trying to find premises I discovered that most people were away. It was difficult to consult with the other commissioners because they too were either on holiday or finishing up their previous employment. However, the Ministry of Justice was very helpful and seconded Manie Steyn to the Commission. A civil servant, he knew his way around the state bureaucracy and was extremely helpful to me. He is a very gentle person, much underestimated, quiet and undemanding, but totally committed. In the end he stayed on for the full life of the Commission.

We stumbled from one vacant building to another, trying to find offices in the centre of Cape Town that would be modest and which would make a spectrum of visitors feel comfortable. We eventually found a building which looked like a vast barn, with no internal walls and not too much flooring or ceiling. We called in a company to draw up

[83]

plans and to renovate the building without delay. While this work was under way I visited a number of furniture factories and, working from a great deal of ignorance, placed orders so that the commissioners would at least have a desk, a chair, and the bare necessities to assist them with their work. We had also decided to decentralise our operations, with our headquarters in Cape Town but with additional offices in Johannesburg, Durban, and East London. We therefore had to secure premises in these three centres as well and also to order furniture, carpeting, equipment, pencils and paper, and everything else needed to run offices. Through delegation and a great deal of travel and head-scratching, we managed to find adequate space and the requisite furniture and fittings.

Manie Steyn was appalled at the pace and method I adopted. It seems I was breaking every rule in the book in terms of regulations laid down by state departments. This was particularly true in that I did not ask for a number of tenders before ordering furniture and fittings. My argument was that we simply had no time to do this, and I consciously decided that I would accept responsibility for making these decisions and would be answerable to the government when the time came. In the end the Auditor-General left us in no doubt that what had taken place was illegal, but confirmed that there had been no malpractice in the sense of any money being abused or favourites being given jobs, so no proceedings followed. Biki Minyuku, who was later appointed chief executive officer of the Commission, made it abundantly clear that this was something that had nothing to do with him and that the blame, if there was to be blame, should be laid at my door. I didn't mind, because I knew that we had to move, and move fast, and I think we got off the ground in record time; that was all I was concerned about. I was strongly of the view that a truth commission should not last too long, and therefore we had no time to waste.

All this preparatory work took an enormous amount of time and energy. Our first hearing was to take place in April 1996. We had so many decisions to make about processes and procedures and staff appointments during that time that it was impossible to hold a hearing any earlier. We had to appoint people to brief the victims, people who would take statements before the public hearings, and deal with the thousand and one administrative details that had to be put in place.

Tutu and I had met earlier to discuss the staff appointments that needed to be made immediately, and the appointment of chairpersons and deputy chairpersons of the various committees. There were three main committees, the Human Rights Violations Committee, the Amnesty Committee, and the Reparation and Rehabilitation Committee. My own view was that we ought to allow the commissioners themselves to make the decisions about which of their colleagues they would like to see heading the committees, but Tutu was adamant that this was something he wanted to do himself and that he would put his decision before the commissioners for their approval. There was a great deal of resistance to this, but, because of Tutu's moral and spiritual stature, there was no real opposition when he announced the appointments. Hlengiwe Mkhize was appointed chairperson of the Reparation and Rehabilitation Committee, with Wendy Orr as her deputy. Tutu decided that he would assume leadership of the Human Rights Violations Committee himself, with Yasmin Sooka and Wynand Malan as his two deputies. The composition of the Amnesty Committee was out of our hands, for the Act authorised the President to appoint the chairperson and several of its members. We were, however, able to appoint two commissioners to the Amnesty Committee, namely Sisi Khampepe and Chris de Jager. Dumisa Ntsebeza was appointed head of the Investigative Unit.

There were also a number of staff appointments to assist the commissioners. Tutu suggested that John Allen, who had worked very closely with him at Bishopscourt, be appointed as director of the Communications Department, and announced that he would bring his own assistant, Lavinia Crawford-Browne, with him into the Commission. He felt that as deputy chairperson I ought to be

[85]

allowed to retain my assistant, Paddy Clark, as well. It was perhaps unfortunate that all three of these early staff appointments were white. I was relieved that it was a black chairperson who had made the proposals! Again, very little comment was made at the time, but on many, many occasions in the future this appointment of whites was referred to by several of the commissioners. The appointments were ratified at the next Commission meeting, almost without comment, but the resentment lingered.

Another staff appointment was Paul van Zyl. Paul was a young lawyer, very committed, full of ideas, and extremely bright. He had worked very closely with me, particularly in the last few months leading up to the appointment of the Commission. The Swedish government had given the Commission a grant to cover the salary of my assistant, Paddy Clark, and one other assistant, whom I had hoped would be Paul because of his competence and our experience of working together. I tried to introduce him very gently, indicating that it was the Commission's decision as to whether he should be employed but that he was available, that he would not be a financial burden, and that he had a great deal of experience and knowledge which could be of great assistance. The problem was that once again a white person was being put forward and while I did it as tentatively and as sensitively as I knew how, I think a number of the commissioners, and Mapule Ramashala in particular, were quite cruel towards Paul, often making him feel extremely uncomfortable. How he stood it I don't know. I don't think I would have lasted a week! Ironically, three months later, after his position had been debated and discussed at every Commission meeting, it was Mapule who said, 'For heaven's sake, we can't go on like this. Let's make him the executive secretary of the Commission because he is clearly very able.' It was one of the best decisions made by the Commission – without Paul van Zyl's skill and dedication, the Commission would have been considerably poorer.

A key appointment very early on was that of the director of the Research Department, and we were very fortunate in securing the services of Professor Charles Villa-Vicencio from the University of Cape Town. He assisted the Commission throughout its life, under almost impossible conditions and circumstances, and, together with his own staff, made it possible for the final report to be available at the appointed time so that we could present the five volumes to President Mandela. Without his hard work, determination, and ability, the report would have been delayed by at least six months. Charles is very much a mixture of conservatism on the one hand and radical action on the other. On many occasions he would storm into my office, using language that would normally be heard in army barracks or on board a ship rather than from a professor of religion! I could appreciate his frustration at the apparent lack of urgency, the difficulty in getting decisions made, and the constant tiresome debates in the Commission. He had been a friend of long standing, and this also presented problems, because some people felt that we were too close and that, together with Paul van Zyl, we were conspiring and planning outside of the Commission. I can understand this suspicion, but it was misplaced. We certainly did talk and meet and plan, but largely because we were given responsibilities in strategic planning and spent many hours preparing for action. However, we always presented our ideas to the Commission for approval. On many occasions we didn't get the nod and reluctantly set our proposals aside. The friendship and support of Charles and of Dumisa Ntsebeza was very helpful during a tempestuous two and a half years.

Among the senior staff members who served the Commission very well were Hanif Vally, a very active human rights lawyer, as head of the Legal Department, Kariem Hoosain, and later Willie Greyvenstein, as Financial Director, and, for quite a while, Sandra Arendse as director of the Human Resources Department. In addition, we had to appoint regional managers. Wendy Watson did this admirably in Durban, Patrick Kelly in Johannesburg, Vido Nyobole in East London, and Ruth Lewin and then Marcella Naidoo in Cape Town. A little later Ruben Richards was appointed as executive secretary of the Human Rights Violations Committee and Thulani Granville-Grey as executive secretary of the Reparation and Rehabilitation Committee. Martin Coetzee was appointed as executive secretary of the Amnesty Committee. A vital contribution was made by Gerald O'Sullivan, our computer systems analyst.

On 1 March 1996 we appointed Dr Biki Minyuku as the chief executive officer of the Commission. He performed the mammoth task of coordinating the various departments and served the Commission throughout its life. He was also the chief accounting officer of the Commission and performed his duties and responsibilities with considerable zeal. I don't think we could have appointed anyone who was more hard-working and dedicated. But in spite of having some valuable management skills he time and time again created friction and difficulties among commissioners and senior staff. No one could ever doubt his bona fides, but he simply could not, it seemed, avoid creating conflict, which was the very last thing we needed. On at least a dozen occasions Tutu and I sat in the chairperson's office and discussed this problem with Biki. We urged him in particular not to write provocative memoranda to commissioners, staff, or anyone else in the heat of the moment. He wore his heart on his sleeve; he had tremendous admiration and even devotion for Tutu, who, I think, was his spiritual adviser as well as his boss. Biki and I had many differences, and inevitably, because part of my responsibility related to strategic planning and organisation, this meant that we would clash. But I felt a very warm affection for him, although that was often severely tested by my perception that he created problems where none existed. Towards the end of the life of the Commission he applied for the post of Vice Chancellor of the University of the North, and was appointed. I hope very much that his undoubted commitment and skills will be matched by an ability to work with and alongside people, because in the end, whether it be in a commission or a university, success in any endeavour depends on being deeply aware that the human factor is the most important.

Another demand placed upon Tutu and me in particular was the stream of visitors that poured into our offices, not only from South Africa, but, it seemed, from every part of the world. There were students who wanted to serve as interns, there were visiting professors, politicians, and heads of state. These meetings were extremely time-consuming, but it was also very encouraging that there was so much interest in the South African model. We received numerous invitations to travel around the world to attend conferences and meetings, which in most cases we could not accept.

We were also visited by hordes of journalists from South Africa and beyond our borders. We simply could not refuse interviews, particularly as it had been decided that Tutu and I would be the only ones authorised to make statements on behalf of the Commission. This meant that the journalists, particularly from radio, were constantly looking for Tutu and me to give them sound bites to enable them to do their job. I had always imagined that the media would be interested in the Commission, and in particular that they would be there in large numbers for our first hearings. Never in my wildest imaginings did I think that the media would retain its insatiable interest in the Commission throughout its life. Not a day passed when we were not reported on radio. We were very seldom absent from the major television evening news broadcasts, and we were, if not on the front page, on the inside pages of every newspaper throughout the two and a half years of our work. Although it was not easy to be under constant public scrutiny, I think the Commission owes the media an enormous debt of gratitude. Through their very conscientious work they involved the whole country in the work of the TRC. Unlike many other truth commissions, this one was centre stage, and media coverage, particularly radio, enabled the poor, the illiterate, and people living in rural areas to participate in its work so that it was truly a national experience rather than restricted to a small handful of selected commissioners.

I also found that many of the journalists became personally involved, and were very deeply affected by what they had to listen to in order to write their stories and

[89]

present their programmes. Many of them were disturbed, emotionally, mentally, and spiritually. On more than one occasion Tutu and I met with the regulars in off-the-record meetings. There they opened their hearts, hard-bitten journalists though they were, and told us of their own feelings and of their own experiences and trauma. It was astonishing to see Tutu in particular ministering to journalists who, understandably, are normally an extremely cynical group of people. We got very close to them and I admired the fact that they never once broke a confidence and never allowed their subjectivity, as far as I could see, to interfere with their objective reporting.

OVER THE NEXT two and a half years, the commissioners were to face extraordinary experiences and crises. Perhaps the most distressing of these occurred in January 1997, when Desmond Tutu was diagnosed with cancer of the prostate. We hoped above all for his recovery but also that he would be able to continue his leadership of the Commission. Tutu's condition involved treatment and rest. He was absent for several weeks, and spent two months in the USA undergoing radiation treatment in the middle of 1997. I found Tutu's absence very difficult. We had worked so closely together and trusted each other implicitly. To manage and lead without him added considerably to the burden we normally faced together. I recall him saying to me earlier, 'I appreciate your friendship and loyalty – I need never look over my shoulder.' It was that intimate companionship we shared that left a huge gap. I think Tutu's illness affected him very deeply but in a strange way enabled him to guide and direct the work of the Commission with even greater sensitivity.

The Commission was made up of strong and independent-minded people, and we often experienced difficulties in working together. Very early on I noted in my diary,

The difficulty of making far-reaching decisions
and learning to function as a group with time binds

is almost soul-destroying. If there was an ounce of
appreciation for every pound of demand, it would
have been a lot easier to bear. There is no doubt
that Desmond and I have much, much to learn
but I would hope that the rest of the bunch will
accept that of themselves as well! The sickness
of racism and separation in our country has left a
ghastly heritage and this threatens to sour so much
of human relations in South Africa, and the
Commission is no exception.

I rather foolishly concluded, 'I am sure the worst is behind
us and soon we will be in a normal working environment,
and I know that everything will be better.' How little I
knew.

One commissioner who was a source of conflict was
Mapule Ramashala. I think she disliked the way Tutu conducted meetings. She burst out on one occasion that she
was 'tired of being treated like a child'. I think the problem
was that Tutu used anecdotes and humour from the chair
in an attempt to relax the meetings and to prevent friction
and confrontation. Mapule, on the other hand, felt that
this was demeaning and patronising. I think she felt that
Tutu's attitude towards women was different from that towards men, and that this offended her strong feminist
stance. Mapule and I clashed very early on and never resolved our acute differences. My impression was that she
felt that as a white male I was attempting to control matters. There is no doubt that, having had maximum freedom
in helping to organise the founding of the Commission, it
was not easy for me in those initial days to appreciate that
I was part of a larger team and that process was at least as
important as action.

At the second Commission meeting, in January 1996,
when Mapule and I had quite a set-to about several matters, I jotted down in my diary, 'Mapule is a very powerful,
very talented person but I wonder if she will last the pace.'
On a number of occasions she and the Commission came
close to parting company. Soon after the last of these close

[91]

calls, we heard that Mapule had successfully applied for the post of Vice Chancellor of the University of Durban-Westville, which again indicated that she is a person of considerable merit and great talent. I have no doubt that she will do extremely well in that post, provided she can curb her tendency to dominate.

Another source of conflict was Hlengiwe Mkhize. Although it was an agreed policy that only the chairperson and deputy chairperson would issue press statements, Hlengiwe made statements in January 1997 implying that the Commission was being run by 'white liberals' headed by me. I responded by saying that it would be surprising if there were no tensions in the TRC: 'The commission is a microcosm of South Africa, which itself is experiencing enormous tensions as it recovers from a period of desperate conflict. Secondly, the commission's work is extraordinarily demanding, both in time and emotions.'[1] But it was Tutu's statement from his hospital bed that put the matter in perspective:

> Newspaper reports on the alleged marginalisation of black members of the TRC have forced me into doing something which I should not be doing, which is issuing a statement from my sick bed. Firstly, all major decisions are taken by the full Commission. Most Commissioners are black. Most members of each of the three constituent committees of the TRC are black. The chairpersons of each of the Committees, as well as the Chief Executive Officer, are black.
>
> Secondly, the suggestion from anonymous sources in the Commission that it is run by a clique of liberals is insulting to me and I take very strong umbrage. The implication is that I am almost a token chairperson who is not in control. Anyone who knows me is aware that I am not a person to be manipulated by cliques. Dr Alex Boraine consults closely with me on what he is doing. He does not take decisions other than those delegated to him without discussing them with me. What is more, when we were appointing a

Chief Executive Officer last year, Dr Boraine was
quite insistent that a suitably qualified black person
should be appointed.

It is sad that anonymous individuals are not using
the existing channels laid down in the TRC to resolve
grievances because it undermines the tremendously
committed and conscientious work being done by
staff, Committee members and Commissioners.[2]

Tutu's statement helped matters to return to normal, but
the Commission, like the wider South Africa, was never
entirely free of tensions, some of which were linked to
racism, conscious or otherwise.

Such tensions affected the white commissioners too.
Mary Burton, for example, was at first held back by her
determination not to be seen as a 'pushy' white liberal.
This was understandable, but, as a result, for the first two
years the Commission was denied her considerable leadership abilities. All this changed in the last nine months. Her
concern for the victims overtook her reticence and she
became a powerful 'mover and shaker'. She began to
recommend several courses of action and led from the
front.

The Commission also experienced conflict from its
right-wing members. Wynand Malan seemed to feel that I
was unduly critical of the National Party and of F.W. de
Klerk. I, on the other hand, felt that he was attempting to
'water down' the Commission's report so that it could be
much more acceptable to those who had implemented
apartheid. It came as no surprise to me when, in the end, he
submitted a minority report, stating his reservations about
some of the Commission's findings. His report must speak
for itself, but I think it ought to be read very carefully in
conjunction with the reply by the Commission.[3] I think
most of us felt that he had every right to issue a minority
report, but felt that by absenting himself so often from
major debates, and by failing to participate in many of the
difficult arguments leading to eventual consensus, he unfairly judged the Commission's process and its ultimate

[93]

findings. Most disappointing was his attempt to offer a sophisticated spin on the formulation of apartheid.

Chris de Jager, who had formerly been a Conservative Party MP, also often disagreed with the decisions that were being made, and said so, although he accepted the majority decision of the Commission. I think in the end the overwhelming allegations of wide-scale atrocities by the security forces became too much for him; he began to realise the direction in which the report was going and didn't want to be part of that. He resigned at the end of the first year. I wrote to him on behalf of the Commission, urging him to withdraw his resignation, but in the end he was transferred from the Commission to the Amnesty Committee, where he seems to have fitted in extremely well.

The commissioners and staff members faced an extremely demanding and hectic programme, which made it difficult for us to face some of these crises and personality clashes with equanimity. Our work left us in a state of permanent, bone-aching exhaustion. The rigorous demands on everyone brought about by a deadline, the seemingly never-ending schedule, and the long days and very often long nights exacted a heavy toll on the lives of the commissioners and many of the staff. The constant travelling, the long absences from home, the suspension of a normal social life, the criticism of family and friends, yet another square box of a hotel room, the persistent calls from an insatiable media, the invasion of privacy, and the tension between the task on the one hand and the process on the other meant that all of us were in survival mode, trying to get though one hour or one day or one week.

There were many highs and lows, which meant that we were often irritable when it came to the actual management of the Commission. We returned from long journeys, short of sleep, barely debriefed from the demand of listening to victims' stories, and then had to sit through countless meetings and engage in what appeared to be fairly humdrum matters on an over-long agenda. This was not conducive to good decision-making. Sometimes the pettiness, the suspicions, the drudgery of countless committee and Commission meetings, and the endless discussions made one dread returning to headquarters. It all seemed out of touch with what we experienced when we were face to face with people who were opening their hearts and minds to us. It was as if we were in real, genuine discourse at the time of the hearings and engaging in almost irrelevant chit-chat when it came to the management of the Commission.

We also faced the trauma of listening to, and in some cases taking upon ourselves, the grief, the horror, and the pain of victims and survivors. Several of the commissioners and many of the staff sought counselling at trauma centres and from the resources within the Commission itself. When one is dog-tired and the pace is relentless, it also brings about a feeling of inadequacy, a questioning of oneself, and a desperate hope that one can measure up to the task.

There was one point when the hearings were to have an even more direct impact on the life of one of the commissioners. In a bizarre twist of events, Dumisa Ntsebeza was publicly accused of being involved in the Heidelberg Tavern massacre, which had taken place towards the end of December 1993. This particularly brutal attack on a pub had left four people dead and six injured, two of them crippled for life. During the investigation of the amnesty applications of those who had committed the atrocity, one of the TRC investigators came across an affidavit from a Mr Bennett Sibaya, who claimed that the getaway car had been driven by Dumisa Ntsebeza. It was to the credit of the Commission that this information was not discarded or obscured in any way but was brought to Desmond Tutu and me. We immediately asked the Investigative Unit to proceed with the investigation. Dumisa was head of the Investigative Unit, but we told him that he ought not to involve himself in any way with the investigation and that the report would be handed to me.

The report stated that Bennett Sibaya insisted that Dumisa Ntsebeza was the man. I discussed this with Tutu and we decided that, as the Amnesty Committee was to

[95]

meet very soon to hear the amnesty applications concerning the massacre, the Commission should serve a notice
on Dumisa to say that he might be mentioned adversely
during that hearing. Looking back, I think we made the
wrong decision. We should have immediately instituted an
investigation, although both of us believed that the
evidence was inconclusive and had absolute faith and trust
that Dumisa had not been involved in any way. At the
amnesty hearing, in a moment of high drama, Bennett
Sibaya walked over to Dumisa, who was sitting in the
audience, and identified him as the one he had seen in the
getaway car on the night of the massacre. This was strenuously denied by Dumisa and his lawyer, but the damage
was done. This was a huge blow not only to Dumisa's
credibility but also to that of the Commission. A week
later, Sibaya appeared at Tutu's office door and confessed
that he had lied and that his accusation had been instigated
by the security police. He then appeared before the full
Commission at a press conference, admitted that he had
lied, offered an apology to the Commission, and shook
hands with Dumisa Ntsebeza.

Despite this, it was decided that an impartial investigation should be held and we asked the President to initiate
it. The President immediately appointed Richard Goldstone as a one-man commission, who later reported his
finding that Sibaya had lied and that he had been put up to
this by the police. He also suggested that legal action
should be contemplated against Sibaya for his act of perjury.

In all this, the man who went through absolute hell
was Dumisa himself. To see someone who was normally
full of laughter and good spirit cast down and depressed
was agony for those of us who had been enriched by his
warmth and friendship. Many of us tried to support him
during this difficult time, and I wrote him a letter urging
him not to be concerned by the accusation, and stating that
he would have to face many such trials during the life of
the Commission, and that I was confident that he would
come through this unscathed and even stronger because of
it. He told me that it was his view that the staff were

divided in their support of him. He was bitterly disappointed because he felt that this division was on racial
grounds: that the white staff believed him to be guilty as
alleged, while the black staff were solidly behind him. This
was yet another example of the incipient racism that
affected the Commission.

4

Breaking the silence:
The TRC hearings

AT THE VERY first TRC hearing, the first person
to appear before us was Mrs Nohle Mohape, whose husband, Mapetla, had been killed in detention in 1976. After
she had taken the oath my opening words were,

> In welcoming you as the first witness in the proceed-
> ings of the Truth and Reconciliation Commission we
> are mindful of the suffering that you have endured in
> the past. Many of us remember as though it was
> yesterday when Mapetla died in police custody. We
> remember the anguish and horror of those days and
> we know also, apart from the personal grief that you
> have experienced, that you yourself have been a
> victim of human rights violations. We know that you
> too have been detained and were in solitary confine-
> ment and we salute you as someone of great courage.
> We thank you for coming here today. This is a testi-
> mony to your commitment, to truth, to justice, to
> reconciliation and to peace between you and all
> people and all South Africa.

Her response was, 'I am very happy today after 20 years to
be present in this commission. Today is the 20th year when
my husband died. I am very happy to get this chance to sit
in front of you to explain to you who killed my husband.'

It was Tuesday 16 April 1996. The place, East London,
in the Eastern Cape. At last the curtain was raised; the
drama which was to unfold during the next two and a half

years had witnessed its first scene. The ritual, which was what the public hearings were, which promised truth, healing, and reconciliation to a deeply divided and traumatised people, began with a story. This was the secret of the Commission – no stern-faced officials sitting in a private chamber, but a stage, a handful of black and white men and women listening to stories of horror, of deep sorrow, amazing fortitude, and heroism. The audience was there too, and a much wider audience watched and listened through television and radio. It was a ritual, deeply needed to cleanse a nation. It was a drama. The actors were in the main ordinary people with a powerful story. But this was no brilliantly written play; it was the unvarnished truth in all its starkness.

We participated in many similar hearings throughout South Africa over the next eighteen months. Because this was the first hearing it was much more dramatic and demanding than any other of the hearings that followed. The City Hall in East London was packed to capacity. The atmosphere was electric with a tangible air of tension and expectancy. Already there had been a bomb scare and the hall had had to be cleared before we could reassemble. The hall was full, not only with people who had come to bear witness and to listen to so many of their friends and colleagues telling their stories, but also with security force members to protect the people and proceedings. This was a moment of absolute irony: that people who had suffered so deeply were there to tell stories of horror and outrage which had been perpetrated by, in the main, policemen. Today they were no longer under siege, no longer harassed, but were protected by the police. They were guests of honour. They were in a liberated zone. It was an astonishing moment, and one that will stay with me for the rest of my life.

Our choice of East London as the venue for the first hearings of victims and survivors of human rights violations was quite deliberate. Many had urged us to begin the public hearings in one of the major cities of the country, but we felt strongly that we should start in the Eastern

Cape, which had witnessed some of the worst features of apartheid persecution, and we wanted to make the point that the Commission's concern was not only for the major cities, but also for the smaller towns, the rural areas, and every area of the country.

I arrived in East London on the Tuesday before the first hearings took place. I went straight to our office there and met with one of my fellow commissioners, Bongani Finca, and some of his staff. Bongani is an unassuming, quiet man with a deep faith and a wonderful sense of humour. He clearly commanded respect, not only among his staff but particularly among those who were flocking to the Commission to tell their stories. We went immediately to Bisho and met with the first witnesses, who were making their statements. A dedicated staff were listening and writing down the sometimes halting, sometimes free-flowing, words of those who were going to be among the first witnesses before the historic Commission.

I was struck by the quietness and the seriousness of the situation. Many people were obviously re-living their ghastly experiences. Most were telling their stories in Xhosa. As I moved among them and shook hands and greeted people I began to realise how heavy was the responsibility resting on the Commission. I felt humbled and vulnerable. I was apprehensive and lost in thought when I drove back to East London for the first of many radio and television interviews. Were we sufficient for the task?

The next day the members of the Human Rights Violations Committee met to make final arrangements for the first public hearing. It was clear that my colleagues were as anxious as I was. One of the issues that concerned us deeply was whether we could allow witnesses to give the names of their alleged torturers and the killers of their loved ones. This was an issue that was to trouble us throughout the TRC hearings, and was the subject of several court cases. How do we reach the truth and ensure due process? Understandably, many of the people who were going to tell their stories wanted to tell the whole story. There was a great deal of anger as well as excitement among those who were ready to tell the whole of South Africa about their particular experience under the yoke of apartheid.

Religion played a very large part in the communities in which the hearings were to be held. Finca himself was a Presbyterian minister and he had been asked to hold a special church service on the Sunday before the first hearing. The church in Mdantsane was packed to the rafters. It was supposed to have been an inter-faith service but it soon became apparent that it was almost entirely a Christian service and very largely Protestant. This was perhaps understandable, but I hoped very much that we were not going to exclude some because of this emphasis. This was to be a recurring issue in the work of the Commission. Archbishop Tutu never hesitated to exercise his role as a church leader and a committed Christian. This was true at the church service but equally true at the hearings themselves. When I suggested to him that he should not wear his purple clerical robes to the hearings, he replied, 'The President knew that I was an Archbishop when he appointed me!' For me the saving grace on that Sunday afternoon was the singing, the dancing, and the traditional enactment of purification, of repentance, of sorrow, of commitment.

The following evening I sat with my wife, Jenny, in the Holiday Inn and anxiously anticipated the next day when Mrs Mohape would appear as the first witness at the Commission's first hearing. It was only in the early hours of the morning that sleep rescued me from a sense of apprehension and even dread. I knew that it could go very badly wrong. Although we had prepared for every eventuality, this was South Africa and we remained a very divided society. We were embarking on a journey into uncharted territory with no map and no compass.

Mapetla Mohape died in detention in 1976. The official verdict was that he had committed suicide. He had been a close friend of Steve Biko and an ardent supporter of black consciousness. In her evidence before us, Mrs Mohape told of how Mapetla and Steve and others had urged them to be proud of their origin:

[101]

They would even make a noise, telling us to stop imi-
tating whites, busy smearing our faces with creams
because we wanted to look like whites, busy stretching our hair because we wanted it to be long. You are
beautiful as you are. We recognise you as you are.
Don't try and imitate other cultures so that you can
become beautiful. It is not important to us. You are a
human being.

This was the major thrust of the black consciousness
movement and it prompted the strong resistance to the dehumanising policies of apartheid. As a result of this resistance many were harassed, imprisoned, tortured, and
killed.

At the hearing, one witness followed after another. The
day seemed to be full of trauma, drama, occasional flashes
of humour, evidence of great pain, intense anger, and yet a
remarkable and wonderful spirit of generosity. Throughout
it I sat on the edge of my seat, my body stiff with anxiety and
my heart filled with great sadness as I listened to ordinary
people telling their extraordinary stories of sorrow and loss.

The second day was in many ways even more moving
than the first. This was especially true of the story told by
Nomonde Calata. She was the widow of Fort Calata, one of
the so-called Cradock Four who had been brutally murdered in the Eastern Cape in 1984.[1] In the middle of her evidence she broke down and the primeval and spontaneous
wail from the depths of her soul was carried live on radio
and television, not only throughout South Africa but to
many other parts of the world. It was that cry from the soul
that transformed the hearings from a litany of suffering and
pain to an even deeper level. It caught up in a single howl
all the darkness and horror of the apartheid years. It was as
if she enshrined in the throwing back of her body and letting out the cry the collective horror of the thousands of
people who had been trapped in racism and oppression for
so long. Antjie Krog was present at the hearing in her
capacity as a reporter for the South African Broadcasting
Corporation. She later commented in her book, *Country of*

my Skull, 'For me, this crying is the beginning of the Truth Commission – the signature tune, the definitive moment, the ultimate sound of what the process is about. She was wearing this vivid orange-red dress and she threw herself backwards and that sound ... that sound ... it will haunt me for ever and ever.'[2]

Nomonde Calata's sorrowful cry was played over and over again by the SABC. Many people told me afterwards that they had found it unbearable and switched off the radio. I had met Nomonde several times and had known her husband, Fort, before his assassination. At an earlier conference to which I had invited her, she spoke not only of her deep despair at the loss of her husband, but also of how her thoughts had turned to the unborn child she had been carrying at the time, who is now a young teenager: 'She keeps asking questions: who was my father? It is hard to explain to her. At times she comes and says, "Can't you draw a picture for me? Can't you say something that he said?" That is very, very hard.'[3]

Another person who stood out for me at that memorable hearing was Ernest Malgas. I had met him years earlier, a veteran of the struggle who had been harassed and arrested many times and spent fifteen years in jail. But this time he was very different from the upright, powerful man I had known before. He had grown old, had suffered a stroke, and was in a wheelchair. Because of the stroke he found it difficult to speak, and his stumbling, tortured speech added extra pathos to an already moving story. His account of his life, his commitment to the struggle, to overthrowing and overcoming apartheid, and the suffering that this brought in its wake was achingly moving. He told the Commission that he had been tortured many times. I asked him to describe his torture, because we needed to verify and corroborate accounts of torture and other human rights violations. He was silent for a while and then tried to describe a particular method of torture known as 'the helicopter', which involved suspending the victim upside down from a wooden stick and beating and kicking him in the process, often until he was unconscious. Revisiting this experience was too much for Malgas and he broke down and cried. It was too much for Desmond Tutu, who put his head on the table and sobbed. I brought the hearing to an end – it was fairly late in the day – because clearly there was no way we could continue. Tutu has always blamed me for his breaking down and sobbing, because I asked Malgas to describe his torture. It certainly was a moment of intense tragedy, but I think it was the accumulation of the events of the days before which brought it to a head. There were to be many, many such moments when, by sheer willpower, many of us, and certainly I, had to bite hard on our teeth or the inside of our cheeks, and blink away the tears which threatened to overwhelm us. We had a job to do and that job was to keep the focus on the victims and as far as possible to keep the attention away from ourselves. But at times it was an almost impossible task.

Another striking testimony in those early days in East London was that of Beth Savage, a white woman, who was one of several victims of a hand grenade attack on the King William's Town Golf Club. King William's Town is a small border town about forty kilometres from East London. At a simple Christmas celebration, armed members of the Azanian People's Liberation Army (Apla), the armed wing of the PAC, had stormed the Golf Club, opened fire, and hurled hand grenades into the clubhouse. After months of medical treatment and still carrying shrapnel in her body, Beth Savage was quite radiant. She ended her account of the attack with these words: 'I would like to meet the man who killed my friends and injured me. I would like to meet that man that threw that grenade in an attitude of forgiveness and hope that he could forgive me too for whatever reason.'[4] Many would strongly disagree with the sentiments that Beth Savage expressed on that day. But in a few short, sensitive words she acknowledged the responsibility of the beneficiaries of apartheid for some of the horror and tragedy of the conflict which had raged in South Africa. Her willingness to forgive and in particular her remarkable plea for forgiveness will forever stand in strong contrast to the refusal by so many white South Africans to accept any responsibility for the system they supported for so long. Her brave testimony was a rebuke to the many white political leaders who played word games to avoid accepting unqualified responsibility for the darkness they had brought upon our land.

During the first week of hearings in East London thirty-three witnesses appeared before the Commission; eight victims testified about abuses they had suffered, and the remaining victims spoke on behalf of deceased husbands, children, brothers, and friends. While most of the witnesses had an ANC affiliation, victims included people with affiliation to the PAC, Azapo, Umkhonto we Sizwe, and Cosas,[5] as well as people who were not politically involved, such as those who had been injured or had lost loved ones in the King William's Town Golf Club attack. The witnesses came from many parts of the Eastern Cape, from the former Ciskei and Transkei, Port Elizabeth and East London, and many towns in between.

The victim hearings, which played such a major role in the work of the Commission, were the subject of considerable debate and activity in the early months of its life. Almost every decision taken in those first hectic months was geared to set in place the staff and the strategy to ensure that the public hearings would be sensitively and efficiently managed.

The decision to operate on a decentralised basis, for example, was largely to allow the Commission to traverse the vast distances in South Africa and to offset logistical difficulties which arose from holding hearings throughout the country. Having offices not only in Cape Town but also in East London, Durban, and Johannesburg enabled us to conduct many more hearings than would otherwise have been possible. We had no doubt that it would be necessary to go where the people were rather than to sit in a central venue and expect witnesses to come to us. But the organisation required to achieve this was overwhelming, and we always felt that we were inadequate for the task. No matter what provisions we made, there always seemed to be additional challenges. Countless meetings were held to plan for every eventuality, and it is no exaggeration to say that the planning of the initial round of hearings dominated every aspect of our work until the first hearing in East London in April 1996.

Although the entire Commission was involved in critical decisions surrounding the hearings, the Human Rights Violations Committee accepted the major responsibility and reported to the Commission. That committee originally comprised Desmond Tutu (chairperson), Yasmin Sooka (vice chairperson), Wynand Malan (vice chairperson), Mary Burton, Bongani Finca, Richard Lyster, Dumisa Ntsebeza, Denzil Potgieter, Fazel Randera, and me. Wynand Malan and Denzil Potgieter were reassigned to the Amnesty Committee during 1997.

We were also very fortunate that in accordance with the Act we were able to appoint a further ten people as Human Rights Violations Committee members. These were Russell Ally, June Crichton, Mdu Dlamini, Virginia Gcabashe, Pumla Gobodo-Madikizela, Ilan Lax, Hugh Lewin, Judith 'Tiny' Maya, Ntsikilelo Sandi, and Joyce Seroke. Tiny Maya resigned at the end of 1997 and was replaced by Motho Msouhli. Both Ntsiki Sandi and Ilan Lax were reassigned to the Amnesty Committee in early 1998.

It was this group of commissioners and committee members that began to work out strategy, to identify the steps that needed to be taken, and to appoint the skilled personnel who were required.

We decided that the only way to identify victims was to invite them to complete a statement which would give us the relevant information, provide a permanent record, and ensure uniformity and consistency. It seemed to take forever for us to agree on the protocol but finally one was adopted unanimously by the Commission. Even though it took a great deal of time, the protocol was important because the way we set out the statement would assist us to identify victims; in this we had to walk the tightrope between too wide and too narrow an interpretation of 'gross violations of human rights'. The Act states that

gross violations of human rights means the violation
of human rights through – (a) the killing, abduction,
torture or severe ill-treatment of any person; or (b) any
attempt, conspiracy, incitement, instigation, command or procurement to commit an act referred to in
paragraph (a), which emanated from conflicts of the
past and which was committed during the period
1 March 1960 to 10 May 1994 within or outside the
Republic, and the commission of which was advised,
planned, directed, commanded or ordered by any person acting with a political motive.

This is a narrow definition and often caused commissioners and staff, as well as many who came to us, great distress. Apartheid masqueraded as a massive experiment in
social engineering, reaching into every aspect of life, and it
was always difficult to appreciate that we were limited to
gross violations of human rights. What then about the
plight of those who were forcibly removed from their
homes? Or those whose basic humanity was diminished
by the tentacles of apartheid which spread through health,
education, housing, and employment? We had to remind
ourselves continually that if the TRC was to carry out its
mandate it had to do its work within a limited time and
adhere to the narrow definition laid out in the Act. If we
were to address the overall consequences of apartheid, we
would need twenty to thirty years before we could complete the task. There were other agencies, commissions,
and committees set up by the state, which were partners in
dealing with the legacy of the past, and the state itself was
taking racist laws off the statute book and introducing new
laws which promised equality before the law and
adherence to the rule of law. Our task was to focus on the
more extreme human rights violations.

Making a statement to the Commission was a voluntary process, therefore we had to be proactive without imposing on anyone. We tried to make it clear from the very
beginning that no one ought to be obliged to complete a
statement, but that the opportunity was there if they

wished to do so. There were three approaches to securing statements from victims. Firstly, trained statement-takers were based in all four offices, and victims were invited to come to those offices and complete statements. Many did, but they were in the minority. Most of the victims were poor, many lived in rural areas, and public transport was costly. On its own, therefore, this method proved to be inadequate.

A second method was to go into the communities and to take statements in a public hall, in a church, or in people's homes. The news of our arrival in a community was widely covered by the media. This was a successful strategy, particularly when we announced that a hearing would be held in a particular area. Statement-takers and support staff would go in advance and meet the community leaders. This caused considerable interest, and many people took advantage of the opportunity to make statements. In some areas we held public meetings and workshops, and this always brought a good response.

It soon became apparent to us, however, that even these two approaches were limited and were inadequate to reach out to all who wished to make statements. To overcome this we introduced a third approach whereby we appointed 'designated statement-takers'. This programme was made possible by a foreign donor. We embarked on a training programme for statement-takers drawn from community-based organisations who acted on behalf of the Commission. Many non-governmental organisations became involved, and in the three months that these designated statement-takers were appointed on a full-time basis they collected close to 4000 statements.

Statement-taking was no simple matter, and the Commission owes a huge debt to those brave and dedicated people who undertook this onerous and challenging task. Many were proficient in several languages. They worked long hours and often listened to gruesome stories. They had to exercise patience with people who had grown old and who sometimes forgot some of the details of the story that they wanted to share with the statement-taker. Their work was an act of love. Their patience and endurance was quite remarkable and they contributed richly to the success of the public hearings.

It was impossible to have public hearings for all those who made statements, and many of those who did submit written statements were not keen to appear in public. The way we approached the matter was to look at the statements that were made and to select a representative group based on types of victims, places, occasions, and dates on which the alleged offences and abuses took place, so that we would have a mix of violations committed to be heard in public and thus shared with the whole nation.

Once the statements were completed they were registered on the Commission's database, photocopies and originals secured in strong rooms. The data processors then entered the details of each violation onto the database. Thereafter it was the turn of the Investigative Unit, whose task was to corroborate the essential facts. This proved to be a daunting task. Often the incidents had occurred hundreds and sometimes thousands of kilometres away from the closest office. Many of the incidents had taken place as early as the 1960s. Over and over again, investigators would go to a police station in search of information, only to find that there were no proper records or that the records seemed to have been destroyed. In some cases all the victims had been killed or had since died and it was difficult to find eyewitnesses. Finally, many incidents reported to the Commission had occurred in neighbouring states or as far afield as Europe.

In addition to the attempt by the investigators to corroborate the facts set out in the statements, the Research Department prepared briefing documents on the history and political background to particular human rights violations which had taken place. This was extremely helpful to the Commission and to the media in understanding the context in which violations had taken place.

Thus it was that the telephone operators, the receptionists, the staff, the committee members, and the commissioners worked to prepare for a hearing, took part in a hearing, or dealt with the many consequences of the hearings.

In addition, we had to consider an overall Commission strategy, a witness protection programme, security, media liaison, and so much more. Separate committees were appointed for all of these matters. I was the chairperson of the Strategy Committee, which straddled many aspects of the Commission's work and constantly had to meet in order to adapt and adjust in relation to new developments. Furthermore, numerous meetings, think-tanks, and seminars were conducted to refine our approach and deal with specific problems such as legal challenges, psychological support services, and the like.

In sum, the Human Rights Violations Committee, in consultation with the Commission as a whole, had to take into account the following demanding factors: the safety and security of all activities and participants, the representivity of victims appearing at hearings, sensitivity with regard to the choice of hearing venues, seating arrangements at hearings, simultaneous translation services, the format and duration of hearings, the length of testimony by victims, legal assistance for victims, psycho-social support for victims and their families who testified, the policy of 'cross-examination of victims' by alleged perpetrators, and the policy on the types of public hearings to be held, including victim hearings where the focus was on the individual victim testifying on her or his experience of suffering.

To ensure that victims were received with compassion and dignity, we appointed 'briefers' to accompany and assist them before, during, and after the hearings. Often a victim would break down during his or her story and the briefer would be there to provide comfort, perhaps with the touch of a hand, sometimes with a hug, or by offering a glass of water or a tissue. These briefers rendered a wonderful service. They were the frontline carers who demonstrated in action the essence of the Commission's aim, namely to bring healing to the badly damaged women and men who came before us to break the silence by sharing their stories and their pain.

[110]

Another group who must be saluted are the translators. We felt it was important that victims tell their stories in the language of their choice, therefore we introduced simultaneous translation. The translators had the difficult and traumatic task of speaking in the first person and therefore in a sense taking on the pain and anguish of the victim. Day after day, working in shifts, they were confined to hot and cramped booths. They were among the unsung heroes of the TRC.

The question must be asked, was all this preparation, activity, hard work, and planning worthwhile? I often asked myself this question, particularly in the lead-up to the first hearing in East London. But the moment Nohle Mohape told us that she was happy to be present at the hearing and grateful to be able to tell the story of her own suffering and the death of her husband, Mapetla, I knew it was all worthwhile.

One of the problems we faced at the East London hearings was the naming of perpetrators in the testimony of victims. According to Section 30 of the Act,

> If during any investigation by or any hearing before
> the Commission – (a) any person is implicated in
> a manner which may be to his or her detriment, (b)
> the Commission contemplates making a decision
> which may be to the detriment of a person who has
> been so implicated or (c) it appears that any person
> may be a victim; the Commission shall, if such
> person is available, afford him or her an opportunity
> to submit representations to the Commission within
> a specified time with regard to the matter under
> consideration or to give evidence at a hearing of the
> Commission.

We were concerned that the victim hearings should not involve additional trauma for those appearing and that they should not be subjected to vicious cross-examination. In addition, we were concerned that if we were to give prior notice to those whose names were going to be mentioned to their detriment, the names of the victims would become known, and, in the light of the past, when so many people had been harassed and worse, we wanted to do everything possible to protect victims already faced with the enormous pressure of reliving past atrocities. What we did, therefore, was to send out somewhat vague notices to people whose names were going to be mentioned by witnesses at that first public hearing. Because of the pressures on the Commission we sent out the notices late and should have realised that we were leaving ourselves open to a court challenge. Some within the Commission and on our staff maintained that at a public hearing no findings were being made but that they would be made only at a much later date, and therefore that no notice was necessary. Nevertheless, while we may have been correct in protecting witnesses who had suffered so much, we did not take sufficient account of due process and the whole question of the *audi alteram partem* (hearing the other side) principle. Also, because of the pressure relating to our first public hearing and our inexperience, it has to be conceded that in those early stages our administrative work was sloppy.

On 15 April 1996 an urgent interim application was lodged against the Commission by Brigadier Jan du Preez and Major General Nic Janse van Rensburg, on the grounds that they had not been given reasonable and timeous notice or sufficient information relating to the charges against them by the witness concerned, at our first hearing in East London. The witness was Joyce Mtimkulu. She was the mother of Siphiwe Mtimkulu, who had disappeared after long periods in prison and after being poisoned while in custody. At that time there was no real evidence of what had happened to him, but the general view was that the security police had been involved in his abduction and killing. The fact that this came to light a little later on didn't help the Commission in its response to the application lodged by Du Preez and Van Rensburg.

The application was opposed by the Commission at the Cape Supreme Court. Judge Edwin King ruled in favour of the applicants and in particular stressed that reasonable and timeous notice should be given to any who might be detrimentally implicated at public hearings. He ruled that the Commission had to furnish Du Preez and Van Rensburg with facts and information which would enable them to exercise their rights in terms of Section 30.

The Commission appealed against Judge King's decision and the matter was heard by the Cape Full Bench on 20 June 1996. In this instance the court ruled that the Commission was not obliged to give prior notice, but that where it made a finding that could be detrimental to an implicated person after a hearing, that person should be granted an opportunity to make representations to the Commission.

Du Preez and Van Rensburg petitioned the Appellate Division in Bloemfontein and the appeal was heard before five judges, with Chief Justice Corbett presiding. In this instance the judgement went against the Commission: we were compelled to give prior notice before evidence was heard publicly, as well as to provide the implicated persons with enough information to enable them to make representations to the Commission. This ruling imposed an almost impossible administrative burden on us. It resulted in long delays, because it was exceedingly difficult to trace a number of the perpetrators and the Commission could not proceed until the individual or individuals concerned had been successfully tracked down. This meant that we had to employ more staff in order to meet the requirements of the ruling. It also had a negative effect on the victims themselves. They felt that the Commission, in following these procedures, was more sympathetic to perpetrators than to them.

What we hadn't fully realised was that this ruling would also have a direct impact on the final report of the Commission. In a sense, the Commission would be obliged to give alleged perpetrators prior sight of the report if they demanded it, which is contrary to any other state commission that I know of.

We thought the judgement handed down by the Appellate Division was unfortunate, to say the least; it seemed to us that the reasons given by the Cape Full Bench were convincing. It was particularly strange in light of the fact that Gideon Nieuwoudt, a member of the security branch in the Eastern Cape, also brought an urgent application against the Commission, trying to prevent Mrs Mtimkulu from telling her story in public. Judge Buchanan, who presided, differed from Judge King and supported the Cape Full Bench. However, the Appellate Division's ruling was the one we had to take into account, and, despite all the difficulties and all the problems, we did everything we could to adhere to the judgement. It is ironic that the same Gideon Nieuwoudt, who tried to muzzle Mrs Mtimkulu, later applied for amnesty for the kidnapping and killing of Siphiwe Mtimkulu!

The East London hearing was followed by hearings in Cape Town, Johannesburg, and Durban. It was decided that Tutu and I would attend all these hearings, and the first month proved to be one of the toughest in the life of the Commission. There was simply no let-up, and trying to be present in these four major areas throughout the week and to deal with so many other issues that were reported to us in the evenings and over weekends proved to be energy-sapping and mind-blowing. Our spirits were often laid low by the enormity of what we heard, but we were inspired by the courage that was revealed time and time again in the midst of tragedy.

Because of the methodology we adopted, those who came to the Commission were a very wide cross-section of South Africans. They were not a partisan group specially selected by the Commission. Those who came to us came voluntarily and they came from every part of the country and from every part of the community. Black and white, women and men, old and young. Despite the public opposition by the leader of the Inkatha Freedom Party, Mangosuthu Buthelezi, by far the most statements were gathered in KwaZulu-Natal. We received 9506 from this area, compared with 3511 from the second-largest area, Gauteng. Of the total of 21 297 statements taken, 86.9 per cent were from the African population and only 1.1 per cent were from the white population. In other words, it was over-whelmingly Africans who came to the Commission to share with us the gross violations of their human rights. The breakdown in gender terms was as follows: more women came to the Commission than men, although more African women came than any other category. Men were in the majority among the white, 'coloured', and Asian deponents. Nationally the proportion of women to men was 54:52. The violence of the past had clearly resulted in the deaths of more men than women, so more of the survivors who came to tell their stories were women. But it should be emphasised that in many instances women played down their own suffering and spoke about that of their families. Many women had suffered in their own right, having been detained without trial, harassed, assaulted, insulted, raped, and tortured. Most of the statements were made by those aged thirty-seven and above, with men in the majority in the younger category and women in the middle-aged to elderly age groups. Those who came to the Commission told of experiences suffered directly by themselves or by someone close to them. In the 21 000 statements made to the Commission, nearly 38 000 allegations were disclosed, of which 10 000 were killings.

Two things should be emphasised. Firstly, there were clearly many more victims in South Africa than those who came to us voluntarily. Many decided that they did not want to come to the Commission and many who attended the hearings did not want to make statements. Further-more, I have no doubt that if we had had more resources in terms of staff and finance and the precious commodity of time, the list would have been very much longer. Secondly, those who came to the Commission cannot be confined and circumscribed by statistics. They were so many, they were so different, most were so poor, so full of anguish, so desperate to tell their stories, that it loses something to classify them as male or female, black or white, young or old. They were all human beings who had been cast aside, badly treated, and severely wronged, and

[115]

were seeking some way back to start a new life. They were all very human.

———

FOR THE FIRST six months of its life, the TRC listened to the testimonies of people who had suffered under apartheid. But the Commission had a second task: to hear the accounts of the people who had committed these atrocities. These testimonies were heard by the Amnesty Committee.

The Amnesty Committee was one of the three statutory committees of the Commission. Initially, five members were appointed, one of whom had to be a judge of the Supreme Court. President Mandela had the right in terms of the Act to appoint three of the five members, and two others had to be commissioners, both of whom had to be legally trained. Mandela decided to appoint not one judge but three so as to indicate the absolute integrity and impartiality of the Amnesty Committee. Judge Hassen E. Mall was appointed by the President as chairperson of the committee, Judge Andrew Wilson as deputy chairperson, and Judge Bernard Ngoepe as the third appointee. The two commissioners appointed to the Amnesty Committee were Sisi Khampepe and Chris de Jager.

The process of appointment of the Amnesty Committee caused considerable delays. President Mandela obviously had many other things to do and he needed to consult widely in order to ensure that the committee was as representative as possible. The difficulty was that judges can't simply walk out of cases that are already under way, and as a result the Amnesty Committee took far too long to get off the ground.

A second problem was that the chairperson of the Amnesty Committee was not a member of the Commission. We invited him to attend Commission meetings, and he did so quite often, but that is very different from being a commissioner. During the drafting of the Act some of us had stressed strongly the need for the chairperson to be a commissioner and also for any amnesty decisions to be reviewed by the full Commission. These proposals had been turned down, in the main by the National Party, because they wanted to ensure that the Amnesty Committee, which would be making major decisions about perpetrators, should be as independent as possible. I understand this view, but it did create major problems in terms of executing the work expeditiously.

I think, too, the mood of the judges was very different from that of the commissioners. Their approach seemed to lack urgency, and they saw themselves as almost beyond contradiction, allowing no one to dare query their decisions. We tried in a number of ways to hurry them on in the work, which was assuming alarming proportions. We had never imagined that we would have as many amnesty applications as we did, and as they poured in we realised that unless we could strengthen the Amnesty Committee, the process would go on for years. We gave them as much administrative back-up as possible, replaced staff who weren't delivering, appointed additional staff and finally additional Amnesty Committee members, but nothing seemed to galvanise the committee into action. To be fair, I think one of their major problems was the fact that everyone applying for amnesty had the right to legal representation, and victims, who were encouraged by the Commission to attend the hearings, very often had legal representation as well. Lawyers are well known for taking the longest time possible for a variety of reasons, and this made life very difficult for the Amnesty Committee.

Furthermore, many of the decisions faced by the Amnesty Committee were very complex and therefore time-consuming. The whole question of amnesty, which is by definition controversial, will be taken up in greater detail in Chapter 8. Suffice to say here that Judge Mall was an absolute gentleman and one could only warm to him, despite his apparent lack of urgency.

The amnesty provision was probably the most controversial aspect of the Truth and Reconciliation Commission. On the one hand, some people urged that there should be a general amnesty with no conditions attached, and they opposed the idea that individuals would have to apply for amnesty and that their cases would be heard in public. On the other hand, others, among the victims in particular and in the human rights community, were suspicious of even a limited amnesty and thought that it would be very unfair to victims and their families and might encourage impunity.

The amnesty provision was faced with a legal challenge, lodged before the Constitutional Court by the Azanian People's Organisation (Azapo), Nontsikelelo (Ntsiki) Biko, Churchill Mhleli (Mbasa) Mxenge, and Chris Ribeiro on 1 July 1996. Had this challenge been successful, it would have paralysed the Amnesty Committee and would have had very serious repercussions for the entire Commission. The sponsors were very well known in the country. Azapo had close ties with the late Steve Biko, Ntsiki was Biko's widow, Mxenge's brother, Griffiths, had been very cruelly hacked to death by the security forces, and Chris' parents, Fabian and Florence Ribeiro, had been assassinated on the instructions of the security police. Many of us in the Commission felt very sympathetic towards both the organisation and the individuals concerned. Thus it was with mixed feelings that we opposed their challenge.

What were the applicants asking of the Constitutional Court? They were demanding that the amnesty provision, Section 20(7) in the founding Act, be declared unconstitutional. The effect of Section 20(7), read with other sections of the Act, is to permit the Amnesty Committee to grant amnesty to a perpetrator of an act associated with a political objective and committed prior to 5 December 1993. The consequence of this granting of amnesty is that the perpetrator cannot be criminally or civilly liable for the violation under consideration. The Act goes even further and lays down that neither the state nor any other body, organisation, or person (and this would include political parties) that would ordinarily have been vicariously liable for such an act could be liable in law.

Several of us attended the hearing in Johannesburg and as we listened first to one side and then to the other, we were extremely worried about what the final verdict would be. However, in a judgement delivered by Judge Ismail Mahomed, then deputy president of the Constitutional Court, the court unanimously upheld the constitutionality of Section 20(7). Clearly the postamble of the Interim Constitution was central to the argument before the court and very prominent in Mahomed's judgement. The court held that amnesty for criminal liability was permitted by the postamble, because without it there would be no incentive for offenders to disclose the truth about past atrocities. The argument went further that the need for reconciliation and reconstruction in South Africa was clear and without truth this would not be possible.

Furthermore, the court noted that the amnesty provision was a critical component of the negotiated settlement itself, without which the Constitution would not have come into being. The possible granting of amnesty was based not on legal terms nor on the human rights argument, but on a political decision taken by the major political actors leading up to the settlement which had brought about the 1994 election and a new democratic government.

The court also argued that amnesty for civil and criminal liability was permitted by the postamble of the Interim Constitution, not only because without amnesty there would be a disincentive for disclosure of the truth, but also because the Act specifically allowed for reparation for victims. This reparation provision would be in lieu of civil damage which could have been claimed by victims. Mahomed went to the heart of the matter when he argued that reparation for victims of gross human rights violations must be seen in the context of the wider suffering and injustices that had taken place:

The families of those whose fundamental human rights were invaded by torture and abuse are not the only victims who have endured 'untold suffering and injustice' in consequence of the crass inhumanity of apartheid which so many have had to endure for so long. Generations of children born and yet to be born will suffer the consequences of poverty, of malnutrition, of homelessness, of illiteracy and disempowerment generated and sustained by the institutions of apartheid and its manifest effects on life and living for so many. The country has neither the resources nor the skills to reverse fully these massive wrongs. It will take many years of strong commitment, sensitivity and labour to 'reconstruct our society' so as to fulfill the legitimate dreams of new generations exposed to real opportunities for advancement denied to preceding generations initially by the execution of apartheid itself and for a long time after its formal demise, by its relentless consequences. The resources of the state have to be deployed imaginatively, wisely, efficiently and equitably, to facilitate the reconstruction process in a manner which best brings relief and hope to the widest sections of the community, developing for the benefit of the entire nation the latent human potential and resources of every person who has directly or indirectly been burdened with the heritage of the shame and the pain of our racist past.[6]

Finally, the Court found that the amnesty provision was not inconsistent with international law and did not breach any of the country's obligations in terms of public international law. Those who believe it is the duty of the state to punish those responsible for gross violations of human rights will argue against this claim for years to come, and we will return to this judgement in a later chapter when we consider the question of amnesty in greater detail.

Because the Constitutional Court was the highest court in the land, its judgement prevented the possibility of any further challenges to the constitutionality of the Amnesty Committee, enabling it to continue its work without this threat hanging over it.

In his judgement, Judge Mahomed revealed understanding and sensitivity to the plaintiffs. He noted that they wanted to

> insist that wrongdoers who abused their authority and wrongfully murdered and maimed or tortured very much loved members of their families who had, in their view, been engaged in a noble struggle to confront the inhumanity of apartheid, should vigorously be prosecuted and effectively be punished for their callous and inhuman conduct in violation of the criminal law.[7]

The task of the Amnesty Committee was to consider applications by people who had committed political acts which had resulted in gross human rights violations. Section 4 of the Act distinguished between four kinds of responsibility. Firstly, those who participated directly in gross violations of human rights; secondly, those who gave orders for gross violations of human rights to be committed; thirdly, those who created a climate in which gross violations of human rights could occur; and, finally, those who failed to act against or punish those responsible for gross violations of human rights and therefore were responsible for sanctioning or ratifying these acts or were guilty of 'official tolerance' of these acts.

As in the case of victims, an application form had to be devised. This seemed to take forever. It had to be very carefully worked out legally and be true to the Act, it had to be simple enough for lay people to understand, and it had to be translated into all official languages. Once the application form was finally adopted, it was widely distributed. It was available in the four Commission offices, and supplies were also sent to police stations, magistrates' courts, prisons, town halls, various organisations, and political parties. It was also made available to the media.

Initially the response was very slow. There was a lot of uncertainty. It seemed that even though the application was cast in very simple language, most people needed

[121]

assistance to complete the form. The initial period that the applications could refer to was from March 1960 to 5 December 1993, but the cut-off date was later extended to 10 May 1994. This was largely at the request of the Freedom Front and the Pan African Congress, so that some of the acts of violence which took place immediately prior to the election could be included in the time frame.

The hearings of the Amnesty Committee were very different from those of the Human Rights Violations Committee where the victims told stories about the wrongs they had suffered. The very fact that the Amnesty Committee was made up of judges and lawyers was one of the reasons for this difference. Furthermore, all amnesty applicants had the right to legal assistance; after their initial submission, their lawyers argued on their behalf. The mood was more judicial, almost like a court. A limited amount of cross-examination was allowed; this was sometimes abused by some of the lawyers who acted on behalf of the applicants, and even those who acted on behalf of victims. The atmosphere of compassion and sensitivity that was so prominent in the victim hearings was lacking. It is easy to be critical; the Amnesty Committee had an extraordinarily difficult job and the very nature of their work made it almost inevitable that there would be a very different climate from that of the victim hearings.

In terms of the Act, priority had to be given to applicants who were in prison. But the Commission decided that a number of 'window cases' should also be heard, from perpetrators who had not been charged, in order to encourage applications from all who had been involved in human rights violations.

There were a number of complicating factors. Firstly, the Investigative Unit had to read through the application forms and then seek corroboration to ensure that the stories told by the perpetrators were accurate and truthful and that they met the standard of full disclosure. This all took time, and sometimes weeks would go by without a single case being resolved. A distinction was made between chamber hearings and public hearings. In terms of the Act, if the case involved a gross human rights violation such as murder, rape, abduction, torture, or severe ill-treatment, it had to be heard in public. Other human rights violations which fell outside these definitions could be heard in chambers, and this enabled quite a number of cases to be processed.

We had enormous difficulty with legal assistance, which was available to all amnesty applicants and victims. This was not of an even standard, because many of the applicants had been employed by the state as security policemen or members of the armed forces, and they had a standard of legal assistance which was much higher than that of the victims, who had to depend on their lawyers being paid by the Legal Aid Board, which limited the amount they could charge. Inevitably, many 'top' lawyers did not want to work according to those rates.

Once an amnesty decision had been made, whether it was favourable or otherwise, it was conveyed to the Commission and was published in the *Government Gazette* and made available to the media.

Because of the many delays and the many applications that were received, Parliament amended the Act in order to allow for additional members to serve on the Amnesty Committee. In 1998 the Act was amended to allow for nineteen members, and, finally, Section 1 of Act 33 of 1998 was amended to allow an unlimited number of members on the committee. When the Commission was suspended in October 1998 and the five-volume report was handed to President Mandela, the Act was amended to enable the Amnesty Committee to continue its work until it had heard every application. It is unlikely that the committee will complete its work before September 2000.

Long before the Commission was appointed, several important events took place which were to play a major role in the life and work of the Amnesty Committee and the TRC as a whole. The first was the confession of Almond Nofemela. Nofemela had been sentenced to death for murdering a white farmer, and was awaiting execution when, in October 1989, he made an astonishing disclosure of his involvement in hit squad activities at Vlakplaas. Vlakplaas was a farm near Pretoria, which was used as the controlling centre of illegal operations by the security police and the askaris, turned members of the liberation forces who now worked for the state, of which Nofemela was one. It was at Vlakplaas that death squads were trained in order to counter ANC insurgents and resistance. Nofemela always thought that the senior police would protect him and would prevent him from serving a long prison sentence or indeed being executed. But when he realised, literally hours before he was due to be executed, that he had been abandoned, he decided to blow the whistle.

At first, many cynics felt that he was simply trying to save his own skin, but when he was joined by Dirk Coetzee, who confirmed that a major death squad ring existed at Vlakplaas, a chain of events began which led to a number of commissions of inquiry. One of these commissions was the Harms Commission, appointed in 1990 by President F.W. de Klerk to investigate these allegations. The commission, which was restricted to a very narrow inquiry, found that the Vlakplaas hit squad allegations were unfounded. The security police were determined to silence Coetzee, and several attempts were made to assassinate him, including the sending of a parcel bomb. Coetzee and Nofemela both applied for amnesty and in their amnesty applications revealed a great deal of the sordid story which included killings, abductions, and torture.

Another major event which was destined to influence the proceedings of the Commission was the trial and conviction of Colonel Eugene de Kock, perhaps the most notorious Vlakplaas operative. De Kock's trial caused shockwaves throughout the security services and the government, because it was clear that he would not remain silent about the names of those who had been directly involved with his own activities. De Kock, who had acquired the nickname 'Prime Evil', was found guilty of scores of murders, of defeating the ends of justice, of abduction, assault, and conspiracy, of fraud for siphoning

more than R360 000 from Vlakplaas funds, and of supply-
ing weapons to the Inkatha Freedom Party. There could be
little doubt that there were many, many other illegal
activities in which De Kock was involved, but the prosecution decided to concentrate on the cases where there was
very clear evidence, and he was found guilty after a trial
lasting for more than a year.

One thing that emerged from the amnesty applications by Coetzee and Nofemela and from De Kock's statements in the dock was that the Harms Commission had
been derelict in its duty and woefully wrong in its conclusions. De Kock made it clear that he and others had lied before that commission and that some police officers had
been paid large sums of money to give false evidence. The
question that Judge Louis Harms, the then Ministers of
Defence and Law and Order, and many of the officials
involved had to ask themselves was, if they had taken the
evidence before them seriously, could lives have been
saved?

During De Kock's trial, the former Minister of Foreign
Affairs, Pik Botha, stated that he was deeply shocked to
hear that De Kock claimed that evidence had been fabri-
cated to justify cross-border raids under the previous
government. All the protestations made by various ministers and generals rang hollow when De Kock revealed that
parties had been held at Vlakplaas after a number of the illegal raids inside and outside South Africa, and that he had
been awarded several medals for excellent work in fighting
terrorism. One thing is patently clear: De Kock could
never have orchestrated such a vast number of illegal activities without a huge budget and support services from his
political bosses and the generals who gave him his orders.
De Kock was eventually given several life sentences, and
he believes – and there are very many who support him in
this – that he was a scapegoat for many of his immediate
colleagues, those in authority over him, and the politicians
who laid down government policy on the conflict with
those who resisted apartheid. De Kock was extremely
bitter, and in many of the amnesty hearings at which he

[125]

gave evidence he lashed out not only at former State President P.W. Botha, but President F.W. de Klerk as well.

However, the real breakthrough in the work of the Amnesty Committee occurred in October 1996, when five high-ranking former security branch officers, several of them colleagues of Eugene de Kock, decided to come clean and to apply for amnesty. The men who came forward as a group were Brigadier Jack Cronje, former commander of Vlakplaas, Colonel Roelf Venter, Captain Wouter Mentz, Captain Jacques Hechter, and Warrant Officer Paul van Vuuren. Theirs were the first amnesty applications, and they resulted in an avalanche of applications from throughout the country. At the time I stated that the Commission had been waiting for a long time for a breakthrough from the police, and I added, 'I don't think this is the last word. This is the start of a river which will become a flood.' The media and many influential commentators had criticised the Commission for simply listening to a long list of victims but not acquiring hard evidence from the perpetrators; now they had to eat their words, with nearly 8000 perpetrators making application to the Amnesty Committee.

The hearing of the five policemen began on 21 October 1996. They owned up to at least forty murders as well as several bombings and assassinations. In their submission they called on the leaders of the National Party to admit authorising actions outside the law. They felt that they had been rejected and thrown aside by the former government. From the very beginning they made it clear that they had not been acting on their own when they committed these gruesome deeds, but had been upholding government policy and apartheid, fighting communism, and resisting the liberation of South Africa. These agents of the government declared that they had been acting on instructions and orders, while high government officials and senior politicians denied that they had known that these activities were taking place. This was a theme that was to continue throughout the Amnesty Committee hearings.

As I read the applications from people such as Coetzee and Nofemela and listened to the evidence given before the

Amnesty Committee, I was struck by the gratuitous violence which accompanied many of the assassinations committed by the agents of apartheid. Nofemela's description of the killing of lawyer and activist Griffiths Mxenge is an example: 'He fought back and did not fall after we had stabbed him several times. I then fetched a wheel spanner and hit him on the head until he fell.' Another participant in the killing, David Tshikalanga, added that Joe Mamasela, another askari, 'slit his throat while he was going on the ground. I don't know who cut his stomach open'. Dirk Coetzee described in vivid detail the killing of Eastern Cape student activist Sizwe Kondile. He explained that they decided to get rid of Kondile's body by burning it, so that there would be no evidence of the murder: 'The buttocks and upper parts of the legs had to be turned frequently to ensure that they were reduced to ashes. We were drinking and having a braai next to the fire.' The chairperson of the Amnesty Committee, Judge Mall, responded at one time by describing the activities of those who were applying for amnesty as 'sheer brutality' – an unusual outburst from a correct and reserved judge. But anyone who listened to these tales of horror, whether they were part of the Amnesty Committee or in the audience or watching television or listening to the radio or reading the newspapers, would react in very much the same way. The awfulness, the darkness, of the deeds was overwhelming and shattered the idea of smart young policemen doing their duty to defend the country. In many ways they came across as thugs who, dare it be said, enjoyed their work.

The ugliness of the conflict is particularly vividly displayed in the actions of John Deegan, a former member of the security police and the special forces unit Koevoet who was responsible for a number of atrocities. According to his testimony, his father had been murdered and this had had an indelible impact on him. He felt desperate as a victim of his father's death. He then described they way he dealt with a wounded member of the South West African People's Organisation:

Even at that stage he was denying everything and I
started to go into this uncontrollable rage and he
started going floppy ... and I remember thinking 'how
dare you?'. Then – and this is what I was told afterwards – I started ripping. I ripped all the bandages, the
drip which Sean had put into this guy ... pulled out
my 9 mm ... put the barrel between his eyes and fuck-
ing boom ... I executed him. I got onto the radio and I
told my Colonel ...'we floored one ...we are all tired
and I want to come in.'

The South African conflict, like conflicts all over the
world, has left many damaged people in its wake. This is
one of the reasons why the work of the Commission,
which began the process of healing and catharsis, needs to
be continued by a much wider range of agencies with
greater resources of people and time so that some of the
trauma which still exists in the hearts and minds of many
people in the country, black and white, can receive further
healing and closure.

Finally, is it possible that the perpetrators, or at least
some of them, were victims as well as perpetrators? My
own view is, very much so. As I listened to so many who
had joined the police force and the army at a very young
age, who were subjected to constant propaganda from their
superior officers, and who were influenced by the militant
speeches made by Cabinet ministers and other politicians,
I can understand, at least in part, what happened to them.
In some instances they truly believed that they were defending the country against communism, against terrorism. They believed the propaganda, and, in the course of
carrying out their duties as the situation deteriorated, their
own consciences seemed to be deadened and dulled, allowing them to participate in the worst atrocities. To think of
the perpetrators as victims is not to condone their actions
or their deeds, nor is it to turn away from the many victims
whose lives they destroyed by their activities. It is simply
to try to understand something of the ambiguity, the
contradictions, of war, of conflict, of prejudice.

To understand that many perpetrators are also victims is not to turn away from the hard fact of racism, which was a dominant factor in many of the atrocities performed by members of the security forces. The harsh fact of the matter is that most whites regarded blacks as inferior and even as sub-human. Certainly, this was the attitude of the majority of the leaders and followers of the apartheid government. The moment one designates a person as sub-human, one can act against them as an object with very little feeling. After all, if they are not quite human, then they don't feel as we do, they don't hurt as we do, and in a sense they don't bleed as we do. They don't care about their children as we do; they are different; they are other; they are pushed aside; they are marginalised; they can be killed and disposed of. I have no doubt that this was one of the major factors which played out in the conflict which had South Africa in its grip for so long. I also have no doubt that even though liberation has taken place, and South Africa has had two free and fair elections, and the majority of people in power are black, deep-seated racism still exists. If reconciliation and stability are to grow, then the pernicious racism of whites against blacks and blacks against whites must constantly be challenged, and this sickness must be ousted from society.

In a very important chapter in the five-volume report, an attempt is made by the Commission to explain or account for the causes, motives, and perspectives of the perpetrators.[8] What made them act as they did? Various excuses were offered by the perpetrators themselves. On the one hand they told the Commission that in many instances their actions were unintentional and that things went wrong, and they simply had to try to cover up. Others were more concrete and declared that, as far as they were concerned, South Africa was at war and therefore the end, namely defeating the terrorists and communists, as they saw them, justified the means that they used.

As has been indicated above, another reason given for the breakdown of behaviour by the security forces was that there was a gap between the leadership and followers. F.W.

de Klerk stated over and over again that he accepted that violations had taken place but that he had never issued any instructions to perform such actions, nor had he known that they were taking place. Eugene de Kock, in his book *A Long Night's Damage: Working for the Apartheid State*, expresses a very different point of view. He says of De Klerk,

> He simply did not have the courage to declare: yes, we at the top level condoned what was done on our behalf by the security forces. What's more, we in- structed it should be implemented. Or – if we did not actually give instruction, we turned a blind eye. We didn't move heaven and earth to stop the ghastliness. Therefore, let the foot soldiers be excused.[9]

The National Party formulated a system of planning and executing counter-revolutionary measures against the threats posed by the activities of the liberation movements. The Nationalist government ordered the security forces to take abnormal action not covered by normal legislation. This created the moral ground for justifying the contraven- tion of existing laws. This is a damning indictment which was repeated many times by members of the security forces but denied as often by the political leadership of the National Party. It was this accusation which brought about the strong disagreement between De Klerk and the Com- mission. On the one hand, political leaders were denying any knowledge, except for isolated cases, of extra-legal pro- cedures carried out by the police and the military. On the other hand, the generals and the foot soldiers were adamant that they had received their instructions and that the pol- iticians were well aware of what was going on and, indeed, created the climate which enabled them to plan their assassinations and torture and other extra-legal actions.

From June to August 1997, the TRC analysed a large amount of evidence presented to it concerning allegations of torture committed by the security forces. Our informa- tion indicated that the rate of torture increased more than tenfold after the declaration of the state of emergency in

June 1986. Furthermore, the TRC had received statements alleging that the security forces had been involved in almost 2000 acts of torture in more than 200 different venues around that time. The Commission possessed information which could point to a failure by the government and the State Security Council to take action against members of the security forces responsible for gross violations of human rights. Nowhere in the SSC minutes are there any expressions of concern about the numerous and vocal allegations of torture made throughout the 1980s, and it follows that no measures were adopted to prevent torture and punish those responsible.

After reading the minutes of the SSC and the Cabinet, we decided to hold two sets of hearings. The first would focus on the role of the various armed forces of the government and the liberation movements respectively, and the second would concentrate on the role and functions of the State Security Council.

During the armed forces hearing, numerous high-ranking members of the South African Police, a general in the South African Defence Force, and a senior Cabinet minister serving on the State Security Council agreed that decisions taken by the SSC could be interpreted to authorise serious illegal acts including the murder of the political opponents of the previous government. This served to reinforce our conviction that it was vitally important to hold a hearing into the role of the State Security Council and to clarify the meaning and status of decisions it took. What follows is a survey of some of the evidence obtained during the course of these hearings.

Firstly, the militarisation of policing. From the mid-1980s members of the SSC came to accept that the threat to South Africa was no longer solely an external military threat in the form of armed Umkhonto we Sizwe insurgents infiltrating South Africa from neighbouring states. They began to realise that attempts to overthrow the government were being planned and organised from within South Africa's borders. The minutes of the SSC reflect that P.W. Botha, the chairperson of the SSC, opened

[131]

one meeting by remarking that he was convinced that the 'brain behind the unrest was now within the country'. This acceptance resulted in a shift in counter-revolutionary strategy which entailed an increasing internal deployment of the South African Defence Force. Whereas the SADF had previously directed its military operations at external targets in the frontline states, it now played an increasing role in support of the police force inside South Africa. This resulted in a militarisation of the policing of internal resistance. This change is reflected in the testimony of Major Craig Williamson, former police spy and Vlakplaas operative, at the SSC hearing:

> I would say the upper echelons politically and militarily in South Africa [thought] that the war was going to move from the South West African/Namibian and Angolan border into South Africa... And therefore the reaction by members of the security forces to start using the type of counter measures that they'd used outside the country inside the country against what was seen as the same enemy didn't surprise me. And I really can't understand why it surprises some of the politicians. I will just add, one quick thing I can throw in, is that the whole Vlakplaas operation was something that was transplanted from outside and brought inside. That was Koevoet that was brought into South Africa and it had a role and a function outside which was naturally just continued internally.[10]

This shift in counter-revolutionary strategy was extremely significant, because military operations aim to eliminate enemy personnel, weaponry, and bases, whereas police operations are generally aimed at arresting individuals in order to bring them before courts of law. As the military approach to policing gained ascendance, so too did the killing or 'elimination', rather than the detention or arrest, of activists. The application of a more military approach to opposing the revolution within the country was accepted by the SSC and the leadership of the security forces, and it is therefore highly improbable that they did not foresee the possible consequences of such a shift in counter-revolutionary strategy.

Secondly, there was a growing acceptance among security force leaders on the SSC and senior National Party politicians that unlawful actions would be necessary to prevent a revolution. Members of the SSC knew and understood the mindsets of the police and soldiers on the ground, many of whom were being placed in increasingly difficult and dangerous positions. There was a growing acceptance in government that the revolutionary onslaught could not be combated by lawful methods alone. The state adopted unlawful methods, both offensive and defensive, against revolutionaries. Craig Williamson delivered a paper at a National Intelligence Service symposium in which he argued that illegal actions should form part of a state strategy to counter terrorism: 'When survival is important it is often necessary for a service to resort to secret actions which do not comply with the laws, morality, norms or values which control the public actions of the state. Secrecy, both defensive and offensive, is important. Coverage is used to allow the operatives to execute secret instructions.'

Williamson notes that this view was not contested at the symposium, nor by the important politicians, all the way to up to the Prime Minister himself, to whom a document containing this perspective was circulated:

> When I was instructed to present a paper at the symposium on 'The use of cover in secret operations', as well as on 'The recruitment of long-term deep cover agents or moles', I discussed the contents of my paper with my colleagues and found no disagreements with the views expressed. At the symposium I was not challenged on my views. The report was also circulated to the highest level as the distribution list shows. And I may add, Mr Chairman, the fact that it quotes part out of a long presentation that I made also says something. In the light of the above and in terms of the knowledge which I had of standard secret and/or special force procedures in the then South

Africa, as well as in many other states, I had no doubt that secret, violent and other actions against the revolutionary enemy were an accepted and approved procedure in our overall arsenal of counter-insurgency weapons.

Members of the SSC knew that the overwhelming majority of security policemen were committed supporters of the National Party, who were implacably opposed to the liberation movements and what they represented. They knew that security force members saw it as their task to halt the revolution and by the mid-1980s were being exhorted to do so at virtually any cost. They knew that members of the security forces often witnessed the attacks and violence of the liberation movements and were at times targets and victims of such attacks. They knew that members of the security forces were engaged in a life and death struggle against the revolutionaries. Johan van der Merwe, former Commissioner of Police and member of the SSC, testified that 'it was the point of departure for the government of the day that for all practical purposes we were in a war situation and that the enemy had to be defeated at all costs'.

They also knew that conventional methods of combating unrest and terrorism, such as arrest, prosecution, and conviction, were becoming less and less effective. The sheer scale of resistance, the time-consuming and resource-intensive nature of prosecutions, and the widespread reluctance of ordinary people to testify in courts of law meant that the security forces, in response to the pressure being brought to bear on them by politicians and their superiors, began to turn to illegal methods of combating resistance. Johan van der Merwe testified that

> All the powers were to avoid the ANC/SACP achieve their revolutionary aims and often with the approval of the previous government we had to move outside the boundaries of our law. That inevitably led to the fact that the capabilities of the South African Police, especially the security forces, included illegal acts.

People were involved in a life and death struggle in an attempt to counter this onslaught by the ANC/SACP and they consequently had a virtually impossible task to judge between legal and illegal actions.

In this context the leadership of the security forces knew that those who served under them were becoming increasingly militarised and were engaging in a range of illegal actions (including assassinations) directed against members of the liberation movements and those perceived to be sympathetic to them. The leadership of the security forces (including the Commissioner of Police and the head of the Defence Force) either took part in these illegal activities or sanctioned them once they occurred. The leaders of the security forces were involved in the cover-up of murders and the frustrating of investigations.

Thirdly, politicians serving on the SSC have themselves conceded that the decisions they approved were ambiguous and that in the South African context they could have been misinterpreted.

Former Minister of Law and Order Adriaan Vlok and others have conceded that they, as they put it, were negligent in not querying the language used in the SSC documents drafted by security force members and placed before them for their approval. Vlok himself testified that 'We at the top took certain decisions and we used terminology without actually really thinking about it and that worked its way through to the people on the ground and they misinterpreted it, and for that I accept responsibility. I should have seen to it that those misinterpretations couldn't arise.'

The adoption of potentially ambiguous decisions by the SSC encouraged a climate in which state crimes could and did occur. A few examples will make the point. In 1986 the SSC discussed a document which stated that the task of the security forces was 'to neutralise or eliminate enemy leaders'. Another document, entitled 'Strategie ter Bekamping van die ANC' [Strategy for combating the ANC], noted the advances made by the ANC in its onslaught against the

[135]

state, and reiterated the goal of neutralising the alliance between the African National Congress, the South African Communist Party, and the Congress of South African Trade Unions. The following recommendations were made:

> (1) to neutralise the ANC leadership, (2) to prevent and control *verhoed* in relation not only to potential terrorists but also to ANC sympathisers and co-workers, and (3) to neutralise the power and influence of key persons and their fellow workers in the ANC.

The SSC produced a document entitled 'Naamlys van Politiessensitiewe Persone' [List of politically sensitive people] and listed it on the agenda as follows: 'Action to be taken against politically sensitive persons and the withdrawal of leadership figures'. Among the names on that list of people who would enjoy the close attention of the security police were those of Archbishop Desmond Tutu and Dr Alex Boraine! In various other documents produced by the SSC the same thread continues: the identifying and eliminating of revolutionary leaders, particularly those with charisma, and the physical destruction of revolutionary organisations inside and outside the country.

In most SSC documents there is a failure to provide a clear and unambiguous definition of the following terms: 'elimination', 'neutralisation', 'physical destruction', 'formal and informal policing', 'taking out', 'methods other than detention'. It was our view that the failure to define these terms, particularly the term 'eliminate', was a cause of great concern.

Members of the SSC have conceded that the language was ambiguous and that a reasonable member of the security forces could have interpreted these words to authorise assassinations. However, they made these concessions only 'with the benefit of hindsight'. Adriaan Vlok testified that

> there's the particular language which was used in this era during these meetings and expressions such as

'eliminate', 'neutralise', 'take out', 'destroy' and similar expressions were used fairly commonly... [T]hat is how it was known in the vernacular. It is a fact that our country, especially during the conflict of the past, was plunged into a war psychosis where these words and expressions which were derived from the military became part of the vernacular, just as other expressions with the same import became part of the revolutionary language. At that stage there was nothing unnatural or unusual in the use of these expressions. It is, however ... with the benefit of hindsight ... an indisputable fact that there wasn't necessary consideration of the perspectives [and] interpretations of other people who did not attend these meetings. With my knowledge and my insight into the mechanisms of the SSC I say that no decisions were taken by it to act illegally but at the same time I knew or I know now that it would have been unavoidable that people who did not experience the spirit and intent of these meetings could very easily come to other conclusions and apparently they have indeed done so, especially the divisional commanders and their troops on the ground who were ... responsible for controlling uncontrollable situations and to normalise abnormal situations and on whom there was extreme pressure from, amongst others, their commanding officers, politicians and society in general ... [T]hese people would not easily have linked an innocent interpretation to these expressions.

The testimony of Pik Botha, former Minister of Foreign Affairs, confirms this view:

These words and phrases were part of the vocabulary commonly used throughout South Africa over many years, since the first murders and bomb attacks by terrorists commenced. The sentiments expressed in these words and far more militant language were used in debates in Parliament, at public meetings, business lunches, Party conferences, social functions and in media reporting and editorial comment. These words and phrases reflected the general reaction amongst the majority of white South Africans whenever a murder or bomb explosion by terrorists was announced. It was reasonable therefore that members of the security forces would have interpreted a phrase like 'wipe out the terrorists' to include killing them, and unless the senior command structures of the security forces made sure that all ranks understood the distinction between a person who is directly engaged in the planning and execution of acts of violence threatening the lives of civilians on the one hand, and political opponents belonging to the same organisations as the terrorists on the other hand, lower ranks would probably not have made that distinction on their own.

Fourthly, senior members of the security forces, some of whom served on the SSC, interpreted the terminology it used as authorisation to commit gross violations of human rights.

Security forces have a particular culture and speak with a particular vocabulary. Members of the security forces who testified before the TRC indicated that they either interpreted the word 'eliminate' specifically to mean 'kill' or that in certain circumstances it might mean kill. Johan van der Merwe testified to this:

> COMMISSION: Do you then accept that it is one of the possible meanings of those words to say that people must be killed?
> GEN. VAN DER MERWE: Yes definitely, Mr Chairman. If you tell a soldier, eliminate your enemy, depending on the circumstances he will understand that means killing. It is not the only meaning but it is specifically one meaning.

Later Van der Merwe testified that the use of this language at the SSC did indeed cause the security forces to take actions resulting in the deaths of activists:

COMMISSION: I am saying, would you agree that that unfortunate use of that language, 'vernietig', 'uit-roei', 'uittewis', 'elimineer' [destroy, root out, wipe out, eliminate] and so on – you describe it as an unfortunate use of language – that that unfortunate use of language resulted in deaths, would you agree with that?

GEN. VAN DER MERWE: 'Yes, Mr Chairman.'

The testimony of Brigadier Oosthuizen, a senior member of the security police, supports that of General van der Merwe: 'If I understand the question, there was never any lack of clarity about "take out" or "eliminate". It meant that the person had to be killed.' Major Sarel Crafford, a senior security policeman, concurred with the view of other senior members of the security forces: '"Elimina-tion" ... had only one meaning and that was to kill... [I]f you look at the compilers of these documents, if they wanted to give any other meaning to the word "elimina-tion" they would have used another word. I think person-ally that "elimination" in this context means to "kill".'

It became crystal clear that the use of certain terms such as 'eliminate' by the SSC was interpreted by the generals to mean they were to kill the enemies of the state.

The Commission was concerned not only with those who had given orders for human rights violations to be committed, or who had created a climate in which such acts could occur, but also with the failure of politicians to act against people who were responsible for human rights violations, thus turning a blind eye to their actions.

At the SSC hearing, Pik Botha testified,

I acknowledge that I could have done more in the State Security Council, in the cabinet and in Parlia-ment to ensure that political opponents were not killed or tortured by government institutions. I could have and should have done more to find out whether the accusations that government institutions were killing and torturing political opponents were true. Not one of us in the former government can say

[139]

today that there were no suspicions on our part that members of the South African Police were engaged in irregular activities.

Leon Wessels, former Deputy Minister of Law and Order, testified in a similar vein,

> I ... do not believe that the political defence of 'I did not know' is available to me, because in many respects I believe I did not want to know. In my own way I had my suspicions of things that had caused discomfort in official circles, but because I did not have the facts to substantiate my suspicions or I had lacked the courage to shout from the rooftops, I have to confess that I only whispered in the corridors. That I believe is the accusation that people may level at many of us. We simply did not, and I did not, confront the reports of injustices head on. It may be blunt but I have to say it. Since the days of the Biko tragedy, right up to the days of hostel activities, hostel atrocities in the late, late eighties, the National Party did not have an inquisitive mindset. The National Party did not have an inquiring mind about these matters.

These sentiments were echoed by Adriaan Vlok, the former Minister of Law and Order, referring to my own interventions in Parliament:

> We also have to remember that we were engaged in war and that makes it even more difficult to really do what you ought to do. And we tended to say ... all these voices that we're hearing and people saying things, somebody referred to the turbulent priest, those are the words that we used. And we made a mistake, we should have listened to people like that and let's be quite honest, that is how it worked and we should have listened more to these credible and honourable people from society, but we were waging a war, we had all been indoctrinated not to listen to each other.

A fundamental note that was sounded through the hearings was that the draconian laws on the statute book, laws which legislated on the grounds of race and colour, were found not to be sufficient to maintain the state's control of the country. The security forces broke the laws; death squads, assassinations, and torture were not legal even in the apartheid state. These were criminal acts, condoned by the silence of the political masters of the time, or even possibly orchestrated by some of the political leaders, and certainly by the generals. These were not the acts of a few 'bad apples' who took the law into their own hands. There was a distinct pattern. Torture was not something that took place in a handful of prisons, performed by perverted warders. Torture was endemic. There was no place we visited, no hearing we conducted, which did not contain stories of torture. Thousands were killed, not merely at roadblocks, in ambushes and raids, but also by abduction and design. Those who were seen as a threat to the apartheid regime were in many instances summarily executed.

Like the members of the security forces working for the apartheid state, some of the ANC cadres also talked about 'being at war' and that it was therefore inevitable that civilians were caught in the crossfire and hurt or killed. There was a cycle of violence, with an act committed by one side followed by another by the opposing side. A typical example of this was in the testimony given by Aboobaker Ismail, former head of the ANC Special Operations, when describing the bombing of the South African Air Force headquarters in Church Street, Pretoria, which was authorised by Oliver Tambo in May 1983. According to Ismail, the attack was carried out 'in the wake of the SADF cross-border raid into Lesotho, killing forty-two ANC supporters and Lesotho civilians, and also in the wake of the assassination of Ms Ruth First in Maputo by the security forces'. In response, the SADF conducted various attacks, including further raids on Maputo. One act followed another, and the conflict escalated as a result. General Andrew Masondo, who was the National Political Commissar of the ANC between 1977 and 1985, explained his actions and those of his colleagues in the ANC camps by stating that 'we were at war'. He said, 'You remember I said we were at war ...there might be times that I will use third-degree in spite of the fact that it is not policy.' He also stated, 'People who it was found that they were enemy agents, we executed them and I wouldn't make an apology. We were at war.'

Mangosuthu Buthelezi also argued very strongly before the Commission that he had never, ever given instructions for any violence or unlawful activities. Yet a number of the members of the Inkatha Freedom Party stated over and over again in their applications that they had been under orders. Particularly striking is the statement made by Mr Dhlamini, who said,

> when I killed people I was never called a criminal. Today they call us criminals and deny knowledge of our activities and ourselves. No IFP leader is prepared to stand before this Commission and admit to these activities ...we were not mad persons who just took weapons and started shooting people at random. Therefore, it hurts me very much for the IFP to desert us and say that they do not know anything about us – when they know that they were in fact responsible for all these things.

This pattern of admission by foot soldiers and senior officers on the one hand, and denial by political leaders on the other, continued throughout the hearings. It was argued in mitigation that a lack of discipline existed largely because people took matters into their own hands, that communication was inevitably bad, or that local young people were incensed and distressed by the activities of the police in the townships and took matters into their own hands. The Pan African Congress stated that the Pan African Students' Association, whose members killed American exchange student Amy Biehl, was not under their command: 'They are a component part of the PAC but not involved in the armed struggle. They wrongly targeted and killed Amy Biehl. We expressed our regret and condolences.'

So we listened to stories of betrayal, of informers, of dirty tricks, of cover-ups, beatings, stabbings, shootings, electric shocks, burning of bodies, homes ransacked, abductions. It was like the opening of a huge sewer spilling out its filth and stench. And through it all the cruelty. Harold Strachan was first detained at Port Elizabeth's North End prison in 1962 and later at Pretoria Central Prison. He described the North End prison as 'a hellish place' and recalled seeing warders assault prisoners as a matter of routine. 'Where purposeful cruelty and vengeance left off, neglect would take over. Nobody really cared you know.' [11]

Those who made the decisions and issued the orders did so secretly and did everything to cover their tracks. Those who followed the orders, the hints, the nudges, and the winks did so under a cloak of darkness. Neither those who formulated deadly policies nor those who carried them out so cruelly ever imagined that one day the darkness would be dispelled, that voices they thought long silent would speak. A single example illustrates this. At the first East London hearing, Babalwa Mhlauli told us that a particular policeman was harassing her mother, searching her possessions, and, as she put it, 'barking like a dog'. 'My mother said, "I am a human being, so are you. So you don't need to speak the way you do." He replied, "The truth will come out one day."' Ms Mhlauli continued:

> That was very ironic because here we are today in
> the truth commission talking about this truth and I
> mean, I never expected him to say that because the
> truth that is coming is based on him now, not us, we
> are the victims. He is the one that committed all this
> pain to us, you know. And after that my mother said,
> 'I agree with you very much. I strongly agree with you.
> The truth is definitely coming out one day.'

In the final report of the Commission we tried to capture the feeling and the mood of the public hearings:

> Above all, the Commission tried to listen, to really
> listen – not passively but actively – to voices that for

[143]

so long had been stilled. And as it listened to stories of horror, of pathos and of tragic proportion, it became aware again of the high cost that has been paid by so many for freedom. Commissioners were almost overwhelmed by the capacity of human beings to damage and destroy each other. Yet they listened, too, to stories of great courage, concluding often with an astonishing generosity of spirit, from those who had for so long carried the burden of loss and tragedy. It was often a deeply humbling experience.

The Commission also listened to perpetrators describing in awful detail the acts of terror, assassination and torture that they inflicted on so many over so long a period. Here the mood was very different. Encouraging, though, were the expressions of remorse and a seeking for forgiveness on the part of some of those who applied for amnesty.[12]

5

'Collective responsibility'? Political parties and institutional hearings

THE DECISION TO hold institutional hearings and special hearings was not limited to the armed forces and state institutions, but also covered political parties and civil institutions. The motivation for these extra hearings is outlined in our report. We stress, quite rightly I think, that

> without some sense of the antecedents, circumstances, factors and context within which gross violations of human rights occurred, it is almost impossible to understand how over the years people who considered themselves ordinary, decent and God-fearing found themselves turning a blind eye to a system which impoverished, oppressed and violated the lives and very existence of so many of their fellow citizens.[1]

It was important, therefore, for us to investigate a number of institutions which reflected the apartheid policies, which were so pervasive.

What we don't say in our report is that the pivotal reason why we held institutional and special hearings arose out of a discussion that Desmond Tutu and I had in early 1996 with the two Deputy Presidents, Thabo Mbeki and F.W. de Klerk. We received a message from the two requesting a meeting with the chairperson and deputy chairperson of the Commission. The major point they made to us at that meeting was that it was important for the TRC to do its work in context. We agreed with that. They went on,

[145]

however, to propose that rather than hold hearings where individuals could tell their stories, whether those individuals were victims or perpetrators, we should invite the political parties, and in particular the two major political parties, the ANC and the National Party, to outline the history of apartheid as perceived from their points of view. They felt that relating that broad background would be like putting together a giant crossword puzzle; political party leaders could fill in most of the puzzle and the gaps could be filled by individual stories.

In a sophisticated way, what was being proposed was that a forum or working committee should be established, representing all those parties and former forces whose members might be expected to appear before the Commission and who wished to participate in that committee. The primary task of the committee would be to facilitate the objectives of the Commission through mutual cooperation and by building confidence in the process. What neither Tutu nor I realised was that there had been considerable discussion, initiated by De Klerk but with the cooperation of Mbeki, with political parties such as the African National Congress, the National Party, the Pan African Congress, the Inkatha Freedom Party, and the Freedom Front, and the respective statutory and non-statutory armed forces, urging them to form such a forum in order to interface with the Commission.

I think the originators of this idea were acting in part from a willingness to cooperate with the Commission and to demonstrate this support to their respective followers, thus spurring them on to cooperate as well. I think, however, it was also an attempt, particularly by the National Party and the security forces, to reduce the inquiry which the Commission was bound to undertake in terms of its mandate. This was a manifestation of the 'collective responsibility' which was so strongly advocated by General Constand Viljoen, the leader of the Freedom Front. Even though we were not fully aware of the background and the consultation that had taken place and thought it was more an initiative of the two Deputy Presidents, neither Tutu nor I felt that we could go along with this approach. We thought there were enormous dangers in working together with a forum comprising representatives of political parties and the security forces, for this would challenge the integrity and independence of the Commission.

When we reported to the Commission we therefore proposed that we ought not to accept the approach as outlined by Mbeki and De Klerk and that we should control our own process; we urged that we should start the victim hearings so that the Commission would be victim-centred rather than institutionally focused. The Commission was unanimous in its agreement and we communicated this to the two Deputy Presidents.

Nevertheless, we went on to propose that the Commission ought to send out an invitation, not only to political parties and the former security forces, but to all institutions and to all South Africans, saying that if they wished to make any representation to the Commission they should feel free to do so. We met with representatives of the major political parties to request them to make public submissions. All the parties agreed to do so, with the exception of the Democratic Party, although after a little persuasion they too agreed to appear. This resulted in a very large number of documents being sent and representations being made to the Commission. These submissions, which are considerable, are found in the final report. We note there that these were the submissions that had been lodged with the Records Management Department and there may well be others when the final archive is made available.[2] Many of the submissions are extremely important, but it was impossible for us to have public hearings to receive all of them. Some of them were received in private meetings with the Commission and then made available to the general public, others were simply sent to us and included as part of the record of the Commission.

THE POLITICAL party hearings were part of a carefully planned process. Despite the impatience of the media, who

[147]

wanted to see the perpetrators and the political parties in the dock, as it were, we stayed with our original plan. One journalist put it this way: 'The fireworks which many observers were waiting for have been conspicuous by their absence. Is this a sign that the Commission has lost its way or that it's battling to make headway?' I responded to him and to many other members of the media that the Commission deliberately chose first to hear the powerless and the voiceless, who had never been heard. I explained that our second priority would be amnesty applicants, whose hearings had already begun. Then we would encourage institutions and people from different strands of society to make representations to the Commission. Our approach could be likened to the opening of many windows in a dark and gloomy house. The first window illuminated people who had never been heard before. The second window would be opened on perpetrators who were in jail, and the third on other perpetrators. Yet another window that needed to be opened was that on the political parties.

Even here, many commentators overlooked that this too was a process. We invited political parties to make presentations. They did not want to release their submissions until they appeared before us. Obviously, if their presentations were very long, it was then impossible for us to digest those submissions. We put certain questions and made certain comments and then reserved our judgment, so that we could invite the parties to make a second representation after we had read their first submission and given them a list of follow-up questions. Some people were cynical about the effectiveness of the political party hearings. The general view was that the politicians would come and tell only as much as they had to; they would focus their attack on their opponents and would show the best possible side of their own history. We were not unfamiliar with politicians and realised that there were many risks involved, but decided it was essential to hear their evidence.

It was in fact astonishing that a former president, F.W. de Klerk, would come before the Commission and seek to explain, acknowledge, and even apologise for past actions and policies, however inadequate some people may think his presentation was. This was a proud political leader recognising the authority of the Commission. In the second place, who would have imagined that the 'President-in-waiting', Thabo Mbeki, would come before the Commission and justify what the African National Congress had and had not done? Who would have imagined the ANC would have included in their submission a list of people who had been killed or tortured or assaulted? For that matter, who would have imagined that Mangosuthu Buthelezi would even turn up for the hearings? After all, he had been very vocal in his criticism of the Commission.

Buthelezi appeared before the Commission with two of his key leaders, Frank Mdlalose, chairman of the Inkatha Freedom Party, and KwaZulu-Natal minister Ben Ngubane. After the initial welcome, the hearing began somewhat bizarrely when Buthelezi informed the Commission and the hundreds of people in attendance that during his quiet time that morning he had come across a hymn that he wanted to share with us. He not only shared it but sang it! It was an old-fashioned evangelical hymn which began with the words 'Just as I am, without one plea, O Lamb of God I come before thee'. I think Desmond Tutu was the only one who joined in, somewhat belatedly, in the singing of those two verses.

Buthelezi didn't speak for very long. He was extremely critical of the African National Congress and made it very clear that he didn't support the Commission: 'The IFP has had reservations about the TRC from the outset. We believed – and we continue to believe – that the Commission as currently composed and operating within its current terms of reference will neither reveal the truth nor bring about the reconciliation we so desperately need.' One of the major reasons why Buthelezi opposed the Commission was his long-term antipathy towards his fellow Anglican, Archbishop Tutu. Referring to many of the IFP leaders who had been killed in KwaZulu-Natal, he pointedly said,

We have not seen any prominent clerics weep at the gravesides of the thousands of IFP members who have been murdered for no other reason than [that] they are members of the IFP ... We have not seen one prominent cleric strive to comfort the thousands of widows and children whose loved ones were put to death simply because they held a particular point of view.

This was quite clearly aimed at Tutu and it was not the first confrontation between the two of them. Tutu remained impassive and listened carefully to Buthelezi's statements. Finally, the leader of the IFP said, 'I have always abhorred violence, I abhor violence now, and I will die abhorring violence. I have never made any decision to employ violence anywhere for any purpose whatsoever.' He did, however, make one concession: 'Although I have not orchestrated one single act of violence against one single victim of the political violence, as the leader of the IFP I know that the buck stops in front of me. Because we are human beings we still hurt each other. I apologise for the past hurts and I do so also on behalf of my followers.' These statements were followed by the presentation of a 750-page memorandum, of which 70 pages were read into the record over a period of three hours.

Buthelezi has been and remains a central figure in the political landscape of South Africa. I lived for a time in Durban in Natal and came to know him very well. We were both members of the South African Council of Churches, which opposed the government and apartheid in particular, and we worked very closely together on a number of projects. It was during this time that he made the agonising decision to accept the leadership of a 'homeland', thus condoning a policy that an overwhelming majority of blacks despised. When I became head of the Methodist Church of Southern Africa, I paid a courtesy call to his home and we exchanged gifts. He gave me a Zulu shield and a spear; I presented him with a New Revised Version of the Bible. We ate together, not only then but on a number of occasions, and were on very good terms.

However, as the violence increased and the conflict between the liberation movements and Inkatha sharpened, we became divided. I had moved into politics and into Parliament and in the course of my work there I criticised the position taken by Buthelezi on a number of issues, in particular his cooperation with the government. He, in the meantime, had a very serious dispute with the ANC in London in 1979 and that was the parting of the ways between himself and them. What really soured our relationship finally, I think, was not something I did but something my son Andrew did, when he was president of the National Union of South African Students in 1981, shortly before he was detained for several months. In a speech at the University of Natal he described Inkatha as a 'Zulu Broederbond', referring to the very secretive, conservative, powerful Afrikaner elite organisation. This infuriated Buthelezi. Not only did he make a public statement criticising Andrew, but he wrote me a letter saying that while he had always had great respect for me, clearly I had fallen down very badly in bringing up my children! I wrote to him suggesting that it was important for people in public life to listen to the voices of young people, whether they were white or black, whether they were critical or uncritical.

At the end of the proceedings I asked the representatives of the Inkatha Freedom Party whether they would be prepared to return for a second hearing once we had had an opportunity to go through their very long and detailed submission. They were non-committal, saying they would think about it and that they would prefer to respond to written questions. I then had a very long and ineffectual exchange of letters with Buthelezi and some of his colleagues. Admittedly, the questions I asked him were very pointed, but we were dealing with matters of history, of life and death, and the questions to all the parties were equally pointed. Buthelezi responded by rejecting the questions, claiming they were loaded, and instead put a long list of questions to the Commission. We then had to make a very difficult decision. Clearly, Buthelezi would not

[151]

come back for a second hearing, because his attitude had hardened considerably. Should we or should we not subpoena him if he refused the invitation? Violence was still very much part of the problem in KwaZulu-Natal during this period, and we debated long and hard about what strategy we should follow. I was among those who cautioned against subpoenaing Buthelezi. We had seen many instances when thousands of his supporters had demonstrated publicly if they felt that he had in any way been insulted or criticised. I had no doubt whatsoever that if we had issued a subpoena, violence could have erupted, and many lives could have been lost. For that reason a majority of the commissioners decided not to proceed. In our five-volume report it is suggested that we were mistaken in that course of action. I don't share this view. I still don't think that the loss of even one life would have been worth the correctness of demanding Buthelezi's presence and subpoenaing him if he refused to come.

What troubled me then and troubles me today was the evidence we received in many hearings – victim hearings, amnesty hearings, and special hearings – which told a very different story from the protestations of innocence made by Buthelezi. After very careful consideration of the evidence before us, the Commission made the following findings concerning the IFP:

> During the period 1982–1994, the Inkatha Freedom Party, known as Inkatha prior to July 1990 (hereinafter referred to as 'the Organisation') was responsible for gross violations of human rights committed in the former Transvaal, Natal and KwaZulu against:
> • Persons who were perceived to be leaders, members or supporters of the UDF, ANC, South African Communist Party (SACP) and Cosatu;
> • Persons who were identified as posing a threat to the Organisation;
> • Members or supporters of the Organisation whose loyalty was doubted.

It is a further finding of the Commission that such violations formed part of a systematic pattern of abuse which entailed deliberate planning on the part of the Organisation.

The Commission based this finding on the following actions of the IFP:

- Speeches by the IFP President, senior party officials and persons aligned to the Organisation's ideology, which had the effect of inciting supporters of the Organisation to commit acts of violence;
- Arming the Organisation's supporters with weapons in contravention of the Arms and Ammunition, and Explosives and Dangerous Weapons Acts;
- Mass attacks by supporters of the Organisation on communities inhabited by persons referred to above, resulting in death and injury and the destruction and theft of property;
- Killing of leaders of the political organisations and persons referred to above;
- Collusion with the South African government's security forces to commit the violations referred to above;
- Entering into a pact with the SADF to create a para-military force for the Organisation, which was intended to and did cause death and injury to the persons referred to above;
- Establishing hit squads within the KZP and the special constable structure of the SAP to kill or cause injury to the persons referred to above;
- Under the auspices of the self-protection unit project, training large numbers of the Organisation's supporters with the specific objective of preventing, by means of violence, the holding of elections in KwaZulu-Natal in April 1994, under a constitution which did not recognise the Organisation's demands for sovereignty. In order to achieve this objective, the KwaZulu government and its KwaZulu police structures were subverted;

[153]

- Conspiring with right-wing organisations and former members of the South African government's security forces to commit acts which resulted in loss of life or injury in order to achieve the objective referred to above;
- Creating a climate of impunity by expressly or implicitly condoning gross human rights violations and other unlawful acts committed by members or supporters of the Organisation.

Chief Mg Buthelezi served simultaneously as President of the IFP and as the Chief Minister of the KwaZulu government and was the only serving Minister of Police in the KwaZulu government during the entire thirteen-year existence of the KwaZulu police. Where these three agencies are found to have been responsible for the commission of gross human rights, Chief Mangosuthu Buthelezi is held by this Commission to be accountable in his representative capacity as the leader, head or responsible minister of the parties concerned.[3]

In their submission, the IFP gave the Commission a list of 400 office-bearers whom they alleged had been deliberately targeted and killed by the ANC. They described this as 'serial killing'. The Commission took these allegations very seriously and, under the leadership of Richard Lyster, the Durban office conducted a very intensive investigation. This was not an easy task, mainly because a significant percentage of the incidents listed were outside our mandate because they had occurred after the cut-off date of April 1994. In the end the Commission investigated 289 alleged murders, of which it was unable to corroborate 136, despite extensive research into inquests, records, police dockets, and government departments. We asked for further assistance from the IFP, but received no reply. With regard to the remaining 153 incidents, it was impossible to verify whether the deceased were in fact office-bearers, but we accepted the bona fides of the IFP in this regard. It should be added, though, that in a small number of cases the death certificates showed that the deceased were children. Nevertheless, the Commission was able to identify the perpetrators and their political allegiance in at least 90 of the 289 incidents. These were identified as United Democratic Front or African National Congress members who were responsible for the killing of at least 76 IFP office-bearers during the period from 1985 to 1994.

What is true is that the internecine warfare between the IFP and the ANC following the release of Mandela and other political prisoners and the start-up of negotiations had led to the largest number of killings of any period in South African history and had made the quest for peace and reconciliation extremely difficult. It is ironic that today Buthelezi, while remaining the leader of the Inkatha Freedom Party, is a minister in the ANC-majority Cabinet.

Like all the other initial submissions, the ANC's first appearance before the Commission was limited in its impact. In its second, however, the ANC delegation, led by Thabo Mbeki, was more forthcoming. The smiling and relaxed Mbeki was accompanied by a strong delegation of senior leaders, and they made it clear from the very beginning that they would all be taking part and thus all took the oath. They tabled a 137-page memorandum which contained new details of the involvement of the organisation's armed wing, Umkhonto we Sizwe. While the early hours of the hearing were fairly relaxed, it became more serious when some tough questions were put to the party by Hanif Vally, the director of our Legal Department. He pointed out that there were disturbing questions which demanded forthright answers. These included torture and executions in ANC camps, attacks on civilian and soft targets, the planting of landmines on farms, 'necklacing' (placing a tyre around the victim's neck, dousing it with petrol, and setting it alight), and rape and abuse of women in ANC camps. Also raised was the use of Radio Freedom and ANC publications to incite violence and unrest. When Buthelezi had appeared before the Commission, he had alleged the ANC had planned to assassinate him. When asked about this, Mbeki

[155]

conceded that one of its units had put forward a plan to kill Buthelezi but this was vetoed by the leadership in Lusaka.

In their responses to the questions put to them, the ANC conceded that abuses had taken place in the camps, that there had been serious problems with sexual harassment and rape, that civilians had been killed or injured in the crossfire, and that a large number of violent incidents had taken place during the period of conflict. They stressed that it had not been ANC policy to kill innocent civilians; if they had wished to, they could have killed thousands of civilians, but they had chosen not to take that route. They explained that whenever they had discovered these fundamental abuses of official ANC policy, they had tried their best, not always successfully, to put a stop to them. They expressed regret that many of these incidents had happened and apologised to the victims and their families. They constantly stressed the problems of trying to control the scattered forces under their command. Their senior leadership had been either in prison or in exile, they explained, and a number of the violations which had taken place had been the responsibility of individuals who were responding to particular incidents of violence by the state.

Mbeki pointedly stated that although the ANC had nothing to hide and was prepared to concede that serious mistakes had been made, 'we must avoid the danger where, by concentrating on those particular and exceptional acts ...we convey the impression that the struggle for liberation was itself a gross violation of human rights'. The hearing lasted a day and a half and it was certainly my impression that the information that the Commission received from the written material and through the verbal exchanges would assist it to fulfill its mandate.

The National Party's first submission in 1996 was in many ways a damp squib, as were most of the other political parties' first submissions. De Klerk led the delegation on behalf of his party and presented the Commission with a long list of alleged atrocities committed by the ANC. On the role of the government and the long years of conflict, he was silent. The media expressed general disappointment in the submissions of all the parties, not understanding that they were the first of two hearings. Several black commentators were much more forthcoming regarding the National Party's submission, however. Sandile Dikeni, a well-known correspondent for the *Cape Times*, was extremely critical:

> There are rare moments when history abandons its cruelty and decides to stretch out a wrinkled, friendly hand. One such moment gave itself to the National Party at the Truth and Reconciliation hearings in Cape Town … but if there was any hope of our giving a goodbye to history, we were mistaken. Badly mistaken, because the National Party decided to spit in the face of history instead of grabbing the hand of political reconciliation and being assisted on the bumpy road ahead.

Dikeni went on to say that the major problem with the submission was the omissions, the gaps, and the denial, and wondered if there was any point to such hearings if the submissions had no significant substance.

However, it was the second National Party hearing in May 1997 which produced the real fireworks. De Klerk appeared, grim faced, with half a dozen of his colleagues, and told us that only he would be answering questions. This was in strong contrast to the ANC hearing the day before, when a number of the party's leaders had answered questions. This meant the pressure and the spotlight were on De Klerk more than they were on Mbeki. Furthermore, the small National Party delegation sat formally and correctly, without a murmur, while the ANC leaders often interrupted each other, adding their own comments quite spontaneously, which gave the proceedings an almost informal atmosphere. We were later blamed for giving the ANC a more friendly reception than was afforded to the National Party. As Sheila Camerer, justice spokesperson for the National Party, put it: 'The TRC dealt with the ANC luminaries in a "comradely" manner and in a quite jolly atmosphere.'[4] But, in actual fact, the mood was set by the delegates rather than by the commissioners, who adopted their normal approach of professional courtesy.

Because De Klerk undertook to be the sole speaker, he had to answer a long list of tough questions himself, and it did, as it were, appear as though he was in the dock. His manner was not that of a political leader discussing the past policies of his party and their consequences, but rather that of a lawyer contesting every point, and he resented very deeply the tenor of the questions which had been very well prepared by the legal team and some of our commissioners. Piet Meiring, in his book *Chronicle of the Truth Commission*, suggests that the way that Glen Goosen, a lawyer working for the Commission, put the questions 'visibly rubbed Mr de Klerk up in the wrong way'. It seems that Goosen was 'an Englishman with an Afrikaans surname'![5] Certainly the questions were tough, but they arose out of the National Party's earlier submission and a further, public submission, as well as the evidence we had listened to from victims and perpetrators. Once again, the contradiction emerged: the security forces carried out their evil deeds on the clear understanding that they were obeying their political masters. But De Klerk would have none of that. He stressed over and over again that he hadn't known about illegal actions and refused to accept responsibility for them.

De Klerk was also very upset when I asked him whether he had ever thought of applying for amnesty. I said to him:

> Mr de Klerk, I want to take you back to your opening statement where inter alia you said that you, as leader, and your party accepts responsibility and offers an apology for policies which hurt people, and you mentioned some of these. I quote your words, 'Forced removals, pass laws, racial discrimination, denial of citizenship, job reservation...' And so on. And you said – and I wrote your words down but I'm not saying that they are exactly what you said – but as

a result of these policies and these laws, tremendous harm was done to millions of South Africans, and that you wish to again affirm your own apology and that of your party. Since then we have listened to a number of cases which took place in South Africa, which you yourself have described as horrendous, awful. In particular, we have had evidence from statements from senior people that torture was routine or widespread, whether they were right or wrong, but the fact that they are saying that they were involved in it suggests that there's some veracity in that.

Now, against the background of these acts which have only come to light, but I must say many people in South Africa were not surprised to hear the confessions of senior policemen – there were many press reports, many international reports, many statements made inside, outside of Parliament about what was happening as a result of apartheid policies. But be that as it may, bearing that in mind, and the tremendous harm done to millions of South Africans, during the last months did you at any time weigh up, at least weigh up, the possibility of applying for amnesty?

De Klerk's response was,

The short answer to that is, yes, I have looked very carefully at the question and I have actually made a public statement on it where I dealt with my reasons for not doing so, and in which I essentially said the following... [A]mnesty is there to get a pardon for a crime of which you believe you could be found guilty if you were charged in court. And I think that is the explanation which was given by the Commission itself. Amnesty is not there, that is, [it is] not the correct channel in which to express your sorrow, your acceptance of responsibility, your repentance for things which are not crimes – and I have not been involved in anything which can be, which can constitute any form of credible charge that I have been guilty of any crime. And therefore the channel for accepting that

[159]

responsibility I said in the statement is a hearing like this, is the submission which I made in August last year, is the submission which I made in reply to questions and is the submission which I made this morning. When Dr Koornhof[6] phoned me a few days before he actually lodged his application, where as anybody who said I have a problem, I might have been involved in this crime, I said go and apply, I supported everybody who wanted to apply for amnesty to do so, but in Dr Koornhof's case, on a personal level, my advice to him was I don't think you need to apply, find another way of saying how sorry you are, because you will be cluttering up the amnesty process and there's no way in which I know that you are guilty of any crime. But that doesn't detract from the earnestness with which we say that people have been harmed.

But in the time when some of the things that you are referring were happening, I must also point out – once again not as justification – as Minister of Education I have been expanding education and improving education standards for all. My fellow minister, the Minister of Housing, was building houses much more effectively than the present government is doing at the moment. New schools were being built. New opportunities were being created. Legislation was reviewed and all forms of discriminatory legislation was removed. You see, what we must realise, and this is why it's important – once again it's not offered as justification – is apartheid ... as a policy did not come to an end in 1994. It came to an end as a policy already in 1986. And from then onwards not only with words but with deeds, apartheid was in a very logical and methodical way dismantled by the National Party.

In this period millions of South Africans who have been at the receiving end of apartheid became supporters of the National Party. So it's not just semantics when I say that looking at phases is important. The National Party is no longer, and for some years now hasn't been, an apartheid party. It is a truly non-racial party. More than 50% of its votes came from people of colour. And to continue to tarnish the National Party as it is now is with the apartheid brush is absolutely unfair and it is factually totally wrong to do so.

I responded,

I think it is true, of course, that the consequences of many of these policies over a 40-year period are also still with us today. And what I want to put to you is that in the Act when a gross human rights violation is defined it also includes the definition, 'severe ill-treatment'. I want to suggest to you that as a prominent member of the National Party, as one of its leaders for a number of years and finally as President, and now head of the National Party, that in terms of your own statement that tremendous harm has been done to millions of South Africans, 17 million people were prosecuted under the pass laws, for example, more than 3 million people were forcibly removed, that I would suggest that it could be defined as severe ill-treatment. As accepting political and moral responsibility for that I would have thought that the amnesty process was the exact place where both in terms of your own statements, the consequences of policies which are with us today and will be with us for a very long time in terms of suffering, and for the sake of reconciliation, that it would have been helpful, and I ask for your comment, if you had taken that step of applying for amnesty.

De Klerk answered,

I am not being legalistic when I say that Parliament made a law, that law instituted this Commission and this Commission has three main tasks. The one is to deal with amnesty in respect of crimes, and only those who are involved in crimes should, to my mind, use the amnesty procedure.

Then the truth. The truth also deals with the harm
done to people, with everything, the whole context
which caused the bitterness which caused the conflict, and apartheid is very relevant and the harm that
it has done with regard to that aspect of your task.
And the right place to deal with one's role that you
have played in that situation is under that heading.

The third is reparation. Reparation has already
started in many instances when apartheid was abolished. But you have a tremendous challenge ahead of
you in conjunction with the government and with
all other role players in South Africa to look at the
question of reparation.

So it is within that framework that I am saying that
I am not just being legalistic. It would be using the
wrong procedure, the wrong aspect of your activities,
to use the amnesty route.

Charles Villa-Vicencio came to see me later and told me
that Pik Botha, former Minister of Foreign Affairs, had
shown him a copy of a fax dated 5 May 1997, addressed to
De Klerk, in which he proposed that the entire National
Party Cabinet should apply for amnesty. De Klerk had
rejected this proposal out of hand.

But it was the statements made by Tutu and me at the
subsequent press conference that angered the National
Party and De Klerk in particular. Tutu had raised his aston-
ishment and distress at De Klerk's demeanour, his defen-
siveness, and his constant refrain that he had not known
what had been happening. Tutu, of course, as one of the
major opponents of apartheid, had on more than one occasion been to see De Klerk and had told him what was happening in the country, and the apparent amnesia now
shown by De Klerk deeply saddened him. At a Commission meeting the next day, while Tutu was trying to explain to his fellow commissioners why he had taken the
stance he had, he started weeping and I had to adjourn the
meeting. It took quite a while before we could meet again.
Tutu's reaction, therefore, was not so much anger at De

Klerk but instead a sense of deep sadness. However, it was interpreted by the National Party as an indication of our total lack of impartiality.

The National Party therefore brought a legal charge against Tutu, me, the Commission, the Justice Minister Dullah Omar, and President Mandela. Their major demand was that Tutu should issue an unconditional apology for his remarks about De Klerk at the press conference. They further demanded that I should resign not only as deputy chairperson but as a commissioner, and that Advocate Glen Goosen, who had led the questioning during the hearing, should have no further part in the National Party's relationship with the Commission. We issued a press statement to the effect that these charges were very serious, and, because they impacted on the entire Commission, this was not a decision that Tutu and I could make, but that the matter should be considered by a full meeting of the Commission. The lawyers acting for the National Party indicated that they could see no reason at all why the Commission as a whole should have to make the decision and asked us to comply immediately with their demands, namely that Tutu apologise unconditionally and that I resign. We declined to do this and the matter was discussed fully at the next Commission meeting. The commissioners unanimously decided to resist the demand, and as a consequence the National Party took us to court. On 20 June 1997 the sheriff served me papers demanding my resignation. As I sat with the papers in my hand, I thought how ironic it was that the very people who had brought so much misery to South Africa through unjust policies and practices should accuse me of partiality.

Throughout this period I felt a real sense of pressure and loneliness in the face of the National Party's attack, their insistence that I resign from the Commission, and their attempt to discredit the Commission by demanding an unqualified apology from Tutu. What helped enormously were the messages of support that both Tutu and I received from many parts of South Africa and the world. Our own colleagues in particular went out of their way to send messages of support, which sustained us enormously. A note to me from the Eastern Cape staff, under the leadership of Bongani Finca, was particularly moving. They wrote,

> We know that you do not need this note because you are strong enough to deal with the situation before you without a word of encouragement from us, but we thought we should just send a word anyway to assure you that we are thinking about you and praying the inner strength that God has provided you will sustain you as it has done through your many years of service to the people of our land.

My reply to them was, 'I am very grateful and deeply moved by the note you sent to me. I may look strong and big and unruffled, but I assure you that I desperately need support, particularly from my colleagues. Please convey to all my very deep appreciation for their thoughtfulness and solidarity.'

I was also encouraged by strong support from President Mandela. He spoke to me about the strong attacks on the Commission from all sides, and reiterated his support for the process. He added, 'I chose you to be deputy chairperson because I have complete confidence in you. When people and organisations attack you unfairly, don't be a sissy, fight back!'

I summed up the importance of the National Party's challenge in a letter to Advocate Jeremy Gauntlett, who was acting for us:

> I want to place on record my own understanding of what is at stake in this court case against Tutu and myself.
>
> South Africa made a decisive choice not to follow the route of amnesia nor of the Nuremberg trials. Our model is a unique experience and has drawn attention from throughout the international human rights communities. If we were to lose the case it would not merely be a blow to the Archbishop and to myself and

indeed the Commission, but the country as a whole. It will almost certainly make it impossible for the Commission to continue its work. It will make even the tiny steps we are attempting towards reconciliation that bit more difficult. The majority of people in South Africa have accepted amnesty because they see it as the price we have to pay for peace in South Africa.

I would ask you to plead with some passion for understanding from the Court as to the wider implications which are involved. As I've indicated above, I have total confidence in you and your team but have tried to indicate what this means to us and the country in layman's language.

I concede that I am biased against apartheid as a system which has dehumanised millions of people, but I have no bias against any individual or party. All of us have been damaged and all of us have a measure of responsibility for what took place in South Africa. I concede that I am biased in favour of human rights and have been so throughout my adult life, but it is a bias which wants to determine a culture of human rights for all in South Africa and not only for some who may have a party political credo or ideology.

I hope you will understand what is behind this letter. It is the essence of deep concern that what is being attempted by the Commission should not be destroyed.

When we finally appeared before the court, Judge Gerald Friedman indicated to both parties that we should do everything we could to resolve the matter out of court. He suggested that it would not be in our interests, or in South Africa's interests, if we proceeded with the action. With the help of Jeremy Gauntlett, we tried hard to compose a statement that would satisfy the National Party. At that time Tutu was in the United States undergoing treatment for prostate cancer. He was out of the country for two months and it was a lonely time without his support and

encouragement. It was an incredibly difficult process trying to contact him and giving him one set of words, while
the NP responded with another. We had tried until 10 p.m.
one night, but without much success. The National Party
was playing hardball. During that time, however, F.W. de
Klerk resigned as leader of the party, and it was decided
that an attempt would be made with the new leader,
Marthinus van Schalkwyk, and Archbishop Tutu on his return from the United States. I left soon after his return for a
meeting in Sicily to participate in the debate to establish
an international criminal court.

I received several phone calls from Tutu suggesting a
way forward; my initial response was that I felt we were
being too accommodating and that if anyone needed to
apologise it was not us but the National Party for the way
that their policies had brought so much human misery to
so many for such a long period. Once again, however, in
order to assist the Commission and keep the peace, I
agreed from distant Sicily that an apology should be offered. Obviously I would not resign, as they had demanded.
In the end, the following agreement was reached:

1   The parties are pleased to announce that the legal
     proceedings between the NP and the TRC in the
     Cape High Court have been resolved.
2   The intervention by the Chairperson of the TRC,
     Archbishop Desmond Tutu, on 4 September 1997,
     which resulted in a personal apology from him for
     publicly criticising the evidence presented on be-
     half of the NP by Mr F.W. de Klerk on 14 May 1997;
     and the willingness of the NP and Opposition
     leader, Mr Marthinus van Schalkwyk, to reach
     a settlement in the interests of reconciliation,
     resulted in the following agreement:
     2.1 The TRC Deputy Chairperson, Dr Alex
          Boraine, associates himself fully with the sen-
          timents of Archbishop Tutu referred to above,
          and expresses the same sentiments as the
          Archbishop in relation to his own public

criticisms of the evidence presented on behalf of the NP by Mr F.W. de Klerk on 14 May 1997.

2.2 For this Dr Boraine personally apologises to Mr de Klerk and the NP.

2.3 The TRC acknowledges, and is deeply concerned at the perception, that such public criticism and conduct reflected negatively on its objectivity and impartiality.

2.4 The TRC acknowledges the obligation imposed upon it by the Promotion of National Unity and Reconciliation Act to function without political or other bias and undertakes to refrain from conduct which would contravene the Act.

2.5 The detail of future cooperation between the NP and the TRC will be discussed by Archbishop Tutu and Mr van Schalkwyk at a later occasion.

2.6 The NP shall, in view of the above mentioned apologies and undertakings, withdraw its application. It is agreed that the parties will bear their own legal costs.

While I reluctantly accepted that it was sensible to keep the Commission out of court, it stuck in my throat to be party to an apology, and still does. I agreed to this decision at the time in order to assist the Commission, but we had no need to apologise for saying that De Klerk had known what had been happening in his own party! If anyone needed to apologise it was De Klerk and his government, not Tutu or me.

In their application, the National Party spent a long time indicating a number of occasions when they believed I had transgressed the need for impartiality. Their demand for my resignation stemmed from my frequent and fiery debates in Parliament over many contentious acts of legislation passed by the government. They detailed my political history, my time in Parliament, my resignation, my co-founding of the Institute for a Democratic Alternative for South Africa with Van Zyl Slabbert, and stated that I had participated 'actively in the political affairs of the country and remained a severe critic of the National Party in particular'.[7] They seemed to forget entirely that every workshop held by IDASA was open to all parties, that the National Party was specifically asked to attend and to participate in many of those conferences and workshops and often did so. They went so far as to quote from my book, *The Healing of a Nation?*, and, remarkably, included the following quotations:

> South Africans desperately need to create a common memory that can be acknowledged by those who created and implemented the apartheid system, by those who fought against it and by the many more who were in the middle and claimed not to know what was happening in their own country... After all, a commitment to search for truth in a country that has for so long been based on deceit will be inevitably worrying for those who have sought to conceal the truth.[8]

I say 'remarkably' because the quotations they refer to reveal a very clear commitment to impartiality.

It was clear from the case against me that they were also very upset by remarks I had made concerning the South African Defence Force public hearing. They stated that I had slammed the 'bland' and 'soulless' submission made by former SADF members in Cape Town, and they quoted me as saying, 'My overall impression is that the submission is breathtaking in its one-sidedness', and 'I find it almost unbelievable that in 80 pages there is no acknowledgement or acceptance of responsibility of a single death during the apartheid era.'[9] They were absolutely right, but I felt that the comments I had made were valid, and it transpired in subsequent hearings that the SADF had done little more than whitewash some of the darker deeds of the military.

One final matter which clearly upset the NP was that I had publicly invited De Klerk to spend a day listening to the testimony of victims of human rights abuses. My invitation was a response to a statement he had made criticising the Commission and claiming that it was simply not promoting reconciliation. My response was that 'There is the beginning of an unfolding of wonder and of some guilt, some shock and some hope that we are coming to terms with our past and that the last word is not revenge but healing.' I added, 'If Mr de Klerk really wants to know what is happening, I would invite him to come and spend the day not to talk but to listen.'[10]

De Klerk seemed to believe that I had some personal axe to grind, some deep-seated animosity towards him. My interaction with him had begun in Parliament. When I arrived there in 1974 he was an ordinary member of Parliament and I watched his rapid progress and his appointment as Cabinet minister and, ultimately, State President of South Africa. My memory of him in Parliament is of a very intelligent thinker, a fine debater, and a true-blue conservative who never deviated from the official policy of his party. When he made his epoch-making speech in 1990, unbanning the liberation movements and releasing political prisoners, I praised him in public and in private, in spoken word and in writing, and stated without any qualification that his contribution to the new democracy was remarkable and unique. I am not sure, therefore, why he felt that there was something personal in what I was saying when I addressed myself to him in terms of his own need – as I perceived it – to apply for amnesty.

In his autobiography, *The Last Trek: A New Beginning*, published in 1999, De Klerk comments on the appointment of the seventeen commissioners and makes it clear that he was unhappy with the appointment of Desmond Tutu as chairperson. Despite his misgivings, however, he felt that the National Party could 'live with him'. But, he goes on to say, 'I had more serious reservations regarding the proposed vice-chairperson.' He then outlines some of my own history in politics, and concludes, 'It was clear from Boraine's writings that he viewed the complex human saga of South Africa in the starkest black and white terms. Beneath an urbane and deceptively affable exterior beat the heart of a zealot and an inquisitor.'[11]

I can understand De Klerk's strong criticism to some extent, because we certainly did differ radically in our time together in Parliament. It is true that I asked many questions there about the basic policies of his party. I also think that most of the time he is cooler and calmer than I am when discussing apartheid and its impact on people (the exception was his second appearance before the Commission). I think the major difference is that he was cocooned in the folds of a party that brooked no opposition. From childbirth he was privileged, his father was prominent in National Party politics, and his own lengthy and very successful career in Parliament isolated him from the real world of the majority of South Africans. This meant that he could talk rationally about apartheid as a policy which theoretically could divide people into a number of ethnic groups, living in distinct areas, and in that way conflict could be avoided. I, on the other hand, through my work in the church, in business, and as an opposition member of Parliament, spent a great deal of my time in the townships and saw at first hand the damage that was done to countless millions of people as a result of this policy. I concede, therefore, that I was often passionate in my pleas and demands that this policy should end so that the human suffering could cease and there could be equality and equal opportunities for all.

De Klerk saw himself, to use his own words, as a 'co-liberator' of South Africa. When he came to see us, he described himself as a man of integrity, needed by the new South Africa to consolidate democracy and to establish stability. He clearly believed that he still had a critical leadership role to play and that we should be careful not to blur his image. He was deeply resentful that he had not received the same praise and acceptance that was afforded Mandela. It is quite astonishing that he should feel that way, bearing in mind what Mandela had stood for, fought for, and suffered for for so long, in strong contrast to what De Klerk had participated in. What he refused to accept was that the policies of the National Party had created a climate which made it possible for some of the worst offences and extra-legal practices to take place, particularly during the 1980s. I have no doubt that he could grasp this intellectually, but it seemed impossible for him to do so emotionally, perhaps because of his father's role as a senior member of the National Party, and because he had spent his own life defending the principles, and therefore the practice, of apartheid.

I also found it extraordinary that he should maintain over and over again that he hadn't been aware of what was happening. During my twelve years in Parliament I had been approached on many occasions by individuals, organisations, and groups, who shared with me and my party something of their personal suffering and sorrow. I went to many areas where forced removals were taking place. I went to morgues and saw the bodies of people who clearly had been shot in the back by police and spoke on these matters in Parliament time and time again. In this regard, the former Minister of Law and Order, Adriaan Vlok, made a telling statement when he appeared before the Commission. On his own initiative, he said that it was true that 'Commissioner Boraine did tell us about some of these things that were taking place but we didn't believe him and did not want to accept what he was saying because we saw him as being part of the enemy of South Africa.'[12] Leon Wessels, a former deputy minister in De Klerk's Cabinet, said in his statement to the Commission, 'It was not that we didn't know, we didn't want to know. We didn't talk about it, we whispered it in the corridors of Parliament.'[13] It may be that De Klerk was unable to hear what some of us were trying to say and couldn't understand the force of Tutu's plea to him. I am deeply saddened that he did not leave politics in 1994. I think he would then have gone out on the crest of a wave, as it were, as a major contributor to our new democracy. But it was not to be. I think he believed that he would continue to be a leader in South Africa on a par with Mandela, which of course was unthinkable.

IN ADDITION TO the political party hearings, the TRC held hearings investigating the role of other institutions.

There were a number of reasons for this. It is true that we needed to see the submissions of individuals in a much broader and wider context, but it is even more true that apartheid was all-pervasive and affected every area of life, and many institutions in the country had participated one way or another in the implementation of the policy. It was with this in mind, and in the context of apartheid's legacy, that these hearings were organised. It would be impossible to assess and to understand the full implication of apartheid without an appreciation of the extent to which the tentacles of an aggressive racial policy reached into every area of life.

I want to set out some part of this legacy, not only because it was important for the work of the Commission, but because it influences and affects South Africa today and will do so for many years to come. It is one of the reasons why it is so difficult to move towards reconciliation and resolution of the problems we have experienced. Apartheid is officially over, but its baggage is apparent everywhere and will continue to hold South Africa back for generations to come.

The cost of apartheid is summed up with great visual force in a well-known poem by Ingrid Jonker, with the stark title, 'The Child who was Shot Dead by Soldiers at Nyanga':[14]

> The child is not dead
> The child lifts his fists against his mother
> Who shouts Afrika! Shouts the breath
> Of freedom and the veld
> In the locations of the cordoned heart
>
> The child lifts his fists against his father
> In the march of the generations
> Who shout Afrika! Shout the breath
> Of righteousness and blood
> In the streets of his embattled pride
>
> The child is not dead
> Not at Langa nor at Nyanga

Not at Orlando nor at Sharpeville
Nor at the police station at Phillippi
Where he lies with a bullet through his brain

The child is the dark shadow of the soldiers
On guard with rifles, saracens and batons
The child is present at all assemblies and law-givings
The child peers through the windows of houses
And into the hearts of mothers
This child who just wanted to play in the sun at
    Nyanga
Is everywhere
The child grown to a man treks through all Africa
The child grown into a giant journeys through the
    whole world

Without a pass

Professor Francis Wilson, an economist at the University of Cape Town, commenting on 'the locations of the cordoned heart', reminds us that 'the march of the generations in the streets of embattled pride is a long one that goes back through three centuries of conquest'. He adds that 'The child has been present at all "assemblies and law-givings" in the country's history. South Africa itself is the cordoned heart and her people, oppressed and oppressors together, are imprisoned by the fetters with which one group seeks to bind the other'.[15]

Ingrid Jonker's poem was written in 1960 and Francis Wilson's comments were written twenty-five years later. Ten years after that, South Africa began to break the 'fetters' which bound the majority of her people in what appeared to be perpetual servitude. Although it seemed impossible that South Africa would achieve a relatively peaceful and democratic election, the transition from oppression, exclusivity, and resistance to a new negotiated democratic order has been realised.

No other country in modern times has made a successful transition from a position such as South Africa's, namely fifteen years of economic stagnation and over ten years of outright decline in per capita income, gross inequalities of income and opportunity, ethnic rivalries, and significant and escalating violence. Yet the miracle has happened. Frank Chikane, former secretary-general of the South African Council of Churches, was rightly amused when he heard politicians, political scientists, and members of the business community talking about the 'South African miracle'. There was no reasonable or logical explanation for our escape from the potential bloodbath.

Yet there remains 'unfinished business', and the magnitude of the challenge is compounded by the fact that apartheid was an intensified, more sophisticated, more cruel, and more far-reaching development of a policy of repression and racism which spans the centuries. A single quote from Cecil John Rhodes (1887) illustrates the historical roots of the attitude which has determined the domination of the black majority by the white minority:

> I will lay down my own policy on this Native question. Either you have to receive them on an equal footing as citizens, or to call them a subject race. I have made up my mind that there must be class legislation, that there must be pass laws and peace preservation acts and that we have to treat natives where they are in a state of barbarism in a different way from ourselves. We are to be lords over them. These are my policies, these are the policies of South Africa ...we have given them no share in the government and I think quite rightly too.[16]

Sixty years later, the same creed of domination and exclusivity was expressed in a speech in Parliament by former State President P.W. Botha:

> Do we stand for the domination and the supremacy of the European or not? We must first answer that question before we can speak about fair treatment and the rights of the non-Europeans. For if you stand for the domination and supremacy of the Europeans then

everything you do must in the first place be calculated to ensure that domination.[17]

The first South African constitution, promulgated in 1910, entrenched white hegemony and was fundamentally undemocratic, excluding the vast majority of the population. It was also structurally racist, because the exclusion of the majority was on the basis of skin colour. This racism was further institutionalised when the National Party came into power in 1948. The NP's policy of apartheid was not only a denial of basic political rights but a systematic piece of social engineering which embraced every area of life from birth to death. The Population Registration Act fundamentally determined one's life chances. Thus the system of apartheid determined state policies relating to the franchise as well as access to land, housing, residence, schools and universities, transport, health services, sport, hotels, restaurants, and even cemeteries.

In other words, apartheid was a system of minority domination of statutorily defined colour groups on a territorial, residential, political, social, and economic basis. It is this legacy which, unless tackled with the same determination and skill as the initial negotiation process, will make it impossible to sustain the miracle, consolidate democracy, and ensure a peaceful future for all South Africans. Indeed, the success or otherwise of service delivery will in large measure determine the success or failure of the Truth and Reconciliation Commission itself.

The institutional hearings involved business and labour, the faith community, the legal community, the health sector, the media, and prisons. Special hearings dealt with conscription, children and youth, and women. A record of the institutional hearings is contained in the Commission's report.[18] My own comments on these hearings will be fairly brief but will hopefully indicate the broad mandate adopted by the Commission and the impact of apartheid on the social fabric of South African life.

[175]

At the business and labour hearing, the relationship between business and apartheid was discussed. The perception of most black South Africans, particularly those active in the trade union movement, has always been that business was 'in bed with government'. At the hearing, the Afrikaans Handelsinstituut [trade institute] acknowledged its commitment to what it called 'separate development' rather than apartheid, but did stress that its active support for this system had been part of the support by the wider white community for the separate development policies of the government. The bottom line was that it acknowledged that it had cooperated intimately and closely with government in the implementation of its policies.

This perception of collusion between business and government was challenged at the hearing by English-speaking business leaders, who claimed to have been marginalised under apartheid and believed that Afrikaner business had been given special treatment. However, the Congress of South African Trade Unions (Cosatu) agreed with Professor Sampie Terreblanche of the University of Stellenbosch, who insisted in his submission before the Commission that, although it is true that the government favoured Afrikaner business, the apartheid policy 'created the conditions for the rapid accumulation of capital by white capitalists in all sectors of the economy'.[19]

The majority of business leaders who made presentations to the Commission argued that they had in fact been hampered rather than helped by the politics of apartheid and that they had, by and large, made a contribution to the ending of apartheid by their criticism of government, their proposing of alternative policies, and their provision of jobs for hundreds and thousands of black workers.

There was an admission that business had not done enough, that if they had erred their sin was one of omission rather than commission, that their calls for substantial change had not been urgent enough, that their employment practices had often been woefully inadequate and discriminatory, and that with the benefit of hindsight 'it may be said that the enormity of the apartheid system

[176]

required stronger responses from business on certain key issues... [I]n the ongoing debate about "gradualism" vs the "all or nothing" approach to get rid of apartheid, the stance of these organisations was to push the gradualism argument to the maximum.'[20]

Business leaders failed to admit that they had deliberately moderated their critique of the government's racial policies because so much of their profit was linked to state contracts. The labour unions, the ANC, and other commentators, on the other hand, were blunt and tough in their criticism. The ANC declared in its submission,

> It is our contention that the historically privileged business community as a whole must accept and acknowledge that its current position in the economy, its wealth, power and access to high income and status positions are the product, in part at least, of discrimination and oppression directed against the black majority. While some of the important business organisations and groups opposed some of the laws introduced by successive apartheid governments, a number of core discriminatory laws were both actively sought and tolerated by business... Historically privileged business as a whole must, therefore, accept a degree of co-responsibility for its role in sustaining the apartheid system of discrimination and oppression over many years.[21]

The Cosatu submission echoed the above but went even further: 'We remain of the view that apartheid with its form of institutionalised racism masked its real content and substance – the perpetuation of a super-exploitative cheap labour system. We all know that the primary victims of this system were the black working class and the primary beneficiaries the white ruling elite.' In this stance they were strongly supported by Sampie Terreblanche, who stated very powerfully that 'Business should acknowledge explicitly and without reservation that the power structures underpinning white supremacy and racial capitalism for 100 years were of such a nature that whites have

[**177**]

been undeservedly enriched and people other than whites undeservedly impoverished.'[22]

Major Craig Williamson, the prominent police spy, lent credence to this view when he said in a memorandum submitted to the Commission at the armed forces hearing in Cape Town on 9 October 1997 that

> Our weapons, ammunition, uniforms, vehicles, radio and other equipment were all developed and provided by industry. Our finances and banking were done by bankers who even gave us covert credit cards for covert operations. Our chaplains prayed for our victory and our universities educated us in war. Our propaganda was carried out by the media and our political masters were voted back into power time after time with ever-increasing majorities.[23]

The mining industry in particular came in for strong criticism for its creation and support of the migrant labour system, which has been responsible for the breakdown of family life, the emergence of social ills such as alcoholism, prostitution, and crime, and the stunting of the development of the workers concerned. For a long time, workers were regarded as replaceable labour units rather than human beings. The fact that nearly 70 000 miners died in accidents during the twentieth century and more than one million were seriously injured starkly reveals the lack of basic care, let alone compassion, in that industry.

In its findings, the TRC accepted that business in general benefited from operating in a racially structured context. However, the Commission was anxious to point the way ahead rather than to dwell on the past, and made recommendations relating to the role of the private sector in the future. Specifically, the Commission stated that

> It will be impossible to create a meaningful human rights culture without high priority being given to economic justice by the public and private sectors. Recognising that it is impossible for the public sector alone to find the resources required to expedite the

[**178**]

goal of economic justice, the Commission urges the private sector in particular to consider a special initiative in terms of a fund for training, empowerment and opportunities for the disadvantaged and dispossessed in South Africa.

The Commission went further and recommended that

a scheme be put into place to enable those who benefited from apartheid policies to contribute towards the alleviation of poverty. In submissions made to the Commission a wealth tax was proposed. The Commission does not, however, seek to prescribe one or other strategy but recommends that urgent consideration be given by government to harnessing all available resources in the war against poverty.[24]

Recognising the political and economic significance of the land question, the Commission also recommended that the business community, together with other interested parties and in cooperation with the Land Commission, 'undertake an audit of all unused and underutilised land with a view to making this available to landless people.'[25] Further recommendations related to affirmative action, compensation for black, Indian, and 'coloured' business people who lost their businesses or other means of income during periods of unrest, and the elimination of child labour wherever it still exists.

The faith community hearing investigated the important role played by religion in South Africa. In the 1991 census, more than 70 per cent of South Africans indicated an allegiance of one kind or another to the Christian faith. In addition there are strong Muslim, Hindu, and Jewish communities in the country. Many members of these faith communities specifically asked if they could make presentations to the Commission concerning their roles during the period under review.

Before the founding of the TRC there was a strong feeling in some quarters that the Commission should not have been set up by the state, but that the search for truth and commitment to reconciliation were matters for the churches in particular and the faith communities in general to undertake. This is a spurious argument, bearing in mind the state's responsibility for apartheid as well as the complicity of many churches and religious groups in the outworking of the policy. Furthermore, it is unlikely that religious bodies, separately or together, would have had the resources, the skills, and the will to undertake such a massive enterprise.

It was confirmed at the hearing that many faith communities, contrary to their central teachings, were active or silent supporters of apartheid. The Dutch Reformed Church gave explicit support and was often regarded as the 'National Party at prayer'. I recall a very prominent member of a death squad, prior to his applying for amnesty, telling me in detail of the support he had received from his community, his culture, and his church. He told me with tears streaming down his cheeks how he often fell on his knees and prayed that God would guide and sustain him on a killing mission. I was particularly distressed by his plaintive cry and appeal to me, which I recorded in my diary as follows: 'I know now that what I did was very wrong but I believed that my political leaders and my church leaders supported me in what I was doing. I believed it was part of God's mission to destroy the ANC who I was told were terrorists and communists who would destroy our country and our religion.' He concluded with this question: 'What can I do now? I have no place to go to. I can never, ever go back to the church which never criticised me but always supported me in what I was doing as a member of the security police.' Many people indicated to the commissioners and our staff that they felt deeply resentful towards a church which had supported apartheid and encouraged them in their work as security policemen with the specific intent of destroying those who sought to resist apartheid.

While the Dutch Reformed Church explicitly supported apartheid, there can be no question that many other branches of the faith communities were lukewarm in their criticism of the policy and very often reflected intolerance and racism. Many congregations deeply resented those in leadership who dared to speak or act against apartheid. There was a false piety which resulted in a faith divorced from the real world. In Dietrich Bonhoeffer's memorable words, they had 'embraced cheap grace rather than the costly grace of the Christian gospel'.[26]

If one looks at the structures of faith communities at almost every level, particularly at the local level, and considers the discrepancies between salaries paid to white and black ministers and priests, it is painfully obvious that the actions of many faith communities were congruent with apartheid rather than opposed to it. Moreover, most of the Christian churches uncritically supported military chaplaincies. Many ministers, as well as State President P.W. Botha, saw the role of the chaplains as one of commitment to state policies rather than a source of comfort and succour to soldiers who were forced to do military service. Of course there were exceptions, but in large measure churches and chaplains gave support, symbolic and practical, to the violent state machine.

On the other hand, it should also be stressed that not only were many faith communities victims of the oppressive policies of apartheid, but a large number, particularly the leaders of the faith communities, were vigorous and heroic opponents of the apartheid government. Many of these demonstrated this opposition in word and deed, participated in special meetings and conferences, marches and publications, and a large number paid a very high price for their opposition. There are many such people, but at least two names stand out as representative of this brave group. The first is Beyers Naudé, who came from a staunchly Afrikaner background and held a leadership position in his own Dutch Reformed Church, but became a pariah in the Afrikaner community because of his brave stand against apartheid on theological as well as human grounds. Desmond Tutu also stands out, not only as a leader of the South African Council of Churches, but also as a very vocal and visible Archbishop of the Anglican community. His name became almost synonymous with the theological criticism of apartheid as a heresy and an apostacy. As a result he became extremely unpopular in official government circles, and many whites within various church communities loved to hate him.

We should also not forget the many unsung heroes, ministers and church leaders who provided shelter for the oppressed. At the very least they provided a church building, a church hall, or a church house where people who were being severely oppressed by the security forces could find shelter and indeed could often be hidden until they could make alternative arrangements. It was a very risky thing to do, but there are many who did exactly that. To offer a simple meal and a blanket to fugitives from the security forces was extremely dangerous.

In the words of the TRC report, faith communities 'enjoy a unique and privileged position in South African society and are widely respected and have far-reaching moral influence. As such they have a special role in healing and reconciliation initiatives.'[27] The Commission therefore urged in its recommendations that faith communities hold special healing services within their own communities and parishes, ecumenically and locally, regionally and nationally. There is to date very little evidence to suggest that this recommendation has been put into practice, but one can only hope that it will, because South Africa remains a very damaged society and faith communities have a special responsibility to the ministry of healing.

In addition, the Commission recommended that, as a practical expression of reconciliation, religious communities undertake 'a land audit, identifying land in their possession which can be made available to the landless poor, and that where religious communities have acquired land as a result of apartheid legislation, this land be returned to its rightful owners'. The Commission also urged faith communities to create a general fund to be financed 'in proportion to their resources, that can be used for the victims of past abuses'.[28]

There can be little doubt that there are enormous resources in terms of skills, land, buildings, possessions, and commitment which can and should be better utilised in the search for healing and restoration in South Africa. It will be very interesting to see how the faith communities respond to contemporary challenges. During apartheid many members and leaders of faith communities allied themselves with the liberation forces. Now that these liberation forces are no longer in opposition, however, now that they have become the governing party, what is the attitude of faith communities to the government? Will they recognise their responsibility to challenge the government if it abuses its power? And what of those people in the Christian church in particular who either supported apartheid or kept quiet because they were fearful and didn't want to get involved? What is their reaction to the new South African dispensation? Will it remain one of acquiescence and neutrality? Or will there be a new spirit of involvement and commitment? There are no clear signs yet as to how the faith communities will face up to these new challenges and demands.

There was a remarkable similarity between the business and labour hearing and that of the legal profession. In the same way that business leaders, while regretting that they hadn't done as much as they perhaps ought to have done, on the whole defended the role of business during the apartheid era, so a fairly large and significant group of lawyers defended the attitudes and behaviour of their profession during that period. On the other hand, organisations such as the Black Lawyers' Association, Lawyers for Human Rights, the Legal Resources Centre, and the National Association of Democratic Lawyers were extremely critical of the performance of the legal community as a whole and the judiciary in particular.

Those who sought to defend the actions or inaction of the legal profession argued that they had had no choice because of the doctrine of parliamentary sovereignty, which meant that they had to obey the decisions taken by Parliament and had little room to manoeuvre. Wherever they could, the argument went, they had done their very best to strive towards a more just and liberal interpretation of the law. They had been nervous that if they took too strong a stand the state might have made even greater incursions into the independence of the judiciary, and any attempt to strive for the maintenance of the rule of law would then have been impossible. Some conceded that they could have taken a stronger stand, and that they ought to have resisted more forcefully government's interference in the administration of justice. On the whole, however, they felt that they had done a reasonable job in the circumstances.

It was also argued very strongly that judges should not appear in person before the Commission because this would call into question their independence and would encourage future commissions constantly to call judges to appear before them. I was astonished when I heard about this decision. To address the problem, we met with Chief Justice Ismail Mahomed and the president of the Constitutional Court, Justice Arthur Chaskalson. They had obviously discussed the matter thoroughly and made it very clear to us early on that they would not appear in person before the Commission, but that they would make written submissions. Bearing in mind the kind of treatment meted out to people like Mahomed during apartheid I had imagined that he would be only too pleased to recount his experience of a racist legal system in the hope that this would be a lesson to all of us and help ensure that it would never happen again. We had imagined that if his story could have been told before the Commission, it would have lent great impetus to the whole process of transformation. I have always held both men in high esteem and thought they would immediately agree that for the sake of transparency and transformation they should appear before the Commission as a signal that all of us in the end were accountable. The meeting became almost embarrassing, with some of us virtually on our knees pleading with them to change their minds. Nothing we said prevailed, however, and we had to accept that judges would not appear before us, although we knew that there were at least some who felt quite strongly that it was right to appear and were ready to do so. However, because of the decision taken by the chief justice and the president of the Constitutional Court, no judges appeared before us.

Frankly, the reasons advanced by the judges in turning down our invitation to appear before the Commission were spurious. According to David Dyzenhaus, a South African emigrant to Canada, who attended the legal hearings, the claim that judicial independence would be compromised is 'hollow once one sees that judicial independence is itself an instrumental virtue: it is instrumental to ensuring the accountability of judges to the law. And the majority of old-order judges had failed to show fidelity to the law, had failed to take seriously a judicial oath which required them to "administer justice".' Another reason advanced for their non-appearance was to keep intact the fragile bond between judges who had served in the old regime and the newly appointed judges. But what kind of collegiality is it that is bought at 'the expense of an open and honest debate about the substance of judicial independence'?[29] I don't question the bona fides of the judges concerned, but I do question their wisdom in declining to participate in a public process which sought to venerate the rule of law.

One of my colleagues, Yasmin Sooka, a lawyer herself, recommended that we should subpoena key judges to appear before the Commission. This was discussed at great length and I concede that I argued against her, feeling that it would not assist the Commission in its work and would be detrimental to the image that we were trying to project against overwhelming criticism. I was wrong in that decision and Yasmin Sooka was absolutely right. We as a Commission should have subpoenaed the judges, because this would have been an indication that all South Africans ought to give an account of their conduct during the apartheid era. No other institutions were exempt, and the refusal by the judges to appear before the Commission confirms the view held by many judges that they are in some way superior to other people, and beyond criticism. The Commission made it abundantly clear that it fully supported the need for the independence of the judiciary but believed that it was not only unfortunate but tragic that judges took the attitude that they did. In its findings the Commission states that

> an appearance before the Commission in such special circumstances would have demonstrated accountability and would not have compromised the independence of the judiciary. History will judge the judiciary harshly. Its response to the hearing has again placed the questions of what accountability and independence mean in a constitutional democracy in the public domain for debate.[30]

The Commission was also very strong in its criticism of the 'complete failure of the magistracy to respond to the Commission's invitation, more so considering the previous lack of formal independence of magistrates and their dismal record as servants of the apartheid state in the past'.[31]

Finally, the Commission found that there had always been a minority, including judges, legal academics, and students, who took a stand against apartheid. Some lawyers refused to be silenced, and took a very risky stance in criticising unjust laws and arbitrary official conduct. Some were prepared to defend political prisoners and other victims of an unjust system. They very often paid a high price for this stand, including harassment by the state in many instances, and ostracism by many of their own colleagues.

A final hearing which must be referred to is that dealing with chemical and biological warfare. We were aghast to read the secret files which came into our possession outlining horrific experiments either considered or carried out in research laboratories under the leadership of the notorious Dr Wouter Basson.

He was arrested in January 1997 on charges of possessing Ecstasy capsules, and a court case is under way so I will not elaborate. Suffice to say that he was a most unsatisfactory witness and refused to cooperate with the Commission, although he did appear before it. He sat throughout the hearing with a half smile on his face as though he was untouchable and regarded us with contempt. We, who had heard so many stories of horror, were nevertheless overwhelmed by the evidence of sinister scientific experiments, the use of poisons against political opponents, and the cultivation of anthrax and cholera to threaten the lives of entire communities. All of this sent a shiver of revulsion down my back. This was much more sinister than the ravings of a mad scientist. The decision to manufacture drugs such as Ecstasy and Mandrax for use in riot control and to undermine the stability of black communities is particularly abhorrent. It seemed to me then that we had only touched the tip of the iceberg, and subsequent allegations and revelations during the court case confirmed my view.

The argument for 'collective responsibility', as held by General Viljoen and as proposed to us by De Klerk and Mbeki, was flawed: we decided that individual accountability was the focus of the Truth and Reconciliation Commission. But in the political party hearings and institutional hearings, we did address the broad responsibility of institutions for the climate in which individual acts took place. There can be no denying that all institutions in South Africa were tainted by apartheid, and none of those who chose participation in an evil system can entirely escape a degree of responsibility for its injustices. For example, I who participated in an undemocratic Parliament have to accept a measure of responsibility for the actions of that Parliament, even though my party opposed the unjust laws and actions sanctioned by that body.

In this connection, it should be recorded that many of those who appeared before the Commission had the grace to offer an apology for the role they played during the years of oppression.

[187]

6

A season of madness:
P.W. Botha

THE COMMISSION was born in controversy and remains controversial long after its final report has been published. Because of its public nature, every move the Commission made was closely scrutinised not only by the media but in particular by its opponents. Almost every week we were told by the media that we were facing an absolutely critical challenge which would make or break the Commission. We survived many of those so-called make-or-break challenges. There can be little doubt, however, that there were two challenges which would be decisive for the integrity of the Commission. The first was what we were going to do about P.W. Botha, former State President of South Africa, who made it very clear from the outset that he would never cooperate in any way with the Commission. We had to make a crucial decision about how to deal with a man who still commanded a great deal of support from the right-wing Afrikaner camp. The other person we had to contend with was Winnie Madikizela-Mandela, who had been associated with a number of abductions and killings. The media constantly asked us about both these people. In a leading article in the *Sunday Independent* of 24 November 1996 this point was forcibly made:

> The Truth and Reconciliation Commission faces its hardest political test in the coming weeks. First, it has to convene the hearing into the Mandela United Football Club, which operated in Soweto in the late eighties. The focus of that hearing is on one woman,

Winnie Madikizela-Mandela, who has been both praised and pilloried across the world. Second, and perhaps even more importantly, it has to stare down the unrepentant man, whom many have called one of apartheid's most brutal rulers: P.W. Botha, the former state president.

What persuaded the Commission to take the action it did was not the pressure of the media, although I am certain that we were influenced by that, but the stories told to us by the victims of gross human rights violations. It was when we listened to what had taken place in their lives and among their families and friends that it became impossible to ignore the responsibility of and the contribution made to this tale of misery and death by P.W. Botha. In the same way, as we listened to the mothers of children who had disappeared when they were linked with members of the infamous Mandela United Football Club, there was no way that we could ignore the involvement and responsibility of Winnie Madikizela-Mandela.

In this chapter and the next, I have selected these two prominent personalities as case studies of the madness and tragedy of apartheid. It may be that this will increase the controversy. Some will be very angry indeed that I have dared to discuss P.W. Botha, the proud leader of the National Party for so many years, in the same breath as Winnie Madikizela-Mandela, who was found guilty of kidnapping. Others will be appalled that I can talk about Madikizela-Mandela, the Mother of the Nation, in the same breath as Botha, who symbolised the ugly face of apartheid.

Of course there are major differences between the two. They are opposites in terms of birth, background, training, ideology, gender, age, experience, and power. In all these ways and in many others, they are different. And yet they were both caught up visibly and powerfully in the unfolding of the South African tragedy.

THERE WERE A numbers of reasons why we felt it was very important for us as a Commission to hear from P.W.

Botha. He had been not only a political organiser but also a member of Parliament of long standing, Minister of Defence, Prime Minister, and State President, and was intimately linked with the policies and practices of apartheid. It was essential to have his testimony, and his refusal to co-operate with F.W. de Klerk when De Klerk was preparing the National Party's submission to the Commission meant that it was inevitable that we would have to approach him directly.

We were sensitive to his age. We knew that he had had a stroke, that he was not well, and also that he was potentially a rallying point for the right wing, and we did not want to do anything to encourage further action from that source. On the other hand, we had a responsibility to the Act as well as to the country. We had been listening to many first-hand experiences from victims across the spectrum; we had begun to hear from applicants for amnesty who described in graphic detail the actions of the security police and the military, and we felt it was extremely important that we should hear directly from the man who had been in charge of the country. Furthermore, P.W. Botha was on record as being extremely critical of the Commission, dismissing it as 'a circus' and as an attack on the Afrikaner community.

We could not ignore Botha's role in the madness and tragedy of apartheid, but we wanted to proceed carefully. There was never any intention of, as it were, letting him off the hook and allowing him to remain silent or unaccountable while we were subpoenaing or inviting others to appear before the Commission. But some people felt we were moving far too slowly and many commentators in the media were extremely impatient with our delay in calling Botha to account. There were equally vociferous voices, mainly from Botha's former colleagues and the major Afrikaans newspapers such as *Die Burger* and *Rapport*, that issued dire warnings against unleashing the tiger and urged the TRC to allow Botha to enjoy his retirement. They, too, joined the chorus, accusing the Commission of being a witch hunt against the Afrikaner and suggesting that by

[190]

touching Botha we were touching the nerve of the Afrikaner.

Pieter Willem Botha was born on 12 January 1916 in the Orange Free State. He was the only son of Pieter Willem and Hendrina Botha and came from farming stock, although his mother was the granddaughter of Hennie de Wet, a former member of Parliament.

He went to local junior and senior schools in small towns and matriculated at the high school in Bethlehem in 1933. Foreshadowing his later career, he became chairman of the school debating society. His parents couldn't afford to send him to university, but he managed to secure a loan and in 1934 he entered Grey University College in Bloemfontein as a law student. His time there, however, was short-lived. As a part-time organiser for the National Party his political skills were recognised, and he was asked to apply for a full-time post in the party. In 1936 he took up his duties as a political organiser in Caledon in the Cape. The area he covered included Caledon, Swellendam, and Bredasdorp.

He worked as a political party organiser for ten years and achieved a reputation as a very hard worker and also as an effective disrupter of opposition party public meetings. One story in particular which has done the rounds relates that P.W. Botha used a bicycle chain to break up opposition meetings. On 1 September 1941 he was appointed assistant secretary of the Cape National Party; his foot was firmly on the ladder to full-time participation in the legislature.

At the beginning of the Second World War Botha became a member of the Ossewa Brandwag, a paramilitary organisation which sought to undermine South Africa's war effort against Germany. In fact, there was a time, because of his involvement in the Ossewa Brandwag, when he was under threat of internment. However, he soon became disillusioned with the organisation and in 1941 he wrote to an Afrikaans newspaper objecting to the direction that it had taken and rejecting its attempt to monopolise the Afrikaner struggle for a republic. So strongly did he feel

[191]

about this that in the same year he resigned from the Ossewa Brandwag.

On 13 March 1943 he married Elise, the daughter of Dr and Mrs S.H. Rossouw. In the same year he became a parliamentary candidate for the first time in the Vasco constituency, but lost to the United Party. In the next few years he was assistant and acting secretary of the Cape National Party's special committee of inquiry into so-called coloured affairs. This was the beginning of a long relationship with the future role of 'coloured' people in South Africa. In 1946 he was promoted to the post of Union Information Officer, dealing with propaganda and publicity, and this too served him well in later years. Part of his responsibility was to produce pamphlets denigrating political opponents.

In 1948, when the National Party came to power and the dreaded apartheid policy was first introduced, Botha became a member of Parliament for the district of George. He was later appointed chief secretary of the party in the Cape Province, a post which he held until 1958. As a member of Parliament he was reputed to be a good constituency man, working hard to develop the constituency and establish, among other things, a modern technical high school, an airport, a civil defence college, and an old-age home.

In October 1958 Botha was appointed Deputy Minister of the Interior by Prime Minister H.F. Verwoerd and held this post until 1961. Once again, he was closely involved with 'coloured affairs' and the implementation of the Group Areas Act. The decision to remove en masse the 'coloured' people living in District Six and dump them in low-income housing on the Cape Flats outside Cape Town was taken while he was Minister of Community Development and of Coloured Affairs. However, he didn't keep that portfolio for long; on 5 April 1966 he was appointed Minister of Defence, a position in which he was to remain until 1980. In 1966 he was also elected leader of the National Party in the Cape Province.

As Minister of Defence, Botha was instrumental in making South Africa largely self-sufficient in arms; a growing arms industry was developed with the establishment of the Armaments Development Corporation (Armscor) as a statutory body. During this time he also became a member of the important State Security Council, a statutory body which was established to advise the government on national policy and strategy with regard to the security of South Africa. He saw himself very much as a soldier's man and regularly visited the border areas; he was in every respect a Minister of Defence.

It was while he held this portfolio that a major South African army incursion into Angola took place in 1975. I was in Parliament then, and I remember Botha, without turning a hair, lying to Parliament and denying that South African troops were in Angola. He and the government were very strongly criticised for covering up this escapade, which was widely reported in the foreign press but denied locally because of Botha's assurances. In a democratic society, he would have been forced to resign for deceiving Parliament and the public.

On 28 September 1978, following the resignation of B.J. Vorster, Botha became Prime Minister of South Africa. He retained the post of Minister of Defence, which was always his favourite calling, and also administered the portfolio of National Intelligence.

To his credit, Botha was the first South African Prime Minister to visit Soweto and the homelands. As a result of some of the reforms he introduced, minor as they were, he began to experience resistance from right-wing elements in his party. In 1979, along with other changes streamlining the government bureaucracy, Botha upgraded the State Security Council, and from that time on it had power and significance out of all proportion to that which it had enjoyed before. The SSC became the main policy-making body as far as security matters were concerned, and the Cabinet became a rubber stamp. In addition, under Botha's leadership the Senate was abolished, and he established the President's Council, with nominated members from white, 'coloured', and Indian groups.

A key feature of Botha's term of office was his develop-ment of what came to be known as the 'total strategy', to counteract the 'total onslaught' against South Africa, linking political, economic, and military forces into a single concerted effort to squash the growing resistance to apartheid.

After the 1981 election a serious clash occurred between Botha and the right wing of his party. The National Party and Andries Treurnicht, who was a prominent member of the party and of the Cabinet, had a number of public rows. In 1982 the right wing, under Treurnicht's leadership, broke away to form the Conservative Party in reaction to Botha's decision to include 'coloured' people and Indians in the so-called tricameral Parliament. It is also noteworthy that Botha did his best to woo the business sector, with considerable success, in order to ensure their cooperation and to maintain a degree of economic stability.

In 1983 Botha called a referendum among white voters for approval of the new tricameral Constitution. He secured a massive mandate for his proposals, although this support was superficial. Black South Africans were incensed at being excluded once again. Protests intensified, resulting in increasing civil unrest and, within a mere seven years, the collapse of the apartheid regime.

On 14 September 1984, in terms of the new Constitution, Botha became State President, a position which combined the functions of head of state and head of government.

At the opening of Parliament in January 1986, Botha announced his intention of setting up a statutory national council to review legislation affecting blacks and undertook to develop a structure to accommodate them in the central government – in a separate institution, of course.[1]

In his last years as State President, Botha's relationship with his Cabinet deteriorated seriously, but this rift was papered over.

On 18 January 1989 Botha suffered a stroke. Thereafter he had almost no contact with his Cabinet except with a senior minister, Chris Heunis, and Willie van Niekerk, who was Minister of Health and a medical doctor. There was intense speculation in the media as to whether Botha would recover sufficiently to take up his responsibilities again. In the National Party a decision was taken to make no public statements and to await Botha's return before any decisions were made about a possible future change of leadership.

On 24 January 1989 Botha was released from hospital and it was clear that he would have to undergo a fairly lengthy period of convalescence. The question of his continued leadership came to a head when he wrote a letter on 2 February to the National Party's parliamentary caucus stating that he would resign as leader of the party but not as State President. This came as a great shock to many of the party leaders and to the caucus. F.W. de Klerk was elected party leader, but this was only a prelude to the inevitable confrontation between Botha and his colleagues. They were not prepared to accept the separation of the offices of party leader and State President. At a meeting of the Federal Council of the National Party on 10 March, a resolution was passed to the effect that the leader of the party should also hold the office of State President. This was in effect to throw down the gauntlet.

Botha reacted very strongly, and the relationship between him and his party deteriorated at an accelerating rate. A number of crisis meetings ensued, and in August an ultimatum was presented to Botha in his official office at Tuynhuys. The ultimatum was that Botha should take sick leave and that an acting State President should be appointed. Botha angrily rejected the proposal and, according to De Klerk, he challenged his colleagues' assumptions about his health, stating, 'I am healthy, I am healthy. Is every one of you in a position to produce a medical certificate that you are healthy? Let me know how many of you are sitting here with pills in your pocket.'[2] However, he finally agreed to resign on condition that he would appear on television, announcing the reasons for his resignation. He did this on 14 August 1989. He made a very muddled accusatory statement, but this was the end of his formal life in politics. He continued to influence matters from his retirement home, but from that moment on he was yesterday's man.

My first encounter with P.W. Botha was very soon after I was elected to Parliament in June 1974. In the first parliamentary session that followed I began to observe him and tried to decide whether or not the account that I had had of him was accurate or not. I soon discovered that he was indeed powerful, often irritable and rude, and that most people seemed to be terrified of him. I gathered that within his caucus he ruled with a rod of iron, and he certainly gave that impression in Parliament. He loved to see people squirm. As a minister he had almost unlimited time in his speeches in Parliament, and he would challenge each one of the few members of the opposition and use ad hominem remarks rather than answer the criticisms that we levelled at him and his party. The image I have is of him literally licking his lips, pointing his index finger, and threatening his political opponent. Very early on in the session, he stated, 'We are after the blood of those persons who, wrapped in a cloak of sanctimoniousness, are trying to prejudice the security of South Africa.'³ This was taken up a week later by one of my colleagues, Colin Eglin, who asked Botha to explain what he meant by this statement. He repeated it and said,

> We are going to act. The Hon Member said that I said I was after the blood of certain people. Of course, sir, I am after Beyers Naudé's blood to be specific ... I am after the blood of those Wits students... These Wits students tell the world that South Africa must lose in this struggle. That is what this attitude amounts to. I am after the blood of such people as Dr Boraine who says 'To be born black in South Africa is nothing short of the kiss of death.' Those people are preaching a dangerous philosophy in this country because they are affecting polarisation between white and black.⁴

Such an attack by a senior minister on a backbencher was unusual, but it was typical of Botha's style. On numerous other occasions he would attack me when I tried to point out the bankruptcy and the immorality of apartheid.

[196]

It is interesting to note the comments of one of his close colleagues, F.W. de Klerk. What did he think about P.W. Botha? In his autobiography, *The Last Trek, A New Beginning*, De Klerk refers to his predecessor on a number of occasions. He admits that he was 'increasingly irritated by his [Botha's] irascible and egocentric behaviour... [I]t became increasingly evident that P.W. Botha's leadership style had also become a major obstacle.' The last years of Botha's presidency, he writes, were marked by a series of unfortunate incidents

> which were usually caused by P.W. Botha himself. In a book entitled *Leierstryd* [Leadership struggle] two leading Afrikaner journalists describe the 'bullying and surly P.W. Botha style' which increasingly caused concern in high government circles. Instead of Tuynhuys [Garden house], the term Kruithuis [Powder house] was heard in political discussions, as President Botha's intemperate clashes with a great number of people became known to a wider circle.[5]

De Klerk reveals that he reached a stage in his political career when he considered resigning from the Cabinet: 'I felt I could no longer serve under P.W. Botha and that the time had come to make a stand. His surliness, aggression and poor, poor human relations were doing serious harm to the National Party and to the country.'[6]

De Klerk reflects on that fateful meeting in August 1989 which led finally to Botha's resignation:

> As I listened to him two emotions in particular were aroused in me. There was sorrow for a man who, in his serious illness, had become isolated because of his irascible and cantankerous nature. But it was also clear to me that he had fallen prey to the suspicion and petty-mindedness which, according to experts, were typical symptoms of some stroke victims. My other emotion was a firm certainty that we had acted correctly and that it was in the best interests of the

party and of the country that he should vacate the office of state president. He was no longer fit to rule.[7]

There are many other people within the National Party who told of strong Cabinet ministers going into Botha's office and coming out in tears. He was certainly a very tough nut. But if Botha's fellow party members feared him in this way, it was black South Africans who suffered under his policies.

As a Commission we thought long and hard about who we should invite to appear before us, always on the basis of what information we needed in order to fulfil our mandate. We talked often about key figures, including P.W. Botha. He had been a full-time, professional political organiser long before he went into Parliament; he was, as it were, a true believer in the apartheid policy.

In October 1996 I was asked a point-blank question at a press conference about what the Commission was going to do about P.W. Botha's alleged role in the period of conflict in South Africa during his tenure as Defence Minister and State President. We hadn't reached a firm decision and Tutu was out of the country at the time. Nevertheless, I suggested that, upon his return, Tutu would visit Botha at his retirement home in Wilderness. I explained that because of Botha's age and his ill health, and because of the importance of the information he held as a result of his former positions, we would attempt to coax him to cooperate with the Commission. I explained that we were well aware of his previous critical attitude and derisory statements against the Commission, but that we nevertheless felt it would be worthwhile making a more gentle approach to see if we could persuade him to cooperate, because the information he held was invaluable. I discussed this later with Tutu and he immediately agreed. We put it to the Commission and they also supported the idea that Tutu, on his own, would visit Botha. The necessary contact was made, Botha agreed to see Tutu, and their meeting took place at the end of October 1996.

The visit was successful in the sense that there was no finger-waving and no shouting match took place. Tutu told us later that Botha had received him with warmth and friendliness and treated him to 'rooibos tea and sausage rolls in the parlour'. Botha had prepared a statement indicating that he was willing to cooperate with the Commission in its investigations but couldn't answer question after question. It was decided that the Commission would prepare a list of questions and send them to Botha for his attention. He added, though, that he had nothing to apologise for and would not seek amnesty. As an act of cooperation, however, he suggested to Tutu that the Commission should meet with former Defence Minister Magnus Malan and former Law and Order Minister Adriaan Vlok 'in the same way and spirit as we have met today'. The Commission felt generally satisfied that the right approach had been made and immediately began to prepare a set of questions for Botha's consideration, which I sent to him on 3 February 1997.

The questions concerned some of the worst apartheid atrocities which had occurred in the 1980s when the Botha administration's total strategy was at its height. As I said in a press statement, 'politicians who actually formulated policy and gave instructions are surely much more responsible than those people who followed orders, and therefore should be held accountable'. I also mentioned in the press statement that some of the questions related to the bombing of Khotso House, the headquarters of the South African Council of Churches, in 1988. According to former Commissioner of Police Johan van der Merwe, the instructions to carry out the bombing had been issued by Botha himself.

Many of the questions were framed in broad and general terms and sought to inquire into Botha's understanding of the overarching historical and political forces that shaped the conflicts that occurred during the Commission's mandate period. We asked Botha to answer the questions as soon as possible. Months went by and we didn't hear a word from him, although his lawyers kept on assuring us that they were busy assisting him to answer the questions. In the meantime, however, we gained access to the minutes of the State Security Council and we also listened to many applicants for amnesty who constantly alleged that their orders had come from the very top; when pressed, they said they had no doubt that their actions had been sanctioned by government with the approval of the State President.

The Commission took two decisions to subpoena Botha. With our time running out and having had no reply from him, and in light of the additional information we had received, it seemed to us imperative that we take action. The first decision to subpoena Botha was taken on 22 August 1997 and the subpoena was issued for him to appear on 14 October at the State Security Council hearing. We were informed by his lawyers that the former State President was not well, and after he furnished the Commission with a medical certificate the subpoena was withdrawn. A second decision to subpoena him was made on 22 October by the Human Rights Violations Committee. Both these decisions to subpoena Botha were made not in a fit of pique, as was suggested by some at the time, but simply to carry out our obligations as set out in Section 4 of the Promotion of National Unity and Reconciliation Act.

As I have already mentioned, four broad categories of responsibility can be distilled from the sub-sections of Section 4. Firstly, those who participated directly in gross human rights violations; secondly, those who gave orders for such violations to be committed; thirdly, those who created a climate in which gross human rights violations could occur; and, finally, those who failed to act against or punish those responsible for such violations and therefore were guilty of 'official tolerance' of these acts. We had no information that Botha had participated directly in gross violations of human rights, but certainly there were strong allegations that he had been involved in the other three categories of responsibility outlined above. In order to accommodate Botha, and bearing in mind his state of health, the Commission decided to hold the SSC hearings in

George, a town close to Botha's retirement home, so that he would have the minimum amount of trouble in attending; we also gave private and public assurances not only that his lawyers could be present at the hearing but that arrangements would be made for his doctors to be there as well. We also indicated that we would conduct the sessions in such a way that there would be maximum opportunity for the hearings to go into recess at any time.

Despite all these assurances, Botha, through his lawyers, told us in no uncertain terms that he would not attend and therefore would disobey the subpoena. In terms of the Act, if anyone refused a subpoena issued by the Commission they were guilty of contempt, and therefore our only recourse was to hand the matter over to the Attorney-General for his consideration. The Attorney-General, Frank Kahn, after considering the papers, decided to act against Botha. Botha appeared in the George Magistrate Court on 23 February 1998. Once again, he excelled himself in his arrogance and dismissal of the Commission, describing his appearance in court as a 'second circus' after pleading not guilty to ignoring the Commission's subpoena. The security was so extensive that the small town of George looked as though it was under siege. Security forces erected barriers at the main entrances leading into the town and put a head-high razor wire barrier around the court building. About a hundred ANC supporters gathered on a traffic island opposite the courtroom and booed the dark-suited Botha as he stepped from his BMW shortly before 9 a.m. to attend the hearing. Some of the placards carried by the demonstrating crowd read, 'Botha's Miaow No Match for Madiba's Roar', 'Afrikaner Tiger Miaow Miaow Miaow', and 'The Tiger in Africa is Behind Bars'. The demonstrators were later joined by several hundred curious onlookers. Another prominent poster read, 'We can forgive him for his past but send him to jail for his arrogance'.

In his defence, Botha accused the Commission of acting in bad faith and with an ulterior motive. He claimed that Tutu and he had entered into an agreement in George on 21 November 1996 according to which the Commission

[201]

was not entitled to require his presence. Tutu strenuously denied this; he said on numerous occasions that he had no authority to enter into any kind of agreement with Botha and that any decisions relating to the TRC had to be taken by the Commission itself. I have to say that, despite this assurance, some of the commissioners were extremely worried that Tutu, in his pastoral demeanour, might have inadvertently given some assurance that if Botha cooperated in the way that he agreed to do, he wouldn't have to appear before the Commission. This worry was intensified by Botha's well-known habit of secretly tape-recording his supposedly confidential discussions. However, Botha's lawyers did not produce any substance to back up their argument that a deal had been struck between Botha and Tutu.

Botha was way out of line in suggesting that the Commission was acting in bad faith. We had leaned over backwards, despite heavy criticism, particularly from newspapers representing the black majority, which argued that we were being far too gentle and were pussyfooting around Botha in a way that we hadn't done with others from the liberation movements or the security forces.

Over and above the attempts by the Commission itself to find some compromise so that Botha should not be taken to court, President Mandela himself had done everything humanly possible to persuade him, but to no avail. Mandela had telephoned Botha on a number of occasions and pleaded with him to appear before the Commission. He had gone so far as to offer to accompany Botha to the Commission hearing. And this from a man who had suffered twenty-seven years of imprisonment with the enthusiastic support of Botha and his colleagues. Mandela had gone one step further and had contacted Botha's immediate family, invited them to a meal in his official home, and urged them to put pressure on their father to attend a Commission hearing.

Nothing had helped. Botha was obdurate and stubborn and the case had to go on. Ironically, Botha appeared before Victor Lugagu,[8] the Western Cape Regional Court chief magistrate, and the case was adjourned until 14 April for trial. I say 'ironically' because Botha's attitude towards black South Africans was well known, but now, ultimately, the former head of state was standing as defendant before a black judge. Several people in the crowd of ANC protesters were overheard saying, 'We don't want Botha to go to jail. The fact that he has appeared before a black South African is enough and we are satisfied that no one is above the law.'

Botha was strongly supported by a number of former generals, including Magnus Malan, former Minister of Defence and former head of the South African Defence Force. Others who supported him and attended the hearing included Greyling Wentzel, former Minister of Agriculture, Constand Viljoen, former head of the Defence Force and leader of the Freedom Front, Johan van der Merwe, former police chief, and other retired military generals. General Viljoen warned that the prosecution of Botha was becoming 'a rallying point for Afrikaner nationalism'. He added that there seemed to be a 'hardening of attitude by the Commission... [T]hat is why I said this is Afrikaner bashing, this is Botha bashing and that is why we stand by him.'[9]

As I have indicated, we were not unmindful of the risk of Botha becoming a rallying point for the more extreme right-wingers in Afrikaner ranks, but we were left with no choice. We could not simply ignore Botha's involvement in the period under review. In the end, the Commission was proven right and Botha did not become a rallying point. By the end of the trial he appeared a pitiful figure, and in the last few days there was hardly anyone there to support him.

Between the adjournment of the initial hearing and the actual trial date we continued to go on record on a number of occasions urging Botha to change his mind. On one particular occasion I was interviewed by *Rapport*,[10] the major Afrikaans Sunday newspaper. In that interview I again pleaded for reason and made it crystal clear that we were not seeking to make Botha into a victim or a martyr but were simply trying to do our work. I was particularly concerned because of a development which had taken place early in April. Two retired neurologists, Derek Philcox and K. de Villiers, had handed in two sworn affidavits indicating that they feared that the damage to the right side of Botha's brain might affect his judgement when he took the stand. They stated that when they discovered the seriousness of Botha's stroke in 1989, they warned him not to resume office, but they were asked to withdraw their services, ostensibly because their opinion jeopardised the State President's political career. My own reaction was to say that if their findings were accurate and could be substantiated, then clearly Botha was not fit to stand trial and we would have to find an alternative method of persuading him to appear before the Commission.

What we decided to do was to send the neurologists' affidavits to the Western Cape Attorney-General and let him make the decision as to whether the former President was medically fit to stand trial on 14 April. In the end, Botha's lawyers made it very clear that he was angry at the suggestion that he was medically unfit and even threatened to sue the neurologists for daring to suggest this. Clearly, therefore, the lawyers and Botha were not going to use medical unfitness as a means of evading the trial. Botha was determined to go on.

In my interview in *Rapport* I said, 'I wish there was a way in which the Attorney-General and former President Botha's lawyers could find a way of resolving the issue.' I acknowledged that Botha saw me as a former parliamentary opponent, but indicated that I didn't live in the past and that among my own former political opponents were Adriaan Vlok, Pik Botha, and F.W. de Klerk, all of whom had agreed to appear before the Commission. I went even further and said that if my presence on the panel was a problem for Botha, then I would recuse myself. I stressed that I wished that this conflict with Botha had never taken place: 'We never wanted him to appear in court. We don't want him to be thrown into jail. All we want is that he should come before the Commission and we would deal with him with sensitivity and respect.'[11]

Responding to a question by a journalist, Freek Swart, as to whether Botha was not too ill to be bothered by a meeting with the Commission, I stated,

> P.W. Botha is a very strong man. He is known as a strong and tough leader and we have noticed that he was strong enough to be engaged to be married, to sell his house, to buy other property and to make very strong criticisms of the Commission. If we would want to insinuate for a moment that there was something medically wrong with him, he would not accept it. He has rejected the report of the neurologists and as a direct result of that we have no other choice but to go ahead with the court case on the 14th of April.[12]

I added that even if at the eleventh hour Botha decided that he would appear before the Commission, we would approach the Attorney-General and ask him either to delay the trial proceedings or indeed to withdraw the charges so that we could continue with the Commission hearing.

A week before the trial, my assistant, Paddy Clark, called me out of a planning meeting where we were preparing for the trial, telling me that she had had a call from the Attorney-General and that he wanted me to call back immediately. I left the meeting, spoke to him, and he asked me to come to see him at once. When I got there he told me that Botha's counsel had read my comments in *Rapport* and were open to the possibility of some kind of deal. According to his lawyers, the court case would adjourn and Botha would appear before the Commission at an in camera hearing, allowed for by Section 29 of the Act. If this was acceptable, the case would then be thrown out. This was a startling development, which was followed by many discussions and phone calls and meetings to set up the hearing. Botha's lawyers stated that the hearing would be on condition that I would not serve on the panel. As I noted in my diary, 'Extraordinary how I seem to have got under the skin of the National Party establishment and Botha in particular.'

[205]

We continued the discussions when we arrived in George on the eve of the hearing, but I began to wonder whether Botha knew anything about the discussions; his lawyers had constantly changed the conditions, and suggested that the Commission should be represented only by Tutu. This we rejected. They then suggested we should change the name of the hearing to something else. This too we rejected. We were a statutory body. We were carrying out our responsibilities, and, while we were prepared to lean over backwards, we couldn't camouflage the fact that this would be an official hearing. We had agreed to a Section 29 hearing because the Act made it possible for us to make public all the deliberations of a hearing held in camera if we decided to. When I entered the court house I bumped into Botha in one of the narrow corridors. His face was like thunder, but I stuck out my hand and said, 'Goeie môre, Meneer' [Good morning, Sir]. He hesitated, shook my hand as though it was a snake, and mumbled, 'Môre' [Morning]. To see him standing in the dock was sad. To hear him described as 'the accused' was almost bizarre, but extremely important. Nevertheless, Botha remained the same arrogant man I had known over the years. It became clear that his lawyers had been trying to nudge him to appear before us, but he saw through it and broke off the negotiations. There would be no Section 29 hearing and the original trial would have to go on.

In a conversation with *Rapport* journalist Freek Swart, Botha recounted a conversation with Tutu, in which he announced that he would not attend the hearing:

> When the court session started, they came to tell me that Tutu was there and that he wanted to talk to me. Bishop Tutu came to join me. I said to him, 'Good morning, good morning!' He then asked whether he could pray. I said to him, 'You can pray if you wish.' After he had said amen, I said to him, 'You tell me, as one Christian to another, what you are proposing to me.' He then told me that his proposal was that I should come back and testify before the Truth Commission. I then

said to him, 'Man, you are now asking me to capitulate. That is what you are asking, and you know that I said that I would not appear before you.' I added: 'You know that when Christ stood before Herod He refused to answer questions.' He then said: 'Yes, but Christ did answer questions before Pilate.' I answered: 'Yes, but what happened to Pilate?' I said, 'I am not Christ. I am his follower.' I added: 'You have the truth at your disposal and I am telling you now, I am prepared to speak to you and President Nelson Mandela, but you will not force me to appear before the Truth Commission. I refuse to be humiliated and you people want to humiliate me. And at the same time, you also want to humiliate Afrikaners who believe in me just like you have already humiliated others.' He then got up and walked away. At that the negotiations failed.[13]

The trial started in June and our major witness on behalf of the TRC was Paul van Zyl, executive secretary to the Commission. Paul's submission was thoroughly researched, and he had often worked until the small hours of the morning in order to have it ready for the trial. He was very closely cross-examined by Botha's lawyers, but they were unable to shake him from the substance of his evidence. Paul divided the Commission's evidence into two categories. The first was the evidence that came to the Commission's attention after 30 January 1997 (the date on which written questions were put to Botha) but prior to the first decision to subpoena Botha (22 August 1997). The second category was the evidence which came to the TRC's attention after the first decision to subpoena Botha (22 August 1997) but prior to the second decision to subpoena him (22 October 1997).

Paul proceeded to lay out the evidence which influenced the first decision to subpoena Botha. He quoted from allegations made in amnesty applications, which suggested that Botha had given orders for human rights violations to be committed. The first of these was presented by Johan van der Merwe, former Commissioner of Police, and

Adriaan Vlok, former Minister of Law and Order. They stated that the order to blow up Khotso House had come directly from Botha. Botha's first response to these allegations was to state that they were incorrect, that they were based on untested evidence, and that the bombing fell outside the TRC's mandate. Botha had not applied for amnesty, however, and there was no guarantee that his version would be subjected to proper scrutiny via cross-examination. The Commission also made the point that there was an inevitable overlap between the work of the Human Rights Violations Committee and the Amnesty Committee, and the fact that Botha might have to appear before the Amnesty Committee did not preclude him from having to appear before the Human Rights Violations Committee. In his answers to the written questions that we had sent to him, Botha had gone into great detail about the fundamental difference between Vlok's version and his own. This was an even stronger reason why Botha should have appeared before the Commission, so that we could clear the matter up. On this score alone we were convinced that the decision to subpoena him was the correct one.

There was also evidence that Botha had been responsible for human rights violations in more indirect ways. It was the Commission's submission that, in his capacity as chairperson of the State Security Council, he had created a climate in which gross violations occurred, and should be held accountable for such violations. The SSC, chaired by Botha, had played a central role in deciding to declare the state of emergency on 12 June 1986. Furthermore, the TRC had received statements alleging that the security forces had been involved in almost 2000 acts of torture in more than 200 different venues during the time in which Botha was either Prime Minister or State President. It was decided that, because of Botha's active role and his chairing of the SSC, he had to be included as one of the witnesses for the hearing, and that is precisely why he was subpoenaed.

In summary, it was considered extremely important for Botha to testify at the SSC hearing for a number of reasons. Firstly, his roles as chair of the SSC and, prior to that, Minister of Defence were intimately linked to the formulation and implementation of state policy. Despite his many public protestations of having nothing to apologise for, the fact that he was a key figure in determining and implementing apartheid policy for so long left him without any defence.

Secondly, only a small percentage of the questions put to Botha in writing had dealt with state security policy. Most of the questions had been formulated without the benefit of the considerable amount of new evidence which emerged after the written questions had been submitted to him. In fact, only one question referred to a minuted decision taken by the SSC, because at that time the Commission had not gained access to the SSC minutes.

Thirdly, it was the Commission's experience that a better quality of evidence is obtained when a witness answers questions in person at a public hearing. It is time-consuming and ineffective to cross-examine a witness via correspondence. The Commission had a limited period of operation and the information it required from Botha was of crucial significance to its mandate. By the time the decision was taken to hold hearings to investigate the SSC, Botha had already taken more than seven months to answer the questions put to him in writing, and at that stage we had received no assurance that the answers would be forthcoming by a clearly specified date.

Fourthly, when a witness testified in a public hearing, his or her testimony became a matter of public record. This allowed others who might in some way be affected by the evidence to respond to it. In addition, the evidence would become the subject of public comment and debate. This subjected the evidence to closer scrutiny and allowed the Commission to make more informed findings.

Fifthly, Section 33 of the Act enjoined the Commission to hold its hearings in public unless there were compelling reasons for it to do otherwise. It was in keeping with the Commission's statutory obligation to conduct its affairs in a public and transparent fashion.

[209]

Finally, the Commission could not wait until it received the written responses to the questions put to Botha before it decided to request that he testify at the SSC hearing. The Commission was running out of time to complete the work assigned to it by statute. At that stage it was required to complete all its work by 31 July 1998, and Botha answered the questions put to him only on 5 December 1997, almost a year after he had received them. In order to begin work on a vitally important section of its final report, it was important that the SSC hearings be completed before the end of 1997. The section of the final report dealing with the SSC had been put on hold, and no findings had been made, because we needed to hear Botha's evidence and question him on a number of crucial issues.

The written questions put to Botha concerning the SSC were no longer relevant, as a result of new evidence received by the Commission in the six months after these questions had been submitted. In particular, the Commission's scrutiny of SSC documents, to which it had not had access at the time it formulated the questions to Botha, opened up new lines of inquiry which could not have been anticipated and which therefore had not been included in the questions.

We had supplied Botha with written questions and asked him for written responses, not as a substitute for his testimony at a hearing, but in order to comply with his request that we provide him with a comprehensive set of questions so that he and his former security ministers would not have to respond continually to ad hoc allegations through the media.

Time and time again Botha's defence had stressed that a deal had been struck, that because of the written questions and Botha's answers, he would not have to appear before the Commission. What is remarkable is that his lawyers had failed to raise this argument in our initial interaction. Even after his attorney had taken instructions from him at a time when Botha knew that he was required to attend the hearing, the attorney only raised Botha's health and not the existence of a 'deal' as a basis for not having to attend a hearing.

To disprove the charge of bias and victimisation of Botha, it should be pointed out that he received R1.6 million in legal assistance to help him answer the questions posed by the TRC. This was a direct result of an intervention by the Commission through its chairperson to President Mandela. This of course was at considerable cost to the state and created tremendous public criticism that the Commission was favouring Botha. We supported assistance because we felt that his appearance before the Commission was critical.

It was our considered view that the evidence placed before the court was compelling. We were fully justified in subpoenaing Botha, and his appearance in court was the result of his wilful refusal to appear before the Commission.

A key witness in Botha's trial for contempt was former police colonel Eugene de Kock. De Kock, together with many of his colleagues and generals, maintained that the actions they had carried out, which can only be described as state violence, had not only been known by senior politicians but had been authorised by them. The former colonel entered the small courtroom looking stern and pale. Botha sat in his chair, glanced at De Kock and then turned away so that he was sitting with his back to him. If Botha imagined that De Kock would be in any way intimidated by being only a few feet away from him when the former colonel read his statement, he was in for a shock. De Kock came out with all guns blazing. I watched him as he passionately described the politicians of the National Party as cowards who sold out the police and the army: 'They wanted to eat lamb but they do not want to see the blood and guts.'[14] De Kock went on to say that he and his colleagues had been told by politicians at the highest level that they, the security forces, were fighting for the protection of their fatherland. But, he said, they were only fighting for the 'incestuous little world of Afrikanerdom'. De Kock went on to say, 'We did well. We did the fighting.

[211]

I am proud of that. But the politicians have not had the moral guts to accept responsibility for the killing.' He described himself as a lowly colonel, but affirmed, 'I am also an Afrikaner.' However, it was as 'cowards that God would deal with the politicians'.[15] I watched Botha carefully as this vitriol was spewed out by De Kock. He was unmoved; he stared ahead and never looked at De Kock again.

In cold and measured tones, De Kock told the court of the bombings of the ANC offices in London in 1981, Cosatu House in 1987, and Khotso House in 1988. He told the court that he had received the Police Star for outstanding service for the London bombings and that the award could have been granted only by the State President himself, who at that time was P.W. Botha.

De Kock stated that he had been very surprised at the decision to bomb Khotso House, but was told by a police general that Botha was irritated and impatient about any delay in destroying the building. He described at great length how he and others carried out the attack with the clear impression that the bombing of the church headquarters was authorised by Botha himself. He told the court that the Minister of Law and Order had warmly congratulated him a few weeks after the bombing. This for him was confirmation that the orders had come from the very top. There was a hush in the small courtroom as De Kock concluded his powerful and at times emotional evidence. One could hear a pin drop as he left the witness box and made his way out of the court.

A witness to the Khotso House bombing was Bishop Peter Storey, a Methodist minister who had been actively involved in the South African Council of Churches. During his testimony, Botha again sat impassively. Storey, who is a powerful public speaker, was very convincing as he described the scene. He spoke as an eyewitness to the effects of the bomb. He told the court that he had seen a group of pensioners covered in blood, cowering in shock from the attack. Residents were wandering around in their night clothes, in a complete daze. Some of them were bleeding; their faces and forearms were lacerated. In his view, he said, they were extremely fortunate to be alive. These were pensioners who lived in a church-owned apartment block opposite Khotso House. Twenty-one people were injured in the attack. Storey's statement was very moving and indicated just how serious the attack had been and why it was important for the Commission to clarify exactly who was responsible.

Tutu was the final witness to be called on behalf of the prosecution. He was a little apprehensive, and it was startling to see Botha in the dock and Tutu giving evidence. One was used to seeing Botha in charge, berating Tutu for his fierce opposition to apartheid. Now the tables were turned. But, as one has come to expect, Tutu was extremely gracious, almost tentative in his opening statement. He began by expressing his greatest possible reluctance at having to appear. He told the court that he was filled with considerable distaste at having to take part in the trial and expressed his belief that it should never have come to this pass. He explained to the court that he had tried to reach out to Botha out of deep compassion for him. He had seen Botha as a brother even though it was not politically correct to do so. But he strongly denied that he had ever agreed to exempt Botha from appearing before the Commission, stressing that he had no authority to do so.

Tutu also tried to answer the many charges that had been made, particularly by the Afrikaans media, the generals, and some politicians, that the Commission was 'out to get Botha'. He said that he had never gloated over Botha's position as the accused in court, and had never intended to humiliate him, but that their interaction had been courteous and friendly. He said that when one examined the events leading up to the court case, there could be no suggestion of malice by himself or by the Commission.

During his cross-examination of Tutu, Lappa Laubscher SC made a very strong attack on my own role as deputy chairperson of the Commission, accusing me of obvious bias and prejudice. Tutu was quick to defend me: 'I would disagree. He is actually a very, very fair person.' When Laubscher continued to attack me on the basis of a paper I had delivered at a conference in Belgium, which outlined the far-reaching consequences of apartheid, Tutu responded, 'I would have to say, where do you live? I live in South Africa and we are dealing with a past and we know that people were killed in this country.'[16]

During one of the recesses, I had a strange experience with Botha, and I quote it as it was reported in the *Cape Argus*:

> Former President P.W. Botha has behaved impeccably this week in contrast to his angry outburst during the April session of his trial, but there was one bizarre exchange during an adjournment that left Truth Commission Deputy Chairperson Alex Boraine feeling uneasy and unnerved. Mr Botha stood up, turned towards Dr Boraine and stared, moved towards him and stared fixedly at him with the slight smile playing on his lips. Dr Boraine, sitting on the bench next to the witness stand, held Mr Botha's gaze with a slight smile in return. But Mr Botha, standing motionless, and without a word, continued staring at Dr Boraine for several minutes before eventually turning away. Dr Boraine told the *Cape Argus* later that he had been concerned by Mr Botha's behaviour. 'It was very odd. It was a scary experience which I didn't enjoy,' he said.[17]

I felt that if Botha could have done me some violence he would not have hesitated. The little smile and the cold eyes said it all.

Botha's counsel attacked Tutu on two other issues. Firstly, he suggested that the Commission's dealings with Botha were very different from its dealings with the ANC. Tutu defended the Commission's conduct, saying that it was legally bound to act even-handedly. However, he went on to say that this did not mean that the Commission should be morally neutral. In his judgement, apartheid itself was a gross violation of human rights, and the Commission did not see apartheid as morally equivalent to the armed struggle: 'There is no moral equivalence between those who used force to maintain an unjust system and those who used force to oppose it.'[18] He added, however, that the justness of the ANC's cause had not given the organisation carte blanche to commit human rights violations.

Laubscher also criticised Tutu for failing to read the 112 pages of written answers provided by Botha in response to the Commission's written questions. But Tutu stated that while he had not read the answers himself, the Research Department had done so. He could have added in his own defence that I had requested the Research Department immediately to summarise Botha's replies to ascertain whether or not they were sufficient for the Commission's needs. That summary was very carefully worked through, not only by me but also by other senior members of the Commission, including the director of the Research Department, Charles Villa-Vicencio, and the executive secretary, Paul van Zyl, as well as Dumisa Ntsebeza and Yasmin Sooka. This was typical of Tutu's approach. He was the centre of the Commission, led by example, and delegated a considerable amount of the work to others. I think this is one of the reasons why the Commission worked as well as it did. It would have been impossible for Tutu to have read every document that came across the desks of the Commission. We reported regularly, indeed on a daily basis, to Tutu so he knew exactly what was taking place.

At the end of the long session in the witness box Tutu was told that he could step down. He paused and, ignoring court protocol, asked if he could say a word to Botha. He looked at Botha and asked him to apologise for the distress apartheid had caused. Giving Botha the benefit of the doubt, Tutu said,

> Even if you didn't intend it, I want to appeal to you, I want you to take this chance provided by this court, for you to say that while you may not have intended the suffering to happen to people, you may not have given orders to authorise anything, but if you are able

[215]

> to say, I am sorry that policies of my government caused you pain. Just that. It would be a tremendous benefit to all of South Africa.[19]

Botha remained silent, and later stated through his lawyers that he was astonished that Tutu should have asked him to apologise, for he was not aware of anything he had done for which he should confess to the TRC.

It was a tragedy that Botha did not enter the witness box to respond to the allegations made against him. It was an even greater tragedy that because of his arrogance and his insensitivity to what apartheid had done to so many hundreds and thousands of people he defied the Commission and refused to appear before it. He maintained to the very end that he was responsible only to God and not to the Commission.

The court was adjourned and in August 1998 Botha was convicted of contravening Section 39(e)(i) and Sections 134 and 29 of the Promotion of National Unity and Reconciliation Act. He was sentenced to a fine of R10 000 or twelve months' imprisonment, plus a further twelve months' imprisonment suspended for five years on condition that he did not contravene any provisions of the Act again.

His lawyers immediately lodged an appeal, which was duly heard and upheld in March 1999. The appeal was upheld on purely technical grounds, namely that the notice issued by the Commission and served on Botha on 6 December 1997 was unauthorised because it was prematurely issued. The judgement of the Appeal Court states, 'This court is mindful of the fact that there will be many who may consider that it is unjust that the appellant should succeed in his appeal upon the basis that the appeal was upheld purely on technical grounds.' But, it concludes,

> This court is duty bound to uphold and protect the Constitution and to administer justice to all persons alike without fear, favour or prejudice in accordance with the Constitution and the law. Suffice it to say

that the same law, the same Constitution which obliges the appellant to obey the law of the land like every other citizen, also affords him the same protections that it affords every other citizen.[20]

It was with great distress that we learnt of the successful appeal, and the question was immediately posed as to whether or not we should appeal against the decision. The fact that the Commission had then finished its work and that its major actors were busy elsewhere, as well as the fact that we had succeeded in making Botha accept that he was answerable to the law and not above it, and that we had been able, in the course of the trial, to outline many of the very questions and allegations that we would have posed to him in a normal public hearing, meant that there was no point in taking any further action against him. It had been conclusively shown that no one is above the law.

It is quite bizarre in a sense that in Botha's press statement following his successful appeal, he expressed appreciation for South Africa's independent judiciary. He was right to do so, but when one bears in mind that the independence of the judiciary was eroded and undermined by his government when he was in power, it is a statement of supreme irony.

In the *Cape Argus* of Monday 7 June 1999, a leading article stated,

> The appeal judgement is a hollow victory for the aging Mr Botha. It was decided on a technical point relating to the TRC's founding legislation and its rights and duties when its life was extended to cope with the overwhelming workload. There was no finding in respect of Mr Botha's duty as a self-proclaimed law-abiding citizen to appear before the TRC and bear witness to what he knew about the multitude of gross human rights violations that occurred during his lengthy term of office... History will be the final judge of Mr Botha and there is no doubt that it will give a harsh verdict.

In the meantime the Commission had published its own findings on P.W. Botha in its final report:

Mr P.W. Botha presided as executive head of the former South African government (the government) from 1978 to 1984 as Prime Minister, and from 1984 to 1989 as Executive State President. Given his centrality in the politics of the 1970s and 1980s, the Commission has made a finding on the role of the former State President:

During the period that he presided as head of state (1978–1989), according to submissions made to, and findings made by, the Commission, gross violations of human rights and other unlawful acts were perpetrated on a wide scale by members of the former South African Police (SAP) and the former South African Defence Force (SADF), among others. Such violations included:

- The deliberate unlawful killing, and attempted killing, of persons opposed to the policies of the government, within and outside South Africa;
- The widespread use of torture and other forms of severe ill treatment against such persons;
- The forcible abduction of such persons who were resident in neighbouring countries;
- Covert logistical and financial assistance to organisations opposed to the ideology of the ANC and other liberation movements both within and outside of South Africa, enabling those organisations to commit gross human rights violations on a wide scale within and beyond the borders of this country;
- Acts of arson and sabotage against the property of persons and organisations opposed to the government, within and outside of the country.

During the period 1979–89, Mr P.W. Botha chaired the State Security Council (SSC), established to advise the government on national security issues which were, or were perceived to be, a threat to the government. Under his leadership, the SSC:

- Placed great pressure on the government's security forces to engage robustly against organisations and persons opposed to the government, in their perceived onslaught against the government;
- Used language in its meetings and recommendations that was highly ambiguous and was interpreted by persons with access to the meetings, their minutes and recommendations, as authorising the killing of people;
- Failed to recommend to the government that appropriate steps be taken against members of the security forces who were involved in or who were suspected of being involved in gross violations of human rights, thus contributing to the prevailing culture of impunity;
- Recommended that the government impose states of emergency, under which gross violations of human rights committed against persons opposed to the government increased, and assisted the government in the implementation of the states of emergency;
- Recommended the adoption of principles of counter-revolutionary warfare which led to the increased deployment of special units of the SADF in support of the SAP in South Africa, resulting in a shift of focus in policing from arresting and charging opponents of the government to eliminating opponents and their bases;
- Recommended that the government support covert projects aimed at opposing and destabilising the governments of neighbouring countries which were supportive of liberation movements;
- Recommended that the government support covert projects to help destabilise and oppose organisations and people opposed to the government.

As a consequence, the SSC created a political climate that greatly facilitated the gross violation of human rights, and in which such violations occurred on a wide scale.

Mr Botha was responsible for ordering former
Minister of Law and Order Adriaan Vlok and former
Police Commissioner Johan van der Merwe unlawfully to destroy Khotso House in Johannesburg (a
building occupied by organisations considered by
Botha to be a threat to the security of the government), thereby endangering the lives of people in and
around the building. This decision greatly enhanced
the prevailing culture of impunity and facilitated the
further gross violation of human rights by senior
members of the security forces.

For the reasons set out above and by virtue of his
position as head of state and chairperson of the SSC,
Botha contributed to and facilitated a climate in
which the above gross violations of human rights
could and did occur, and as such is accountable for
such violations.[21]

Botha was a proud and spiritual man, nurtured in Afrikaner
nationalism, whose passion for his country was in the end
deeper than his religious values. Or, to put it differently, his
God was the god of the narrow, exclusive white race and his
destiny was inextricably tied to blood, soil, and language.
For Botha, the end justified the means. Whites were chosen
as the conveyers of Christian faith and Western civilisation. Apartheid was essential to maintain white domination, and those who resisted this scheme of things could
not be tolerated. As I sat in court watching Botha's reaction
to the proceedings, I often wondered what he thought about
his life-long political career and how, in his final years,
everything had been turned upside down. Did he ever dare
to ask, 'Was I wrong?' Can the leopard change its spots? I
think he remained stubborn and intransigent to the end.
This once immensely powerful man, surrounded by the
trappings of power and flattered by sycophants, cut a very
lonely figure as he left the court. He won his appeal on a
technicality, but he will forever be remembered as a leader
who took his country to the edge of a precipice in his determination to maintain white domination at all costs.

7

A South African tragedy:
Winnie Madikizela-Mandela

WHILE UNDOUBTEDLY a controversial figure, Winnie Madikizela-Mandela has enjoyed wide and enthusiastic support in South Africa and abroad. In South Africa she became known as 'the Mother of the Nation'. Many African-Americans have been very vocal in their criticism of the Commission's treatment of her. According to the Nation of Islam leader, Louis Farrakhan, Madikizela-Mandela is known throughout the black world 'as a fighter for justice'. He argues that 'She is the "mother of the struggle" and the Truth and Reconciliation Commission was used to sully her reputation and destroy her chances of being a political force.'[1]

I thought about her reputation when I was sitting on the panel listening to nine successive days of hearings concerning the Mandela United Football Club and Winnie Madikizela-Mandela's critical involvement in the nefarious actions of this group of young miscreants. We heard many witnesses and many statements during those nine traumatic days, but one that stood out for me was the testimony of Bishop Peter Storey of the Methodist Church, who had been very much involved during the period when children and young people belonging to the Mandela United Football Club were committing their reign of terror in the townships. One of his ministers, Paul Verryn, from whose home young people were abducted and later viciously assaulted at Madikizela-Mandela's home, became one of the central characters in the unfolding drama.

[221]

After giving his evidence and answering questions from lawyers and commissioners, Storey made a closing statement:

> I really hope and pray that these hearings will give us the truth, because throughout this saga I believe the truth has been trimmed to prevailing political whims by politicians very often, by people with political interests. Or the truth has been suppressed because people have vanished and feared for their lives. I really believe that to dispel this suffocating fog of silence and lies is very important for the future of this country.

He talked about the erosion of conscience, the devaluing of human life, and the reckless resort to violence:

> The primary cancer may be and was and will always be the apartheid oppression, but the secondary infection has touched many of apartheid's opponents and eroded their knowledge of good and evil. One of the tragedies of life is that it is possible to become like that which we hate most and I have a feeling that this drama is an example of that.

He concluded, 'it is not enough to become politically liberated. We must also become human. This case is about becoming human again and recognising the inhumanities which some of us were capable of because of the times we used to live in.'[2]

On many occasions we were to hear about 'the times in which we were living'. There can be little doubt that the ANC succeeded in making many parts of the country 'ungovernable' in its effort to end apartheid. But the price paid was and remains very high. During the 1980s South Africa witnessed the toughest security legislation ever introduced by the state, and the state of emergency imposed in the second half of the 1980s brought a state of siege to most townships. Many leaders were detained, others were on the run and in hiding, and this dearth of leadership resulted in something close to a state of anarchy. It was during this time that the Mandela United Football Club was founded, and its members seemed to operate without any discipline, without any checks or balances, becoming a law unto themselves. The one to whom its members swore total allegiance, the one who directed their movements, whose home became their refuge and their headquarters, was Winnie Madikizela-Mandela. Who is Winnie Madikizela-Mandela? Is she a saint or a sinner? The Mother of the Nation or the Mugger of the Nation? This was the question then and remains the question now.

Nomzamo Zaniewe Winnifred Madikizela was born on 26 September 1934 at Bizana, Pondoland. She was the daughter of Nomathamsanqa and Columbus Madikizela, a teacher and later Minister of Agriculture and Forestry in the Transkeian government. She attended school at Bizana and Shawbury, enrolling at the age of sixteen at the Jan Hofmeyr School of Social Work. Thereafter she took a post as the first African medical social worker at Baragwanath Hospital in Soweto.

In 1957 she met Nelson Mandela, who was then a member of the African National Congress executive and an accused in the Treason Trial. They married a year later. Three months after their marriage she was arrested for the first time for her role in an anti-pass campaign. From that day on she became not only a prominent member of the ANC, but also someone who was constantly in the media spotlight. She served on the national and provincial executives of the ANC Women's League and chaired the Orlando branch of the ANC until the organisation was banned in 1960.

Not only was she married to a political activist who was utterly committed to the anti-apartheid struggle, not only did she lose her husband to the prisons of Robben Island and Victor Verster for twenty-seven years, but she herself was subjected to years of harassment and persecution by the security police. In 1962 she was banned in terms of the Suppression of Communism Act and restricted to Orlando West in Soweto. She couldn't continue her job as a social welfare worker. Further banning orders, even tougher than the first, were served on her in 1965 and 1966. She remained under these banning orders, which restricted her movements, until 1975. During this period she was charged at least twice for contravening her banning order and was sentenced to one year's imprisonment, suspended after she had spent four days in prison.

But worse was to follow. In 1969 she was detained under Section 6 of the Terrorism Act and held in solitary confinement for seventeen months. During the period 1970–74 she was charged on numerous occasions for alleged contraventions of her restriction order. In 1974 she served a six-month jail sentence for such a contravention. When her banning order lapsed in October 1975, she became more openly active again. She helped found the Black Women's Federation, and, in response to the 1976 Soweto riots, helped to establish the Black Parents' Association, which arranged legal and medical help for those affected by police action. She was detained again late in 1976; the following year the banning orders were amended and she was banished to Phatakahle township in the small town of Brandfort in the Orange Free State. In August 1985, after her home in Brandfort was firebombed by the security police, she returned to her home in Orlando West in defiance of her restrictions. From then on she was subjected to a number of additional banning orders and restrictions, constant harassment, arrests, and detention by the security police. In this impossible and trauma-filled existence she was also trying to raise two daughters.

In April 1986 she made a public statement which caused great controversy and brought her into considerable disrepute. She was quoted as saying in a public meeting that the liberation of black people would be achieved by means of matches and tyres. She was referring to the infamous 'necklace killings', which involved placing a car tyre around the neck of a victim, pouring petrol over the tyre, and setting it alight. It became a notorious method of dealing with those who were alleged informers for and collaborators with the state. Despite her regular denials, this statement has continued to haunt her.

In June 1988 her Soweto home was burnt down. Inevitably the security police were blamed, but it turned out that those responsible were a group of schoolchildren reacting to the actions of the Mandela United Football Club, whose members were even then alleged to be involved in abuse, rape, and assault. Madikizela-Mandela had started the Football Club to assist young people who were victims of the raging conflict in the townships. It was never a bona fide soccer club, and its members acted as her bodyguards and constantly accompanied her when she appeared in public. They were, as it were, her 'muscle'.

In January 1989 Madikizela-Mandela was involved in a controversy surrounding the abduction of four youths from a Methodist mission house by members of her 'football club'. One of the abducted youths, Stompie Moeketse Seipei, was subsequently found murdered. The leadership of the ANC in exile and Nelson Mandela in prison urged Madikizela-Mandela to disband the club and disassociate herself from its members. She was stubborn about this and refused to take advice from those in leadership. Finally, on 16 February 1989 the United Democratic Front and the Congress of South African Trade Unions issued a statement disassociating themselves from her and blaming her for the conduct of the Football Club. The ANC tried to exercise damage control and urged that she ought not to be cast aside but should be brought back under the discipline of the movement.

Subsequently, the coach of the Football Club, Jerry Richardson, was charged and convicted of the murder of Stompie Seipei. Madikizela-Mandela was implicated in assaults on Stompie and other abducted youths, and in April 1991 was charged with eight counts of kidnapping and assault. She was convicted on four counts of kidnapping and on four counts of being an accessory to assault, and was sentenced to six years' imprisonment. She was granted leave to appeal, and in 1993 the Appeal Court found her guilty of kidnapping but not of assault, and ordered her to pay a fine of R15 000 plus R15 000 compensation to the three surviving victims of the kidnapping and assault which had taken place at her home.

On 11 February 1990, Nelson Mandela was released from jail and the couple was reunited. However, it was an uneasy and difficult relationship which finally ended in separation in 1992 and divorce in 1996.

Nevertheless, Winnie Madikizela-Mandela continued to exercise considerable influence, and in 1991 she was elected to the ANC's National Executive Committee. In December 1993 she was elected president of the ANC Women's League and in the same month was elected deputy president of the South African National Civic Organisation.

In the first democratic election held in South Africa in April 1994, Winnie Madikizela-Mandela stood for Parliament and was placed number 31 on the ANC's list of candidates. She continued to enjoy considerable grass-roots support and in December 1994 was placed number 5 on the list of candidates for the ANC National Executive Committee. She was also appointed Deputy Minister of Arts, Culture, Science, and Technology. However, in 1995 President Mandela announced that his former wife's appointment as a deputy minister had been terminated with immediate effect. In 1998 she was nominated as Deputy President of the ANC, but was not elected. In the 1999 general election she was number 9 on the ANC candidates list for Parliament; she was duly elected and serves in the National Assembly. She was not appointed to the Cabinet, however, nor to any key executive position.[3]

That is the stark outline of her curriculum vitae, but it doesn't explain or capture who she really was or is. Those who know her well – her family, her colleagues, her friends, her political allies – all have different points of view about what makes her tick. She has many detractors. Many of those who have followed the media coverage regard her as dangerous and are vicious in their attacks on her. Who, really, is she? Fatima Meer, a long-time friend of the Mandela family, and author of a biography of Nelson

Mandela entitled *Higher than Hope*,[4] wrote of her own impressions of Winnie Madikizela-Mandela in the *Sunday Times*. She begins her article,

> I like her for her warmth and her common touch. Oh, she can be exasperating; she can work up a fine temper; she can be arrogant and imperious. When she chooses, she can barricade herself behind a wall of icy chill but this is almost always in defence or anger when attacked or suspecting an attack. Winnie is most usually down to earth, frank, even shy, with a sense of humour that easily dissolves into a fun giggle. She is vulnerable and easily moved to action by individual appeals. This is the social worker in her.

Fatima Meer tried to express her unhappiness about the group of young people that surrounded Madikizela-Mandela, but to no avail. She believes that Madikizela-Mandela tried to discipline the Football Club members and believed that she was succeeding, 'but she was really deluding herself.' Overall, Meer seems to believe that Madikizela-Mandela was a victim of a 'vicious media which not only headlines every conceivable bad news against her, but regurgitates it endlessly so that one bad multiplies into many in the public mind.' She concludes her article by writing,

> I admire Winnie for her capacity to keep her cool and maintain her dignity in the face of repeated trials by the media. She heroically faced the persecutions, the torture, the bannings and banishments of the national government for 27 years, but she has faith in herself and that faith accounts for her survival.[5]

A very different picture emerged during the Commission hearings. Early on we heard from Phumlile Dlamini that Winnie Madikizela-Mandela had assaulted her while she was pregnant, and had arranged for others to assault her as well. We heard from many witnesses about her ruthlessness, and, if they are to be believed, she was the one who orchestrated savage beatings, bloody attacks, and even murders, such as the murder of Stompie Seipei. Whatever else is true, she certainly surrounded herself with young thugs, people of limited intellect, who clearly considered themselves to be above the law and answerable only to her.

It was this contrast between the high esteem in which Winnie Madikizela-Mandela was held, not only in South Africa but in many parts of the world, as a noble example of the anti-apartheid resistance, and the allegations and accusations that we knew we were going to hear, that made the opening of the hearing so fraught with trepidation and anxiety. The nine-day hearing began on 24 November 1997. The hall in Johannesburg was packed to capacity, with scores of people waiting outside. There were, it seemed, hundreds of journalists from the local and international media. Outside the hall there was a small group of women carrying placards saying 'Winnie for President', others saying 'An Injury to One is an Injury to All'. There was a large contingent of police, and dogs sniffed the hall for explosives before we could start. We desperately wanted this hearing not to become a spectacle which would obscure the search for truth and a concern for the victims.

The Commission's task was all the more difficult because it was dealing with events in the turbulent and violent 1980s, and therefore it would not be easy to separate saints from sinners. Winnie Madikizela-Mandela's life and work was writ large, and to decipher the truth was problematic to say the least. Many people had great sympathy for her, and many were scared of her. Our responsibility was to try to establish some degree of truth in a web of deceit. We looked for some semblance of morality in a story of political expediency. Our work was to protect victims, but it was difficult, agonisingly so, to decide who was the victim and who was the perpetrator. As Oscar Wilde put it, 'The truth is rarely pure and never simple.'[6]

The hearing was chaired by Desmond Tutu, and the commissioners who sat on the panel throughout the hearing were Dumisa Ntsebeza, Yasmin Sooka, Hlengiwe Mkhize, Khoza Mgojo, Fazel Randera, and me. Acting for the Commission was our legal advisor, Hanif Vally, assisted by Piers Pigou and investigator Leila Groenewald. About fifteen lawyers were there, representing their clients. Winnie Madikizela-Mandela was represented by Ishmail Semenya. Winnie herself was undoubtedly the centre of attention, dominating the proceedings, even though she appeared as a witness only on the last day. She overshadowed not only the commissioners but also, tragically, the parents who had come to plead for the return of their children or at least to know where the bodies were buried.

On the first day her appearance set off a series of scuffles, with what seemed like hundreds of photographers and journalists jostling for position. She cut a dignified figure as she took her place in the hall. Accompanying her were her daughters, Zinzi and Zenani, and her bodyguards. She wore a floral dress on that opening day, but every day she wore a different outfit, and, although the hall was stifling, temperatures high, and the atmosphere electric, for the most part she looked cool and calm. Occasionally she would mutter something under her breath or make signs, seemingly in an attempt to intimidate the witnesses. But for most of the time she sat listening to the litany of terror being described in great detail.

Tutu opened the proceedings very wisely on a low-key note, welcoming all those present and emphasising that this was a hearing, that the Commission was not a court of law, and that it was guided by the Promotion of National Unity and Reconciliation Act. He stressed repeatedly that because we were not a court of law there would not be any verdict of guilty or not guilty at the end of the hearing. Our goal was to find the truth, he said, and, 'as always, we are here concerned primarily for the victims and survivors. We seek the truth not for the purpose of prosecution. We seek the truth for the healing of our land.' After Tutu's welcome and introduction, the first witness, Thami Hlatswayo, was called. The interpreters, the lawyers, the commissioners, the large crowd, the media, the victims, the witnesses, and

Winnie Madikizela-Mandela herself were ready to start the marathon proceedings.

In the next nine days, witness after witness testified that Madikizela-Mandela had wrongly accused Methodist minister Paul Verryn of sodomising young people, and had participated in the kidnapping of four youths and in the savage beating of these youths after they were taken from the Methodist church home. She was accused of murdering Stompie Seipei, beating Lolo Sono and ordering his death, as well as that of Siboniso Shabalala, arranging the murder of Andrew Ikaneng, ordering the murder of Sibeso Chili, organising the attack on the Chili house in which thirteen-year-old Finkie Msomo died, planning the assassination of Dr Abu-Baker Asvat, and arranging for Katiza Cebekhulu to be spirited out of the country so that he could not testify against her. In the 1991 court case, Madikizela-Mandela's alibi for 29 December, the day that Stompie and three others were kidnapped and assaulted, had been that she was miles away in Brandfort. The two people who had backed her alibi, Jerry Richardson and Xoliswa Falati, both of whom were serving jail sentences, withdrew their support, however, and stated that they had lied to protect their employer.

It is impossible to go into all the sordid details of the hearing, so I will focus on the testimony of only a few of the key witnesses. Among those who had requested the Commission to find out the fate of their children were Nicodemus Sono and Nomsa Shabalala. Mr Sono testified that his son, Lolo, had been a member of the Mandela United Football Club and had been working closely with Madikizela-Mandela. On one particular weekend, when Mr Sono arrived home, a stranger knocked on his door and told him that there was somebody outside who wanted to see him. When he went outside he saw a kombi, with Madikizela-Mandela sitting in the front seat. His son, Lolo, and a number of other young men were in the back of the vehicle. Mr Sono was concerned because it appeared that his son was being held by two young men, one on either side. Madikizela-Mandela said that she had brought Lolo so his father could see him because 'he is a police spy'.

Mr Sono's lawyer asked him whether he had had a good look at his son. His reply was, 'Yes, because when I opened the slide door the light in the kombi went on and I could see Lolo at the back. He was beaten up. His face was bruised. It was actually pulped. He was like, you know, thick, as if someone had beaten him up and crushed him against the wall.' He told us that his son had tried to speak to him, but had been told to shut up by Madikizela-Mandela, who explained to Mr Sono that Lolo was a spy. He pleaded with her to 'leave Lolo with me because he has already been beaten.' 'She refused. I urged her again, please won't you leave my son with me because he has already been beaten. I mean, if you leave him with me I will see what to do from here.' She refused once again and told the driver to drive off. As they drove away, he continued to plead with her until she finally said to him, 'I am taking this dog away. The movement will see what to do.' 'That was the last time I saw my son Lolo in the company of Mrs Mandela and some young men that were not known to me.'

Mr Sono also testified that he had subsequently visited Madikizela-Mandela's home on several occasions, asking about the whereabouts of his son. When the news broke that Stompie Seipei's body had been found, Mr Sono again approached Madikizela-Mandela several times, but she refused to give him a clear answer; the last time he approached her, just before Nelson Mandela was released from prison, she refused to see him. Mr Sono was vigorously cross-examined by Advocate Semenya, Madikizela-Mandela's lawyer, but he stuck to his story.

Mrs Shabalala testified that on 14 November 1988 certain young men from the Mandela United Football Club had come looking for her son, Siboniso. When her son returned home she told him about the visit and he said he would go to Winnie Madikizela-Mandela's house to find out what the problem was. Siboniso disappeared and his mother never saw him again. During question time I asked Mrs Shabalala what she wanted to ask Madikizela-Mandela. 'I want to speak to Winnie', she said. 'I am the one who went to report the matter that Winnie had abducted my son. She is the one who committed this atrocity. I do want to speak to her but I was told I'm not supposed to speak to her.' When Madikizela-Mandela's lawyer cross-examined Mrs Shabalala, she repeated that she had wanted to approach Madikizela-Mandela but had been afraid to: 'I used to see her scaring other people or threatening other people and now today it is the first time that I face Mrs Mandela and I am scared of her even now.' Turning to Madikizela-Mandela, she said, 'I would request Winnie to give Siboniso back to me. I want him or his bones and remains. If Winnie doesn't know anything, that is what she says, I also say that she knows, deep down inside of her she knows.'

Tragically, neither Lolo Sono's nor Siboniso Shabalala's bodies have ever been found. Madikizela-Mandela, when she took the stand, denied categorically the accounts given by Mr Sono and Mrs Shabalala.

The Rev. Paul Verryn (now Bishop Verryn) gave evidence that was not only helpful to the Commission but also poignant and very moving. He had lived in a church house in the township and ten or twenty people had stayed there at a time. He had been accused by Madikizela-Mandela, members of the Football Club, and many others of abusing young people who had stayed there. It was on this pretext that the young people were removed on the instructions of Madikizela-Mandela and under the directions of Jerry Richardson and Xoliswa Falati, and were taken to Madikizela-Mandela's house. Subsequently, everyone who had made this accusation and who appeared before the Commission admitted that they had lied and that they had been told to make the accusation, several of them mentioning Madikizela-Mandela by name. The only person who did not apologise or withdraw the allegation during the hearings was Madikizela-Mandela herself.

Paul Verryn testified to the fact that young people had been living in his home, and that while he was on holiday he had received the distressing news that four of the young people had been abducted from the house. He was warned by several people not to return to the township, because his life was in danger. However, on 7 January 1989 he received information that one of the young men, Kenny Kgase, had escaped from the Mandela house. He testified that he had met with Kenny; his 'eyes were bloodied, [and] he had marks on his back where the skin was broken, the kind of marks that would come from being beaten with a sjambok.' On 16 January, two other young men, Thabiso Mono and Pelo Mekgwe, were released from the Mandela house. That evening a community meeting was called and the youths described their abduction. They said they had been forced to accuse Verryn of sexual abuse and they retracted the allegations.

In his testimony, Paul Verryn made a number of remarkable statements, which showed his sense of love and his commitment to forgiveness and reconciliation. During the discussion of Stompie Seipei's death, he said,

> I see that Mrs Seipei is in the audience here today and
> the thing that has been most difficult for me is that
> having heard the allegations I did not remove him
> from the Mission House and get him to a place where
> he could be safe and I think if I had acted in another
> way he could be alive today and so I want to apologise
> to Mrs Seipei for my part in that.

This was an astonishing statement, seeing that he had done so much for those young men and could hardly be accountable for Stompie's death, and it revealed the depth of his own feelings. Verryn also made a moving statement to Winnie Madikizela-Mandela. 'I don't know Mrs Mandela really. We have met face to face briefly in my Mission House once.' Then, addressing her directly, he said,

> And my feelings about you have taken me in
> many directions, as you can imagine. I long for our
> reconciliation. I have been profoundly, profoundly
> affected by some of the things that you have said
> about me, that have hurt me and cut me to the quick.
> I have had to struggle to come to some place of

learning to forgive, even if you do not want forgiveness or even think that I deserve to offer that to you.
I struggle to find a way in which we can be reconciled
for the sake of this nation, for the people that I believe
God loves so deeply. So I sit before you and want
to say that to you.

A little later Desmond Tutu addressed Winnie Madikizela-
Mandela's lawyer and asked him whether there would be
any response to Verryn's very moving words. Semenya
replied, 'Mrs Mandela would want to communicate with
the Bishop but holds the view that if the Bishop had meant
to communicate he could have done so earlier, outside of
what we believe to be a camera scenario.' Tutu tried to
push very strongly for a response, speaking more as a pastor than as chairperson of a commission, but this was the
final word from the lawyer and Madikizela-Mandela.

Another witness, Bishop Peter Storey, gave a fascinating
insight into the extent of the Football Club's activities and
Winnie Madikizela-Mandela's involvement therein when
he recounted a visit to Nelson Mandela in prison by the
then Presiding Bishop of the Methodist Church, Stanley
Mogoba, who is now the leader of the Pan African Congress. In 1988 Mogoba had been given a memorandum by
Storey outlining the problem and asking for Mandela's
intervention. On his return, Mogoba related the conversations he had held with Mandela. According to
Mogoba, Mandela had said, 'The fault is hers. I owe an
apology to the church but why could not Bishop Peter have
come closer to her instead of it being discussed in the
press?' Mogoba told Mandela that Storey had in fact tried
to meet with her but that she had failed to keep an appointment, and he added that Winnie was the one who had
broken the press silence. Mandela acknowledged this and
said, 'I owe Peter an apology for what I have been thinking.
It is an ugly situation.'
    Mandela then sought advice from Mogoba and won-
dered if it would make good sense to tell Winnie to call a

press conference to make a public apology, to admit that she had done wrong, to seek forgiveness, and to express a desire to begin again. Mogoba's response was very brief: 'Your idea has merits but it may be too late.'

It is clear that the stories surrounding Winnie Madikizela-Mandela and the Football Club had aroused the concern and interest, not only of the local community and the leadership of the larger Soweto community, but also of the leadership of the ANC in Lusaka as well as Nelson Mandela himself in prison.

In the immediate community in those fateful days of 1988–89, a special group, which later became known as the Mandela Crisis Committee, was set up to try to resolve the threatening conflict surrounding Madikizela-Mandela. The committee included Beyers Naudé, the well-known Afrikaner clergyman and church leader; Sydney Mufamadi, former secretary-general of the National Union of Mineworkers and later Minister of Safety and Security; Frank Chikane, former general-secretary of the South African Council of Churches, later key assistant to Deputy President Thabo Mbeki, and currently director-general in President Mbeki's office; Aubrey Mokoena, then leader of the Release Mandela campaign and currently a member of Parliament; Sister Bernard Ncube, then president of the Federation of Transvaal Women's Organisations and now a member of Parliament. Another member, Cyril Ramaphosa, former general-secretary of the National Union of Mineworkers, prominent politician, and now a leading businessman, was unable to attend the hearing.

It is easy for those of us who were outside that cauldron of rumour and fear to sit in judgement on the Crisis Committee and its attempt to resolve the situation. However, listening to the testimony of the members of the committee, I must say I was overcome with a sense of deep unease, and I came to the conclusion that, while there was a commitment to and a concern for the children and young people who had been mistreated or who had been missing or found dead, the key priority of the Crisis Committee had been to control any political fallout which could

[235]

impact on the ANC and the opposition to apartheid. Furthermore, although all the committee members were asked point-blank if they were intimidated by Winnie Madikizela-Mandela and all refuted this, there is no doubt in my mind that a nervousness came through in their account of what had happened in those tragic days. Her stature in the ANC and her powerful personality seemed to have cowed almost everyone.

It would seem that, initially, the Mandela Crisis Committee had been set up to deal with the burning down of the Mandela house and to prevent further conflict between members of the Mandela United Football Club and the schoolchildren who were responsible for the act of arson. It also planned to rebuild and restore the house. Only subsequently did the Crisis Committee become concerned with the alleged kidnapping of young people from the Orlando West Methodist Church. The committee was approached by representatives of the community, who were deeply concerned about the alleged kidnappings and the accusations of sexual abuse. Their objective was to persuade Madikizela-Mandela to let the community leadership take over responsibility for young people instead of having them live in the back of her house and working with her as members of the Football Club.

The second objective of the committee was to close down the club, not only because of the accusations of criminal behaviour but also because it was suspected that the club was being infiltrated by members of the security branch. It was particularly important that the four young people who had been taken away from the Methodist Church house should be released and that the community should be shown that they were safe and well. During their attempts to achieve these objectives, the Crisis Committee members were in contact with Oliver Tambo, then president of the ANC in exile, and he, according to the evidence led by Frank Chikane, personally called Madikizela-Mandela and asked her to close down the Football Club. As a result, the ANC in exile made a statement concerning all these matters and wrote in their ANC publication, Sechaba,

The ANC shares the concern of the people and has all the time tried to intervene to find an amicable solution to the problem. In the light of reports about its activities in the recent past, our organisation, complementing the initiatives of leading personalities of the Mass Democratic Movement, tried to use its influence to bring about the disbanding of the group... Unfortunately our counsel was not heeded by Comrade Winnie Mandela.

The ANC expressed their concern not only that the Football Club should be disbanded but that a hand should be stretched out to Madikizela-Mandela: 'It is necessary that Comrade Winnie Mandela is helped to find her way into the structures and discipline of the Mass Democratic Movement.'[7] The implication was clear. Winnie was a loose cannon and her unpredictable behaviour could cause considerable harm to the ANC.

It would appear that, despite entreaties by the ANC leadership outside the country, its representatives within the immediate community, and Nelson Mandela from jail, Madikizela-Mandela was not willing or ready to cooperate with her own party structures and leadership. In her evidence in camera and in the public hearing, she rejected the account as laid out by members of the Crisis Committee and stated that she had no recollection of their request that she disband the club and release the young people being held in her house. Any statements that they had made at the time she believed were the work of the security police rather than the Crisis Committee.

Despite their tentative approach to Madikizela-Mandela, the written statement of the Crisis Committee is very clear: 'She seems to think that she is above the community. That was our opinion. She shows utter contempt for both the Crisis Committee and the community.'

The crunch question was put by Mr Vally:

One of the youths breaks down and tells you that they have been assaulted, that is Katiza Cebekhulu. The other two youths have got fresh wounds on their

[237]

bodies which you note. Zinzi Mandela advises you that Kenny has escaped and the fact that she doesn't mention Stompie concerns you in that you were worried about his whereabouts. Surely there was some degree of urgency by this stage. Surely you could have taken more drastic action. Why didn't you?

The question was not satisfactorily answered.

Following the evidence of the Crisis Committee we listened to evidence led by Dr Nthato Motlana, who was a major leadership figure in Soweto and personal physician to the Mandela family, Rev. Otto Mbangula, a Methodist minister working in the township, and Father Mhkatshwa, a Catholic priest who is now a member of Parliament. They had visited Madikizela-Mandela's home, out of concern for the young people who had been abducted and in order to ascertain their well-being and their whereabouts, but it was clear from their testimony that they had been reluctant to challenge Madikizela-Mandela. They had been at great pains not to incur her wrath. For example, Dr Motlana, a man of enormous integrity and courage whom I have known for many years, told the Commission that he had visited Madikizela-Mandela to try to secure the release of the young people, but that he had not asked to see them. We asked him why, as a medical doctor, he hadn't thought it important to see the young people to establish their well-being, but he could give us no answer.

When we questioned Rev. Mbangula and Father Mhkatshwa, they gave us the same impression. During question time after their evidence, I put it specifically to both religious leaders,

> Kenny was not released. He escaped and he tells the community that he has been very badly assaulted and has scars and wounds to prove it. He also expresses a very deep concern about Stompie's safety and health and possible death. Now you went to visit Mrs Mandela after that. You were concerned about the safety and security of the children, or of the young men, but you go there and you are assured that they are safe and

sound. You must have asked her about Stompie. It has already been established that he was badly hurt and that he may be dead or may be dying. You must surely have considered asking to see him and on what basis did you accept from Mrs Mandela that the children were safe and sound?

Rev. Mbangula agreed with the point I was making and acknowledged that he hadn't asked the question. But because he did not explain why he hadn't, I put a further question to them:

You didn't try to see the children or the young people. You didn't ask about Stompie. I ask you, therefore, was there a political reason? Were you afraid to put these questions because of the status of the person like Mrs Mandela? You are deeply caring men. You go to the house, you don't ask about the children, you don't ask to see them, you conclude the meeting with prayer and you leave.

Rev. Mbangula claimed that this had been an oversight.

Father Mhkatshwa's reply was equally unconvincing. He stated that the purpose of the visit was not to be confrontational, that it was a pastoral visit to discuss allegations that young men had been removed from the Methodist Church into Madikizela-Mandela's custody. He specifically stated that he couldn't remember asking too many questions. I put it to him that at that time he had believed that the matter wasn't very important, that the meeting had been amicable, and there had been no confrontation. However, subsequent events showed that the matter was extremely serious and that not only were young men assaulted but Stompie was killed. 'In other words,' I said, 'your accepting of Mrs Mandela's assurance that the children were safe and sound and quite healthy, to use your words, turned out to be very different.' He replied, 'Obviously in this world certain things happen that you cannot in any way humanly speaking foretell that they are going to happen.' My response was, 'But you could have asked to see them because then you could have had greater knowledge about the condition of the children and you would have known at least that one was either missing or desperately ill or dead. Right?' His reply was non-committal. I then put a final question to him:

> If you look back and see the context of all these con-
> cerns and your attempt to get to the root causes,
> surely it would have been logical, sensible and com-
> passionate to have gained some assurance for your-
> selves that these young people were all right, just by
> at least greeting them, seeing them, getting some
> assurance from them so that you could go back to
> your community and say, look, it's all right, these kids
> are OK. You don't have to be concerned about them.

Father Mhkatshwa's reply was, 'Well, if they had been in prison or if they had been in detention, I would have in-sisted on seeing them but this was a very different situa-tion.' Clearly the fact that Winnie Madikizela-Mandela was who she was, that she was, as was often stated, a com-rade, meant that the normal sensitivities that would have obtained were simply put to one side. This confirmed our earlier view that because of Madikizela-Mandela's status there had been a clear reluctance to put any pointed questions, to challenge her in any way.

It is interesting to note that it wasn't only Winnie's friends and admirers who were apparently afraid of her. Evidence was led by several security police officers, includ-ing Superintendent André Kritzinger, who stated that 'she was untouchable' because of her high political profile: 'There was sufficient evidence for a prima facie case against Mrs Mandela, but because of her high political profile the Attorney-General decided not to prosecute her.'

In sharp contrast, the evidence given by Azar Cachalia and Murphy Morobe of the United Democratic Front and the Mass Democratic Movement was refreshing and convinc-ing. This was particularly true of Azar Cachalia, who made what I thought was an extremely brave statement to the Commission. Cachalia is an attorney by profession and was employed by the new democratic government as head of the Secretariat for Safety and Security within the department of the same name. He recounted the events leading to the issuing of a statement by the MDM on 16 February 1989 in which it publicly distanced itself from the conduct of Winnie Madikizela-Mandela and the Mandela United Football Club.[8] In his statement he reminded the Commission that a state of emergency was in force after June 1986. During 1988 repression was intensified and the UDF, the trade unions, and all key affiliates were prohibited by government proclamation from engaging in any political activity. All Soweto-based affiliates were restricted and virtually the entire leadership of the UDF was either in detention or on trial, and those who were not incarcerated were severely restricted. In his estimate, about 5000 people were detained during 1988. In Soweto, large numbers of members of the Soweto Students' Congress, the Soweto Youth Congress, and civic associations were in jail. A ban on all outdoor gatherings remained in force under the Internal Security Act. Cachalia summed up the situation by saying, 'To say that it was difficult to operate politically under these conditions was therefore an understatement. Nevertheless, despite this and at the risk of sounding too clichéd, the struggle continued.'

He pointed out that, in spite of this determination, structures had been considerably weakened and in particular linkages with youth groups had become tenuous:

> The youth and children bore the brunt of the state's brutality. As a result, thousands of unaffiliated youths, lacking direction or cohesion, many of them badly affected by beatings, by harassment, by being in detention, formed themselves into street patrols, hunting down other trouble-makers, hooligans and vandals. The effect of these gangs on the community was extraordinarily destabilising. Township residents were horrified by the disorder and the challenge to their

[241]

authority by some of these 'young thugs'. This is the climate in which Mrs Mandela created her own personal vigilante gang, the Mandela United Football Club.

Cachalia said that he had begun to hear disturbing reports of what could only be described as criminal activities by the Football Club. He referred to three broad themes which began to emerge. Firstly, the Football Club often dispensed its frightening brand of justice, and it was clear that the general view in the community was that Madikizela-Mandela often directed these operations. Secondly, there were stories that children had disappeared from the Mandela home. Thirdly, the Football Club was infiltrated by the police and some of its members actually worked for the police. He referred in particular to the abduction of two youths by members of the club; they were taken to the Mandela home and were accused of being informers. 'On one of them the letter M was sliced into his chest with a penknife and the words "Viva ANC" was carved down his thigh. Battery acid was then poured over his open wounds. The second youth also had the words "Viva ANC" carved on his back.'

Matters were brought to a head with the abduction of four young people from the Methodist church house and their incarceration in the Mandela home. Cachalia made a very strong allegation about this: 'At best for Mrs Mandela she was aware and condoned this criminal activity. At worst, she directed it and actively participated in the assaults.' He and his colleagues in the UDF became desperate. Stompie Seipei's body had been positively identified and their worst fears had materialised. It was ironic that this was taking place against the background of a campaign by the UDF for the release of children from prisons. One of their major concerns was the brutalisation of children in the townships. It seemed to Cachalia that the sickness of apartheid in the brutalisation of children in detention was now being mirrored in the actions of one of the most well-known and revered leaders of the ANC, Winnie Madikizela-Mandela.

It was for this reason the UDF and Cosatu decided to distance themselves publicly from her actions. 'For me,' Cachalia said, 'it was one of the most difficult decisions I have ever made but I think it was also one of the proudest moments that I can remember... I hope that if I am ever confronted with having to make a similar decision I will have the moral courage to do it again.'

Murphy Morobe also made a very strong statement against Winnie Madikizela-Mandela, which he concluded by emphasising the ANC's need at that time to stand up for those things that they believed in and for what they were fighting against:

> It is important that we become uncompromising against issues relating to violations of human rights because it is precisely because we were fighting against that from the system of apartheid that some of us went to jail. Some of us were tortured in jail. It was therefore important that we shouldn't get to a situation where we condoned these activities.

He acknowledged that one of the reasons why they hadn't acted sooner was that in 1989 South Africa was on the eve of its liberation: 'We didn't want the name of our movement, namely the ANC, to be tarnished.' But he also went on to say, 'Mrs Mandela is a powerful person, a powerful figure, so before you mess with a powerful person you must be clear of your facts and that was the situation.'

Both Cachalia and Morobe were very closely cross-examined by Advocate Semenya on behalf of Madikizela-Mandela, but they did not budge from their original position that Madikizela-Mandela was responsible for the criminal activities of the Mandela United Football Club.

Azar Cachalia made one final comment before leaving the witness box. He directed the statement to Madikizela-Mandela:

> I want to say to Mrs Mandela that I have known you for years. I deeply admired and respected you. The Cachalia and Mandela families go back a long way.

> And as I sit here I am deeply conflicted. There is one
> part of me which wants to in a sense go over and hug
> you and to say let's walk away from all of this because
> it is a bit of a bad nightmare. But there is another
> part of me which says we actually cannot go forward
> unless there is some level of accountability.

This comment from Cachalia to Winnie Madikizela-Mandela in a crowded hall revealed the intimacy of the hearing and, more importantly, of the relationships which had existed during the tragic years under review. Such sympathetic closeness made the work of the Commission so much more difficult and made it almost impossible to separate the lies, the truths, the half-lies, and the rumours which seemed to be part and parcel of the overall hearing. Witnesses like Cachalia were nevertheless honest, although others may have obscured the truth through loyalty. But Cachalia's comment was also extremely important in stressing the need for accountability. As a Commission we were compelled by our mandate to set aside our personal feelings and follow the truth no matter where it led.

Another very interesting and difficult aspect of the hearing was the discussion of the murder of Dr Abu-Baker Asvat. Ebrahim Asvat, brother of the murdered man, gave evidence and expressed his dissatisfaction with the original police investigation. Evidence was also put forward that the two men who had been convicted of the murder, Thulani Nicholas Dlamini and Cyril Mbata, had claimed that they were promised R20 000 by Winnie Madikizela-Mandela if they killed Dr Asvat. In his evidence, Katiza Cebekhulu, one of the members of the Football Club, alleged that she had asked him to point out the location of Dr Asvat's house and surgery to the two men. Throughout the long discussion and the testimony of the many witnesses, it seemed clear that the original police investigation was far from satisfactory. The police claimed the motive was robbery, but according to Dr Asvat's brother no money had been taken, although money was readily available in a cash box and on the body of the deceased. Furthermore, the allegation made by Dlamini that the killers had been promised R20 000 by Madikizela-Mandela to kill Dr Asvat had never been placed before the court.

Also of great significance was the question of whether Winnie Madikizela-Mandela had visited Dr Asvat on 29 or 30 December 1988. Stompie Seipei was assaulted on 30 December and Katiza Cebekhulu accused Madikizela-Mandela of stabbing him to death. Jerry Richardson claimed that he had killed Seipei on Madikizela-Mandela's instructions. Cebekhulu also said that Madikizela-Mandela had taken him to Dr Asvat's surgery on 30 December to prove that he, Cebekhulu, had been raped by Verryn. However, Dr Asvat apparently could find no evidence to prove this claim. Madikizela-Mandela insisted that she had been in Brandfort on 30 December and therefore could not have participated in Seipei's assault or murder. Yet the medical card made out in the name of Cebekhulu was date-stamped 30 December 1988.

A key witness was the deeply respected and revered Albertina Sisulu, a stalwart in the ANC and wife of Walter Sisulu, Nelson Mandela's life-long friend, fellow prisoner, and confidante. She had been Dr Asvat's receptionist and assistant. In an interview with her on South African television earlier in the year, Fred Bridgland, author of the book *Katiza's Journey: Beneath the Surface of South Africa's Shame*, showed Cebekhulu's medical card to Mrs Sisulu and asked her whether it was her handwriting on the card:

SISULU: That is my handwriting.
BRIDGLAND: Is that Dr Asvat's writing?
SISULU: Yes, it's his writing.
BRIDGLAND: Is that the date you would have
   stamped on it? Was that part of your job?
SISULU: Yes it was and that date is the 30th of
   December. I wouldn't have stamped that date if
   that wasn't the date.

[245]

In his questioning of Mrs Sisulu, Hanif Vally, the TRC counsel, asked her, 'Do you recognise the handwriting at the top of the card?' To his utter surprise and dismay, Sisulu replied, 'I don't recognise the handwriting noting down the particulars on Cebekhulu's card. I have never seen Cebekhulu.' Despite many questions from the commissioners and lawyers, Mrs Sisulu starkly contradicted the story she had told in the interview with Bridgland. This moved Dumisa Ntsebeza to say,

> My initial impression, and it can be changed by all the evidence that might come from Mrs Mandela and from any other evidence, but my impression as I sit here is that you are trying your very best to say as little as possible anything that might implicate Mrs Mandela. If that is so, I am trying to get the reasons for this ... if I am right, what you are trying your very, very best to do is to say as little as possible about your colleague, your comrade, and to say as little that might incriminate her or implicate her and is this the reason why you are now changing your story? You don't want to be the one who is identified in South African history as having dared to speak about your comrade in terms that seem to suggest that she was involved in something like the death of Dr Asvat.

Mrs Sisulu denied this emphatically and stuck to her story.

When we went into recess late that evening, the commissioners expressed to each other their deep dismay and disappointment at the turn of events and found it impossible to understand how Mrs Sisulu could say one thing in an interview, identifying her handwriting on the card and confirming the date, and then say something entirely different at the Commission hearing. This contradiction was widely reported in the media. We received a request a little later from Mrs Sisulu to be allowed to appear again to clarify the situation. Tutu repeated the point that in the documentary interview she had identified her own handwriting on the card, but that she had said exactly the opposite in her testimony before the Commission. He asked her finally which was the correct version: what she said when she was being interviewed on video or what she said in her evidence before the Commission? Her reply was quite simple and straightforward: 'What I said in the Commission is my version.' Tutu then replied, 'Yes, and what you said in the documentary was a mistake?' Mrs Sisulu responded, 'That might have been a mistake.'

Many people were relieved to hear this statement, so much so that Dumisa Ntsebeza went on record as saying, 'I am the first person to want to say publicly here that you have vindicated yourself and that in my eyes you remain not only the friend of my family but the person you have been – an icon of moral rectitude in all that we have been fighting for. I am pleased for you.'

There were many in the media who were still puzzled and disconcerted, however, and I must confess that I felt the same way. I didn't think that Mrs Sisulu's explanation had resolved the apparent contradiction. The question that kept reverberating in my mind was, could it be possible that Winnie Madikizela-Mandela was so powerful and that people were so afraid of her and her links with Nelson Mandela and the ANC that even a person of such great integrity as Albertina Sisulu could back away when her original evidence could have implicated Madikizela-Mandela? There is no way that one can answer this question with any certainty, but I thought then, and think today, that Madikizela-Mandela wielded such power that to cross her would take enormous courage and could be foolhardy. Ntsebeza's response, on the other hand, in particular his personal references, reinforces the difficulty that even the Commission had in being objective in the context of the struggle against apartheid.

Finally the day came when Winnie Madikizela-Mandela herself took the witness stand. She wore a black suit with a green blouse, quite a lot of jewellery, and dark glasses. Her family and friends were present and there was an enormous sense of expectation in the assembled crowd. The atmosphere, while electric in one sense, was also very restrained, largely because Madikizela-Mandela's lawyer led her very quietly and deliberately. His mien, contrary to his attitude when cross-examining witnesses, was even-paced and subdued. Halfway through the proceedings, Dumisa Ntsebeza whispered to me, 'Damp squib'. Madikizela-Mandela was so quiet herself that some wondered if she was under sedation.

For the next several hours Advocate Semenya, the attending lawyers representing their clients, the Commission's counsel, and the commissioners themselves put questions to her relating to the damning allegations that had been made during the preceding eight days. Madiki-zela-Mandela's response was consistent. When statements were put to her, her reply was that they were 'lies', they were 'ludicrous', 'ridiculous', 'hallucinations' by the persons concerned, 'media distortions', 'police harassment', 'pure fabrication', and 'nonsensical'. She described Cebekhulu as 'a mental patient', and when persistent questions were asked about days and times and events, she simply replied that she couldn't remember or she didn't know. At the bottom of it all, she claimed, was a conspiracy of lies against her. Certainly she did not accept any responsibility. When presented with a long list of people who had been close to her or who had stayed in her home, and who were now serving prison sentences for very serious criminal charges, she shrugged the matter off. When presented with a list of Umkhonto we Sizwe people going in and out of her house, she dismissed that as well. Paul Erasmus, a policeman, had stated under oath that Madikizela-Mandela's house had been under twenty-four-hour surveillance. When the question was asked how, if this was the case, it was possible for people to bring weapons to the home, for MK people to come in and out, for assaults to take place, for murders to take place, without any response from the police, Madikizela-Mandela was at a loss to explain, except to repeat that her house was like a police station, constantly monitored. One lawyer was so frustrated that he finally burst out, 'The truth in your hands is like putty which you simply mould to suit your own ends.'

[248]

When my turn came to ask her questions, I began by putting a brief statement to her: 'We have heard a great deal about the Mandela United Football Club. If I were to suggest, after having listened to all the evidence, that this was a very good idea that went very badly wrong, how would you respond?' Her response was straightforward, 'That is correct.' I then asked her why, when she found that the young people had been brought to her home, she didn't immediately take them back, if she hadn't authorised their removal in the first place. Her reply was vague and unsatisfactory. I then asked her about the many people who had expressed their concern to her – the Crisis Committee, Dr Motlana, church leaders, and many others – and asked her,

> Wouldn't it have been easier if from the very beginning you said to them, listen, I can understand your concern. You say you care for these kids. Come on, let's meet them and if you have any accommodation for them, take them away. They seemed to be of the opinion firstly that they couldn't see them and second that you were reluctant to let them go. Is that true?

Madikizela-Mandela replied, 'No, that was a wrong impression, Deputy Chairperson.'

I then reminded her that a number of allegations of assault on her property had been made during the course of the hearing, and that some of those allegations were that she herself had participated in those assaults. I said to her,

> I think you are a very powerful, charismatic person, a leader. How was it possible for some of these things to take place when they were in the back of your own house? I mean, if they took place you would hear them scream, surely? Wouldn't you go and say, what the hell is going on here? I'm in charge. What is happening here? This is what is confusing me. Please try and help me.

Her reply was that these alleged assaults must have taken place when she hadn't been there, and, in any case, 'It is a total fabrication.' I then reminded her of what Judge

[**249**]

Stegman had said in his finding in the 1991 trial when she was found guilty of kidnapping and assaulting the youths. He had said in his summing up, 'Mrs Mandela punched and slapped each one of them … and called for a sjambok to be brought to her. Each of the four was beaten by Mrs Mandela.' I said to her, 'That was his finding. What do you say now to that against the background of so many of these allegations?' Madikizela-Mandela described the judgement as vicious and said that she had not been there at the time.

I persisted and said to her,

> Stompie has become almost a symbol in South Africa. We all know now that he died a very cruel death and you yourself had acknowledged your own sorrow about that. Again, how was it possible for this youngster to be so badly assaulted and then finally killed on your own property and then taken from your property, according to Jerry Richardson, and killed without you knowing anything about it?

She didn't answer the question, so I put it to her again: 'He was there for a number of days and according to a range of witnesses he was looking very, very ill, badly assaulted, his head was swollen, his hands, he couldn't hold a cup and so on. Was this never brought to your attention, that he was there in the back of your house, in that condition?' Madikizela-Mandela responded, 'Not at all sir.'

The final word was left to the chairperson, Desmond Tutu. After he thanked everyone who had been involved with the arrangements for the hearings, and those who had attended, he made a very personal statement about his relationship with the Mandela family. He was clearly moved, and there was a hush as he described the relationship:

> We live in the same street in what is sometimes called Beverly Hills. Our children went to the same school in Swaziland. They call me uncle. Mrs Mandela is godmother to one of my grandchildren. When I was Bishop of Lesotho I used to visit Mrs Mandela when

she was in Brandfort. I have immense admiration for her and there is no question at all, she was a tremendous stalwart of our struggle, an icon of liberation, who was banned, harassed, under surveillance, banished, with a husband away serving a life sentence. She had to bring up two girls.

He went on in this vein for some time. Then he referred to the sordid accounts that we had heard over the past nine days: 'Some of us were devastated, but also found it exhilarating what happened during this hearing. Devastated by the performance of some eminent leaders of the struggle. There were splendid exceptions who stood out in stark contrast. Azar Cachalia, Murphy Morobe, the two Methodist bishops, Sydney Mufamadi.' Tutu also referred to Mrs Sisulu's testimony and said he was now 'over the moon over what happened to rehabilitate someone I hold in the highest possible regard.' He stressed the need to demonstrate that the new dispensation was different qualitatively and morally and the need to stand up to be counted for goodness, for truth, and for compassion. Then, getting closer to the critical issue, he stated, 'I acknowledge Mrs Madikizela-Mandela's role in the history of our struggle and yet one has to say that something went wrong, horribly, badly wrong. What, I don't know.'

Then Tutu spoke his closing words, which became a source of considerable debate in the media:

It was marvellous seeing Winnie as she walked hand in hand with her husband then, leaving the Victor Verster prison... I don't know that we will ever know all the details of what it is that went wrong. Many, many love you. Many, many say you should have been where you ought to be, the first lady of this country... I speak to you as someone who loves you very deeply. Who loves your family very deeply. I would have said to you, let us have a public meeting. And at that public meeting for you to stand up and say there are things that went wrong, there are things that went wrong and I don't know why they went wrong.

[251]

There are people out there who want to embrace you.
I still embrace you because I love you and I love you
very deeply... I beg you, I beg you, I beg you please.
You are a great person and you don't know how your
greatness would be enhanced if you were to say sorry,
things went wrong, forgive me, I beg you.

There was a hushed silence and then Madikizela-Mandela
responded:

Thank you very much and I would like to thank the
panellists and I would like to thank you all. Save to
say thank you very much for your wonderful wise
words and that is the father I have always known in
you. I am hoping it is still the same. I will take this
opportunity to say to the family of Dr Asvat how
deeply sorry I am. To Stompie's mother, how deeply
sorry I am. I have said so to her before a few years
back, when the heat was very hot. I am saying it is
true, things went horribly wrong. I fully agree with
that and for that part of those painful years when
things went horribly wrong and we were aware of
the fact that there were factors that led to that, for
that I am deeply sorry.

The nine day hearing was adjourned.

I was stunned as we left the stage, exhausted and troubled. I had no idea that Tutu was going to conclude the way
he did, and I was still trying to come to terms with that. I
thought afterwards that it was a great pity that he had per-
sonalised the issue to the extent that he had. This is an
even more powerful example of the moral dilemma in
which the Commission found itself, and understandably it
gave rise to criticism. Tutu's impassioned plea was that of
a pastor rather than a secular commissioner. His intimate
relationship with the Mandela family in this instance was
a disadvantage, and I think he should have been more cir-
cumspect and more judicial. His hugging of Madikizela-
Mandela during the hearing, and his declaration of love and
admiration, left the Commission wide open to the charge

of bias. The contrast between this hearing and the trial of P.W. Botha only added fuel to the flames of criticism. Tutu's attitude was not wrong so much as unwise. He cared so deeply that he did not contemplate for a moment the misconceptions that could ensue. I know Desmond Tutu too well and have too much respect for him ever to doubt his bona fides. I think he genuinely believed that he could elicit from Madikizela-Mandela some apology, some acceptance of responsibility, some accountability. Such a response was not really forthcoming, and we thought a great deal about this when we were working on our findings for our final report.

Most of the media were very critical of Tutu's final statement and felt that Winnie Madikizela-Mandela had made no real concessions whatsoever. Gwynne Dyer, a London-based independent journalist and historian, was particularly harsh on Tutu. It was his view that Tutu should have discredited Madikizela-Mandela when he had the chance, and he wrote in very strong language, 'The monster is still on the loose and South Africa will pay the price for years.' In his article he praises Tutu as a brave man, in particular for his role in the anti-apartheid struggle, but says that 'He had no way of dealing with Winnie Mandela, who simply denied all her alleged crimes regardless of the evidence.'[9] Other commentators, including Antjie Krog, felt that Tutu had 'saved the day' by pleading with Madikizela-Mandela to acknowledge that 'things went horribly wrong'. For me, as someone who sat through the entire hearing, who read carefully the account of the in camera hearing, and who has now read well over 3000 pages of the transcript of the hearing, I can only conclude that anyone who participated in that hearing, who listened to the many witnesses and Madikizela-Mandela's responses, would have to be naïve or blindly committed to the point of worship if they believe that she had not been aware of what was going on in her own home and had not been party to much of what took place. I think Bishop Storey is right. There was a sickness in the heart of South Africa called apartheid. But there were secondary symptoms as well, and Madikizela-Mandela and her Football Club were part of that sickness when she imitated what she hated most. The adoration she received from crowds of desperate people and the power she wielded were too much, too strong. She began to believe what her adoring fans said about her. She began to believe that she could do no wrong, that she was at war and the end justified the means. As W.H. Auden put it,

> I and the public know
> What all schoolchildren learn,
> Those to whom evil is done
> Do evil in return.[10]

In the final analysis, Winnie Madikizela-Mandela was both victim and perpetrator. She is a woman of immense personal charm and power whose passion for justice turned into a vengeful crusade which struck terror into the hearts of friends, comrades, and security police alike. In many ways she is more to be pitied than to be blamed. I still admire her courage in standing up to the forces of a criminal state and her solidarity with the poor and the oppressed. We must never forget the context in which she lived and worked. Frank Chikane described the situation in 1986 as

> A world made up of teargas, bullets, whippings, detention and death on the streets. It is an experience of military operations and night raids, of roadblocks and body searches. It is a world where parents and friends get carried away in the night to be interrogated. It is a world where people simply disappear, where parents are assassinated and homes are petrol bombed.[11]

I still have deep sympathy for the heavy personal burden she carried as the wife of the imprisoned Nelson Mandela. Itumeleng Oa Mahabane gives us a glimpse of why it is important not to judge her too harshly, nor to cast her aside. In a letter to the *Star* newspaper he writes,

> Racist though this might seem, only one community can judge Winnie and that is the very community

that she betrayed. The Truth Commission was white South Africa's chance to get a glimpse of the ghetto of P.W. Botha's state of emergency; it was an opportunity for them if not to understand what went down to get some idea and examine their country's past and their role in it. They rejected it. Madikizela-Mandela is a product of that ghetto and none but those who were residents of it can judge. Madikizela-Mandela's refusal to show contrition is contempt for residents of that ghetto. Only those who lived under those conditions can judge her, only those who bothered to commit to the new South Africa and her past can sit on her jury.[12]

There is considerable food for thought in Mahabane's letter, especially for white South Africans. When we bear in mind that many of apartheid's political leaders and generals have retained their positions of power and privilege, then we begin to see Winnie Madikizela-Mandela and her deeds in context. Furthermore, all of us are capable of evil. As Max Frankel asks, 'Is there a beast in each of us waiting to be unleashed by extraordinary fear, greed or fury?'[13] His reply, and mine, has to be: yes!

A final word. I deeply regret that Winnie Madikizela-Mandela did not apply for amnesty. Acknowledgement of accountability could have led to pardon. This is where the ANC leadership failed South Africa and in a strange way failed Winnie herself. While I admire Thabo Mbeki's gospel of the second chance and share his revulsion for the cold, merciless approach of so many, I think one thing more is required. To forgive after the acceptance of accountability and responsibility by the person concerned is an act of grace and gives the offender a second chance. To ignore or overlook the offence is an act of impunity.

The Commission's findings on Winnie Madikizela-Mandela and the Mandela United Football Club were included in our final report. They are as follows:

The Commission finds that Ms Madikizela-Mandela was central to the establishment and formation of the

Mandela United Football Club, which later developed
into a private vigilante unit operating around Ms
Madikizela-Mandela and from her houses in both
Orlando West and Diepkloof. The Commission finds
that the community anger against Ms Madikizela-
Mandela and the Football Club manifested itself in
the burning of the Mandela home in Orlando West in
July 1988, which led to political, community and
church leaders requesting that she disband the
Football Club.

The Commission further finds that the Mandela
United Football Club was involved in a number of
criminal activities including killing, torture, assaults
and arson in the community. It is the Commission's
view that Ms Madikizela-Mandela was aware of
the criminal activity and the disquiet it caused in the
community, but chose deliberately not to address
the problems emanating from the Football Club.
The Commission finds that those who opposed
Ms Madikizela-Mandela and the Mandela United
Football Club, or dissented from them, were branded
as informers, and killed. The labelling by Ms
Madikizela-Mandela of opponents as informers
created the perception that they were legitimate
targets. It is the finding of this Commission that
Ms Madikizela-Mandela had knowledge of and/or
participated in the activities of Club members,
and/or that they were authorised and/or sanctioned
by her.

The Commission finds that Ms Madikizela-
Mandela failed to account to community and political
structures. Further that she is accountable, politically
and morally, for the gross violations of human rights
committed by the Mandela United Football Club.
The Commission finds further that Mrs Madikizela-
Mandela herself was responsible for committing
such gross violations of human rights.[14]

Winnie Madikizela-Mandela and P.W. Botha are indeed two very different people. So far apart in culture, position, and race, yet brought together as key actors in the South African tragedy. Tutu made a desperate appeal to both of them to acknowledge their own part in our tragedy. Neither responded with genuine remorse. Both continue to claim that they were right and without fault. At opposite poles, repressor and repressed, they sum up the sickness of the soul of South Africa during the years of racial conflict. 'The primary cancer may be and was and will always be the apartheid oppression, but the secondary infection has touched many of apartheid's opponents and eroded their knowledge of good and evil'.

South Africa has begun the healing process – we are becoming human again. We must be eternally vigilant that we never allow unbridled power to destroy our future full of promise and possibility.

8

Amnesty in exchange for truth: Evaluating the South African model

MANY PEOPLE from around the world have asked me to what I attribute the achievement of the South African Truth and Reconciliation Commission. In my response I have referred to a number of favourable conditions which helped the Commission to achieve a degree of success in relation to its stated objectives.

Firstly, as has already been mentioned, the ANC was the first body to call for a truth commission. In other words, from the very outset the largest political party favoured such a commission and took this commitment with them when they became the new government in South Africa. Without this it would have been impossible for the Commission to come into being and to emerge as the important contributor that it became to truth, knowledge, acknowledgement, and accountability.

In an unpublished paper entitled 'Fourth D.T. Lakdawala Memorial Lecture', Judge Albie Sachs refers to the seminal meeting of the ANC National Executive Committee in August 1993 at which the recommendation was made for a truth commission to be appointed in South Africa. He describes it vividly: 'It was a passionate meeting, sharp, uncomfortable. The issue was how to respond to a report of a commission of inquiry set up by the ANC to investigate violations of human rights committed by ANC cadres in Angolan camps during the liberation struggle.'[1] The report of the Motsuenyane Commission had left no doubt that members of the ANC security forces had committed gross human rights violations in dealing with those who for one reason or another had been placed in captivity in the ANC camps.

This was clearly a very sensitive issue and one which caused a great sense of embarrassment and shame to many, but also anger that they, as a liberation movement, should be criticised in this way in the face of the overarching violations that had taken place at the instigation of the state. It was critical for the future development of a human rights culture that the ANC did not sweep these serious allegations under the carpet. To their credit, they decided that it was impossible to ignore the findings of the commission and that there had to be a serious response to serious charges. Again, in the words of Albie Sachs,

> Some people said forcefully: we set up the Motsuen-
> yane Commission, it has reported, we have to follow
> through. And others responded with equal vehemence:
> how can we do that, we were fighting a freedom
> struggle in terribly difficult conditions in the bush in
> Angola, the enemy was ruthless and they stopped at
> nothing, we had young people quite untrained in inter-
> rogation techniques, they did their best, they protected
> the leadership, how can we punish them now?[2]

Clearly, it was a moment of crisis. Against those who argued that the ANC should do nothing, Pallo Jordan, who later became Minister of Environmental Affairs and Tourism, stood up and 'with his well elocuted, high pitched voice said, "Comrades, I've learnt something very interesting today. There is such a thing as regime torture, and there is ANC torture, and regime torture is bad and ANC torture is good; thank you for enlightening me!" And he sat down.'[3]

In light of the ANC's subsequent displeasure with the TRC, followed by Deputy President Thabo Mbeki's criticism of it during the discussion in Parliament on the TRC report,[4] it is important to bear in mind Jordan's ironic comment, and we will need to return to it.

After a long discussion, according to Albie Sachs, someone stood up in the meeting and asked, 'What would my mother say?' Albie Sachs explains that the figure of 'my mother' 'represented an ordinary, decent, working-class woman, not sophisticated in politics but with a good heart and an honest understanding of people in the world, a person whose hard life experiences had promoted a natural sense of honour and integrity'. The person who raised this question went on to say that the 'mother' would consider the ANC to be completely mad. Here they were, examining with deep agony their own weaknesses and faults, but in the meantime those responsible for state violence, those accused of a crime against humanity, were apparently getting away scot free.[5]

It was at that moment that Kader Asmal stood up and said, 'The only answer is a truth commission which can look at the violations of human rights on all sides from whatever party.' It is not clear whether Albie Sachs is quoting Kader Asmal directly, but he continues, 'human rights are human rights, they belong to human beings, whoever they might be. Any torture or other violation has to be investigated on an even-handed basis across the board, not just by one political movement looking at itself, but at a national level with national resources and a national perspective.'[6]

But the major point that concerns us here is that the ANC decided not only to face up to the charges against them in terms of gross human rights violations, but also to enlarge the terrain so that all human rights violations committed in the past would come under the spotlight. It was this commitment by the leadership of the ANC which of course made it so much easier for the Truth and Reconciliation Commission to come about.

The fact that the ANC won the election by an overwhelming majority enabled them to push swiftly for the appointment of a truth commission. It also meant that they were willing and ready to commit financial resources so that the Commission could be conducted efficiently and effectively. There are many countries that have considered the same approach, but simply lacked the backing of the government and/or the financial resources which are necessary for such an undertaking. Such support enabled the Commission to hire premises, to have a very large travel budget enabling commissioners and staff to travel throughout South Africa, and of course to hire an adequate, professional staff which, at the height of the Commission's life, numbered more than 300 people.

The second favourable feature which gave both prominence and stature to the Commission was the person of Nelson Mandela. He is the embodiment of truth and reconciliation in his own life and person. I am still amazed at the remarkable lack of bitterness that he has consistently displayed. From the day of his release to the present time, he has focused on the need to come to terms with the past, but always with a readiness to forgive and to move on. It is not merely in the words that he uses, powerful as they are, but in his actions of reaching out to the very people who had put him in jail, who had kept him there, who had decimated his own party, who were responsible for torture and deprivation, detention without trial, mass removals, and so on. He stretched out a hand of reconciliation and friendship.

There are countless examples to illustrate this. One which had a bearing on our own work was told to Desmond Tutu and me during one of our breakfast meetings with him. Mandela told us that he had been approached by the head of his security unit, who informed him that he was going to release one of the security officers protecting him because it had been discovered that this particular young officer had been directly involved in the bombing of Khotso House, the headquarters of the South African Council of Churches, in 1988. Mandela told us that he had informed the head of security that he knew the young man, that he felt that this was something that had happened in the past, that he should be given another chance, and that he, the President, would not allow the officer to be removed from his personal protection unit. A couple of days later the young man came up to the President and began to thank him for having faith in him, but then broke down; he started weeping and expressed his appreciation to Mandela

[**261**]

for giving him a second chance. It is this spirit which infused the Commission itself and led Tutu on many occasions to echo it by stating, 'There is no one who is devoid of possible redemption. We cannot give up on anyone.'

The fact that the President supported the establishment of the Commission, and that he was directly involved in appointing the commissioners and selecting the chairperson and deputy chairperson, gave the Commission his personal stamp, not so much of authority but of compassion and support. Throughout the life of the Commission he insisted on its independence, but was never slow to defend it when it came under severe attack. I remember one occasion when General Bantu Holomisa testified before the Human Rights Violations Committee and made some very serious allegations about members of Mandela's Cabinet. Holomisa at the time was a senior member of the ANC and served as a deputy minister. Very soon after that he was sacked from his post and was strongly criticised by the ANC for his disloyalty. What troubled us was not that the President had decided to fire one of his own ministers and appoint someone in his place; that was his right and his business. What concerned us was that it might discourage other ANC people from coming to the Commission. I made a press statement to that effect. President Mandela replied quite strongly in his own press statement, saying that it was his right to appoint members of his Cabinet and deputy ministers, and that he didn't have to give any reason for doing so. I was pursued by the press to respond and I simply stated, publicly, that I would be writing to the President. Very soon afterwards I was asked if I had heard from him. I reiterated that I had written to him and was awaiting his reply. The next day I received a call from Mandela indicating that he had not received my letter, that he received over 1000 letters a day, and that the special group charged with the responsibility of passing on to him only those letters which were appropriate had erred in not putting my letter before him, because he personally wanted to see all communications from the TRC. He then asked if I would come and see him immediately.

I went that afternoon and told him that we as a Commission had never demanded that reasons should be disclosed for General Holomisa's dismissal, nor were we interested in interfering with the normal process of government or of party politics. I did say to him, and had stated this in my letter, that it would be 'unfortunate and of great concern to the Commission if General Holomisa's dismissal discouraged people from coming before the Commission'. I added that it would be helpful if it could be made clear that these events would in no way affect the support which the ANC had given the Commission thus far. His reply was that he agreed with what I had said and that he would welcome a public statement from me to that effect. I immediately issued a statement informing the public of our meeting; I said that there was no conflict between the President and the TRC, and that the ANC and the President in particular reaffirmed their request to all South Africans to cooperate in every possible way with the Commission. This is one of many examples of Mandela's fairness and his readiness to support the TRC.

He was enormously supportive of Tutu and me; he would take it upon himself to call us at times of extreme stress and would invite us to meet with him, usually over a very early breakfast, never to tell us what to do but to allow us to tell him what we were doing and what our concerns and anxieties were. There is no doubt that there were times when he disagreed with the actions we took. I think he hoped very much that we would simply ignore former State President P.W. Botha, and was not happy that we finally subpoenaed him. His own actions in telephoning Botha, urging him to appear before the Commission, offering to accompany him to the hearing, and discussing the matter with Botha's immediate family and friends are an indication of his total commitment to reconciliation rather than recrimination. But never did he intervene and suggest that we should stop what we were doing or do something that we were not doing. His persona reflected all that was good about the Commission – a deep horror of human rights violations, an anger at the horrific treatment

[263]

of so many hundreds and thousands of people, and yet a commitment to truth which would simultaneously work towards reconciliation. There are many countries whose representatives came to South Africa and many countries to which I travelled whose people were deeply envious, with good cause, of the fact that we had such a person as Nelson Mandela as the leader of our fledgling democracy, but no one appreciated him more than those of us who were in the cauldron of the Commission. It certainly assisted us enormously to do the work entrusted to us.

A third favourable condition was that the Commission was building on the successful political negotiations which had led to peaceful elections and the appointment of a democratic government. There was a sense that if we could succeed in the almost impossible task of bringing former enemies together at the table to negotiate a new Constitution and a new administration, then we could also try to deal with the past to help to consolidate that new democracy and to build a human rights culture, which until that time had never existed in South Africa.

A fourth feature was the existence of a very strong civil society. The fact that the overwhelming majority of South Africans had for so long been excluded from the parliamentary process and government at local, regional, and national level meant that there had been no point in forming political parties; a great deal of innovation, energy, and passion had therefore gone into the development of a strong civil society with one of the largest numbers of non-governmental organisations in the world. Some NGOs focused on legal issues, others on education, others on matters of religion, others were committed to caring for the victims of apartheid; they were involved in almost every area of life in the country. This meant that when the decision was made to have a truth commission in South Africa there were many who had had long experience working within NGOs who were available to serve on the Commission, as senior committee members and staff. It also meant that there was a cradle of support, and many

NGOs were directly involved in the numerous drafts of the Bill which finally became law.

After all, it was an NGO, Justice in Transition, that had created opportunities for conferences, workshops, discussion, and debate about the TRC, thus ensuring a very strong democratic process. Throughout the life of the Commission, a number of NGOs were directly involved, and many of them did outstanding work. But I think that the very busyness of the Commission made it impossible for ideal cooperation to exist, and the Commission itself must take some blame for not having had an even closer marriage with civil society. Some of this was by design, due to the belief that the Commission ought to keep a distance from various NGOs which had been very clearly anti-apartheid and therefore could be seen as being partial, for partiality was one thing the Commission sought to avoid. It is clear to me, however, that without the help of so many South Africans who had been directly involved in one NGO or another, the Commission would never have been able to achieve what it did.

A further factor which assisted the Commission was the interest of the international community in its initiative. Not only were many governments, institutions, organisations, and individuals willing to offer advice, but several governments responded to our request for assistance, with direct financial contributions to the President's Fund, the fund set up to help victims with reparation and rehabilitation. In addition, a number of countries agreed to second staff, mainly policemen and women who could assist our Investigative Unit in their huge task of following up the stories told by victims and perpetrators. They not only provided a far greater degree of impartiality, but accepted responsibility for their airfares, accommodation, and salaries, so that we could have more than sixty investigators from the international community and South Africa working throughout the life of the Commission.

Another condition which has earned both praise and criticism was the religious character of the Commission. I have already indicated that the overt religious character exemplified by Desmond Tutu, the ecclesiastical dress, the offering of prayers, and the use of Christian metaphor was both positively and negatively received. When the commissioners were first appointed, a special service of dedication was held in St George's Cathedral in Cape Town. While it was a Commission decision, it was certainly at Tutu's suggestion. At the service, which was attended by political, community, and religious leaders in large numbers, there was participation from Muslim and Jewish community leaders, who led the congregation in prayer. There were readings from sacred texts by members of the Buddhist, Christian, and Muslim communities. There was also a time of silence so that people from any religion, or no religion, could simply reflect on the challenge of searching for truth and working towards reconciliation. Each commissioner was called by name to move forward and receive a candle and an olive branch. Each candle was then lit from the large peace candle and the commissioners stood in a semi-circle facing the congregation. Following the order of service, the words of dedication were read by the congregation:

> We call upon you who have been appointed as commissioners of the Truth and Reconciliation Commission to acknowledge and recognise as a sacred trust the awesome responsibility that has been given to you.
>
> We pledge you our support and give you our blessing in the task that lies before you. And we ask that, in your work for truth and reconciliation, you will be guided by a wisdom greater than your own, a wisdom that knows and encompasses all truth.
>
> Will you dedicate yourselves to carry out the task that has been entrusted to you with the highest integrity, with impartiality and compassion for all, for the purpose of healing our nation?

The commissioners responded one by one, 'I will.' The service of dedication concluded with an address by President

Mandela, a response by Archbishop Tutu, and the singing of the national anthem, 'Nkosi Sikelel' iAfrika'.

I was somewhat critical of the general emphasis on the Christian faith, but there were many others who offered even sharper criticism than I did. Some felt that it excluded those from other faiths and thereby diminished the value of the Commission's work. Others who were of no particular faith felt embarrassed by the prayers and the singing of hymns and the occasional sermon at the end of the day's proceedings.

Against this criticism it must be noted that religion has played a dominant role in South African society. In the 1991 census more than 70 per cent of those who responded indicated some relationship with one or other of the major denominations of the Christian church. The remarkable growth of the so-called African independent churches is a further indication of the importance that religion plays in the day-to-day life of the overwhelming majority of people in South Africa. Of course it is true that there were many, particularly in the Dutch Reformed Church, who used religion to support the pernicious doctrine of apartheid and all its attendant horrors, but there were also many who, in the name of their Christian faith, opposed apartheid. Even when we as a Commission made no attempt to begin the day's proceeding with prayer or hymns, such action often came quite spontaneously from those who were attending.

One example occurred during a particularly difficult hearing in the small township of Boipatong. On 17 June 1992, forty-eight people, many of them women and children, had been massacred there. We therefore went there with a sense of foreboding. It was a cold and gloomy day, and people huddled together in the dilapidated hall in their hundreds. All the memories of that fateful night when so many people were killed in their homes came crowding back. The hall seemed full of ghosts. I stood outside in the minutes before the proceedings started. I was very nervous, as I think were my fellow commissioners. As we went into the hall we heard the sound of singing. Quite

[267]

spontaneously, those depressed, poor people of great sorrow and loss had started to sing a well-known hymn. It filled the hall, bringing a measure of light and hope, and was an indication of how religion, in the best sense of that word, had given an enormous amount of security, of comfort, to so many black people in particular who had had no place in the white man's scheme of things.

In other words, the search for truth, the truth-telling, was not something foreign. It was something that many, many people had experienced to a degree in their own churches and cathedrals. So, too, the commitment to reconciliation. This was a theme which resonated with so many of the victims who came to the Commission. Thus, even though there is certainly room for criticism, I think the religious nature of the wider South African community helped the Commission in its work. In a later chapter I will refer directly to the concept of *ubuntu*, which is very close to religious culture and African values.

A final factor which I think assisted the Commission enormously was the person of Archbishop Desmond Tutu. There is no doubt that the commissioners who were appointed had been publicly tested and tried, and each, in his or her own way, had a contribution to make, and made it. However, none of us was indispensable. There were other South Africans who could have served equally well on the Commission. With one exception. I don't think the Commission could have survived without the presence and person and leadership of Desmond Tutu. A Nobel Peace Prize laureate and a tireless fighter for justice in South Africa, he was a household name long before he came to the Commission. He had demonstrated in his life and work an enormous compassion for the underdog. His sense of humour, his twinkling eyes, his tiny stature, his presence rather than his performance, meant that he was and is an icon in South Africa. His choice by President Mandela was an inspired one. He assisted the Commission enormously in every possible way to become an instrument for healing, perhaps because he always saw himself and his colleagues on the Commission as wounded healers, not better than anyone else, not wiser than anyone else, but simply people who had been given a job to do and who cared very deeply for victims and perpetrators alike. As Antjie Krog puts it,

> The process is unthinkable without Tutu. Impossible. Whatever role others might play, it is Tutu who is the compass. He guides us in several ways, the most important of which is language. It is he who finds language for what is happening. And it is not the language of statements, news reports and submissions. It is language that shoots up like fire – wrought from a vision of where we must go and from a grip on where we are now. And it is this language that drags people along with the process.[7]

These, then, are the favourable conditions which assisted the Commission to do its work. There are, moreover, some unique features which distinguish the South African model from any other truth commission that has taken place anywhere else in the world, and we will consider these now.

IT IS IMPORTANT to emphasise that the Commission was unique in nature and form. It is the only truth commission which has included amnesty as part of its proceedings. Every other commission has happened after, or has resulted in, a general amnesty. When we consider the nature of the South African amnesty provisions later in this chapter, we will look more carefully at the comparisons and contrasts, but suffice to say now that the main distinctive feature of the South African Commission is that it included not only victim hearings but also amnesty hearings. This was a very ambitious undertaking, and not without considerable risk. When the decision was first taken not to declare a general amnesty, there were many who stated that very few people, if any, would seek amnesty in light of the conditions that were imposed. We ourselves as a Commission never anticipated that we would receive nearly 8000 applications.

In the words of the Promotion of National Unity and Reconciliation Act itself, the Commission was charged with firstly 'facilitating the granting of amnesty to persons who make full disclosure of all the relevant facts relating to acts associated with a political objective and comply with the requirements of the Act', and secondly 'establishing and making known the fate or whereabouts of victims and restoring the human and civil dignity of such victims by granting them an opportunity to relate their own accounts of the violations of which they are the victims and by recommending reparation measures in respect of them'. The holding in tension of these two objectives gave a unique character to the South African Commission.

It has already been emphasised that another distinctive feature of the South African Commission was the democratic process that was followed. We need not go into detail here, except to stress that the role of civil society, the churches, opposition parties, and the government in drawing up the Act ensured maximum participation. The several drafts which were freely available to any person or organisation, the number of workshops and conferences held throughout the country, the public hearings by the parliamentary Portfolio Committee on Justice, and the manner of selecting the commissioners resulted in widespread participation. The fact that it was not a presidential commission, appointed by the President, but a commission established by a democratically elected Parliament, is also unique.

Thirdly, the proceedings of the TRC, unlike the Argentinian, Chilean, and Salvadorean commissions, or any others, were not held behind closed doors, but were open to the public. This resulted in maximum transparency as well as remarkable participation by many in South Africa and beyond her borders. We debated for a fairly long time whether or not we should allow cameras into the open hearings. What concerned us was that the cameras might intimidate victims who were already facing the challenging task of telling very personal and horrifying stories. We consulted widely and in the end made the decision that cameras would be permitted, but that there would be a measure of control to protect victims from abuse. The general view among the NGOs which we consulted was that the stories the victims were going to tell were stories that the whole of South Africa needed to hear. I have no doubt that this was the right decision, and we were extremely well served by the media's coverage of the Commission and its hearings throughout its life. On the whole, the media were very cooperative, and the Commission was able to reach an agreement on guidelines for the presence of cameras at hearings. Overall, I think these guidelines met the criteria required for good media coverage but at the same time ensured dignity and sensitivity.

The judges serving on the Amnesty Committee were initially adamant that they would not allow cameras in their hearings. They were accustomed to the normal dignity of a court and felt that the cameras were a foreign intrusion and should not be allowed. I recall vividly the meeting Desmond Tutu and I had with the three judges at Bishopscourt to try to reach an agreement on this difficult issue. The Commission had already made its decision, but we felt that we had to give consideration to the judges and their concerns. We met over supper and we put our case as best we could. They were quite stubborn and were not inclined to change their minds. What I think decided the issue in the end was not the meeting of minds but the fact that there was a very important soccer match that Tutu wanted to watch on television, and so he finally said, 'The Commission has decided. We have listened very carefully to your objections, but they are overruled and now I must go upstairs!' He padded off in his tracksuit and left me with the three judges. One of them simply put his head on the table and bewailed, 'This is supposed to be a democracy!' After further discussion, feathers were smoothed and the judges grew a little calmer and agreed to allow, at least on an experimental basis, the use of cameras in the amnesty hearings. We never heard another word on the subject, and cameras were used in all public hearings.

I think what was appreciated by many, particularly in the rural areas of the country, was the opportunity to participate in four hours of live radio coverage every day, which, of course, included hearing the victims speak in their own language without commentary. Many people in South African can neither read nor write and depend on radio for information. Radio penetrates even the most remote areas of the country, which again meant that people who could never get to a public hearing, who knew very little about the finer details of the Commission, could listen and could participate in the hearings. There were regular features on all SABC news bulletins. There was also a regular forty-five-minute summary on television each Sunday evening, presented by Max du Preez. Tribute should be paid to Du Preez and his crew for the sensitive and professional way in which they covered the preceding week of TRC hearings. This particular programme attracted one of the largest audiences each week.

A further advantage of full media access to the public hearings was the generation of film and photographs far in excess of what has appeared in the media. This material will hopefully be used in the proposed archive for the benefit of scholars, academics, and interested parties for many, many years to come.

Finally, because the Commission decided not to hold public hearings in the major centres only, but travelled the length and breadth of the country, many people could attend these hearings and participate personally in the ritual which was being played out in the work of the Commission.

A fourth unique feature of the South African Commission was the powers granted to it by the Act. These included search and seizure as well as subpoena powers. The former was particularly important because we knew that long before the 1994 election, instructions had been given for the destruction of documents. This would have denied us access to a great deal of material and we were quite sure that certain state departments which were opposed to the new democracy would attempt to destroy even more material or at least confiscate it and spirit it away. We also appreciated that many civil servants would do their best to obstruct the Commission's work. The powers of search and seizure were therefore extremely useful and were used on a number of occasions, particularly with regard to the former South African Defence Force.

The power of subpoena was used more as a threat than anything else. We rarely had to make use of it, but in the case of P.W. Botha it was of vital importance that we had this power. As I have recounted in Chapter 6, the former State President not only ridiculed the Commission and dismissed it with contempt, but also made it very clear that he would not attend any of its hearings. After thinking long and hard, we decided to subpoena him. We served the subpoena on his lawyers, but it was dismissed out of hand. We had no alternative then but to cite him for contempt, and we handed the matter over to the Attorney-General in Cape Town. After careful consideration the Attorney-General decided to proceed against Botha, and he was tried in a small magistrate's court in the town of George. Although his appeal was upheld, the sight of the once very powerful head of the armed forces, who had virtually held life and death in his hands, having to appear in court was a strong reminder that no one is above the law. Without the power of subpoena we would not have been able to bring so powerful a leader to answer to the law of the land.

In most instances we started off by inviting people who we thought had information that was necessary for us to fulfil our objectives. In the majority of cases the people who were invited, particularly from the police and the military, agreed to attend the hearings, and those who initially declined and were warned about the possibility of a subpoena very quickly changed their minds.

A fifth unique feature was the extensive mandate which the Commission chose to adopt. Instead of confining itself to hearing individual victims of human rights violations and perpetrators applying for amnesty, the Commission decided to hold special hearings and institutional hearings, because of apartheid's impact on every

area of life. As has already been discussed, the major benefit of following this course of action was that it gave institutions and senior people in those institutions an opportunity to account for the role that they played in the
apartheid years, and also to point towards a new dispensation where institutions could be much more accountable
in terms of fundamental human rights.

Commenting on the Commission's five-volume
report, Albie Sachs states,

> It is not a dry governmental report, but a passionate
> memorial that resonates with the emotion of the
> hearings themselves. In addition it contains a serious
> reflection on how evil behaviour is condoned and
> spreads itself and on what institutional mechanisms
> and what kind of culture are necessary to prevent its
> reappearance.

He adds, 'That was one of the greatest objectives of the
Commission, not simply to let the pain come out but to explain the conditions that permitted gross injustice to flourish and so to ensure that these things did not happen again.'[8]

Some argue that by focusing on gross human rights
violations the Commission let off the hook the beneficiaries of apartheid, who were able to ascribe the responsibility for the worst of these atrocities to the police, the military, and the liberation movements. But this is to miss the
impact of the hearings, which made it impossible for the
beneficiaries to persist in denial. Furthermore, because
there were institutional and special hearings, many powerful people who complied with apartheid could not escape
their own accountability. As Albie Sachs puts it,

> Business, where were you? Business was making
> money, business was cooperating directly with the
> security forces, supplying explosives, trucks and in-
> formation. The press, where were you? There were
> some brave newspapers and wonderful journalists,
> but by and large the press was racist in its structure
> and fearful in its thinking. The legal profession, the

[274]

judges, where were you? We judges, old and new, had hard debates in our own ranks. The strongest view was that the judiciary had contributed substantially to injustice by enforcing racist laws and showing an unacceptable lack of vigilance in the face of accusations of torture and abuse.[9]

In the recommendations made by the Commission to government it is hoped that the lessons learnt from sins of omission and commission, not only by individuals, political parties, and state machinery, but also by institutions, will guide all of us into a more decent and just society.

A last point to stress is that after considerable discussion it was decided that the Commission would make public the names of the alleged perpetrators. This was in strong contrast to the Chilean and Argentinian commissions. Some names were mentioned in the Salvadorean Commission, but those people were immediately granted general amnesty by the President of that country when he received the report. We decided that the naming of perpetrators, while raising the risk of denying due process, was important in terms of accountability and acknowledgement. The main point was that we gave people who were named an opportunity to make their own response. We followed this procedure in the hearings, where we stressed that at the time of the hearing no findings were being made. Before we included names in the final report, we sent notices informing people of our intention, and invited them to respond in writing if they had any objections to being so named.

As ALREADY indicated, one of the most far-reaching unique features of the Commission was its approach to amnesty, and we will need to consider this in some detail.[10]

Amnesty was made possible in exchange for truth. The South African model was very different from one that grants general amnesty. Firstly, amnesty had to be applied for on an individual basis; there was no blanket amnesty.

[**275**]

Secondly, applicants for amnesty had to complete a pre-scribed form, published in the *Government Gazette*, which called for very detailed information relating to the specific human rights violations. Thirdly, applicants had to make a 'full disclosure' of their human rights violations in order to qualify for amnesty. Fourthly, in most instances applicants would appear before the Amnesty Committee, and these hearings would be open to the public. Fifthly, there was a time limit set in terms of the Act. Only those gross human rights violations committed in the period 1960 to 1994 would be considered for amnesty. Further-more, there was a specified period during which amnesty applications could be made, from the time of promulgation of the Act in December 1995 to 10 May 1997.

Only those acts which were demonstrably political would qualify. These were to be judged according to strict criteria:

> Whether a particular act, omission or offence… is an act associated with a political objective, shall be decided with reference to the following criteria:
> * The motive of the person who committed the act, omission or offence;
> * The context in which the act, omission or offence took place, and in particular whether the act, omis-sion or offence was committed in the course of or as part of a political uprising, disturbance or event, or in reaction thereto;
> * The legal and factual nature of the act, omission or offence, including the gravity of the act, omission or offence;
> * The object or objective of the act, omission or of-fence and in particular whether the act, omission or offence was primarily directed at a political opponent or State property or personnel or against private property or individuals;
> * Whether the act, omission or offence was commit-ted in the execution of an order of, or on behalf of, or with the approval of, the organisation,

institution, liberation movement or body of which the person who committed the act was a member, an agent or a supporter; and

- The relationship between the act, omission or offence and the political objective pursued, and in particular the directness and proximity of the relationship and the proportionality of the act, omission or offence to the objective pursued.

However, acts committed for the following reasons would not qualify:

- For personal gain: provided that an act, omission or offence by any person who acted and received money or anything of value as an informer of the State or a former state, political organisation or liberation movement, shall not be excluded only on the grounds of that person having received money or anything of value for his or her information; or
- Out of personal malice, ill-will or spite, directed against the victim of the acts committed.

The provision of amnesty to perpetrators of gross human rights has been and remains a source of heated debate and controversy in the international human rights community. South Africa, despite the uniqueness of its amnesty provisions, has not escaped this debate. Many prominent jurists and human rights activists are utterly opposed to any form of amnesty; this opposition arises in the main from the many cases of general or blanket amnesty which have been granted in countries that have moved from dictatorship to democracy. The following quotes sum up the contradiction in 'blanket amnesty':

'How can I ever have peace when every day I risk meeting my unpunished torturer in the neighbourhood?' – tortured ex-political prisoner, Argentina

'How is reconciliation possible when lies and denials are institutionalised by the responsible authorities?' – human rights activist, Chile

[277]

'No government can forgive, no commission can forgive. They don't know my pain. Only I can forgive and
I must know before I can forgive.' – widow testifying
at a TRC hearing in South Africa in 1997

I first came across the general antipathy towards amnesty
in human rights circles when I attended a conference in
Guatemala in 1995. There were representatives from many
parts of Latin America, and when I presented my paper on
the proposed South African Truth and Reconciliation Commission, underlining that a limited form of amnesty was
being envisaged, there was an outcry from many of those
present. There was little willingness to distinguish between one kind of amnesty and another; all amnesties were
anathema. Although I was surprised at the time, I realised
soon after that most of the sharp criticism of amnesties
came from people who had suffered themselves or who had
worked directly with victims of human rights violations
and had seen perpetrators getting away without any punishment or prosecution, or even accountability. The fact of
the matter is that many countries in Latin America in the
last decade or more have granted amnesties to perpetrators.
An obvious example was the granting of blanket amnesty
by General Pinochet in Chile in 1978. This was soon followed by the Brazilian military in 1979 and the Argentinian
military in 1983. Amnesties were granted by the civilian
government in Uruguay in 1986 and, following the report
of the United Nations Commission on the Truth for El
Salvador, by President Duarte in El Salvador a year later. I
share the view that general amnesties in relation to gross
human rights violations granted by previous regimes are
unacceptable and should not be respected by the international community.

While the South African amnesty model has been described as the most 'sophisticated amnesty undertaken in
modern times, if not in any time, for acts that constitute
violations of fundamental international human rights',[11] it
has nevertheless been the subject of considerable debate;
there are those who, while recognising the uniqueness of

the South African approach, still have reservations about whether or not prosecutions would have been the better course of action. Even those who acknowledge that South Africa made the correct decision do so with a measure of reluctance, largely, I think, because they are nervous that other societies may want to follow our example. Therefore there is usually a strong emphasis on the special circumstances which obtained in South Africa, and it is argued that the South African model cannot be imposed on other societies. There is merit in this argument, but it can be taken too far. There may well be countries in transition which could, with profit, learn from the South African approach.

At the same time, it should not be overlooked that many individuals and families who had themselves been victims of gross human rights violations, or who were relatives of those who had undergone harrowing experiences, expressed their unhappiness and anger at amnesty being granted and demanded their day in court. Their approach was very much along the lines of 'an eye for an eye'; they argued that perpetrators should not be allowed to get away with their crimes, that justice was being denied, and that the only source of comfort to them would be to see the perpetrators in court. We have already discussed the view of the Biko family and others, and a number of victims who attended amnesty hearings urged the Amnesty Committee not to grant amnesty because in their view the offences were such that the perpetrators ought to stand trial.

In a more formal sense, there has been a long, ongoing debate in the international human rights community, where the classic response to gross human rights violations is prosecution. This point is well articulated in a seminal article by Diane Orentlicher, entitled 'Settling Accounts: The Duty to Prosecute Human Rights Violations of a Prior Regime'.[12] Orentlicher argues that states have a duty to prosecute and that the international community should take action against states that refuse to do so. It is her contention that amnesty contradicts the rule of law and damages perceptions of justice which require that people be answerable for what they have done. Carlos Nino, replying to Orentlicher's unqualified stance, argues, 'Rather than a duty to prosecute, we should think of a duty to safeguard human rights and to prevent future violations by state officers or other parties.' Nino concedes that there are instances, which ought to be condemned by international law, in which certain governments violate human rights in a direct and active way, but he argues that 'The factual context may frustrate a government's effort to promote the prosecution of persons responsible for human rights abuses except at the risk of provoking further violence and a return to undemocratic rule.'[13] Despite this very important qualification to the dogmatic demand on states to prosecute, the model followed by international law remains that of the Nuremberg trials held in Germany in 1946, as well as the International War Crimes Tribunals set up in The Hague to prosecute human rights violators in the former Yugoslavia and Rwanda.[14] It should be noted, however, that these tribunals are the exception rather than the rule, because they were appointed to address extreme situations such as genocide. Usually the responsibility to act has fallen on the states concerned.

There is no doubt that there are a number of advantages to prosecutions for gross human rights violations. Firstly, prosecution establishes the general principle of retributive justice, that perpetrators cannot be allowed to get away with their actions, that there is a price to be paid, and that it is not only fair but right that accounts must be settled.

Secondly, prosecution reduces the possibility of private revenge. It is argued that if a state does not take action through its normal criminal justice system, then individuals and groups could be tempted to take the law into their own hands. In a fair trial, the accused is given an opportunity to defend him- or herself, to explain and even to justify his or her actions. It is no longer a private matter; it is part of the community process and part of the record and history of that community.

Thirdly, by its very nature a trial will give access to a considerable amount of information about the crimes that have been committed. This information is not merely subject to the whim of the accused or even of the prosecutor but is subject to strict cross-examination and rules of evidence which make the information quantitatively more reliable.

Fourthly, prosecution can educate the populace about the extent and definition of the violations committed. This form of education could serve as part of the record available to the general public and to an extent could be a strong signal that those who transgress will not go unpunished. Thus, prosecutions are a guard against impunity and the risk of future violations.

Fifthly, prosecution has the potential to grant closure to both perpetrator and victim. When the final decision is reached, there is a sense of relief; the matter has been dealt with and the victims can now get on with their lives. There is, therefore, a return to normality and a facing up to the consequences of the acts committed.

All the above advantages of prosecutions must be taken very seriously, particularly in light of the need to restrict impunity. However, trials and prosecutions are not above criticism. In the case of widespread gross human rights violations over a long period, a critical question is, whom do you prosecute? Even in the Nuremberg trials it was impossible to deal with any except some of the very top echelon of Nazi leaders, and many escaped the net. In the subsequent trials that were held, 85 882 cases were brought to trial in a country where hundreds of thousands of people had been directly involved in the Holocaust (it is worth noting that from these more than 85 000 cases, only 7000 convictions were secured).[15] In more recent times, more than 9000 people disappeared in Argentina during the military dictatorship. It was impossible for the criminal justice system to place everybody on trial; instead, the state decided to prosecute only a handful of leaders of the junta.

An even greater problem surrounds the attempts to deal with perpetrators in the former Yugoslavia. Very few of the large number of perpetrators will be prosecuted.

Inevitably, arbitrary decisions have to be made, and it becomes impossible for even an international war crimes tribunal to try everyone directly involved in 'ethnic cleansing' or genocide. How fair then is the process? What about those who are not tried, and how just is the system for the few who are put on trial? Are they the scapegoats who must bear the sins of the many? The most relevant case is that of Rwanda. It is estimated that over 800 000 people were killed there in three months. Thousands of people have since been arrested, but such was the nature of the butchery that took place, which was not by aerial bombing or massive instruments of war but largely by one individual killing another, that at the very least more than half a million people ought to have been arrested. More than 100 000 people have been incarcerated in very crude and inadequate conditions, and have been awaiting trial for more than five years. It is clearly going to be impossible to have a fair, meaningful trial for every one of them. Thus, ironically, the search for justice is shot through with injustice.

There are cynics who argue that if one has enough money one can get away with almost anything. It is true that wealthier perpetrators have access to excellent legal representation, and it is an extremely difficult task for the prosecution to produce irrefutable evidence leading to their conviction. Thus, in many court cases the charge is not proven, which leaves the victim frustrated and often angry.

It is also a fact that in a criminal court it is always difficult and very often impossible to achieve accountability beyond that of the individual or individuals who are on trial. In other words, it is difficult in a trial for account to be taken of those institutions which created the climate, and in some instances gave the orders, for human rights violations to take place.

In a criminal trial, punishment is seen as the final word. But in a deeply divided society, punishment cannot be the final word if healing and reconciliation are to be achieved, because the human rights violations have taken place within a particular context. It can be argued that when abnormal situations become so constant as to make them seem almost normal, abnormal measures have to be used, because the law on its own cannot be expected to deal with the consequences of large-scale massacres, crimes against humanity, genocide, 'ethnic cleansing', and the like.

In the last decade, an alternative to criminal trials which has been used in many parts of the world is what has come to be known as a truth commission.[16] While there are wide differences between the various truth commissions around the world, the main theme is the attempt to get at the truth of the past in relation to gross human rights violations and to record the findings so that they are publicly available. However, as has been emphasised, the South African Truth and Reconciliation Commission is the only commission that has incorporated amnesty within its framework, and it is this commission that is the focus of our study.

The South African Commission deliberately avoided granting a general or blanket amnesty; instead, amnesty was exchanged for truth. It is worth noting why South Africa chose this route rather than prosecutions. As has already been discussed, the transition from oppression to democracy was achieved not through a violent overthrowing of the state but through negotiations between the state and the liberation movements. Therefore a compromise was inevitable, and one of those compromises was the provision for amnesty. Judge Marvin Frankel's comment in this regard is particularly helpful and instructive:

> The call to punish human rights criminals can present complex and agonising problems that have no single or simple solution. While the debate over the Nuremberg trials still goes on, that episode – trials of war criminals of a defeated nation – was simplicity itself as compared to the subtle and dangerous issues that can divide a country when it undertakes to punish its own violators.
>
> A nation divided during a repressive regime does not emerge suddenly united when the time of

repression has passed. The human rights criminals are fellow citizens, living alongside everyone else, and they may be very powerful and dangerous. If the army and the police have been the agencies of terror, the soldiers and the cops aren't going to turn overnight into paragons of respect for human rights. Their numbers and their expert management of deadly weapons remain significant facts of life... The soldiers and police may be biding their time, waiting and conspiring to return to power. They may be seeking to keep or win sympathisers in the population at large. If they are treated too harshly – or if the net of punishment is cast too widely – there may be a backlash that plays into their hands. But their victims cannot simply forgive and forget.

These problems are not abstract generalities. They describe tough realities in more than a dozen countries. If, as we hope, more nations are freed from regimes of terror, similar problems will continue to arise.

Since the situations vary, the nature of the problems varies from place to place.[17]

It is worth referring again to the postamble to the Constitution, which incorporates the agreement reached between the two major parties, the African National Congress and the National Party. The emphasis from the outset was on reconciliation in order to achieve unity:

In order to advance such reconciliation and reconstruction, amnesty shall be granted in respect of acts, omissions and offences associated with political objectives and committed in the course of the conflicts of the past. To this end, Parliament under this Constitution shall adopt a law determining a firm cut-off date, which shall be a date after 8 October 1990 and before 6 December 1993, and providing for the mechanisms, criteria and procedures, including tribunals, if any, through which such amnesty shall be dealt with at any time after the law has been passed.

With this new Constitution and these commitments, we, the people of South Africa, open a new
chapter in the history of our country.

Another important reason for offering amnesty as part
of the TRC was the threat by the security forces that they
would not defend the peaceful process of the election and
indeed would make a peaceful election impossible. Bearing
in mind that the security forces had protected the negotiation process, without which the transition to democracy
would have come to a dismal halt, it was felt that the
threat had to be taken very seriously and that amnesty
would have to be provided for.

There are, however, a number of other factors which
would have made prosecutions in the South African context very difficult. Firstly, the very nature of apartheid was
all-pervasive, and it would have been extremely difficult to
know whom to prosecute and whom not to prosecute. If all
those responsible for the policy and the implementation of
apartheid were to be prosecuted, the numbers would have
been in the hundreds of thousands and the criminal justice
system would have been strained far beyond its limits.
Secondly, a decision would have had to be made about
what time span the prosecutions would cover, because
apartheid had been in existence for decades. Thirdly, the
resources available to the state were extremely limited in
terms of human skills, and, because the overwhelming
majority of officers of the courts, including magistrates
and judges, were white, prosecutions may have resulted in
a large number of resignations or at least a lack of cooperation. Fourthly, the criminal justice system had relied very
heavily on harassment and torture in order to secure convictions, and the entire police force would need to be reformed before they could be entrusted with the responsibility of maintaining due process when bringing people to
trial. Fifthly, the costs of trials would have taken resources
away from essential social development. The demand on
the fiscus for housing, education, health care, job creation,
and so on meant that virtually all social services would

[285]

have had to be put on hold if a huge outlay were to be expended on long and protracted trials.

I think it has to be accepted that it is no simple matter to obtain a conviction in a court of law. If there had been trials in South Africa there is a strong possibility that the majority of those accused would have been found not guilty because of a lack of skilful prosecutors and a lack of evidence.

Now that we have looked at the advantages and disadvantages of prosecution, let us consider briefly what the South African TRC model can and does offer over the benefits of prosecution that have been referred to above. Firstly, insofar as information is concerned, both qualitatively and quantitatively, the TRC has been able to secure information far beyond what any trial could have elicited. The information is contextual, exploring people's motives. The victim hearings in particular meant that thousands of those who had endured human rights violations could, in their own languages, in their own styles, at their own pace, and without cross-examination, tell what happened to them. In the case of perpetrators, because amnesty was conditional on telling the truth, full disclosure was part of the demand. In the confessions offered by those applying for amnesty, very wide and detailed information was made available, not only to the Amnesty Committee but to the whole of South Africa, because of the public nature of the hearings. The silence was broken and at least a measure of truth was revealed.

The Constitutional Court noted how the amnesty provision would deal with the problem of getting to the truth and dealing with the hurt of the past:

> The Act seeks to redress this massive problem by
> encouraging these survivors and the dependents of
> the tortured and the wounded, the maimed and the
> dead, to unburden their grief publicly, to receive the
> collective recognition of a new nation that they
> were wronged, and crucially, to help them to discover

what did in truth happen to their loved ones, where and under what circumstances it did happen, and who was responsible. That truth, which the victims of repression seek so desperately to know, is, in the circumstances, much more likely to be forthcoming if those responsible for such monstrous misdeeds are encouraged to disclose the whole truth with the incentive that they will not receive the punishment which they undoubtedly deserve if they do. Without that incentive there is nothing to encourage such persons to make the disclosures and to reveal the truth which persons in the positions of the applicants so desperately desire. With that incentive, what might unfold are objectives fundamental to the ethos of a new constitutional order.[18]

It is understandable that many are suspicious of any commission labeled a 'truth commission'. It has ominous, Orwellian overtones which put people on their guard. Antjie Krog, in her inimitable way, puts it well when she tells of her own difficulty with the word 'truth':

> The word 'truth' makes me uncomfortable. The word 'truth' still trips the tongue. I hesitate at the word. I am not used to using it. Even when I type it, it ends up as either 'turth' or 'trth'. I have never bedded that word in a poem. I prefer the word 'lie'. The moment the lie raises its head I smell blood. Because it is there ... where the truth is closest.'[19]

Despite the understandable reservation regarding the search for truth, it is a fact that a commitment to history involves a search for an objective truth. The Commission therefore unapologetically set out to try to reach a public and official acknowledgement of what happened during the apartheid era. If only to counter the distorted and partial recording of history in South Africa it was necessary that there should be an accurate record of the period under review. Colin Bundy reminds us that 'The establishment of the objective truth is part of the struggle for the control of history. It plays a central role in society's redefinition of itself.'[20] Bundy argues that the provision of accurate and authentic facts discredits the distorted version of history provided by the previous regime and prevents that version from being perpetuated in school and university textbooks and in people's memories. The truth that emerged in the stories told by victims and perpetrators challenged the myths, the lies, and the half-truths conveyed and distributed at every level by the former regime. I am unashamed in my belief that, in the South African context, history has to be rewritten and that the TRC has made a significant contribution to this end. This is not to argue for one group's truth to be replaced by another, but rather for the enlarging of the boundaries, a testing of different claims, so that a fuller and more precise picture begins to emerge.

In its final report, the Truth and Reconciliation Commission distinguishes between four kinds of truth. The first is objective or factual or forensic truth. The Act which governed the work of the TRC required it to 'Prepare a comprehensive report which sets out its activities and findings based on factual and objective information and evidence collected or received by it or placed at its disposal.'

This requirement operated at two levels. Firstly, the Commission was required to make public findings on particular incidents with regard to specific people – concerning what happened to whom, where, when, and how, and who was involved. In order to fulfil this mandate, the Commission adopted an inclusive policy of verification and corroboration to ensure that findings were based on accurate and factual information. The Investigative Unit, which had more than sixty trained investigators at its disposal, did a yeoman task in seeking to corroborate and verify testimonies, whether they were from victims or perpetrators. Secondly, the Commission was responsible for findings on contexts, causes, and patterns of violations. It was this search for patterns underlying gross violations of human rights that engaged the Commission at a very broad and deep level.

While the Commission, through its Investigative Unit, its database, and its Research Department, attempted to do all of the above with the highest degree of efficiency possible, there were always limits in the search for truth and even in truth-telling. While I think Michael Ignatieff underestimates the influence and impact of some truth commissions, nevertheless his comments are salutary:

> All that a truth commission can achieve is to reduce the number of lies that can be circulated unchallenged in public discourse. In Argentina, its work has made it impossible to claim, for example, that the military did not throw half-dead victims in the sea from helicopters. In Chile, it is no longer permissible to assert in public that the Pinochet regime did not dispatch thousands of entirely innocent people.[21]

It follows that in the South African context it is no longer possible for so many people to claim that 'they did not know'. It has become impossible to deny that the practice of torture by the state security forces was not systematic and widespread, to claim that only a few 'rotten eggs' or 'bad apples' committed gross violations of human rights. It is also impossible to claim any longer that the accounts of gross human rights violations in ANC camps are merely the consequence of state disinformation.

The second kind of truth is personal or narrative truth. Through the telling of their own stories, both victims and perpetrators have given meaning to their multi-layered experiences of the South African story. Through the media these personal truths have been communicated to the broader public. Oral tradition has been a central feature of the Commission's process. Explicit in the Act is an affirmation of the healing potential of truth-telling. One of the objectives of the TRC was to 'restore the human and civil dignity of victims by granting them an opportunity to relate their own accounts of the violations of which they were the victims'.

It is important to underline that the stories we listened to didn't come to us as 'arguments' or claims as if in a court of law. They were often heart-wrenching, conveying unique insights into the pain of our past. To listen to one man relate how his wife and baby were cruelly murdered is much more powerful and moving than statistics which describe a massacre involving many victims. The conflict of the past is no longer a question of numbers and incidents; the human face has shown itself, and the horror of murder and torture is painfully real.

By facilitating the telling of 'stories', the TRC not only helped uncover the existing facts about past abuses but assisted in the creation of 'narrative truth' – the personal story told by a witness. This enabled the Commission to contribute to the process of reconciliation by ensuring that the silence shrouding individual subjective experiences had at last been broken, by 'restoring memory and humanity'.[22] A great deal of this material has been recorded in the Commission's report, but together with the report must be seen the transcripts of the hearings, individual statements, a mountain of press clippings, and video material. This material will be an indispensable resource for historians and other academics and researchers for years to come.

The third kind of truth is social or 'dialogical' truth. Albie Sachs, even before the Commission began its work, talked about 'microscope truth' and 'dialogical truth': 'The first is factual and verifiable and can be documented and proved. Dialogical truth, on the other hand, is social truth, truth of experience that is established through interaction, discussion and debate.'[23]

People from all walks of life were involved in the TRC process, including the faith community, the former South African Defence Force, NGOs, the media, the legal and health sectors, and political parties – and obviously the wider South African population through the media and public scrutiny. What I am emphasising here is that almost as important as the process of establishing the truth was the process of acquiring it. The process of dialogue involved transparency, democracy, and participation as the basis of affirming human dignity and integrity.

Finally, the fourth kind of truth is healing and restorative truth. The Act required the TRC to look back to the past and to look to the future. The truth which the Commission was required to establish had to contribute to the reparation of the damage inflicted in the past and to the prevention of it ever happening again in the future. But for healing to be a possibility, knowledge in itself is not enough. Knowledge must be accompanied by acknowledgement, an acceptance of accountability. To acknowledge publicly that thousands of South Africans have paid a very high price for the attainment of democracy affirms the human dignity of the victims and survivors and is an integral part of the healing of the South African society.

In summary, one of the major advantages of a truth commission committed to discovering the truth is that it involves what could be termed inclusive truth-telling. The TRC had a specific and limited mandate, but its attempt to help restore the moral order must be seen in the context of social and economic transformation. These are two sides of a single coin. Truth-telling is a critical part of this transformation which challenges myths, half-truths, denials, and lies. It was when listening to ordinary people relating their experiences under apartheid that one was able to understand the magnitude and horror of a system which damaged and destroyed so many over so long a period. It also reminded the Commission forcibly of the maldistribution of assets and the legacy of oppression which makes transformation so difficult. Therefore the work of the Commission was not a one-off event, a kind of cure-all. The process has only started and has to continue, and the public and private sectors have to accept leadership in this regard. In particular, those who benefited from the long years of discrimination and inequity have a particular responsibility.

This means that dealing creatively and honestly with the past isn't a question of laying the blame on the

military, the police, the politicians, the liberation movements, but also on the beneficiaries of apartheid, who were
largely white. In searching for the truth, political accountability is important, but apartheid could never have survived without being buttressed by those who benefited
from it.

There are several other differences between a trial and a
truth commission. The first concerns the quality and
quantity of information and access to the truth. In an article in *Africa News*, Babu Ayindo makes a contrast between
the International War Crimes Tribunal for Rwanda held in
Arusha, Tanzania, and the Truth and Reconciliation Commission in South Africa. He observes that in the Tribunal
witnesses were brought into a foreign world where legal
representatives were dressed in Western attire, and the
proceedings were formal and followed the tradition, both
in procedure and in dress, of a court of law. He contrasts
this to the South African Commission, where witnesses
were embraced and supported throughout the proceedings,
where there was time and space to 'weep and lament'.[24]

Ayindo also observes that the witnesses at the Tribunal
seemed to be on trial rather than telling their stories. The
stories had to be consistent with what they had told the
investigators. The witnesses had to restrict themselves to
what they had seen and heard and not describe what they
had felt. There was little opportunity for them to embark
on a journey of recovery. The witnesses desperately needed
to know why their loved ones had been maimed or killed.
Answers to such questions, which are vital in the healing
process, are not what a tribunal or a court of law deals with.
Ayindo argues further that while he has a respect for history
he believes that a fixation on the past will not foster a
healthy future for Rwanda. In his view, the Tribunal stub-
bornly focused on the past. The South African TRC, he
writes, seemed more focused on the future 'so that the dark
history illuminates the present and guides the future'. He
concludes that the TRC, despite its apparent lack of a comprehensive recovery programme for apartheid victims and

its occasional theatrics, 'serves as a more assured path for the restoration of relationships and the peace of posterity'.[25]

Secondly, the point was made earlier that a benefit of prosecution is to limit the likelihood of revenge being taken by victims in the absence of state action. This may well be true, but the same advantage could be attributed to a truth commission which performs its work in public so that victims can at least see that the truth is being sought and in many instances told, and that a measure of accountability is realised. It is noteworthy that there was not a single case of vengeance taken by any victim or family of a victim in response to the grotesque stories told by security force members and other perpetrators. As far as I am aware, no perpetrators received even a threatening telephone call after giving public evidence of killing or torturing people. Although we had a witness protection programme, there was never any serious threat to those who received such protection. Furthermore, the public shaming of the perpetrators was at least as effective in this regard as conviction in a criminal trial. It was no easy thing for perpetrators to describe their evil deeds with family, friends, and society looking on.

Thirdly, as has already been mentioned, in a trial the accused participates, detailing the violations and sometimes even justifying them. A truth commission, however, affords an opportunity not only for perpetrators but also for victims to tell their own stories. In a court case this is very often through the mouth of the legal representative, and indeed in many instances even those on trial do not have to take the witness stand themselves to account for the charges against them. In a truth commission the application is completed by the person seeking amnesty, and the applicant faces the Amnesty Committee in public and can be cross-examined by legal representatives of the victims and by the victims themselves. Therefore, victims and perpetrators appear together in a truth commission. This is a ritual, if you like, played out with all the actors present and speaking for themselves, and can be part of the healing process.

[293]

Fourthly, in terms of upholding, enforcing, and strengthening the rule of law, in amnesty hearings the emphasis is not only on obtaining knowledge but also on acknowledgement. This is at the very heart of the applicant's story. While the applicant may argue that he or she was under orders, he or she describes the events as a participant in the atrocities committed. He or she accepts accountability. But his or her actions are also put in context. The applicant very often describes the training he or she received as a soldier or as a member of the police force, the orders that were given, the chain of command, the process which involved the violations of human rights. Therefore the rule of law is strengthened in an amnesty hearing, as it is in a trial.

Fifthly, I would suggest that a truth commission is more able and better equipped to provide education for the general public about human rights than is a court of law or a tribunal. In South Africa the amnesty hearings were open, and were made available to the general public through the media. A five-volume report outlining the TRC's findings was presented to President Mandela and to Parliament and is freely available to all. This report contains not only the information that was gathered but also a large number of recommendations. A key recommendation is that the report should be made available to the general public not merely in its final form but also through paraphrasing, editing, through video and audio cassettes, to schools and tertiary institutions, non-governmental organisations and churches, workshops and conferences. Built into the South African model is a process of education which far exceeds that of a war crimes tribunal or a normal trial. The life and legacy of the Commission are geared towards education of the general populace.

Sixthly, a truth commission is far better able to ensure reparation and rehabilitation for victims. The Act governing the South African Truth and Reconciliation Commission required that a special reparation committee had to devise a policy of reparation and rehabilitation and to make it available to Parliament for a final decision. It

should be stressed, however, that reparation and even rehabilitation can begin to take place only when the silence
is broken and people are empowered to tell their own
stories for the very first time. This is probably the greatest
reparation and rehabilitation anyone can be offered. The
Reparation and Rehabilitation Committee worked out an
elaborate and extensive programme, details of which can
be found in the final report.[26]

Seventhly, the holding of trials certainly can and does
act as a powerful deterrent. But a truth commission of the
South African model allows for the disclosure of names,
which is rare among truth commissions and certainly reminds its very wide audience of the consequences of not
applying for amnesty. In other words, amnesty has a short
shelf life. There was an end date and if people had not applied by that time they could not qualify for amnesty. This
resulted in a certain urgency. Furthermore, the Commission recommended in its report that those who had not
applied for amnesty and who were strongly suspected
of committing human rights violations ought to be
prosecuted.

Finally, what a truth commission can do, and what the
South African Commission certainly attempted to do, is to
seek not only knowledge, acknowledgement, and accountability, but also restoration. One of the primary motiva-
tions for and objectives of the Commission was to bring
about a measure of healing to a very deeply divided society
in which many citizens have been severely hurt. The search
for reconciliation and restoration is in my view an integral
part of coming to terms with the past. It is not enough simply to punish perpetrators. Not only is broader reconciliation and restoration necessary and morally right, but it also
places the focus not so much on the past but on the present
and the future. We come to terms with the past not to point
a finger or to engage in a witch hunt but to bring about
accountability and to try to restore a community which for
scores of years has been broken. The South African Truth
and Reconciliation Commission unashamedly sought to
advance the process of reconciliation, despite all the

problems inherent in that task. The act of amnesty involves pardoning offences, bringing the perpetrator back into society, and helping to restore to victim and perpetrator the dignity which both have lost. In this regard a truth commission, especially in the South African context, was not 'second best'. As Aryeh Neier, president of the Open Society Institute in New York, puts it,

> Indeed, in the specific circumstances of South Africa, it is not easy to quarrel with Archbishop Tutu when he contends that the Truth and Reconciliation Commission process of providing amnesty in exchange for acknowledgement and full disclosure, with prosecution as an alternative for those who do not acknowledge and disclose, served the country better than a process that would have relied solely on prosecutions.[27]

The question of reconciliation will be dealt with in a later chapter, but suffice to make the point that a truth commission has a greater potential for achieving this than prosecution and trials.

Even in the case of genocide or 'ethnic cleansing', where punishment is necessitated by the very nature of the crimes committed, there ought to be scope for additional strategies so that we do not rely only on trials and tribunals. Certainly we must take very seriously the gravity and extent of the violations, and accountability is demanded. But that is not the last word. In a deeply divided society like Bosnia, for example, perhaps there should not only be the War Crimes Tribunal in The Hague, but consideration should be given to a form of truth commission which would not include amnesty but would create an opportunity to stake out a common truth where truth is in dispute. Attempts could also be made to bridge the wide cleavages which exist between Serbs, Croats, and Muslims in that region. Certainly the War Crimes Tribunal on its own will not achieve this and may even exacerbate existing hostilities between opposing groups. Serious consideration should be given by the international community, and above all by the people of Bosnia themselves, to the introduction of additional mechanisms to bring about a measure of unity and healing in that country.

The same could be said of Rwanda, which remains at great risk, not only because of the instability of Burundi and the Democratic Republic of Congo, but also because of continuing internal strife and friction. Trials on their own will not bring about a restored society, and the possibility of a truth and reconciliation commission should not be ruled out.

The South African Commission, with its amnesty provisions, meets international obligations in a number of important respects. It has consistently sought to establish truth not only about victims but also about perpetrators. It has stressed the need for the development of a human rights culture and has made a number of recommendations in order to try to bring that about. A comprehensive policy of reparation is now before Parliament and awaits implementation. The emphasis in the amnesty process has been on full disclosure, and the very fact that some applicants have been denied amnesty strengthens the integrity of the amnesty process. It can be argued very persuasively that the Commission prevented further violence, and this is a major international obligation.

The decision against amnesia on the one hand and trials on the other was not merely a choice by one particular party or group but arose from a very careful parliamentary process and involved all the major political parties. The nature of apartheid crimes was so extreme and so pervasive that it would have been impossible to draw a line as to who should be prosecuted and who should not. Finally, the emphasis is not merely on the past but very much on seeking reconciliation and healing in the new dispensation.

It is clear that South Africa did not transgress any of the demands of international law, as embodied in the Geneva Conventions. It is true that the Conventions refer to 'grave breaches' which constitute war crimes for which states have a duty to prosecute. It is also a fact that South Africa signed the Geneva Conventions in 1948. But the Conventions apply only to international conflicts, and

[297]

there is no obligation for states to prosecute these 'breaches' when no international conflict exists.

Many commentators have described the South African conflict as a low-level civil war or as an 'undeclared war'. But neither the state nor the ANC ever formally described the conflict as a state of war.

In an unpublished MA dissertation, Cherry Annette Hill refers to Article 1(4) of the First Protocol of the Geneva Conventions, which 'recognises the struggles of national liberation movements or specifies that they are to be considered subject to the international laws of armed conflict'.[28] But any technical obligation upon South Africa to prosecute those guilty of gross human rights violations falls away as far as the period of the TRC is concerned, because South Africa signed the additional Protocol of the Geneva Conventions only in 1995.

It is my view, therefore, that the South African decision not to prosecute does not in any respect put it in breach of international law. It should be borne in mind, however, that although South Africa said no to prosecutions it also said no to amnesia, and the TRC, through its public hearings, its findings, and its final report, went beyond the accumulation of knowledge to acknowledgement and accountability of human rights violations which had so grievously harmed the majority of South Africans.

It is very important to bear in mind the Commission's determination to avoid impunity. In Volume 5 of our report, we emphasise the need for accountability in the following terms:

> Where amnesty has not been sought or has been denied, prosecution should be considered where evidence exists that an individual has committed a gross human rights violation. In this regard, the Commission will make available to the appropriate authorities information in its possession concerning serious allegations against individuals (excluding privileged information such as that contained in

amnesty applications). Consideration must be given to imposing a time limit on such prosecutions.

Attorneys-General must pay rigorous attention to the prosecution of members of the South African Police Service (SAPS) who are found to have assaulted, tortured and/or killed persons in their care.

In order to avoid a culture of impunity and to entrench the rule of law, the granting of general amnesty in whatever guise should be resisted.[29]

9

'Artificial even-handedness'? Responses to the TRC report

THE POINT HAS been made several times that the Truth and Reconciliation Commission was subject to considerable criticism before and during its life. When its five-volume report was published at the end of October 1998, it received considerable acclaim both in South Africa and internationally. But there were also negative comments, sometimes from the most unexpected sources. A great deal of the criticism arose out of ignorance, political bias, and from people simply being uninformed.

An example of the kind of criticism which the Commission endured throughout its life was that by Thami Mazwai. Mazwai is a well-known journalist and editor who has recently been appointed to the board of the SABC. His ill-informed comments therefore take on serious overtones. The best example I can give is to quote from a letter which I wrote to *Business Day* on 15 May 1998 responding to some of the criticisms which he offered on a regular basis:

> Dear Sir, Thami Mazwai argues (as does the leader of the National Party!) that the TRC 'should pack up and not even complete its remaining two months'. He bases this absurd demand on gross inaccuracies and by flying in the face of the facts.
> 1 He states, 'Dumisa Ntsebeza was accused of driving the St James Church getaway car'. WRONG. The attack in question was the Heidelberg Tavern;

2 He states, 'Because of these allegations Dumisa
Ntsebeza was asked to leave'. WRONG. He was
never asked to leave, nor was he suspended;

3 He states, 'A committee has been appointed to write
a book on the TRC'. WRONG. The Report of the
Commission is being written by the Commission. A
group of journalists and writers was appointed (three
black and one white) to produce (in consultation
with the TRC) an edited, single-volume version of a
five-volume report to make it more accessible to all
South Africans. I did not appoint the group. When I
received Mazwai's letter stating that he and three
colleagues ought to be mandated to appoint the writing team, I told him it would be considered by the
Commission. It was and the Commission ruled that
existing contracts extended to the four journalists
should be honoured. This was communicated to
Mazwai by letter. The Commission consults widely
but reserves the right to make its own decisions
without being dictated to by any individual or group;

4 He states, 'The Amnesty Committee is bent on
punishing the PAC by refusing its people amnesty'.
WRONG. The Amnesty Committee is bound by the
Act and is headed up by judges of the Supreme
Court. The Amnesty Committee does not grant
amnesty when whites kill blacks and refuse
amnesty when blacks kill whites. The Committee
has refused amnesty in several matters in which
white applicants killed black people. Two examples
should suffice: the four Van Straaten brothers who
murdered two black men were denied amnesty because their crime was not viewed as political. In the
Van Eyk and Gerber matter, the applicants were denied amnesty for the killing of a black security
guard because the crime was not considered political. In short, the Amnesty Committee does not consider the race of the applicant as a factor in its decisions to grant amnesty – it applies its mind in terms
of the requirements set out in the Act;

5 He states 'Tutu and Boraine fell over themselves to
challenge the granting of amnesty to ANC leaders'.
WRONG. The Commission unanimously voted to
take its own Amnesty Committee to court. It was a
painful decision but it did so because it believed
that the criteria laid down in the Act were not ad-
hered to. The Commission should be commended
not denigrated for carrying out its mandate. The
ANC did NOT oppose the court order and two
judges of the Supreme Court upheld the opinion
of the Commission.

Finally, Mazwai accused me of being the 'Archangel
of the country's liberals' (he should read the message
of the Archangel as recounted in the New Testament!). This label is amusing, bearing in mind that
I am regularly attacked by so-called liberals. I don't
like labels and I am not about to attach one to
Mazwai. Readers of his column can draw their own
conclusions. One thing is clear – when it comes to
responsible journalism he is no angel!

There were, however, a number of more serious criticisms
which will have to be responded to as the Commission is
evaluated by supporters and critics alike.[1] Several books
have been written on the Commission and I have little
doubt that many more will be written in due course. The
debate will continue for a long time. This is not the place
to respond to criticism and praise; I will deal only with the
immediate responses by F.W. de Klerk and the ANC, and
the criticisms surrounding the issue of reparation.

IN ACCORDANCE with its laid-down procedures, the Commission sent notices to those persons, institutions, and
organisations that were mentioned adversely in its report,
informing them that a particular finding had been made
against them. They were given twenty-one days in which to
reply in writing if they wished to take issue with the findings. More than 400 notices were sent out, and it would

have been impossible to grant interviews to all of those concerned. That is why we stipulated written responses only. We received several written representations and these were dealt with on their merits.

F.W. de Klerk was incensed when he received the Commission's findings about his role. The findings we sent him read as follows:

> Mr F.W. de Klerk presided as head of the former government in the capacity of State President during the period 1989 to 1994. On 14 May 1997, he testified before the Commission in his capacity as head of the former government and as leader of the National Party. In his submissions, Mr de Klerk stated that neither he nor his colleagues in cabinet and the State Security Council authorised or instructed the commission of unlawful acts.
>
> Given the centrality of former State President de Klerk to the transformation of South African politics and his role in the 1990–94 period, the Commission has made the following finding:
>
> • The Commission finds that, when Mr de Klerk testified before the Commission on 21 August 1996 and 14 May 1997, he knew and had been informed by his Minister of Law and Order and the Commissioner of Police that they had been authorised by former State President P.W. Botha to bomb Khotso House.
>
> • The Commission finds that the bombing of Khotso House constitutes a gross violation of human rights.
>
> • The Commission finds that former State President F.W. de Klerk displayed a lack of candour in that he omitted to take the Commission into his confidence and/or to inform the Commission of what he knew, despite being under a duty to do so.
>
> • The Commission finds that Mr de Klerk failed to make full disclosure of gross violations of human rights committed by senior members of government and senior members of the SAP, despite being given the opportunity to do so.

- The Commission finds that his failure to do so constitutes material non-disclosure, rendering him an accessory to the commission of gross violations of human rights.
- The Commission finds Mr de Klerk morally accountable for concealing this from the country when, as the executive head of government, he was under obligation to disclose the truth known to him.

We sent these findings to De Klerk on 1 September 1998 for his response, as required by law. He brought an urgent action, asking the Cape High Court to forbid the findings against him from being included in the Commission's report, which was about to be published. De Klerk had responded to the Commission timeously, but our response to him was that we saw no reason to change the findings; that is why he went to court. The hearing took place on the morning of Wednesday 28 October 1998, the day before the report was due to be published, with Judge Edwin King presiding. In order not to delay the publication of the report, an agreement was reached between the Commission and De Klerk's lawyers, which Judge King made an order of the court. The agreement was that the TRC would make no finding on De Klerk and the hearing relating to the dispute over the intended findings was postponed to 4 March 1999.

The outcome of the court action taken by De Klerk was that the Commission had to remove in one way or another the page containing its findings on the former State President. Charles Villa-Vicencio, director of research, was told on the Wednesday morning that the page would have to be removed. He nearly had a heart attack. The books had already been loaded onto a truck and were ready to be transported to Pretoria. Fortunately, the truck had not left Cape Town on time, because the security personnel were late. All copies of Volume 5 were removed and the so-called 'finding page' excised and reprinted. We insisted, however, that a black square be printed to indicate that something had been removed. The new page was then stitched manually into all 500 volumes. By 2:30 p.m. on the Wednesday the page was complete, but as Villa-Vicencio noted at the time, 'We had to put interleaves behind the new pages because the ink still needed time to dry.'[2]

Ever since the court action, the two parties have been negotiating in an attempt to reach a compromise in order to make the court case unnecessary. At the time of writing, the negotiations are still under way. The TRC submitted a revised version of the findings to De Klerk's lawyers, but they were still not satisfied and in return offered a further amended version. This was not acceptable to the Commission, and De Klerk's lawyers have been informed of this. If the parties cannot agree, the court case will proceed. It must be pointed out, however, that De Klerk responded to the Commission's findings within the stipulated time limit.

THE FINAL MEETING of the Commission prior to the handing over of its five-volume report was held in Cape Town on 26 October, a mere two days before that report was due to be handed over. It was a very special meeting signalling that two and a half years of challenging and traumatic experiences had come to an end. The Amnesty Committee would continue to hear applications, but the bulk of the work had been completed. The record of the life, experience, and findings of the Commission was with the printers. In a couple of days the report would be handed to President Mandela at a public ceremony. We had given considerable thought to how this final act should take place. One of the key decisions we made was that a representative group of victims would take pride of place on this occasion. Cabinet ministers and a large number of dignitaries would witness the handing-over ceremony, which would, in keeping with the spirit of the Commission, be open to the media. There would be singing, and speeches from Mandela and Tutu. It was imagined that the ceremony would be a joyous occasion bringing to an end a very painful and demanding process which had involved thousands of victims and perpetrators and which had touched the lives of most South Africans.

Prior to the public handing-over ceremony, in the intimacy of the Commission boardroom, there would be an opportunity for us to take leave of each other, to share final experiences, to make last-minute plans about the handing-over ceremony, and to ensure that the ongoing work of the Amnesty Committee would be supported by adequate staffing and by representatives from the Commission. Certainly that is what I expected. But that was far from the reality of a meeting which threatened to split the Commission from top to bottom. The key issue was the dispute between the Commission and the ANC over the findings against the party. The ANC had insisted on meeting with the Commission face-to-face; correspondence had been entered into on this matter and they had been told on a number of occasions, both verbally and in writing, that their request was out of the question, and they had been urged to send in their written submissions. They did not do so timeously and in fact failed to meet not only one but two deadlines.

I thought that the matter had been amicably resolved and I was therefore thunderstruck when Fazel Randera proposed that we should consider granting the ANC an audience. The fact that we were a mere two days away from the handing-over ceremony in Pretoria and that the report was already being bound and had to be delivered to Pretoria was not the most worrying feature. What concerned me was that we would be granting the ANC an opportunity denied to everyone else. If we followed this course of action it would be ammunition for those critics who had accused the Commission of being biased in favour of the ANC. We had tried to play by the rules and I thought that everyone else should do so as well. As I listened to the debate, which seemed to go on interminably, I had no doubt that the Commission faced its most severe challenge. To succumb to ANC pressure would be to surrender our fiercely guarded integrity. We would be more than a laughing stock; we would shoot ourselves in the heart, and the Commission would be mortally wounded.

I was astonished that several of my colleagues supported the proposal and were apparently oblivious to the consequences. What was ultimately at stake was party loyalty on the one hand and even-handedness on the other. Thus far the latter had prevailed, but in the end some were wavering. Clearly, some of the commissioners were under immense pressure. After a protracted and heated debate, the matter was put to the vote. To my great relief the proposal was narrowly rejected. But unfortunately this was not the end of the story. The Commission had by now belatedly received the ANC's submission. I for one hadn't seen it and I don't think any of the other commissioners had had sight of it either. Nevertheless, it was proposed that we consider their representations, even at this late stage. After another long debate, tempers were becoming frayed; there was considerable argument and pleading before the matter was again put to the vote. My heart was in my mouth when the vote was deadlocked at seven for and seven against. Tutu, however, used his casting vote and the motion was defeated. Without fail, in many critical moments experienced by the Commission, Tutu always came through. The integrity of the Commission was the driving force for him.

As I reflected on the debate, I realised that more than one of my colleagues must have been in close contact with the ANC over this period and that they saw it as their responsibility to try to persuade the Commission to bend to pressure from the party. Despite the narrowness of the vote I was very proud that the Commission had not buckled under the stresses and strains of competing loyalties.

In order to respond to the reaction of the ANC it will be helpful to list the relevant findings made by the TRC. It is important, however, to view the findings on the ANC against the background of the Commission's primary finding, which reads as follows:

[307]

The predominant portion of gross violations of human rights was committed by the former state through its security and law-enforcement agencies.

Moreover, the South African state in the period from the late 1970s to early 1990s became involved in activities of a criminal nature when, amongst other things, it knowingly planned, undertook, condoned and covered up the commission of unlawful acts, including the extra-judicial killings of political opponents and others, inside and outside South Africa.

In pursuit of these unlawful activities, the state acted in collusion with certain other political group-ings, most notably the Inkatha Freedom Party (IFP).[3]

What were the Commission's findings on the ANC? Because of the furore which flowed from these findings, I want to give them in full. Firstly, there were findings concerning violations committed in the course of the armed struggle:

While it was ANC policy that the loss of civilian life should be 'avoided', there were instances where members of MK perpetrated gross violations of human rights in that the distinction between military and civilian targets was blurred in certain armed actions, such as the 1983 Church Street bombing of the SAAF headquarters, resulting in gross violations of human rights through civilian injury and loss of life.

In the course of the armed struggle there were instances where members of MK conducted unplanned military operations using their own discretion, and, without adequate control and supervision at an operational level, determined targets for attack outside of official policy guidelines. While recognising that such operations were frequently undertaken in retaliation for raids by the former South African government into neighbouring countries, such unplanned operations nonetheless often resulted in civilian injury and loss of life, amounting to gross violations of human rights.

[308]

The 1985 Amanzimtoti Shopping Centre bombing
is regarded by the Commission in this light.

In the course of the armed struggle the ANC,
through MK, planned and undertook military operations which, though intended for military or security
force targets, sometimes went awry for a variety of
reasons, including poor intelligence and reconnais-
sance. The consequences of these cases, such as the
Magoo's Bar and Durban Esplanade bombings, were
gross violations of human rights in respect of the
injuries to and loss of lives of civilians.

While the Commission acknowledges the ANC's
submission that the former South African government had itself by the mid-1980s blurred the distinction between military and 'soft' targets by declaring
border areas 'military zones' where farmers were
trained and equipped to operate as an extension of
military structures, it finds that the ANC's landmine
campaign in the period 1985–87 in the rural areas of
the northern and eastern Transvaal cannot be condoned, in that it resulted in gross violations of the
human rights of civilians, including farm labourers
and children, who were killed or injured. The ANC
is held accountable for such gross violations of
human rights.

Individuals who defected to the state and became
informers and/or members who became state witnesses in political trials and/or became askaris were
often labelled by the ANC as collaborators and regarded as legitimate targets to be killed. The Commission does not condone the legitimisation of such
individuals as military targets and finds that the
extra-judicial killings of such individuals constituted
gross violations of human rights.

The Commission finds that, in the 1980s in particular, a number of gross violations of human rights were
perpetrated not by direct members of the ANC or
those operating under its formal command, but by

civilians who saw themselves as ANC supporters. In this regard, the Commission finds that the ANC is morally and politically accountable for creating a climate in which such supporters believed their actions to be legitimate and carried out within the broad parameters of a 'people's war' as enunciated by the ANC.[4]

Secondly, the Commission made certain findings on gross violations of human rights committed by the ANC in exile:

> The Commission has studied the reports of the Stuart, Skweyiya, Sachs and Motsuenyane commissions of inquiry appointed by the ANC, as well as that of the Douglas Commission, into various forms of human rights abuse in exile. It also took evidence both from alleged victims of abuse in the camps and from those in positions of authority. The Commission has also heard evidence from the ANC on persons executed in exile for a variety of different offences.
>
> On the basis of the evidence available to it, the Commission finds that the ANC, and particularly its military structures responsible for the treatment and welfare of those in its camps, were guilty of gross violations of human rights in certain circumstances and against two categories of individuals, namely suspected 'enemy agents' and mutineers.
>
> The Commission finds that suspected 'agents' were routinely subjected to torture and other forms of severe ill treatment and that there were cases of such individuals being charged and convicted by tribunals without proper attention to due process, sentenced to death and executed. The Commission finds that the human rights of the individuals so affected were grossly violated. Likewise, the Commission finds that the failure to communicate properly with the families of such victims constituted callous and insensitive conduct.

The Commission also finds that all so-called muti-
neers who were executed after conviction by military
tribunal, irrespective of whether they were afforded
proper legal representation and due process or not,
suffered a gross violation of their human rights.

With regard to allegations of torture and severe ill
treatment, the Commission finds that although torture was not within ANC policy, the security department of the ANC routinely used torture to extract
information and confessions from those being held
in camps, particularly in the period 1979–89. The
Commission has taken note of the various forms of
torture detailed by the Motsuenyane Commission,
namely the deliberate infliction of pain, severe ill
treatment in the form of detention in solitary
confinement, and the deliberate withholding of food
and water and/or medical care, and finds that they
amounted to gross violations of human rights.

The Commission further finds that adequate steps
were not taken in good time against those responsible
for such violations.[5]

Thirdly, the Commission made findings concerning gross
violations of human rights committed by the ANC after its
unbanning:

While the Commission accepts that the violent conflict which consumed the country in the post-1990
period was neither initiated by nor in the interests of
the ANC, the ANC must nonetheless account for the
many hundreds of people killed or injured by its members in the conflict. While the ANC leadership has argued that its members were acting in self-defence, it is
the Commission's view that at times the conflict assumed local dynamics in which proactive revenge attacks were carried out by both sides. This situation
was exacerbated by high levels of political intolerance
among all parties, including the ANC. Further, the
Commission contends that the leadership should have

been aware of the consequences of training and arming members of SDUs in a volatile situation in which they had little control over the actions of such members.

The Commission therefore finds that in the period 1990–94, the ANC was responsible for:

- Killing, assaults and attacks on political opponents including members of the IFP, PAC, Azapo and the SAP;
- Contributing to a spiral of violence in the country through the creation and arming of self-defence units (SDUs). Whilst acknowledging that it was not the policy of the ANC to attack and kill political opponents, the Commission finds that in the absence of adequate command structures and in the context of widespread state-sponsored or -directed violence and a climate of political intolerance, SDU members often 'took the law into their own hands' and committed gross violations of human rights.

The Commission takes note that the political leadership of the African National Congress and the command structure of Umkhonto we Sizwe has accepted political and moral responsibility for all the actions of its members in the period 1960–94 and therefore finds that the leadership of the ANC and MK must take responsibility, and be accountable, for all gross violations of human rights perpetrated by its membership and cadres in the mandate period.[6]

The Commission also made certain findings on the United Democratic Front (UDF). They are as follows:

The Commission acknowledges that it was not the policy of the UDF to attack and kill political opponents, but finds that members and supporters of UDF affiliate organisations often committed gross violations of human rights in the context of widespread state-sponsored or -directed violence and a climate of political intolerance.

[312]

The UDF facilitated such gross violations of human rights in that its leaders, office-bearers and members, through their campaigns, public statements and speeches, acted in a manner which helped create a climate in which members of affiliated organisations believed that they were morally justified in taking unlawful action against state structures, individual members of state organisations and persons perceived as supporters of the state and its structures. Further, in its endorsement and promotion of the 'toyi-toyi', slogans and songs that encouraged and/or eulogised violent actions, the UDF created a climate in which such actions were considered legitimate. Inasmuch as the state is held accountable for the use of language in speeches and slogans, so too must the mass democratic and liberation movements be held accountable.

The Commission finds that factors referred to in the paragraph above led to widespread excesses, abuses and gross violations of human rights by supporters and members of organisations affiliated to the UDF. These actions include:

- The killing (often by means of 'necklacing'), attempted killing, and severe ill treatment of political opponents, members of state structures such as black local authorities and the SAP, and the burning and destruction of homes and properties;
- The violent enforcement of work stay aways and boycotts of, among others, private and public transport and private retail shops, leading to killing, attempted killing, and severe ill treatment;
- Political intolerance resulting in violent inter-organisational conflict with Azapo and the IFP, among others;

The UDF and its leadership:
- Failed to exert the political and moral authority available to it to stop the practices outlined above, despite the fact that such practices were frequently

[**313**]

associated with official UDF campaigns such as consumer boycotts or campaigns against black local authorities. In particular, the UDF and its leadership failed to use the full extent of such authority to bring an end to the practice of necklacing, committed in many instances by its members or supporters.

- Failed to take appropriately strong or robust steps or measures to prevent, discourage, restrain and inhibit its affiliates and supporters from becoming involved in action leading to gross violations of human rights, as referred to above;
- Failed to exert sanctions or disciplinary action on member organisations whose members were involved in the gross violations of human rights described above, or failed to urge such member organisations to take appropriate actions against their members.

The Commission notes that the political leadership of the UDF has accepted political and moral responsibility for the actions of its members. Accordingly the UDF is accountable for the gross violations of human rights committed in its name and as a consequence of its failure to take the steps referred to above.[7]

The day after the fateful Commission meeting, I flew to Johannesburg, only to receive the news that the ANC had taken the Commission to court. They had applied for an interdict to prevent the publication of those sections of the report which contained the findings on the ANC. I can only surmise that Fazel Randera and some of my other colleagues had been in regular contact with the ANC and knew that the party would take legal action against the Commission if we refused to consider their representations. Hence their very determined attempt to prevent this from taking place. It was an unsavoury end to a long and demanding process.

Early on the morning of 29 October we gathered in Pretoria to await the court's decision. Tutu was so disillusioned and saddened that he remained in his hotel room. At about 10 a.m., a mere two hours before the handing-over ceremony was to begin, representatives of the media were becoming increasingly restive and asked me to make a statement about the state of play and what our intentions were. I climbed onto a chair and explained that we were in telephonic contact with our staff at the court in Cape Town and were awaiting the decision. I stated that we were confident that the decision would be in our favour and that the handing-over ceremony would take place as scheduled. I must admit that I was not nearly as confident as I appeared. I was terrified and had no idea which way the decision would go. If the judge ruled against the Commission, the report could still have been handed to the President but the ceremony would have been private. All our preparations for making the report simultaneously available to the whole world via the Internet and to the hundreds of journalists outside would have been aborted. I was in the middle of answering questions from the media when someone came up to me and whispered, 'We've won!' I nearly fell off the chair in sheer relief and joy and quickly announced that the court had dismissed the ANC's application with costs.

The ceremony, understandably, was a muted affair. Many of us felt dejected and depressed at the turn of events, and even Mandela was not his usual exuberant self. But even in the midst of a less than joyful occasion I had a lump in my throat and tears in my eyes as I watched the victims and survivors file in and take up their seats in the front rows. I recognised so many of them and my mind went back to the public hearings; I heard again their simple but powerful stories and knew that nothing could take away from them the restored dignity and the breaking of the silence which had made them prisoners for so long.

Tutu, as I have mentioned, was deeply saddened, and this certainly showed in his demeanour during the handing over of the five volumes to Mandela. Earlier, reacting immediately to the news that the ANC had taken the TRC to court, he had expressed his feelings very strongly: 'I have struggled against tyranny. I didn't do that in order to substitute another, and I believe if there is tyranny and an abuse of power then let them know that I will oppose it with every fibre of my being.'[8]

On reflection, this statement may have been too harsh and may have given the impression that the TRC took exception to people taking us to court. The Commission had been taken to court many times during its life, and, while some of those actions were frivolous and partial, we never complained or denied people the right to take this step. At a press conference held immediately after the handing-over ceremony, some of us, including Yasmin Sooka and Dumisa Ntsebeza, after consultation with Tutu, made a public statement to the effect that the ANC had had every right to take the TRC to court, that our concern was not so much a legal one but a concern that a party which had supported the formation of the Commission had sought to muzzle its findings, and that we felt that this reflected very badly on the ANC. This I think was what Tutu was driving at. I think the ANC's argument was wrong, and that as matters unfolded this became clear, although there are very prominent members of the ANC who still maintain that their cause was right and their decision to take us to court was the correct one.

The media made a great deal of the fact that Mandela was receiving the TRC report while his deputy, Thabo Mbeki, had been directly involved in the decision to take the Commission to court. In the weekend following the release of the report, Mandela made a major statement which was viewed by the media as a 'bombshell'. In so many words, Mandela reiterated that the ANC had been fighting a just war, but he added that in the course of fighting that just war it had committed gross violations of human rights. He went on to say, 'No-one can deny that because some people died in our camps and that is what the TRC said.'[9]

The problem arose from the contrast between the statements made by Mandela on the one hand and by other prominent members of the ANC on the other. For example, ANC spokesperson Ronnie Mamoepa was quoted in the *Sunday Times* as saying, 'No member of the ANC can ever concur with the scurrilous attempts to criminalise the liberation struggle by characterising the heroic struggles of the people of South Africa ... as gross human rights violations.'[10] Thabo Mbeki stated, 'We should avoid the danger whereby concentrating on these particular and exceptional acts of the liberation movements, which could be deemed as constituting gross human rights violations, we convey the impression that the struggle for liberation was itself a gross violation of human rights.'[11] Mandela explained his apparent difference of opinion with Mbeki during an address to community leaders in Kimberley. He stated that he and Mbeki had differed because, whereas he had seen a full copy of the report, Mbeki had seen only part of it:

> It is not easy for me to be questioned about whether there is a difference between me and Deputy President Mbeki on the publishing of the report. There is no doubt that Thabo Mbeki had good intentions and may have seen extracts of the report. I am convinced my approach was correct and on the basis that he may not have seen the report he responded on the information he had.

Mandela said, 'No doubt if the report had been read perhaps the response of the ANC would have been totally different.' He concluded, 'As a man who read the report and set up the Commission and has the highest respect not only for Archbishop Desmond Tutu but all the Commissioners, I am satisfied they have done a good job even if there are imperfections. There is no clash.'[12]

Matters were complicated by the fact that Kgalema Motlanthe, secretary-general of the ANC, stated that any suggestion of division over the TRC was 'a figment of the journalist's imagination'. Regarding the report's findings on the ANC he said, 'Most of the violations said to have been committed by us were survival techniques which should have been taken in an historical context. We will continue to ensure that the glorious part of our struggle should be not depicted in such a way that our future generations will be ashamed of it.'[13] Even worse, ANC National

Executive Committee member S'bu Ndebele said, referring to the execution of informers, 'To equate the actions of
[Eugene] de Kock or [Adriaan] Vlok with planting a landmine to liberate the country is unheard of and contrary to
the Geneva Convention. Murder has never been a shame;
it's recognised like that in the Convention.'[14]

The only good thing to come out of this dispute was
the consternation of those who had accused the Commission of bias and who had confidently predicted that the
report would exonerate or excuse the ANC and vilify the
National Party. The ANC's criticism of the report gave
the Commission enormous credibility and made its
right-wing critics look very foolish indeed.

I had hoped that Mandela's strong statement of support would have ended the divisions between the ANC and
the TRC, but they were to resurface very powerfully in a
parliamentary debate on 25 February 1999. This was the
occasion when the Commission's report was formally
presented to Parliament.

Introducing the debate, the Speaker of Parliament,
Frene Ginwala, referred to the publication of the TRC report in 1998 as 'a seminal event in our country's transition
to democracy'.[15] She reported to the members of the joint
sitting that immediately upon receiving the report from
the TRC the President had handed it over to the Presiding
Officers of Parliament, thereby acknowledging the pivotal
role that Parliament had to play in taking the next steps in
addressing the report and its recommendations. The Presiding Officers had called the joint sitting; the President
had agreed to attend and to open the debate.

In his speech, President Mandela made it very clear
that the debate on the TRC should not simply last for an
allocated time set aside in Parliament but should continue
as a protracted effort by the whole nation. He went on
to say,

> Above all, the TRC interim report is a call to
> action and as we put our thoughts together on the
> challenges ahead we need to remind ourselves that ...

reconciliation was the fundamental objective of the people's struggle to set up a government based on the will of the people and to build a South Africa which indeed belongs to all.

He reminded Parliament that the major reason for setting up the TRC was the quest for reconciliation, and that the task ahead was to take forward the work and findings of the Commission so as to continue the search for reconciliation. Mandela expressed his appreciation formally to the TRC:

> I would like once again to record our appreciation of the Commission, Archbishop Desmond Tutu, his fellow Commissioners, their staff and field workers for the service they have rendered to the country and for the continuing work of the Amnesty Committee. Their dedication to a difficult and painful task has helped us through a historic stage in our journey towards a better society... They made it possible for tens of thousands of South Africans to make known the inhumanities they had endured. They made it possible for others to disclose their part in inflicting or acquiescing to those inhumanities by acts of commission or omission.

Mandela then paid tribute to those who had helped the Commission:

> To all the men and women who helped the Commission in these ways, we owe a debt of gratitude for their courage and honesty. They have helped us begin to change from what we were towards the nation we aspire to be. For all these reasons I had no hesitation in accepting the report of the TRC presented to me in October last year, with all its imperfections.

Despite his affirmation of the report, Mandela referred to the criticism of the TRC by some of his colleagues: that it was guilty of 'an artificial even-handedness that seemed to place those fighting a just war alongside those whom

they opposed and who defended an inhuman system.'[16]
This evaluation is more in line with the criticism made by
the ANC secretary-general and Thabo Mbeki when the
report was first published.

Thabo Mbeki, in his capacity as executive Deputy
President, followed President Mandela in the debate.
He, too, placed on record the ANC's appreciation to the
Commission

> for the work it has done in various areas. These include
> the discovery and exposure of the truth with regard to
> many instances of gross violations of human rights;
> the tracing of missing persons including their graves;
> their encouragement of reconciliation between perpe-
> trators and victims of violations of human rights; the
> cultivation of a spirit of remorse among those who did
> wrong; and the identification of some of the people
> who are entitled to receive reparation.

He acknowledged the recommendations made by the Commission and committed government to following these up.

Mbeki very quickly moved into a more critical mode,
however. He began by stating that the ANC had tried to
meet with the Commission to discuss its findings against
the party, but that 'The TRC decided for reasons we still do
not know to this day not to meet us.' This statement is regrettable in light of the procedures set out not only for the
ANC but for all who received notification of adverse findings. These procedures had been debated publicly, and
everyone knew that their responses had to be in writing
and that the Commission could not play favourites. Mbeki
stated that what the ANC had wanted to discuss with the
TRC was 'such obviously important matters as the definition of the concept of gross violations of human rights in
the context of a war situation and other issues relating to
war and peace and the human conduct of warfare'. He
added,

> One of the central matters at issue was and remains
> the erroneous determination of various actions of our

liberation movements as gross violations of human rights, including the general implication that any and all military activity which results in the loss of civilian lives constitutes a gross violation of human rights ... The net effect of these findings is to delegitimise or criminalise a significant part of the struggle of our people for liberation and to detract from the commitment made in our Constitution to honour those who suffered for justice and freedom in our land.

Mbeki continued,

Indeed, it could also be said that the erroneous logic followed by the TRC, which was contrary even to the Geneva Convention and Protocols governing the conduct of warfare, would result in the characterisation of all irregular wars of liberation as tantamount to a gross violation of human rights. We cannot accept such a conclusion, nor will the millions of people who joined in the struggle to end the system of apartheid.[17]

This is a very tough statement and must be answered.

The first point to make is that the major thrust of the TRC report is a strong condemnation of the apartheid regime, and all other criticism should be seen in the context of this indictment. The Commission could not be any clearer than it is when it states in its report,

Any analysis of human rights violations which occurred during the conflicts of the past and any attempt to prevent a recurrence of such violations must take cognisance of the fact that at the heart of the conflict stood an illegal, oppressive and inhuman system imposed on the majority of South Africans without their consent.[18]

In other words, although the Commission, rightly in my judgement, insisted on moral even-handedness, nowhere in the report does it suggest that there is a moral equation between the liberation movements and the apartheid state. The Commission accepted that apartheid was a crime against humanity, and therefore that 'those who fought against the system of apartheid were clearly fighting for a just cause, and those who sought to uphold and sustain apartheid cannot be morally equated with those who sought to remove and oppose it'. However, in our distinction between justice of war and justice in war we made it very clear that 'the strict prohibitions against torture and abduction and the grave wrong of killing and injuring defenceless people, civilians and soldiers "out of combat" required the Commission to conclude that not all acts in war could be regarded as morally or legally legitimate even where the cause was just'.[19]

In reaching this conclusion, the Commission was following international law and international conventions. The Geneva Conventions are quite clear when they allow for the possibility of a 'just war', but they are equally clear that if gross human rights violations are committed during the course of this just war, then those who engage in such actions must accept moral and political responsibility for them. For this reason, we concluded that there was sufficient evidence from the ANC's submissions as well as those from victims both inside and outside South Africa that such violations had taken place and that we were justified in holding the ANC, and the PAC, responsible morally and politically for them.

I can understand the difficulties faced by liberation movements fighting an unconventional war against a powerful state. I can understand the harm and death and injury that was caused and could be caused by the work of state informers. But the crisp question that must be answered by the ANC is, is it an offence when the state tortures or kills an opponent of that state? And can the same offence of torture or killing be condoned because the cause of the liberation movements is just? This, in my view, is something that simply cannot be accepted. Torture is torture, no matter who commits that torture and who the tortured is; murder is murder, whether it is committed by the state or by a liberation movement. Pallo Jordan's ironic comment referred to in an earlier chapter bears repeating:

'Comrades, I've learnt something very interesting today. There is such a thing as regime torture, and there is ANC torture, and regime torture is bad and ANC torture is good; thank you for enlightening me!'

It should also be stated very clearly that the Commission's findings that the liberation movements committed gross human rights violations do not criminalise the entire liberation struggle; this is a point that we made very carefully and consistently.

In sum, I find it extraordinary that someone of the calibre of Thabo Mbeki could describe the Commission's findings on the ANC as 'artificial even-handedness'. There is nothing artificial about moral even-handedness. According to many victims inside South Africa and in ANC camps, serious violations took place. And the ANC itself is on record as admitting that this was so.

André du Toit, in an unpublished paper entitled 'Perpetrator Findings as Artificial Even-Handedness? The TRC's Contested Judgements of Moral and Political Accountability for Gross Human Rights Violations', points out cogently and powerfully that, in its submissions to the Commission, the ANC acknowledged that gross human rights violations had taken place in its armed struggle against the apartheid state. 'In sum,' he argues,

> the ANC's submission to the TRC was marked by a number of profound ambivalences: it set out to provide the framework of just war theory as the theoretical basis for the TRC's investigations, but also participated in and subjected itself to the TRC process by appearing before the Commission; it announced that as a just cause the ANC's armed struggle was not subject to the TRC's investigation and its conduct could not constitute gross violations of human rights, but then itself proceeded to provide a review and discussion in just those terms; it claimed that the ANC consistently maintained a principled approach to the conduct of the armed struggle while providing ample evidence of the slippages in this principled commit-

ment occurring at certain crucial junctures; it admitted that mistakes were made but in its discussion of such cases essentially attempted to rationalise these.[20]

Du Toit recalls that there had been an earlier confrontation between the TRC and the ANC in 1997, when it appeared that the ANC had decided that it was not necessary for any of their members to apply for amnesty. Tutu took a very strong stand and even threatened to resign as chairperson of the TRC on this issue. The ANC's National Executive Committee issued a statement which in the end helped to resolve the stand-off between the Commission and the party; in that statement it claimed that 'in the case of the ANC neither it nor any of its members were ever involved in any crime against humanity. On the contrary, the ANC was involved in a just and heroic struggle. However, where during the course of that struggle violations of human rights did occur these must be acknowledged.'[21] Du Toit concludes his argument by asking the question,

> Did the ANC have reason to be outraged by the TRC's findings and to charge that the Commission had 'grossly misdirected itself' in the interpretation of its mandate? More specifically, could it be argued that by making such findings of gross violations concerning the ANC and its conduct of the armed struggle next to its 'primary' findings on the political atrocities committed by the apartheid state and its functionaries, the TRC in following its even-handed approach in the end made the fatal error of 'a moral equation' between the inherent evils of apartheid and the just cause of the liberation struggle?[22]

Du Toit's answer is an unequivocal no. 'In committing itself to the TRC process,' he argues, 'the ANC had started on a path which logically and morally led to this outcome.' He goes further:

> One could even argue that, difficult as it might be for the ANC leadership to stomach the TRC's verdict, it was very much in its own interest as well as that of the

[324]

TRC process to do so since that would enable it to take the moral high ground and focus the attention squarely on the TRC's 'primary' findings as a devastating and systematic indictment of the apartheid state.[23]

How do we explain the response of people of the calibre of Mbeki and other ANC leaders to the findings of the Commission? It would be easy and trite to suggest that he and his advisers had not read the report, or that having read it they hadn't really understood the delicate balance held by the TRC in relation to state crimes and human rights violations committed by the ANC and other liberation movements. It would be equally superficial to dismiss their criticisms as evidence of a growing authoritarianism or arrogance as a movement which could do no wrong. How then can we understand the continued and passionate negativity of Mbeki and others towards the Commission?

One possible answer is to look back into history and in particular to look at the attitude and actions of the Allied forces at the end of the Second World War. The Allies, very understandably, believed they were locked in combat with an evil monster. Hitler, his Nazi cohorts, and his Japanese allies were, in the minds of most people, the personification of evil. At all costs the Allies had to stop this diabolical force in its tracks. They believed they were fighting a just war to prevent darkness from spreading over the world, fighting for freedom from servitude under the German nightmare. Right was on the side of the Allies. At the Nuremberg trials, theirs was a victor's justice and the only people on trial were those who were responsible for the invasion and occupation of other countries, and in particular those who were responsible for the horror of the Holocaust. It was the struggle between good and evil. When a few voices were raised and questions asked about the bombing of Dresden in Germany, the fire-bombing of Tokyo, and in particular the atom bombs dropped on Hiroshima and Nagasaki with their ghastly consequences and thousands of civilian deaths, the world leaders and the generals were simply unable to accept this criticism. It was

[325]

as if they said, how dare you point a finger at us? We were not the antagonists. We were fighting for the freedom of the world. It is the Nazis who should be in the dock, no one else. Only later, many years later, would some leaders, historians, and scholars begin to feel uncomfortable with some of the actions taken by the Allied forces, particularly those which led to severe loss of civilian lives.

Is it too much to suggest that a liberation army and the ANC in particular could see the struggle in South Africa in black and white terms only, with no shade of grey? That the monstrous evil of apartheid was so grotesque that it would be invidious to criticise or call into question any of the actions taken by those who, at great cost, sought for decades to confront and overthrow this regime? It becomes clear that the expectations of some in the ANC were that the TRC would condemn the National Party and its many allies for their inhuman policies and that the ANC would emerge as the hero that had stopped the villain in its tracks and ushered in a new democracy with a human face.

Such expectations are understandable, and I have strong sympathy with them. But the goal of the TRC was to hold up a mirror to reflect the complete picture. In particular, its objective was to identify all victims in the conflict and to confront all perpetrators of gross human rights violations. South Africans of all persuasions owe a huge debt of gratitude to those who fought so long and hard and at such great cost against a tyrannical regime. Never should it be forgotten that there were people who not only confronted that regime but also ushered in a new peace, a new democracy, and a more gentle, kinder, more decent society in which all can feel they belong. But if the truly astonishing beginning is to flower into a human rights culture and a consolidated democracy, it must be accompanied by an acknowledgement of mistakes made, an acceptance of responsibility, and a determination that these mistakes will never be repeated. This is perhaps asking a great deal of a new state which has accomplished so much, but to acknowledge and come to terms with its own actions would only crown the efforts already made and accomplishments already secured.

It is nothing short of a tragedy that the ANC, represented by its senior leadership, responded in the way it did to the findings of a commission which they in large measure brought into being. They did themselves no credit, nationally or internationally. In our efforts to develop a culture of human rights, South Africa cannot afford double standards. It is correct to condemn violence and human rights violations when they come from the state. It is as important to condemn violations of human rights when they come from those who fought for the liberation of our country. It would only strengthen the ANC if it could unequivocally accept responsibility for its own shortcomings.

In the course of the debate in Parliament Mrs Limpho Hani, widow of Chris Hani, put it so much better than anyone else when she said at the conclusion of her speech,

> I say to my brothers and sisters that we must remember that the TRC findings are only words. It is we who are going to have to make the findings a living reality. These reports must not be removed from the reality of our daily lives. They are an expression of the real distress we face daily. To me they represent the collective sigh of our black people, the heart, soul and spirit of the conditions that we face.

She concluded by saying,

> I believe that most South Africans are committed to breaking from the past, to healing the wounds of history, to building a future based on respect for human rights. This reality places a responsibility upon all of us. Human rights are the birthright of each and every citizen. It is the task of each one of us to help illuminate the way, to chart the way forward and provide South Africa with enlightenment. Our task is huge, but we need to start here, in our homes, in our streets,

in our communities and with the local civil structures. We must guard against the dangers and pitfalls.
We must embark upon the journey from the past into
a bright future.[24]

It would be wonderful if the ANC and all of us could follow
her wise plea. Dealing with the conflicts of the past starts
with knowledge, but it doesn't end there. It must also
embrace acknowledgement and responsibility. I hope the
time will come when the conflict between the ANC and
the TRC is resolved so that all of us can concentrate on
building a human rights culture.

While the ANC was strongly criticised by many
within South Africa and in the international community,
there was obviously support for the party's position from a
large number of people within the party (although I have
been approached by leading members of the ANC, including current and former Cabinet ministers, who told me
that they disagreed very strongly with the ANC's position
and that the TRC was correct to identify human rights violations in the ANC's just war against apartheid).

I was surprised by the support given to the ANC by
Barney Pityana, chairperson of the South African Human
Rights Commission. Barney Pityana is a long-standing
friend who was a close colleague and companion of Steve
Biko. He endured a great deal of harassment and was
imprisoned before he left the country to study for the
priesthood in England. He later joined the staff of the World
Council of Churches and headed its programme to combat
racism. He has the unusual distinction of having senior
degrees in theology and in law.

Pityana expressed very strong views about the TRC
when he addressed the Provincial Anglican Synod in Durban in July 1999. He dealt firstly with the TRC's recommendation that perpetrators who had not applied for
amnesty be prosecuted, and secondly with the findings on
ANC violations. He made it clear that he was speaking in
his personal capacity and not as chairperson of the Human
Rights Commission. However, in his address he said,

The Human Rights Commission has cautioned against selectivity in prosecutions. We have noted that prosecutions as recommended by the [Truth and Reconciliation] Commission would drag on for a long time without any guarantee of convictions. They would raise the hopes of the victims and commit resources required to finance other pressing national priorities. They would also mean the perpetuation of a reference back to the past which we hope to have bridged. We counsel against such a course of action. The simplest solution is to say that those who have escaped the net of the Commission must receive forgiveness by the nation.[25]

This very unclear statement caused great consternation among those who were strongly opposed to the recommendations Thabo Mbeki and others made for some kind of additional amnesty or even a general amnesty. Pityana, when pressed, stated that he wasn't calling for a general amnesty but that the intended prosecutions ought to be frozen. Again, it is not clear what this means. Pityana said those who escaped the net of the Commission must receive 'forgiveness by the nation'. How does a nation forgive? Does he mean that there ought to be a state pardon? This matter is so critical in the debate on justice and impunity that it deserves a more precise formulation. Also, what must we say to victims who have been denied full justice but who have at least had the opportunity to know the circumstances under which their loved ones were abducted, murdered, or tortured? This would of course be denied them if there was some sort of blanket forgiveness 'by the nation'. Furthermore, such an approach is hardly fair on those perpetrators who came to the Commission to apply for amnesty and had to appear in public to tell the full story of their involvement in death squads and the like. They had to endure notoriety in public as well as the discovery by their families and friends of what they had been involved in. Pityana doesn't seem to have thought about this, but because there are many people who would

[329]

conclude that he speaks on behalf of the Human Rights Commission, one has to take a very serious view of his proposal. My own view is that it should be ignored by the state and that the TRC's recommendation that those who refused to take advantage of the amnesty provisions should now face the consequences of a court of law be accepted. Of course no one, let alone anyone on the Commission, wants this matter to drag on indefinitely. But it should not be beyond the wit and ability of the relevant authorities to examine the evidence which has been laid before them by the TRC and decide whether or not to prosecute. If their decision is in the affirmative, it should not be too difficult to conduct those trials without excessive delay and cost. The Commission did not suggest that thousands of people ought to be prosecuted. The numbers are few, but the principle involved is critical to the integrity of the Commission's work and indeed to the rule of law in South Africa.

Pityana, in a very tough paragraph, comes down hard on the TRC and squarely on the side of the ANC. Referring to Tutu's foreword in the Commission's report, which seeks to answer some questions raised by critics, Pityana states that

> the TRC was over-anxious to please especially those who questioned the impartiality and integrity of some members... It bent over backwards to accommodate those who had been part of the oppressive system. How else does one explain the manner in which the intransigence of P.W. Botha was handled? The accommodation with F.W. de Klerk, even as the TRC was refusing the ANC a hearing? Or the hostile grilling that was meted out to Winnie Madikizela-Mandela? Or the ease with which the TRC took the unprecedented decision to apply to court for the setting aside of the group granting of amnesty to some 37 leaders of the ANC?

He concludes, 'The TRC was so anxious to be even-handed that they bent so far backwards as to be biased against those who resisted the apartheid regime.'[26]

His statement is breathtaking in its misinterpretation of events. Firstly, we subpoenaed P.W. Botha, and when he refused to appear we handed the matter over to the Attorney-General and Botha was tried in a court of law. We could not have done more. As far as F.W. de Klerk is concerned, he felt that he was so badly treated that the National Party took Tutu and me to court, demanding that Tutu should apologise and I resign. The charge that we gave the ANC no hearing is absurd and simply not true. We met with the ANC on a number of occasions, as we met with other groups. But in the instance of the findings, we were even-handed in that all those who received notice of them were asked to reply in writing. De Klerk did so and we considered his objections. The ANC did not respond in writing, despite a number of pleas made to them by the Commission. They demanded special treatment. They demanded to meet with the Commission to discuss the findings. They were given an adequate hearing and this is brought out very forcibly by the fact that the court dismissed their interdict against the Commission, with costs. As far as the hostile grilling meted out to Winnie Madikizela-Mandela is concerned, it should be borne in mind that when we asked her to appear before the Commission she could have appeared in camera in terms of the Act. But she made a public statement demanding a public hearing. The questions posed by the Commission were certainly strong and sharp, but they were based on requests made to us by parents whose children had disappeared when they had been in Madikizela-Mandela's care. Our decision to apply to court for the setting aside of the group granting of amnesty would have been done whether or not the group comprised ANC leaders. The fact of the matter is, and the law of the matter is, the decision made by the Amnesty Committee was *ultra vires*. We had no choice but to challenge our own committee and I think the TRC ought to be congratulated rather than criticised for having stood up for what was right. Again, the fact that the court agreed with the Commission, against its own Amnesty Committee, suggests that this was the case.

What I think really worried Pityana is what worried the ANC: we made very tough findings against the ANC, who were involved after all in a liberation struggle against the evils of apartheid. Here Pityana is on very shaky ground and goes to great lengths to justify the torture and killings that took place in the ANC camps. He says, 'Not enough consideration was given either to the extraordinary circumstances which existed at the time when the guerrilla army did not have the resources of the state to detain and hold people in facilities that met the minimum rules.' To be fair to Pityana, he does go on to say, 'Nonetheless, the treatment of prisoners in ANC camps was utterly reprehensible.' That is all the Commission stated: that torture, whether by the state or by the liberation armies, is unacceptable. Pityana's quarrel with the TRC is that 'some moral distinction had to be made', and he states bluntly that the report fails to do this. Again he is wrong. As indicated above, the Commission makes that distinction in black and white. Finally, Pityana states that most of the gross human rights violations referred to by the Commission occurred in the ANC detention camps and there was 'little objection to the way in which the ANC carried out its guerrilla war'. He is wrong on both counts. Because the human rights violations took place inside ANC-controlled camps, they should be regarded more seriously than he seems to suggest. Furthermore, we did refer to a number of violations of human rights in the conduct of the war itself. Responding to victims who appeared before us, the TRC report refers specifically to the 1983 Church Street bombing, when civilians were injured and killed. We refer to instances where members of Umkhonto we Sizwe conducted unplanned military operations using their own discretion without adequate control and supervision, such as the 1985 Amanzimtoti Shopping Centre bombing, which killed and injured civilians. The ANC, through MK, targeted so-called military or security forces, but these operations sometimes went awry through poor intelligence or planning, for example the Magoo's Bar and Durban Esplanade bombings, again with civilian casualties. The

ANC landmine campaign in 1985–87 in the rural areas of the northern and eastern Transvaal resulted in injury and death to civilians, including farm labourers and children. I could go on. The fact of the matter is that, while we conceded in our report that 'the targeting of civilians was not ANC policy, MK operations nonetheless ended up killing fewer security force members than civilians'.[27]

I have dealt at some length with Pityana's criticisms and comments, not only because he has a very proud record of resistance to apartheid at great cost to himself and to his family and friends, but more so because, as chairperson of the South African Human Rights Commission, whether he likes it or not, the words that he utters in public are taken to mean that he speaks for that commission. It is my considered view that the statements that he made at the Anglican Synod and which he commented on in newspaper articles thereafter are unfortunate and do not reflect the findings in the final report of the TRC. Ironically, I had written to Pityana when we were drafting the Commission's recommendations and asked him if he or his commission had any proposals or suggestions that we should include. This referred specifically to the 'unfinished business' of the TRC and the need to continue the work after the Commission had closed down. I did not hear from him, and I hope that the Human Rights Commission will read the more than forty pages of recommendations made by the TRC and will take it upon itself, together with other organs of civil society, to challenge the state for its lack of response to those recommendations and to carry some of them forward itself.

A MORE SERIOUS criticism of the TRC came from many victims' organisations, particularly the Khulumani Support Group, and some non-governmental organisations, relating to the question of reparation. From the very beginning, those of us who worked on the draft Bill had emphasised that the Commission ought to have a three-pronged focus: victim hearings, perpetrator hearings, and reparation for victims. The three committees were set up for this reason. The focus on reparation is evident in the founding Act which governed all our work.

In my view, both the TRC and the state have to accept responsibility for reparation not being as effective as it was hoped it would be. One of the major reasons for this is that when we were writing the Act some of us felt very strongly, and I was one of them, that we ought not to lay down a hard and fast reparation policy until we had heard from the victims themselves. I think this position was well intentioned and was in many ways the ideal approach. After all, the victims were the ones who knew best what form reparation should take. It was for that reason that we asked every victim who appeared before us what they thought the Commission could do for them. We made it clear that our means were limited and that there were many other demands on the state's resources, but we asked them to give us some idea of what they would expect in terms of reparation. In most instances we were over-whelmed by the modesty of the requests. Very few of those who appeared before the Commission even talked in monetary terms. Their first concern was to know the truth. That was the greatest reparation we could give to them, to break the silence. They wanted to know where the bodies were buried. They wanted to have some part of that body, to which they could give a decent burial. They wanted to know why people had done these terrible things to them and to their families. Some talked of memorials, the naming of a school after a young boy who was killed. Others talked about the possibility of a peace park, a place where they could go to be quiet and to mourn. Others talked about the possibility of assistance in education, or, because of ill health, some guarantee of treatment for physical, mental, and spiritual problems. Some of course talked about money in order to repair housing or to assist them generally, because many of them were unemployed.

The suggestions made by the victims were extremely valuable. The problem was that we had never anticipated that so many people would voluntarily come to the

Commission. Months and months went by during which we continued to receive victims, conduct victim hearings, take statements, and analyse those statements, and this meant an inevitable delay in responding to the requests, however modest, made by the victims.

This problem was compounded by the fact that, in terms of the law, when we began the amnesty hearings and people were granted amnesty, those who were in prison had to be released within a matter of hours. This caused a great deal of consternation and anger among the victims. Once again, they were left waiting, while the very people who had caused their suffering and their victimhood were being released. I don't think any of us anticipated this, and it caused a great deal of agony among the members of the Reparation and Rehabilitation Committee and the Commission as a whole.

Where I think the Commission failed was in the inordinately long time it took that committee to come forward with manageable and cohesive proposals. It seemed to the Commission as a whole that hours and hours were spent debating the issue but that very little progress was made. One of the problems was that the question of reparation is very complex and very difficult. Another, regrettably, was that there was often a breakdown in communication and cooperation among the members of that committee. Hlengiwe Mkhize, the chairperson, was very jealous of her position, failed to give adequate and timeous leadership, and yet resented any criticism of herself or the committee. In particular, she made it impossible for her deputy, Wendy Orr, to take any action which she hadn't initiated herself. Furthermore, Glenda Wildschut, who was a tower of strength in the Reparation and Rehabilitation Committee as well as in the Commission itself, was stifled in her attempts to hurry the procedures along and to try to report some progress. I think, to be fair to the committee, that several commissioners kept on stressing – and rightly so – that the Commisson had no right to implement reparation. Our responsibility was to devise a policy. We had no budget for reparation, and some commissioners on a number of occasions paid money out of their own pockets to assist victims to get to a hospital, to apply for a death certificate, to apply for a scholarship to a university, to get psychiatric treatment, and the like.

We failed too, I think, to distinguish strongly enough and soon enough between urgent interim reparation and general reparation.

In the end, however, a very good policy on reparation was worked out by the committee and approved by the Commission. We were mindful that there are many other victims in South Africa and many other demands on the state, such as the need for clean water, health care, education, and employment creation. We made that clear in our report. But what has distressed us most is that although we handed over our report in October 1998 the government has failed to indicate whether or not it accepts the TRC's recommendations, whether or not it wants to accept some and reject others, or what it is going to do about people who have waited so long. I find it understandable that many victims are angry and feel that the work of the TRC was a waste of time and has aggravated their suffering rather than relieving it. All I can argue is that we handed in our recommendations regarding reparation a very long time ago, and the government has made no attempt to implement any of these, except for the urgent interim relief, which took a long time to happen. The government owes an answer, not merely to the Commission, but to those victims who came to tell their stories and hoped that there would be some practical response other than the words of compassion which were expressed in the public hearings.

In Volume 5 of the Commission's report, the reparation policy is laid out as follows:

> The proposed reparation and rehabilitation policy has five components:
>
> *Urgent Interim Reparation*
>
> Urgent interim reparation is assistance for people in urgent need, to provide them with access to

appropriate services and facilities. It is recommended that limited financial resources be made available to facilitate this access.

Individual Reparation Grants

This is an individual financial grant scheme. It is recommended that each victim of a gross human rights violation receive a financial grant, according to various criteria, paid over a period of six years.

Symbolic reparation/legal and administrative measures

Symbolic reparation encompasses measures to facilitate the communal process of remembering and commemorating the pain and victories of the past.

Amongst other measures, symbolic reparation should entail identifying a national day of remembrance and reconciliation, erection of memorials and monuments, and the development of museums.

Legal and administrative measures will also be proposed to assist individuals to obtain death certificates, expedite outstanding legal matters and expunge criminal records.

Community rehabilitation measures

The Commission consulted with relevant government ministries in preparing its proposals for the establishment of community-based services and activities, aimed at promoting the healing and recovery of individuals and communities that have been affected by human rights violations.

During the life of the Commission, a number of victims were referred to the relevant government departments for assistance. It is recommended that the process continue after the Commission closes.

Institutional reform

These proposals include legal, administrative and

institutional measures designed to prevent the recurrence of human rights abuses.[28]

In Volume 5 of the Commission's report, we state,

> The granting of reparation awards to victims of gross violations of human rights adds value to the 'truth-seeking' phase by:
> - enabling the survivors to experience in a concrete way the state's acknowledgement of wrongs done to victims and survivors, family members, communities and the nation at large;
> - restoring the survivors' dignity;
> - affirming the values, interests, aspirations and rights advanced by those who suffered;
> - raising consciousness about the public's moral responsibility to participate in healing the wounded and facilitating nation-building.

With this in mind, the Commission recommended that

> a structure be developed in the President's Office, with a limited secretariat and a fixed life-span, whose function will be to oversee the implementation of reparation and rehabilitation policy proposals and recommendations... The secretariat will also apply itself to:
> - Facilitating mechanisms for financial reparation;
> - Facilitating the issuing of death certificates by the appropriate ministry;
> - Expediting exhumations and burials by the appropriate ministry;
> - Facilitating the issuing of a declaration of death in those cases where the family members request it;
> - Facilitating the expunging of criminal records where the political activity of the individual was criminalised;
> - Facilitating the resolution of outstanding legal matters related to reported violations;
> - Facilitating the renaming of streets and community facilities in order to remember and honour individual or significant events;

- Facilitating the building of monuments and memorials and the development of museums to commemorate events of the past.

The Commission further recommended that 'the government declare a national day of remembrance' and that 'the President, in consultation with organised business and civil society at large, establish a trust fund whose finances will support reparation and restitution initiatives as prioritised by different ministries and civil society'.[29]

The Commission's report has already elicited considerable debate within South Africa and in the wider world as well. This debate includes praise and criticism. This is exactly as it should be. I have no doubt that the debate will continue for many years to come. After all, the Commission dealt with truth and lies, reconciliation and hate, good and evil, and sought to come to terms with a bitter past and to point the way ahead towards a more humane society. The world has witnessed so much that is evil. There seems to be no end to 'ethnic cleansing', crimes against humanity, and even genocide. As Robert Burns put it, 'Man's inhumanity to man makes countless thousands mourn.'[30] It is understandable therefore that there are many who are looking for creative and effective ways to counter the tendency towards evil, and South Africa has become a focus of the debate. It is necessary that the TRC should be subject to critical scrutiny from international agencies, national states in transition, and human rights practitioners. Hopefully historians, poets, writers, and scholars will join the party, as it were, and participate in the never-ending search for clues to cope more effectively with the unfolding drama of human endeavour and the search for the elusive peace which always seems to be beyond our grasp.

10

What price reconciliation?
The achievement of the TRC

M A N Y   C O M M E N T A T O R S   who have commended
the Truth and Reconciliation Commission have also
criticised one particular aspect of its work. The criticism
runs something like this: the Commission has certainly
told some home truths and uncovered significant knowledge about our past, but it offers very little in the way of
reconciliation.

Athol Jennings, the former director of Vuleka Trust,
responding to a survey assessing the impact of the
Commission, stated, 'The TRC has been good at revealing
the truth. The reconciliation side of things appears to be
almost an afterthought that was tagged on.'¹ Gilbert
A. Lewthwaite of the *Baltimore Sun*, reporting from
Johannesburg, wrote, 'The Truth and Reconciliation
Commission ends its investigation of this nation's past
tomorrow, having produced horrifying truths and not
much reconciliation.'² R.W. Johnson, a very harsh critic
of the TRC since its inception, commented on the
Commission soon after its final report was handed to
President Mandela. In an article published in the *New York
Times* he argued that 'The final report of South Africa's
Truth and Reconciliation Commission – a 3000-page
verdict on the entire apartheid era that was released on
Friday – appeared to have done something for truth but
very little for reconciliation.'³ I was in New York at the
time and when I read the column I wrote to the editor:

History will judge whether or not Johnson's criticism is accurate. It is, nevertheless, worth making two points in this regard. The first is that while truth may not always lead to reconciliation, there can be no genuine, lasting reconciliation without truth. Certainly lies, half-truths and denial are not a desirable foundation on which to build the new South Africa. Second, it is readily conceded that it is not possible for one commission, with a limited time-span and resources, on its own to achieve reconciliation against the background of decades of oppression, conflict and deep divisions.[4]

In a more serious and reflective vein, *The Times* of London published an editorial when the Commission's report was released. The editorial praises the report and states,

> Sometimes an official document can truly capture the essence of an era. The report of South Africa's Truth and Reconciliation Commission has done much to illustrate both the corrupting character of apartheid and the degree to which that evil served as an excuse for violence within as well as against the black majority.

The editorial points out that these revelations have not endeared the Commission to most political parties, but adds, 'The purpose of the Commission was the pursuit of the truth, not to court popularity with political parties.' Significantly, the editorial goes on to say,

> The critics – black and white – have claimed that truth has been emphasised at the expense of reconciliation. This argument cannot be sustained. It would have been inexcusable to censor incriminating material simply to avoid embarrassing South Africa's past and present leaders. Any attempt at such an exercise would have rightly led to the charge of political bias. It is hard to see how a litany of lies could serve as the foundation of meaningful reconciliation.

[341]

The editorial concludes, 'No committee can ever absolve the horrors of past atrocities. They can point towards a more civilised future – and in this case have done so.'[5]

The *New York Times* entitled its editorial on the Commission's report 'South Africa's Stinging Truths'. The editorial describes it as 'the most comprehensive and unsparing examination of a nation's ugly past that any such commission has yet produced... [I]t has fulfilled its mandate of telling the fullest truth possible, which is one reason why every political party in South Africa has denounced it.' The editorial continues,

> The controversy has added to widespread complaints that the Commission has not helped the process of reconciliation. This is wrong. True reconciliation, which occurs when a society is no longer paralyzed by the past and people can work and live together, cannot be based on silence. No society can be restored to health by papering over as much pain as South Africans have suffered. A noisy and informed debate about the complicity and the crimes of the apartheid era is necessary if uncomfortable.

With insight not commonly displayed by commentators on the TRC, the editorial acknowledges the healing process of the Commission's work:

> The hearings themselves which allowed victims of human rights violations to tell their stories in public helped the country heal and opened the eyes of many whites to the unpleasant truth about apartheid. The amnesty process, while permitting many important criminals to escape justice, is allowing families to know exactly what happened to their loved ones in dozens of cases that would likely never have gone to trial in South Africa's fragile judicial system.

The editorial concludes, 'No commission can transform a society as twisted as South Africa's was but the Truth Commission is the best effort the world has seen and South Africa is the better for it.'[6]

Phylicia Oppelt, a South African journalist writing for the *Washington Post*, criticises the Commission very strongly, particularly for its granting of amnesty to those guilty of human rights violations. But, very interestingly, she concludes,

> For me the Commission has one, and only one, accomplishment ... and I am not sure whether it is healthy or not ... [U]ntil it began, I had never re-counted personal incidents as I do now. Nor had I examined personal cost. There has never been time. But often now I get glimpses of just how much I have lost growing up in South Africa. Now more than ever before am I aware of the chasm that exists between white and black South Africa. The Commission, with its quest for truth, has not healed my wounds. It has opened ones I never knew I had.[7]

There are many who would argue that an achievement of the Commission was not to perpetuate the myth of the so-called rainbow nation where everyone claims to love one another, but to reveal the serious divide that does exist; the acknowledgement of this divide is the first step towards bridging it. It could be added that someone who has never come to terms with deep hurt and anger will be blighted by unresolved memories forever. I think the Commission can claim some credit for helping many to face up to the truth of the past, with all its horror and shame, not in order to dwell there but to deal with that past and move into a freer existence. Anger acknowledged can be as healing as the outpouring of suffering and grief.

Advocate Richard Penwill, reflecting on the TRC's capacity for reconciliation and much else that courts cannot do, tells of his apprehension when he heard about the establishment of the Commission, and his fears that it could only harm South Africa's future rather than resolve any of its problems. However, writing in early 1998, when the Commission had been in progress for about two years, he acknowledges that he has changed his mind. He writes,

Unlike a court, the Commission does not aim at a conclusion so much as a process. This process was designed not for the purposes of recrimination but instead aimed at confronting the injuries and injustices of the past and coming to terms with them. It is in this light that a picture emerges of a new kind of institution which has achieved what a court could never achieve.

Penwill continues, 'Effecting reconciliation is a process which requires confronting the truth and thereafter aiming at bridging differences, healing and understanding.' He adds,

A conspicuous achievement of the TRC's open policy of hearing evidence is that a large number of victims and their families have been able to come forward and tell their stories. Often these stories have not formed a part of any inquiry or trial, or if they have, have been heard by very few. Much of the testimony has consisted of profoundly moving descriptions of human suffering which would have otherwise gone unacknowledged and unknown on a broader basis by the rest of society. The message has been a clear portrayal of the tragic face of South Africa.

He acknowledges that many South Africans have been distressed at the provision of amnesty, but, he concludes, 'One of the most strikingingly successful aspects of the amnesty system is that it has encouraged people to testify and resulted in the hearing of evidence which would otherwise never see the light of day.'[8]

Penwill refers to his own experience as a practising advocate. He tells of many clients who came to him and told him that their 'confession' had been as a result of torture by the police. One form of torture that was often described to him was the practice of placing a bag over the suspect's head and threatening him or her with death by asphyxiation. Even though many such stories were told in court, the police in their evidence would deny that they had ever been involved in any kind of torture, and in most instances it was their word that was accepted by the court. Penwill refers to a particular hearing before the Amnesty Committee when a policeman finally admitted having practised this form of torture and actually demonstrated the horrifying process not only for the Amnesty Committee but also for the television cameras.[9] Penwill concludes, 'The secrecy of the "wet bag" procedure has finally been publicly broken and many victims will feel exonerated and derive some comfort to know that at last the police have admitted it and everyone has been able to see for themselves.' The advocate was so impressed by the TRC process and its promotion of reconciliation that he urges, 'Once the TRC has finished its work, let us seriously consider a permanent body to be known perhaps as the Truth and Reconciliation Board – which could guard against the wrongs of the future.'[10]

As I have indicated above, my first reaction to the criticism that the TRC has achieved a measure of truth but little or no reconciliation has been to acknowledge this and to point out that the Commission never claimed to be able to reconcile the country; reconciliation is a process that has to be achieved by the entire South African community. But I have thought a great deal since this initial reaction and feel that I was overly defensive. Thinking about South Africa, with its many divisions and its bitter past, and wondering what I could write about reconciliation, I suddenly realised afresh that it is absolute nonsense to suggest that the process of reconciliation hasn't yet begun in South Africa. In fact it began before the Commission was set up. Reconciliation, as conflict resolution, began with President de Klerk's announcement in Parliament on 2 February 1990 that the liberation movements were to be unbanned, that political prisoners would be released, and that negotiations would start. This was the beginning, and a very important beginning, of reconciliation in South Africa. If one compares South Africa before and after 1994, one has to concede that we are not the same country, that the major conflict, which hopelessly and devastatingly divided our society, has been resolved. But in examining the period since 1990, one appreciates that reconciliation is a process, and an extraordinarily difficult one. The period between 1990 and 1994 was characterised by meetings and breakdowns, arguments, stand-offs, disagreements, threats, warnings, and – overshadowing the political discussions – the exploitation and undermining of the process by those who were determined that it wouldn't work, and, worst of all, countless instances of bloody violence.

The first-ever democratic election in 1994 was a watershed. For a brief moment South Africans stood on the mountain top, witnessing a spectacular, almost violence-free election, and watched in awe the transformation which had begun. It was an intoxicating, thrilling experience, but one couldn't stay on that mountain top forever, because there was so much work to be done in the valley below. Post-1994 South Africa has experienced some bitterness by some of the losers, some indulgence by some of the winners, racial incidents, complaining, blaming, whingeing, emigration. The list is endless. Crime has escalated and corruption is a blot on the new democratic landscape. Reconciliation, in other words, is not a sure-fire escalator which takes one consistently and steadily to new heights. It is a process of fits and starts, of going forward and going back, of reaching heights and plumbing depths. But already, as one looks back on the years since 1994, one can see a growing maturity. This was particularly evident in the 1999 election. South Africa has witnessed a shift from traditional voting patterns, and the white right wing, which had seemed so threatening, has almost disappeared. White Afrikaners have made new choices in terms of their political allegiance. So-called coloured South Africans, many of whom had supported the National Party in the previous election, voted for other opposition parties and indeed for the ANC itself. This is part of reconciliation, but it is a process and an extraordinary, exquisitely painful journey.

Professor Jakes Gerwel comes to the discussion on reconciliation in South Africa and on the TRC in particular from a slightly different angle. He states,

In its report the TRC acknowledges that it was impossible for it to 'reconcile the nation' because of limitations of time, resources and mandate. The latter is the most relevant and decisive of these limitations as the Commission was charged not with the initiation or conclusion, but the promotion of national unity and reconciliation, i.e., the advancement or encouragement of a process or result.

But, he adds,

South Africa, notwithstanding the complex of divisions and differences of various sorts, levels and intensities that may exist within it, is decidedly not an un-reconciled nation in the sense of being threatened by imminent disintegration and internecine conflict. On the contrary, on the scale of world affairs it serves as a singularly successful example of a country with racial and ethnic diversity, histories of strife and strongly competing interests, that has resolved its potentially destructive conflicts consensually and has demonstrated within itself the political will and institutional means to cohere.

Gerwel makes two important points. The first is an acknowledgement and a reminder that the Commission was never expected to reconcile the nation, that the process of reconciliation had begun before its establishment, and that its job was to encourage the continuation, development, and promotion of that reconciliation within every area of society. Secondly, he acknowledges that there is a very long way to go in the process of reconciliation: 'While many individual victims and perpetrators of gross human rights violations are not reconciled and group-based memories of discrimination will probably remain for a long time, the country has progressed far on the road of political reconciliation.' But Gerwel feels very strongly that in the obsession with perfect reconciliation we must not undermine the progress towards political coexistence which has already taken place. His appeal is that 'We do not pathologise a nation in relatively good health, by demanding a perpetual quest for the Holy Grail of reconciliation.'[11]

Gerwel does South Africa a great favour by emphasising this need for balance in our approach to reconciliation in South Africa. A distinction ought to be made between acts of personal reconciliation between individuals and reconciliation which comes about through political and social structures, whether these be national, provincial, or local.

Thabo Mbeki, when he was still Deputy President, delivered a very important speech in the South African Parliament in May 1998.[12] The occasion was the opening of a debate on 'Reconciliation and Nation-Building'. The fact that there should be this kind of debate at the highest level of government is significant in itself, and illustrates again the corporate commitment by the state to the search for reconciliation.

In his address, Mbeki refers to the 1993 Interim Constitution of the Republic of South Africa and in particular to the postamble entitled 'National Unity and Reconciliation'. He quotes from the postamble: 'The pursuit of national unity, the well-being all South African citizens and peace require reconciliation between the people of South Africa and the reconstruction of society.' He links this with the 1996 Constitution, which states in its preamble,

> We the people of South Africa recognise the injustices of our past and believe that South Africa belongs to all who live in it, united in our diversity. We therefore adopt this Constitution as the supreme law of the Republic so as to heal the divisions of the past ...[and] to improve the quality of life of all citizens and free the potential of each person.

Mbeki then sets out what he thinks is necessary if we are to take the question of national unity and reconciliation seriously. Firstly, he asks that Parliament commit itself again to the pursuit of the objectives outlined in the Constitution. Secondly, he underlines the need to answer the question honestly as to whether we are indeed making

[348]

progress in the creation of a non-racial and non-sexist society; whether we are healing the divisions of the past in order to achieve the peaceful coexistence of all our people. His major stress is on the need to create opportunities for all South Africans, irrespective of colour, race, class, belief, or sex, and to improve the quality of life of all citizens. Reconciliation and reconstruction are two sides of a single coin. Furthermore, he explicitly defines reconciliation as the creation of a non-racial and non-sexist society, the healing of the divisions of the past, and the improvement of the quality of life of all citizens.

Mbeki links the process of reconciliation with economic justice: 'A major component of the issue of reconciliation and nation-building is defined by and derives from the material conditions in our society which have divided our country into two nations, the one black and the other white. We therefore make bold to say that South Africa is a country of two nations.' He develops this point by indicating that one of the nations is white and well off, and, because of their background and their economic, physical, and educational infrastructures, they are able to exercise their right to equal opportunity and the development opportunities which flow from the new Constitution. 'The second and larger nation of South Africa', Mbeki continues, 'is black and poor with the worst affected being women in the rural areas, the black rural population in general and the disabled. This nation lives under conditions of a grossly underdeveloped economic, physical, educational, communication and other infrastructure.' But he takes the debate one step further by emphasising that not only are we a country of two nations, but we are not making progress towards becoming one nation, and therefore the objective of national reconciliation is not being realised.

Mbeki acknowledges that reconciliation is more than a mirage and that it is inevitably going to take a very long time to deal with the apartheid legacy. He quite ruthlessly criticises the powerful for dragging their feet and for failing to assist in closing the poverty gap between black and white. Some of the contradictions he highlights are the fact

that 30 per cent of South Africa's corporations are not registered for tax purposes but at the same time do not hesitate
to condemn the government for failing to deliver social services, and that many politicians demand that more money
and energy be spent on service delivery but at the same
time demand that taxes be cut and the budget deficit reduced. He also criticises the opponents of affirmative
action who argue that 'black advancement equals white
brain drain' and 'black management in the public service
equals inefficiency, corruption and the lowering of standards'. He pleads for an appreciation of the historical origins
of many of the divisions which exist in South Africa and is
particularly harsh on those who were responsible for or
benefited from the past but now abdicate their responsibilities. He concludes his address with an encouragement and a
solemn warning. On the one hand he stresses that the overwhelming majority of people in South Africa have not abandoned the objective of unity, of peace, of reconciliation, nor
have they lost hope that these dreams will come true. On
the other he states his conviction that we dare not be com-
placent in the face of wide-scale deprivation which could
lead to 'a mounting rage to which we must respond seriously'. He quotes the African-American poet Langston
Hughes, who asks, 'What happens to a dream deferred?'
Hughes' conclusion is that it explodes.

In his inaugural address on 16 June 1999, Mbeki returns
to the same theme:

> Because we are one another's keepers, we surely must
> be haunted by the humiliating suffering which con-
> tinues to afflict millions of our people. Our nights
> cannot but be nights of nightmares while millions of
> our people live in conditions of degrading poverty.
> Sleep cannot come easily when children get perma-
> nently disabled, physically and mentally, because of
> lack of food. No night can be restful when millions
> have no jobs, and some are forced to beg, rob and
> murder to ensure they and their own do not perish
> from hunger. Our days and our nights will remain

forever blemished as long as our people are torn apart
and fractured into contending factions by reason of
the racial and gender inequalities which continue to
characterise our society.

Neither can peace attend our souls as long as
corruption continues to rob the poor of what is theirs
and to corrode the value system which sets humanity
apart from the rest of the animal world. The full meaning of liberation will not be realised until our people
are freed from oppression and the dehumanising legacy
of deprivation we inherited from our past.[13]

I have deliberately quoted Mbeki at some length because
his words help us to understand that while reconciliation
in South Africa is the goal, it is a process which can be encouraged and accelerated or deferred and undermined.
Moreover, Mbeki very powerfully links reconciliation to
the alleviation of poverty, to reconstruction at every level
of society.

Even before the Commission came into being, I too
tried to emphasise the link between the restoration of
the moral order and economic justice. At a graduation
ceremony at the University of Cape Town in 1995, I said,

For the words of reconciliation to be heard, it must be
accompanied by economic justice. Those who have
been oppressed for so long must believe that there
can be a change in their own lifetimes if there is to be
a commitment to genuine peace and stability. There
are a number of instances where this is beginning to
take place...

Every time the Land Claims Court meets, every
time the Department of Agriculture releases land to
people who have been deprived for so long, it speaks
of new opportunity and reconciliation. Every time a
simple home is erected so that people who were once
squatting in bushes can have some shelter, it speaks
not merely of goodwill, of possessions, but is a genuinely concrete action which helps to reconcile a
deeply divided society...

Reconciliation without the anchor of restitution is not merely false reconciliation, not only a travesty of justice – that is, to make victims of people who have suffered – but it is to confirm people in their suffering rather than to affirm them in their survival and create new opportunities for their future.

Mbeki warns all South Africans there is no room for complacency, that much remains to be done. However, he leaves little room for individual reconciliation, for people dealing with their own anger, bitterness, and grief. I think this is an unintentional but serious oversight and that it is important to encourage reconciliation within individuals and between people.

In my view, the Commission held in tension individual and corporate reconciliation. I will try to illustrate this firstly by referring to a number of incidents that took place during the life and work of the Commission. The Commission's report, particularly Volume 5, points to many such examples and is a window onto the individual catharsis that took place at many levels. I can refer here to only a few.

There can be little doubt that many of those who appeared before the Commission felt an enormous sense of relief, simply because they had an opportunity for the first time in their lives to tell their stories publicly and to regain their sense of human dignity. One such person was Lucas Sikwepere, who appeared before the Commission in Cape Town in 1996. He had to be led up to the platform because he was blind. He had been shot in the face by the police and had later been very badly tortured after becoming more politically active as a direct result of losing his sight. He told his story in some detail, and when asked if there was anything else he wanted to add he said, 'I feel what has been making me sick all the time is the fact that I couldn't tell my story. But now it feels like I got my sight back by coming here and telling you the story.'[14]

Tim Ledgerwood, a former conscript in the South African Defence Force, alleged that he had been severely tortured by the security police. The process of telling his story to the Commission, he said, had deeply affected his life, because he now felt an enormous freedom to talk about his experiences to others as well. He said that he had been 'freed from a prison in which I have been for 18 years. It is also as if my family has been freed... The silence is ending and we are waking up from a long bad nightmare.'[15]

Duma Khumalo, speaking on behalf of the Khulumani Support Group, reported a similar healing process after meeting with many of the victims who had appeared before the Commission:

> It is the intervention of the Commission that brought about the dignity of the people that was lost during the political era in our country. People had no one to listen to their griefs or pay attention to some of those griefs until the establishment of the Commission. Then many of the victims came forward and started for the first time to talk about their past griefs.[16]

Cynthia Ngewu, whose son was killed by the police in the infamous 'Guguletu Seven' incident,[17] explained to the Commission that reconciliation, in her view, involved the healing of perpetrators as well as victims: 'What we are hoping for when we embrace the notion of reconciliation is that we restore the humanity to those who were perpetrators. We do not want to return evil by another evil. We simply want to ensure that the perpetrators are returned to humanity.'[18] Ngewu was bereaved and deeply angry, but, remarkably, she thought not only of her own particular needs, which were great, but of the needs of the very people who killed her son. If this is not the beginning of reconciliation in a particular person as well as in a particular community then I don't know what is.

I have already referred to the remarkable testimony by Beth Savage, who was seriously injured in an attack at a golf club function. She not only talked about the circumstances and the injuries that she sustained, but expressed a wish to meet those who were responsible for her injuries. Her wish was fulfilled in April 1998 when Thembelani

Xundu sought amnesty. Beth Savage said in a newspaper interview that as a result of her meeting with Xundu her nightmares relating to the attack had ceased.[19]

The willingness to forgive, to start again, cut across men and women, black and white. Johan Smit, whose son was killed in a bomb planted by an ANC supporter in the Amanzimtoti Shopping Centre in 1985, told the Commission that he had forgiven those who had killed his son and had met the parents of the young man who had planted the bomb. He told the Commission, 'It was a great relief seeing them and expressing my feelings towards them, that I felt glad that I could tell them that I felt no hatred for them. I bore them no grudge.' When he was asked by one of the commissioners whether he had found some relief in knowing what had happened and being able to talk to the family of the man who had killed his son, he replied,

> Yes, it gave me peace because I knew what was happening. I thought that if I placed myself in the other person's shoes, how would I have felt about it? How would I have liked not to be able to vote, not to have any rights, and that kind of thing? So I realised that I would not have liked it, so I realised how it must have felt for them.[20]

J. Msweli told the Commission in 1996 that her son, Simon, had been tortured, violated, and mutilated, and had died as a result of this torture. She felt very strongly that it was important for those responsible to acknowledge that responsibility: 'I want the people who killed my son to come forward because this is a time for reconciliation. I want to forgive them, and I also have a bit of my mind to tell them.'[21]

There were several cases of perpetrators asking for forgiveness. When Colonel Schobesberger, former Chief of Staff of the Ciskei Defence Force, appeared at the Bisho Massacre hearing, he told the Commission and the packed hall,

> We are sorry, the burden of the Bisho massacre will be on our shoulders for the rest of our lives. We cannot

wish it away. It happened. But please, I ask the victims not to forget but to forgive us. To get the soldiers back into the community, to accept them fully, to try to understand also the pressure they were under then. This is all I can do.[22]

After a moment of stunned silence the entire audience, which included many of the victims of the massacre and their relatives, burst into applause. The fact that this soldier was willing to apologise and acknowledge brought about an immediate response even from those who had suffered such grievous losses at the time of the massacre.

A final example of the countless incidents involving forgiveness and reconciliation is the story of Neville Clarence and Aboobaker Ismail. Clarence was a former South African Air Force captain who had been blinded in the bombing of the Air Force headquarters in Church Street, Pretoria. Ismail had planted the bomb outside the building. He told the Amnesty Committee that he regretted the deaths of people in the course of the armed struggle. When he met Clarence before the hearing, he said to him, 'This is very difficult. I am sorry about what happened to you.' The blind Clarence said that he understood, adding, 'I don't hold any grudges.' They agreed to meet again. A little later, Clarence spoke to the media: 'I came here today partly out of curiosity and hoping to meet Mr Ismail. I wanted to say that I have never felt any bitterness towards him. It was a wonderful experience … [R]econciliation does not just come from one side. We were on opposite sides and in this instance I came off second best.'[23]

But many others who appeared before the Commission told us that it was impossible for them to forgive, that they needed more time, that they didn't know if they would ever be able to forgive. Many of them expressed a hope that those responsible for their loss and injury would come before the Commission and said that then perhaps they would be able to forgive, once acknowledgement had been made. It also has to be said that, when full acknowledgement was made at the amnesty hearings, many victims and families of victims still found it difficult to forgive. As I have stressed, it was not the intention of the Commission to demand forgiveness, to pressurise people to forgive, but to create an opportunity where this could take place for those who were able and ready to do so.

I think the great strength of the story-telling, which about 22 000 people brought to the hearings, was that not only was the silence broken, but a process had begun. Many organisations, including churches, schools, and universities, set up their own story-telling exercises so that the experience of the Commission was duplicated many times in many parts of the country. These examples of individual reconciliation are important, and while they do not mean that the country is reconciled, we cannot overlook the generosity of spirit characterised by so many of those who appeared before the Commission. Many of them were helped by the experience, and many of them sought to stretch out a hand to those who had caused their suffering.

The Commission not only played a role in assisting individuals to pick up the pieces of their lives and indeed to stretch out a hand of friendship to the perpetrators, but also acknowledged frankly and frequently that reconciliation cannot be achieved by a single commission in a limited period and with limited resources. This we said over and over again, and in our final report we set out a number of recommendations for the continuation of reconciliation by all South Africans. We felt so strongly about this that in our recommendations we requested the President of South Africa to call a national summit on reconciliation, not only to consider the recommendations listed by the Commission, but also to involve as many constituencies as possible, at every level of government and civil society.

The Commission accepted that if reconciliation is to have any chance at all, a strong human rights culture must be developed, and recommended a number of actions to make this possible. One of the recommendations was that the reports, the findings, and the audio and visual material should be made available not only to community leaders but to every part of the country so that young people in particular can have first-hand information about the experience of the Commission.

A particularly strong recommendation by the TRC was that

Government accelerate the closing of the intolerable gap between the advantaged and disadvantaged in our society by, among other things, giving even more urgent attention to the transformation of education, the provision of shelter, access to clean water and health services and the creation of job opportunities. The recognition and protection of socio-economic rights are crucial to the development and the sustaining of a culture of respect for human rights.[24]

The Commission went further and said that all South Africans should recognise that the public sector alone cannot bring about economic justice; the private sector has a major responsibility, and the Commission urged it to consider special initiatives in the form of a fund for training, empowerment, and opportunities for the disadvantaged and dispossessed in South Africa.

The Commission specifically recommended that

a scheme be put in place to enable those who benefited from apartheid policies to contribute towards the alleviation of poverty. In submissions made to the Commission a wealth tax was proposed. The Commission does not, however, seek to prescribe one or other strategy but recommends that urgent consideration be given by government to harnessing all available resources in the war against poverty.[25]

In other words, the Commission recognised in public utterances and in its written report that reconciliation without economic justice is cheap and spurious.

In its final report the Commission includes more than forty pages of recommendations to government and to Parliament. These recommendations cover a wide field and

[357]

include specific areas ranging from health care, prisons, business, land, children and youth, to international human rights instruments and apologies to neighbouring states for the destabilisation that took place during the apartheid era. All of these recommendations should be seen as being of a piece. Reconciliation is distorted when it is seen only in terms of individual relationships or of matters which have a direct bearing on healing and education alone. The structures of society can and should be effective in the process of reconciliation; therefore we found it imperative to include recommendations relating to those structures.

Implicit in the Commission's work and its recommendations to government is the acceptance that, although reconciliation between individuals is important and critical, to assume that everyone is going to be reconciled to his or her neighbour is to assume the impossible. It is true that through the work of education and the religious communities in particular people can undergo conversions in their attitude towards their fellow South Africans. There is ample evidence that this has taken place and is continuing to do so. But this is the exception rather than the rule. It is wrong-headed and even dangerous to claim that reconciliation and unity are not up to government or political structures, but simply require that we all behave kindly towards each other in individual acts and encounters. Frankly, this is not enough. South Africa is riddled with racism, divisions, and stereotyping; most whites don't trust blacks, and certainly many whites don't like blacks. Anything that goes wrong in the new dispensation will therefore be blamed on blacks' alleged inferiority or inability to govern. There is abundant evidence that many whites still cling to the old racist instincts which have been so well drilled for so long. On the other hand, most blacks don't trust whites. They see them as a symbol of past oppression and constantly watch for signs of racism to emerge.

In South Africa today, the treatment meted out to the majority of blacks in the past is simply unacceptable. While many white people mouth platitudes about reconciliation without believing them, there are benefits to

[358]

their changed behaviour. The farmer who pays his workers a better wage and provides improved working conditions and housing may not like what he is doing, but he accepts that it is necessary and therefore changes his behaviour. The way whites treat blacks in institutions, in shops, and on city streets is vastly different from what it was a few years ago. Their behaviour has changed for the better and has resulted in a commitment to coexistence, an almost unconscious recognition that we share the same space, the same country, and therefore we simply have to get on. But changed behaviour is not a deep, fundamental, religious experience of reconciliation. Accepting coexistence is merely a step in what we should be working towards: a deeper, more abiding, and more caring concern for each other as fellow South Africans and fellow human beings. But we must face up to the reality that in many cases it is not hearts that have changed but circumstances.

This raises the important question of how government can encourage greater cooperation and changed behaviour from those who were in power for so long. In its final report, the Commission identified a number of obstacles to reconciliation which needed to be addressed. In a section on the prevention of gross human rights violations in the future, the Commission recognised that

> One factor militating against the establishment of a human rights culture is the high incidence of serious crime. Security of person and property is a fundamental human right. To address the unacceptably high rate of serious crime, government is requested to give consideration to the introduction of community policing at all levels as a matter of urgency.[26]

A further problem identified by the Commission which makes reconciliation difficult is the widespread corruption in both the private and public sectors in South Africa: 'If there is to be an enthusiastic response by the general public to the war against poverty and crime there also has to be a corresponding ruthless stand against inefficiency, corruption and maladministration at every level of the

public and private sectors.'[27] If white people in particular
can see the government to be committed to and reasonably
successful in bringing down the crime rate and rooting out
corruption, particularly where it exists in state departments, this can only be an incentive for cooperation and a
commitment to coexistence.

The Commission's recommendations will remain
words on paper unless the government and Parliament are
serious about assessing their relevance and their worth in
the ongoing pursuit of national unity and reconciliation.
At the time of writing, the jury is still out as to whether the
government is going to take the TRC seriously enough to
weigh up its recommendations, discard those regarded unnecessary or not worthy of consideration, and accept those
that could make a meaningful difference to society. Unless
there is pressure from civil society in particular, the state
is likely to follow the adage, 'Defer what you can, do what
you must.'

An intriguing question is whether or not a nation can be
reconciled, can be healed. Is it only possible for individuals
or groups of individuals to be reconciled, to be healed, to
forgive and start again? Or can we talk in meaningful terms
of the healing and reconciliation of a nation? In order to
address this question, which relates not only to South
Africa but to all nations that have been caught up in violence and conflict, we should start by considering various
approaches to reconciliation. Two important approaches
are the Christian understanding and the African philosophy of *ubuntu*.

In the Christian religion reconciliation is not something that can be earned. It is seen as a gift from God, which
can be accepted but is not deserved. However, reconciliation with God always also involves reconciliation with
one's neighbour. There are a number of steps that take place
in the reconciliation process: confession, repentance, restitution, and forgiveness. The focus in traditional Christian
religion is very much on the covenant between God and the
individual, and the bridge to that relationship is Jesus

Christ. At its best, reconciliation involves sacrifice and commitment. At its worst, it is an excuse for passivity, for siding with the powerful against the weak and dispossessed. The church in many instances has joined with those who exploited and impoverished entire populations rather than with the wretched and the miserable and those who were enslaved. When reconciliation calls for forgetting or for concealing, then it is spurious. In Argentina, for example, the concept of reconciliation was regarded with deep scepticism. The dominant religion, the Roman Catholic Church, supported the military junta, and the perpetrators of human rights violations were always the first to call for reconciliation. Such false reconciliation has been widely rejected.

Walter Wink reminds us that reconciliation can be grossly perverted by religious authorities who urge the oppressed to accept a society built on violence and injustice. Another perversion of reconciliation is that which preaches a gospel of personal salvation at the expense of social action. Wink quotes a poem by the Filipino poet J. Cabazares to give point to his argument:

Talk to us about reconciliation
Only if you first experience
The anger of our dying.

Talk to us of reconciliation
If your living is not the cause
Of our dying.

Talk to us about reconciliation
Only if your words are not products of your devious
    scheme
To silence our struggle for freedom.

Talk to us about reconciliation
Only if your intention is not to entrench yourself
More on your throne.

Talk to us about reconciliation
Only if you cease to appropriate all the symbols
And meanings of our struggle.[28]

[361]

In South Africa, Desmond Tutu and other Christian leaders have fought long and hard against the use of religion to uphold the status quo and to justify oppression, arguing instead for social action and reconciliation in the name of religion.

Tutu's theology echoes the African philosophy of *ubuntu*. Justice Yvonne Mokgoro helps us to appreciate the rich meaning of this Nguni word. It describes an African world view, a guide for social conduct as well as a philosophy of life.[29] *Ubuntu* represents personhood, humanity, group solidarity, and morality; its core belief is 'umntu ngumntu ngabantu, motho ke motho ba batho ba bangwe', literally translated as 'a human being is a human being because of other human beings.'[30]

Anton Lembede, the founding president of the ANC Youth League, argues that the African

> regards the universe as one composite whole, an organic entity, progressively driving towards greater harmony and unity whose individual parts exist merely as interdependent aspects of one whole realising their fullest life in the corporate life where communal contentment is the absolute measure of values. His philosophy of life strives towards unity and aggregation, towards greater social responsibility.[31]

Lembede's definition of humanity is particularly important because of his position in the ANC Youth League. As president, he strongly influenced the holistic approach of the ANC, an approach which reflects the philosophy of *ubuntu*. It is particularly striking to note Lembede's influence on Nelson Mandela, Oliver Tambo, and Walter Sisulu, all of whom played a leading role in the founding of the Youth League. When one bears in mind the leadership positions held by Mandela, Tambo, and Sisulu, it is not surprising that during the negotiations of the 1990s and in the writing of the Interim Constitution, there was such strong emphasis on forgiveness, reconciliation, and *ubuntu*. Mandela exemplified this humanity not only in his words and speeches but in his life.

There are numerous examples in South Africa where the commitment to reconciliation, religious or secular, has transformed lives and has brought about a change of behaviour and a genuine attempt to right the wrongs within society. Despite our country's history of conflict and prejudice, there are countless examples of black and white finding each other and working together.

If we accept reconciliation at its very highest and best, can it ever transcend the individual and involve the larger community or the nation? Can a nation confess? Can a nation repent and make restitution? Can a nation seek forgiveness? Pepe Zalaquett, the well-known Chilean human rights activist and member of that country's Truth Commission, suggests that there is a correlation between the work of the Chilean Commission and the 'same philosophy that underpins Judeo-Christian beliefs about atonement, penance, forgiveness and reconciliation'.[32] Hannah Arendt, a Jewish philosopher, who certainly did not see the Judeo-Christian faith as the ultimate authority, nevertheless sees Jesus of Nazareth as the 'discoverer of the role of forgiveness in the realm of human affairs'. The fact that Jesus made this discovery in a religious context and used religious language to describe it, she adds, is 'no reason to take it any less seriously in a strictly secular sense'.[33] Donald W. Shriver, in his important book *An Ethic for Enemies*, reminds us that Arendt used two terms, 'promise' and 'forgiveness', to explain how societies can overcome an evil past and change for the better. Arendt puts it this way:

> The remedy against the irreversibility and unpredictability of the process started by (human) acting does not arise out of another and possibly higher faculty, but is one of the potentialities of action itself. The possible redemption from the predicament of irreversibility – of being unable to undo what one has done though one did not and could not have known what he was doing – is the faculty of forgiving. The remedy for unpredictability, for the chaotic uncertainty of the future, is contained in the faculty

[363]

to make and keep promises. The two faculties belong together in so far as one of them, forgiving, serves to undo the deeds of the past, whose 'sins' hang like Damocles' sword over every new generation; and the other, binding oneself through promises, serves to set up in the ocean of uncertainty, which the future is by definition, islands of security without which not even continuity, let alone durability of any kind, would be possible in relationships.[34]

The work of Karl Jaspers can help us to understand the potential for a nation, and not only individuals, to reconcile. In his lectures and writings he discusses the question of German guilt after World War II. In a remarkable essay, he distinguishes between criminal guilt, political guilt, moral guilt, and metaphysical guilt. Criminal guilt is assigned by a court of law, when a person is found guilty of breaking the law. Political guilt, however, concerns the acts of politicians, in particular those responsible for policies which led to human rights violations, as well as civil servants and others who promoted and supported such policies. Moral guilt is a more embracing concept which includes criminal, political, and military actions, but also 'indifference and passivity'.[35] Those who accept moral responsibility are remorseful and accept responsibility for the consequences of their actions or inaction: 'It is an unease that contradicts the "aggressive silence" of those who in their "self isolating pride" refuse to admit culpability of any kind.'[36] Metaphysical guilt is a concern between the individual and his or her god.

Martin Niemoller, an outstanding leader of the Confessing Church in Germany, was sent to a concentration camp for his opposition to Hitler. It is interesting that despite his remarkable bravery and courage he talked in terms not only of the crimes of the Nazis themselves but of the moral guilt of the entire nation, including himself: 'We have let all these things happen without protest against these crimes and without supporting the victims.'[37] Elsewhere he writes, 'We should not blame the Nazis only.

[364]

They will find their prosecutors and judges. We should blame ourselves and draw logical conclusions.'[38]

It follows therefore that responsibility and acknowledgement, which could well be another word for confession, ought to come not only from those who committed criminal actions but also from the political leaders of the time. In the South African context this surely means that P.W. Botha, F.W. de Klerk, and other prominent leaders of the National Party ought to have accepted and acknowledged their own direct involvement in human rights violations.

There are many examples of other leaders who have apologised for human rights violations, even if they were not directly involved in them. Willy Brandt, the Chancellor of West Germany, signed a treaty in 1970 which resulted in 40 000 square miles of German territory being granted to Poland. Both symbolically and practically, Brandt, as leader of the German nation, apologised to the Polish people who had suffered so grievously as a result of the Nazi policies of a generation before. Many will recall his kneeling silently at the Warsaw War Memorial as an act of confession and repentance for offences against the Polish people. What was remarkable about his words and deeds was that he had clearly been opposed to Hitler from very early on, and had spent the war in exile in Norway. In strong contrast, Botha and De Klerk, even though they were directly involved in implementing apartheid, offered qualifications, excuses, and explanations rather than genuine atonement. In other words, it is possible and desirable for nations to repent through their leaders who seek forgiveness, but in many instances this fails to happen because of the intransigence and insensitivity of the leaders concerned.

Another example of a leader's apology on behalf of his country is that of Richard von Weizsacker, one-time President of West Germany. Von Weizsacker had served in the German army which invaded Poland in 1939 and precipitated World War II. He also served on the Russian front, where he was wounded. His father, Ernst von Weizsacker, former Chief State Secretary in the Nazi foreign office,

[365]

appeared in the Nuremberg trials. Von Weizsacker made a speech in the German Parliament on 8 May 1985, the fortieth anniversary of Germany's defeat in the war, a speech that was all the more powerful and memorable because of his direct involvement in the Nazi period. In the speech he unambiguously condemned the Nazi crimes: 'We cannot commemorate the 8th of May without making ourselves aware how much conquest of self the readiness for reconciliation demanded of our former enemies. Can we really identify with the relatives of those who were sacrificed in the Warsaw ghetto or the massacre of Lidice?' Referring to the millions of people who suffered under the Nazi regime, he comments, 'they are all people who were not asked, people who have suffered injustice, people who were defenceless objects of political events and for whom no compensation for justice, and no disputation of claims, can make good what has been done to them.'[39]

Von Weizsacker does not focus merely on the Nazi Party and its leadership but holds Germans in general accountable for many of the crimes committed. He points out that it wasn't a question of Germans not knowing what was happening, but rather a determination not to know. He urges a turning away from amnesia: 'Whoever closes his eyes to the past becomes blind to the present. Whoever does not wish to remember inhumanity becomes susceptible to the dangers of new infection.' He reminds Parliament and the German people that the Jews remember and will always remember what happened:

> As human beings we seek reconciliation. Precisely for this reason we must understand that there can be no reconciliation without memory. The experience of millions of deaths is a part of the inner life of every Jew in the world, not only because men cannot forget such an atrocity but also because memory is a part of Jewish belief.[40]

Finally, Von Weizsacker does not remain morbid about the horrors of the past and the need for accountability, but towards the end of his address he calls for action to result from memory and responsibility. He not only appeals to his audience to remember that mentally ill people were killed but reminds them of the need for care for psychologically ill people today. In the memory of those who were persecuted by the Nazis on the grounds of race, religion, or politics there must be a constant warning never to shut the door on those who are persecuted in contemporary times. It is the responsibility of the German community to protect those who are so persecuted. Appealing for liberal values, Von Weizsacker stresses the need to protect freedom of thought, even of criticism, however much it may be directed against the Germans themselves.

Towards the end of his speech, Von Weizsacker addresses the young, the new Germans, who had not been born when the Second World War began. He reminds young Germans that Adolf Hitler persistently stirred up prejudices, hatred, and enmity. He appeals to young people not to be driven into enmity and hatred against any people, whether they be Russians or Americans, Jews or Turks, radicals or conservatives, blacks or whites. His final word is to the politicians: 'Let us honour freedom, let us work for peace, let us uphold the law, let us serve our inner standards of justice. Let us on the present 8th of May look the truth in the eye as well as we are able.'[41]

This is a remarkable speech which cannot have left the powerful German Parliament and the German people unmoved. It illustrates the fact that, while one cannot talk about national reconciliation as a mass movement, when the leaders of a nation are ready and willing to confess, to seek forgiveness, to be accountable and responsible, they do this not merely for themselves but for the nation as well. This former German soldier spoke with great courage which assisted his country to seek its own redemption.

Chancellor Helmut Kohl of Germany underscored what his President had uttered when he stated, 'Reconciliation with the survivors and descendants of the victim is only possible if we accept our history as it really was, if we Germans acknowledge our shame and our historical responsibility and if we perceive the need to act against any efforts undermining human freedom and dignity.'[42] It would have been easy for Chancellor Kohl to point the finger at those who had been directly responsible. He could have told his audience that while he regretted the crimes of the past, he hadn't been aware of them at the time, and it would be quite wrong to blame the present generation for past offences. Instead he assumed responsibility and accountability, and in doing so as Chancellor of his country, he invited and enabled those whom he represented to accept their responsibility as well. It is in such an act that reconciliation becomes possible.

Another example is taken not from Nazi Germany but from the United States of America. A year after the Japanese air force's attack on Pearl Harbour in 1941, the American leadership ordered the internment of 120 000 Americans of Japanese ancestry. These innocent people, who had nothing to do with the attack and whose only crime was that they originated from Japan, were summarily rounded up, lost their homes and property, and were subjected to humiliation and persecution. It took forty years for the United States government to grant compensation. In 1976, in the Bicentennial Year of the Declaration of Independence, President Gerald Ford issued an official apology to Japanese-Americans and their families who had been so unjustly incarcerated:

> In this Bicentennial Year, we are commemorating the anniversary dates of many of the great events in American history. An honest reckoning, however, must include a recognition of our national mistakes as well as our national achievements. Learning from our mistakes is not pleasant, but as a great philosopher once admonished, we must do so if we want to avoid repeating them.
>
> February 19th is the anniversary of a sad day in American history... We now know what we should have known then – not only was that evacuation wrong, but Japanese-Americans were and are loyal Americans.[43]

Gerald Ford revoked Executive Order 9066, which was still on the statute book; this was the order which had enabled 120 000 people to be sent to the camps. He added that 'We have learned from the tragedy of that long-ago experience forever to treasure liberty and justice for each individual American, and resolve that this kind of action shall never again be repeated.'[44]

A final example is the solemn apology issued by Pope John Paul II in March 2000 for the errors of the Roman Catholic Church over the past 2000 years. This was part of the Sunday mass in St Peter's Basilica in Rome. In his apology the Pope acknowledged the errors and cruelty which had taken place during the history of the Roman Catholic Church, including the Inquisition, the forced conversion of native peoples in Africa and Latin America, and the support for the Crusades, whose victims included Muslims, members of the Eastern Orthodox Church, and Jews. This apology was widely welcomed, but some argued that it was in very general terms and that there were some important omissions. For example, the Pope made no mention of discrimination against homosexuals. And while his apology for discrimination against women was timely, he made no reference to his continued opposition to abortion and birth control, or to the denial of a woman's right to enter the priesthood. Regrettably, there was no acknowledgement or apology concerning the failure of Pope Pius XII to speak out against the Holocaust. Despite these limitations, however, the Pope's public apology was a courageous act, and his successors can build on it and open the way for even greater reconciliation.

At critical moments in a country's history, leaders have emerged who have dared to go against the tide, to apologise, and to open the door to reconciliation. Regrettably, great leaders of sensitivity and compassion are few and far between. There are many who have failed to seize the opportunity. One that comes to mind is the Prime Minister of Australia, John Howard, who refused to apologise for the abduction of Aboriginal children by social organisations, churches, and the state a hundred years earlier. When the account of the theft of children was published under the title *The Stolen Generation*,[45] the Aboriginal leadership called upon the Prime Minister and Parliament to identify with and apologise for the complicity of the state in earlier years.

I was in Australia at the time as the keynote speaker at the Australian Reconciliation Convention, which was held in Melbourne in 1997. Before the conference I had been interviewed on numerous occasions by the Australian media. I tried very hard to limit my comments to South Africa and its quest for reconciliation, but there was no way I could evade the tough questions relating to events unfolding in Australia. I went on record as saying that there are times when a nation's leaders can assist the process of reconciliation by offering an apology. The irony was that Prime Minister Howard was to be one of the key opening speakers at the Reconciliation Convention. He was not at all complimentary when we met in the anteroom before the conference. In his address he expressed his regret at past injustices to Aboriginal children, but refused to identify with the actions of the state in the past, to apologise, or to offer reparation. He had lost a major opportunity to assist in healing the festering sore of Aboriginal hurt. It was a strange sight to see thousands of people at that convention standing up and literally turning their backs on their Prime Minister.

After I had delivered my address I was again interviewed by the media. After expressing my immediate feelings of great sadness that such an opportunity had been missed, and after comparing Howard with Mandela, I said, perhaps unfairly, in response to a question, 'I think Mr Howard has got balls to be present at what was inevitably going to be a hostile audience but he shows a complete lack of heart.' This statement was picked up by the media throughout Australia. It would have been so easy for Prime Minister Howard to have identified himself with the feelings of rejection by the very small group of Aboriginals who have survived in Australia. If only he could have been with me when I met many of their leaders before and after this great convention on reconciliation, to see how hurt they were by his attitude. It is possible to advance reconciliation through courageous leadership. It is also possible to hinder reconciliation through a lack of wisdom and courage.

When I returned to South Africa and heard again the dismissive comments made by former State President P.W. Botha and listened to F.W. de Klerk constantly qualifying his own expression of regret and insistently denying any knowledge of the gross human rights violations which had been committed by members of the security forces, I felt again a sense of deep sadness at an opportunity missed. I wished that De Klerk could have sat with the many black South Africans who throughout the period of the Commission's work again and again expressed their longing for an unambiguous acknowledgement by former leaders of the National Party of their role in the years of repression.

Michael Ignatieff, well-known writer and journalist, makes the same point when he refers to political figures responsible for the war in the Balkans:

> If instead of writing books niggling at the numbers exterminated at Jasenovac President Franjo Tudjman of Croatia had gone to the site of the most notorious of the Croatian extermination camps and publicly apologised for the crimes committed by the Croatian Ustashe against Serbs, gypsies, Jews and partisans, he would have liberated the Croatian present from the hold of the Ustashe past... [H]ad he lanced the boil of the past, the war of 1991 might not have occurred. He chose not to, of course, because he believed Serbs as guilty of crimes against the Croats but sometimes, a gesture of atonement is effective precisely because it rises above the crimes done to your own side.[46]

In the same article Ignatieff warns that

> It is perilous to extrapolate from traumatised individuals to whole societies. It is simply an extravagant metaphor to think of societies coming awake from a

nightmare. The only coming awake that makes sense to speak of is one by one, individual by individual in the recesses of their own identities. Nations, properly speaking, cannot be reconciled to other nations, only individuals to individuals. Nonetheless, individuals can be helped to heal and to reconcile by public rituals of atonement.[47]

It was with such a philosophy in mind that Desmond Tutu called upon the political leaders in South Africa to make some symbolic act of atonement. Showing great sensitivity and awareness of the human psyche, he did not ask this only of the former apartheid leaders. He asked Nelson Mandela to make a public act of atonement at the site of the Church Street bombing by ANC cadres, which had led to the loss of civilian lives. He asked Mangosuthu Buthelezi to make a similar act of atonement at KwaMakhutha in KwaZulu-Natal, where women and children had been massacred by IFP supporters. He asked the leader of the Pan African Congress, Stanley Mogoba, to hold a special service to symbolise atonement at the St James Church in Cape Town where a massacre had taken place in 1993, the perpetrators of which were members of the PAC. Finally, he asked De Klerk to go to the scene of the Boipatong killings. Tutu appealed to all of them, 'Would it not be wonderful if the leaders of these political parties could go to the site of a notorious atrocity committed by his side and say, "Sorry – forgive us." With no qualifications, no "buts or ifs".'[48]

Tragically, none of the leaders accepted this challenge. I think the cause of reconciliation suffered as a result.

In the book *The Healing of a Nation?*, which records the proceedings of the 1994 conference held prior to the setting up of the Truth and Reconciliation Commission, Antjie Krog refers to the Anglo-Boer War, which took place in South Africa from 1899 to 1902. Introducing this subject in relation to the conditions for reconciliation, she quotes a poem by Eugene Marais which, she explains, was interpreted at the time as the thoughts of a lonely guard beside the scorched veld during the war:

Oh cold is the slight wind
And lean.
And gleaming in the dim light
And bare,
As vast as the mercy of God,
Lies the veld in starlight and shade.
And high on the ridges,
Spreading among burnt patches,
The seed grass is moving
Like beckoning hands.

Oh sad is the tune
On the east wind's pulse,
Like laments of a girl
Forsaken by love.
In each grass blade's fold
Gleams a drop of dew,
But quickly it bleaches
To frost in the cold![49]

Krog points out that 26 000 women and children died in British concentration camps and elsewhere during the Anglo-Boer War. After the war, a Royal Commission on War was appointed, but it did not investigate crimes against the local population. The intriguing question that Krog asks is, 'Wasn't the mere fact that the abuses of the war were never exposed perhaps ... a key factor in the character that formulated apartheid's laws?' She continues by asking the penetrating question as to what might have happened if a British commission had recorded reports of injustices during the war. Even more to the point, she asks the question, what would have happened if acknowledgement had been made of British wrongs and if forgiveness had been requested? She speculates as to whether, if there had been some public recognition of the intrinsic humanity and equality of all inhabitants, South Africa's subsequent history would have been different. Of course British abuses, while never officially acknowledged or condemned by the British themselves, were officially recorded by Afrikaners. These accounts entrenched the view of the Afrikaners as a

[373]

threatened and victimised group, and a steely determination emerged that they would never, ever be victims again. Furthermore, the English became the scapegoat of the Afrikaners; as Krog puts it, the English 'became the devil so that we, the Afrikaners, could be the angels'.[50]

It is difficult to know with any degree of certainty whether a public confession by the British concerning the deaths of women and children in concentration camps would have drastically altered the history of South Africa, particularly in relation to race and power. But there can be little doubt that the resentment felt by many Afrikaners helped to shape their own determination to survive at whatever cost. This strong sense of nationalism was fed by German nationalism in the 1930s, leading ultimately to the policy of apartheid. Perhaps history could have been very different, but we will never know. Whatever has happened in South Africa, I have little doubt that if the British had held a truth commission following the Anglo-Boer War, or at least made some public act of atonement for the horrifying results of their concentration camps, it could only have helped to heal the deep wounds which were left after that war.

In trying to assess what contribution, if any, South Africa's Truth and Reconciliation Commission made towards the noble goal of 'unity, reconciliation and reconstruction', in the words of the Constitution, it will be helpful to remind ourselves of the fundamental philosophy contained in the postamble, without which there would never have been a commission:

> This Constitution provides a historic bridge between the past of a deeply divided society characterised by strife, conflict, untold suffering and injustice and a future founded on the recognition of human rights, democracy and peaceful coexistence and development opportunities for all South Africans, irrespective of colour, race, class, belief or sex.
>
> The pursuit of national unity, the well-being of all South African citizens and peace require reconcilia-

tion between the people of South Africa and the reconstruction of society.

One claim that can be made by the Commission is that it was successful in tearing away the mask which had covered the truth about human rights violations for so long. If the Commission had never begun this painful, precarious, and always incomplete journey towards uncovering deception and deceit, what would have been the consequences? Judge Ismail Mahomed, in his judgement relating to *Azapo and Others vs the President of the Republic of South Africa*, answers this question:

> The alternative to the grant of immunity from criminal prosecution to offenders is to keep intact the abstract right to such a prosecution for particular persons without the evidence to sustain the prosecution successfully, to continue to keep the dependants of such victims in many cases substantially ignorant of what precisely happened to their loved ones, to leave their yearning for the truth effectively unassuaged, to perpetuate their legitimate sense of resentment and grief and correspondingly to allow the culprits of such deeds to remain perhaps physically free but inhibited in their capacity to become active, full and creative members of the new order by a menacing combination of confused fear, guilt, uncertainty and sometimes even trepidation.

He continues,

> Both the victims and the culprits who walk on the 'historic bridge' described by the epilogue will hobble more than walk to the future with heavy and dragged steps delaying and impeding a rapid and enthusiastic transition to the new society at the end of the bridge, which is the vision which informs the epilogue.

As Mahomed himself makes clear, the obverse is also as true and as powerful:

The families of those unlawfully tortured, maimed or traumatised become more empowered to discover the truth, the perpetrators become exposed to opportunities to obtain relief from the burden of a guilt or an anxiety that they might be living with for so many long years, the country begins the long and necessary process of healing the wounds of the past, transforming anger and grief into a mature understanding and creating the emotional and structural climate essential for 'the reconciliation and reconstruction' which informs the very difficult and sometimes painful objectives of the amnesty articulated in the epilogue.[51]

This points to the very heart of what the Commission attempted to do. In its public hearings for both victims and perpetrators, some truth has been revealed, some healing has taken place, and some reconciliation has been achieved. This is not to claim that truth exposed necessarily brings reconciliation in its wake. The only claim that I am making is that without this truth it would have been less likely that reconciliation would have been accepted and worked for than was the case; the exposure of the truth dealt a body blow to denial and gave deep encouragement to victims and survivors to put the past behind them and reclaim their lives without the constant shadow of uncertainty, and loss of dignity and recognition.

Furthermore, reconciliation is not something that is achieved and can hang on the wall like some picture representing the past or even the future. It is a process – a process which began before the life of the Commission. The process of reconciliation began at the negotiation table with the basic acceptance by all parties that we have to share this territory called South Africa with our former enemies. A former prisoner of the communist regime in his native Poland speaks eloquently and thoughtfully about transformed attitudes:

The image of the enemy is a moral and political burden because you are negotiating with someone whom only yesterday you called an oppressor, a murderer or a terrorist. You promised your followers that this person would be severely punished as a reward for the oppression they had lived through. Your followers, meanwhile, are telling you justice requires punishment. They ask: 'How can you negotiate and talk to a person who is responsible for all the disasters of our people?'

His reply is, 'I am negotiating because I have chosen the logic of peace and abandoned the logic of war. This means my enemy of yesterday must become my partner and we will both live in a common state. He may still be my opponent but he is an opponent within peace, not within war.' [52]

Reconciliation in South Africa is a process which started not only when enemies sat on opposing sides of a table but also when victims told their stories and perpetrators confessed their atrocities. It is a process which must continue long after the Commission has completed its task.

I have already pointed to the dangers of cheap reconciliation, particularly when it has come from those directly responsible for apartheid's hell who cry 'peace, peace' where there is no peace. A sure and certain test for reconciliation is whether it is accompanied by, or at least points to, the need for economic justice. As Wilmot James, the former executive director of IDASA, states in the organisation's quarterly *Siyaya*, 'The TRC did valuable ground work and now the nation's task is to underwrite emotional healing with material redress.' [53] As has been emphasised earlier, unacceptable anachronisms exist in South Africa, and only when the mass of people who have been not only emotionally but economically prejudiced by apartheid begin to believe that there is a new horizon to which they can aspire will they be enabled to embrace with some enthusiasm the commitment to reconciliation.

I have also stressed the distinction between individual and national reconciliation. Examples have been given which illuminate the many instances of individual reconciliation in the course of the TRC hearings. The question remains whether one can speak with any concreteness of the healing of a nation. The answer remains ambiguous. It may be that to speak of a nation being healed after deep wounds have existed for so long, or to speak of the uniting of a nation which has been so long divided, is to speak the language not of fact but of faith. But that doesn't make it illegitimate. It is to challenge society to be what it is called to be, even though it is not there yet. It is the promise of what is possible in the future. It is the language of poetry. But we must never make the mistake of assuming that we are talking about something that is already present. That is the danger of talking about South Africa as the 'rainbow nation'. When Tutu does this, he understands this as the potential, the promise, the hope, but sometimes the term is misunderstood and misinterpreted as a claim that this is where we are now and dismissed as cheap rhetoric. Michael Ignatieff, whom I quoted earlier, puts it well: 'Societies and nations are not like individuals but the individuals who have political authority within societies can have an enormous impact on the mysterious process by which individuals come to terms with the painfulness of their society's past.'[54] I think, however, he is wrong to limit the intervention to individuals who have political authority. There are others who have moral authority, like Tutu, who can make the same significant difference by means of courageous leadership. I think it is also possible that such impact can be made not only by individuals who have political authority but also by institutions such as the Truth and Reconciliation Commission in South Africa. I believe the TRC contributed to a national process of acknowledgement, accountability, and responsibility which has unlocked the greater possibility of a measure of reconciliation, not only for individuals, but also for the nation.

11

Beyond the TRC:
The South African model and
the international community

LOOKING AT MY notes for a lecture I delivered in
Northern Ireland, I notice that the first line reads, 'South
Africa is not Northern Ireland!' It is important to recognise
that it is neither possible nor desirable to impose the South
African model on any other society. This is not to suggest,
however, that South Africa cannot contribute to other
countries in transition. On the contrary, I think our experience can inform and influence many of those countries that
are undergoing transitions from dictatorship or authori-
tarian rule to a form of democracy. These countries include
Argentina, Chile, El Salvador, and Guatemala, and Eastern
and Central European countries such as Hungary, the
Czech Republic, Poland, and Bulgaria. These countries
share with South Africa a number of similarities: a shift
from totalitarianism to democracy, a legacy of oppression
and serious human rights violations, a fragile government
and a precarious unity, a commitment to a culture of
human rights and a respect for the rule of law, and a
determination that past violations will never be repeated.

There are other countries which could also look to the
South African model for some guidance. These are countries which are aspiring to democracy but remain in conflict, such as the former Yugoslavia, Rwanda, and Cambodia. I would go even further and suggest that there are
some mature democracies which are facing challenges to
their own incomplete transitions and which find it difficult
to come to terms with their past. Japan, for example, is

facing challenges over its use of Korean 'sex slaves', and China is demanding an unqualified apology for atrocities committed by Japanese soldiers before and during World War II. Switzerland has recently been accused of alleged collaboration with Nazi Germany and of withholding money in bank accounts of Holocaust victims. A number of major German corporations have only recently reached a settlement by giving compensation to thousands of Jews and others who were used as slave labour during World War II. It should not be forgotten that there was at least a degree of complicity by American companies in the use of people as slave labour. It wouldn't be stretching matters to refer to the challenge to the United States, with its residue of denial and misunderstanding flowing from the bitter experience of slavery in its earlier history, which still impacts on contemporary life in that country. In recent months I have spoken at many universities and colleges in the United States. Almost without exception the first question from the audience is, 'Do you think that the United States should have a truth commission?', and without exception the question is asked by an African-American. Those who raise the question make it very clear that they believe it is crucial that such a commission should be established to deal with the unresolved tensions and questions relating to slavery.

I have little doubt that the South African experience speaks to many of these situations and may well have something unique to offer, but I want to underline that South Africa was characterised by a number of features which are not necessarily congruent with most other societies. Therefore, if the South African model is to be considered by any other society, it will have to be on the basis of that society's experience, history, needs, and resources.

When South Africa was trying to find ways of coming to terms with its own past, we considered many models. The two conferences referred to in Chapter 1 considered models from a variety of countries and areas, including Argentina, Chile, El Salvador, Germany, Bulgaria, Hungary, and Czechoslovakia (now the Czech Republic and Slovakia). We realised early on that we would not be able to

[380]

replicate any of these models, and we sought instead to learn from their successes and failures and to apply those features which matched our own experience. While we are indebted to those countries and borrowed much from them, we also created something unique which arose out of our own particular and peculiar circumstances. This is certainly the advice I would offer anyone approaching us in relation to their own situation. Therefore, although I and several of my fellow commissioners have been asked to assist in many diverse situations, the first sentence I utter is, 'The South African model cannot be imposed on any other country.'

Aryeh Neier, in his review of the Commission's report, writes,

> Of the nearly 2 dozen 'truth commissions' world-wide during the past decades – most in Latin American and Africa – the South African Truth and Reconciliation Commission is the best known and by common agree-ment has played the largest part in helping a divided nation to come to terms with its past... Its significance goes far beyond the borders of South Africa. The Com-mission's work is a factor in the thinking of people in many other countries about how to deal with questions of individual or collective responsibility for great crimes committed under the authority of their own governments. To cite one current example, in the wake of the forced exodus from Kosovo in the early months of 1999 and the Nato bombing that eventually ended it, some Serbs are now looking to the example of the TRC in South Africa as they consider how to understand what took place, where to apportion blame and whether they can join with other Balkan tribes in planning a future in the new Europe.[1]

There is another very important reason why we ought not to impose our own country's experience on others, which is quite different from the one I have outlined above, but of equal if not greater importance. Despite the heavy emphasis on the duty to punish, the fact of the matter is that, in the majority of transitions, the deciding factor has not been international law. Many scholars and commentators argue that, in practice, decisions made by transitional governments around issues of retroactive justice are not choices at all and are little affected by moral or legal considerations. Instead, such decisions on the form that justice can take – be it trials, truth commissions, ad hoc international tribunals, or amnesty – are dictated in most instances by the mode and politics of the particular transition.

Modes of transition can be defined in terms of four categories: (1) full defeat in an armed war (for example the treatment of Germany after World War II); (2) transition through a dictator's loss in an election (for example Chile); (3) transition through compromise and negotiations (for example South Africa); and (4) transition from a long-standing communist regime (for example Eastern European countries).

Each mode presents its own set of institutional and political constraints which in turn delineate the form of justice, from the most retributive model (prosecutions and trials) to more restorative models of justice (truth commissions and disqualification from public office) to no justice at all (impunity). In the context of a military victory (category 1), the only restriction is the victor's own sense of justice and long-term strategic considerations. For instance, Germany's military defeat in World War II was absolute in that the Nazi regime lost both political and military power. The Allied forces, because of their total victory, were able to opt for the most retributive model, the Nuremberg trials.

Where transitions from totalitarianism occur after elections (category 2), greater political restrictions arise. Very often the former dictator maintains a strong power base (whether in the military or in civil society) and, prior to his or her departure, passes laws to grant amnesty for past human rights abuses. The new democracy, faced with an unstable political and social situation and no clear legal remedy, often seeks an amalgam of retributive and restorative models of justice, via truth commissions, reparations, and limited prosecutions.

[382]

Where transitions occur through a process of peaceful negotiation between the democratising force and the previous totalitarian regime (category 3), the political constraints become even more heightened. Negotiation politics require compromise, first and foremost. Thus, in a country that is attempting to accommodate all factions in a new democracy, justice by necessity becomes a restorative project of establishing moral, if not legal, truth. In such contexts, justice takes the form of truth commissions and limited amnesty. South Africa is a noteworthy example of this approach.

In the case of transitions from totalitarian communist regimes to democracy (category 4), political constraints all but preclude more retributive forms of justice. The nature of communism's teaching and practice has arguably had two discernible consequences: firstly, to rob even dissidents of the initiative and will, for a very long period, to act against those in authority, resulting in a weakness or absence of civil society; and, secondly, to create a technocratic government of such pervasiveness in society that large numbers of individuals in communist countries achieved a level of complicity with the regime unparalleled even by other non-communist totalitarian regimes. Post-totalitarian transitions to democracy in former communist countries are thus characterised by little retribution in the form of trials and little truth-seeking in the form of truth commissions. Instead, these nations have taken refuge in general laws of lustration, which only implicitly admit a history of misdeed by barring the guilty from future participation in government.

Interestingly enough, Timothy Garton Ash, referring to the problem of dealing with the past in Central Europe, makes two points:

> I would say two things. First, the problem is unavoidable. It is intrinsic to the path chosen. Second, I believe with benefit of hindsight that all the countries of Central Europe could and should have tried the expedient of the truth commission – although without

involving the quasi-judicial business of granting amnesty as happened in South Africa. A truth commission before which the political leaders of the former regime and those accused of crime under it have to testify brings both greater public knowledge of the misdeeds of the past and a formal, almost ceremonial, acknowledgement of the victims. It symbolically draws a line between the new era and the old without calling for forgetting or even necessarily forgiving. It is probably the closest a non-revolutionary can come to revolutionary catharsis.[2]

While I agree with Ash that truth commissions could well have been useful in many countries in Eastern and Central Europe, I am not sure that I would be as dogmatic about excluding amnesty in every case. It would be extremely difficult to persuade former political leaders and those accused of crimes to testify unless there was some carrot to encourage that confession. Furthermore, as we have seen, the socio-political circumstances sometimes demand some form of amnesty in order to achieve peace.

NEW DEMOCRACIES IN TRANSITION AND RETROACTIVE JUSTICE

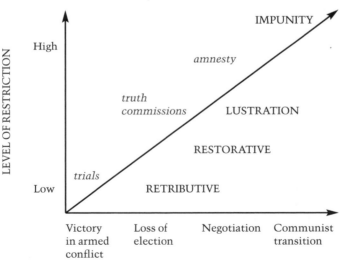

Thus, a country's particular mode of transition and level of political restriction define the parameters of the choice between the competing theories of retroactive justice. The more that peaceful coexistence is a stated goal of the transition, the greater the political restrictions faced by the transitional government. Moreover, history bears out that as the level of restriction increases, transitional societies turn away from retributive models and towards more restorative models of justice.

To sum up, one must proceed cautiously when asked to assist other countries in transition, bearing in mind that the socio-political situations are very different in each country. It is these circumstances which often dictate the limits to which prosecutions can go and indeed where successful truth commissions can be held. Timothy W. Ryback, writing on the conflict in Bosnia, comments,

> Since November 1995, when Dayton halted the Balkan slaughter, Bosnia has been awash with well-intentioned foreigners. In just the past year or so, the Pope has come to preach tolerance, Princess Diana to clear land mines (less than a month before her death), U2 to hold a 'goodwill concert', Woody Harrelson to make a politically relevant film and Bianca Jagger to, well, many people in Bosnia are still trying to figure that out. 'Bosnia is like a desperately ill patient with a different physician treating a different symptom every day,' says Chris Bennett of the International Crisis Group, a human rights monitoring organisation in Sarajevo. Bosnia's 1997 aid directory registers more than 400 foreign organisations working in the region.[3]

We must be careful not to barge into situations of conflict offering solutions which may be unworkable or which may even exacerbate the conflict. It is always preferable to be invited, and even then one should tiptoe into traumatised societies with great sensitivity. That is not to say we should do nothing. Many societies do not have the resources to bring about even a semblance of normality, of restoration, accountability, and reconciliation.

[385]

Not only are individual states deeply influenced by their own socio-political circumstances when deciding how to deal with their transitions. The international community, international organisations, and single countries often determine their course of action on the basis of political considerations and self-interest. A single example will suffice. In an essay in *Time* on 27 September 1999, Charles Krauthammer asks the question, 'Why did the US go to war over Kosovo but not East Timor?' He acknowledges that the Australians headed up the somewhat belated entry into East Timor, but points out that there are a number of stark differences in US policy vis-à-vis East Timor and Kosovo:

> Firstly, the peacekeepers did not bomb their way into Timor as they did into Kosovo; they waited for permission from Jakarta. Before intervening in Kosovo the West had championed the case of Kosovo. East Timor, on the other hand, had been championed by no-one. Thirdly, there will be no American infantry in Timor. The US will help others go in but they will not be babysitting the Timorese as they are the Kosovars.

Why was America so deeply involved in Kosovo and the backing of the extreme action of the Nato bombing of Serbia and so absent in real assistance towards East Timor? Krauthammer argues that the real reason is that 'Serbia does not count for the US; Indonesia does'. In other words, because the former Yugoslavia has no strategic importance for American foreign policy, the US could very easily bomb Serbia in order to bring an end to the Serbian offensive in Kosovo. Serbia is not on the United States' map, but Indonesia controls the Strait of Malacca and has the largest population in the Muslim world. To sum up, in the words of Krauthammer, 'When China oppresses Tibet, Russia ravages Chechnya or Indonesia reduces East Timor to rubble, we do not intervene. China, Russia and Indonesia matter. But Serbia doesn't. So when Kosovo is overrun, we strike.'[4]

It is clear, therefore, that even when one is in areas which are in conflict and receive the attention of international agencies, it is not always legal and moral considerations that come into play but instead the limitations of the international organisations concerned or the political self-interest of the major powers. For all these reasons we must proceed cautiously and with circumspection if we are to be successful in sharing the South African experience with the international community.

Many countries have indicated their interest in learning from the South African model. These include Ethiopia, Indonesia, Cambodia, Nigeria, and Sierra Leone. In the rest of this chapter I shall discuss the cases of the former Yugoslavia, Rwanda, and Northern Ireland.

THE TRAGIC VIOLENCE which has characterised the Balkans for over a thousand years erupted in an epidemic of killing, assault, and destruction in the former Yugoslavia between 1992 and 1995. The eventual response of the international community to this bloodletting was the appointment of the International War Crimes Tribunal for the Former Yugoslavia, based in The Hague. The responsibility of the Tribunal is to identify individuals who were responsible for the upsurge in violence and who either ordered or took part in the killings. The intention was that indictments would be served upon identified individuals, arrests would be attempted, and prosecutions and sentencing would follow. This was an extremely important response, and it was hoped that it would not only result in those people chiefly responsible being brought to trial and punished, but also act as a serious deterrent in the future.

The Tribunal has certainly had its moments of success, but its work has been limited; fewer than a dozen perpetrators have been sentenced. I have always felt that a war crimes tribunal will inevitably be limited as a response to a major human tragedy. If the last word is punishment, then there is very little likelihood of or hope for any measure of restoration and reconciliation of the societies concerned. It is not a question of whether there should be a tribunal, but whether a tribunal on its own is sufficient response to the

[387]

frequent outbreaks of crimes against humanity, 'ethnic cleansing', and genocide. At the moment there are three separate communities living side by side in Bosnia – Serb, Croat, and Muslim – but peace is maintained only by the presence of a large peacekeeping force. It is important that over and above the work of the Tribunal there should be a complementary attempt to bring a measure of unity, stability, even peace and reconciliation, to that territory. Otherwise there is a danger that the moment the peacekeeping force is removed the violence will flare up again.

In July 1997 the United States Institute for Peace (USIP), in collaboration with the OSCE[5] Office for Democratic Institutions and Human Rights and the Council of Europe, sponsored a workshop attended by twenty-one justice officials from the Federation of Bosnia and Herzegovina and the Republic of Serbia. Neil Kritz of the USIP subsequently reported that there was no intention at the beginning of the workshop to push for a truth commission. During the workshop, however, the head of one of the war crimes commissions in Bosnia declared that he and his colleagues were 'in the process of creating three conflicting versions of the truth and if we keep going along this path, 50 years from now our grandchildren will fight again over which one is correct'.[6] According to Kritz, there was almost unanimous agreement from all three major ethnic groups that a truth commission should be appointed, and the USIP was asked to assist in the subsequent development of the idea.

Since that time Neil Kritz and several of his colleagues have done a great deal of hard work consulting and holding meetings in Bosnia and other countries to try to measure the level of support for the establishment of a truth commission. During this time there has been a great deal of heated debate and controversy as to whether or not such a commission should be formed. This despite the fact that in a letter attached to the Dayton Peace Accord there was a suggestion that a commission of inquiry should be appointed. At the 1997 workshop, all Bosnia's ethnic communities concurred:

[**388**]

Beyond prosecution, the establishment of a historical accounting of abuses suffered during the war can contribute to the process of healing and reconciliation. Under current arrangements, however, the work of the three war crimes commissions represented at the Round Table risks producing three conflicting versions of truth and history... [O]ne joint truth commission should be established for Bosnia and Herzegovina including appropriate membership from each ethnic group and an international chairperson to provide a collective forum for victims on all sides of the conflict and to establish one consensus history regarding these painful matters.[7]

Despite this apparent support for the idea of a commission, however, there have been many dissenting voices, including the former president and prosecutor of the International War Crimes Tribunal for the Former Yugoslavia. They argue that the establishment of such a commission would confuse people and would make the work of the Tribunal more difficult. Judge Richard Goldstone, the first prosecutor of the Tribunal, has a different view, however. He has argued publicly that he sees no conflict between the Tribunal and a truth commission and regards them as complementary rather than contradictory. Furthermore, more than 100 political, religious, and intellectual leaders in Bosnia and Herzegovina have endorsed the idea of a truth and reconciliation commission, and the Citizens' Alternative Parliament, a key NGO in Bosnia, has issued an appeal to the Presidency to establish a commission without delay. They argue as follows:

A national consensus and acknowledgement of the abuses suffered by all victims during the recent war and an analysis of the factors which facilitated these atrocities is a prerequisite to any process of reconciliation. The attainment of a lasting peace in our country is threatened by the development of multiple and conflicting versions of the truth regarding these abuses.

We believe that it is in the best interest of the citizens and nations of Bosnia and Herzegovina and their collective desire to avoid renewal of the conflict in the future, to establish the national Truth and Reconciliation Commission. The Commission should, in a professional and objective manner, examine and report on the nature of the abuses suffered, and the societal, political and historical elements which made this pattern of abuses possible. Based on this examination, the Commission should also develop recommendations for steps to be taken to deal with this painful legacy and to prevent the recurrence of such inhumanity in Bosnia and Herzegovina. Such a broad historical accounting is a necessary complement to the crucial judicial process of determining individual criminal responsibility.

The members of the Truth and Reconciliation Commission should be chosen through a process in which the public plays the primary role. Individuals selected must be of high moral standing, unimpeachable integrity and objectivity, and [be] credible to all the public as representing an honest search for the truth regarding our common history rather than the interests of any ethnic or political group.

The Commission should be provided all due legitimacy and support by the government, but must be wholly independent and autonomous in its work. The people of Bosnia and Herzegovina, and the generations yet unborn, deserve no less.[8]

In a discussion I had with the chairperson of the Citizens' Alternative Parliament, he pleaded for assistance from South Africa. In his view, which he said was shared by a large number of NGOs in Bosnia, not only should such a commission be established, but the South African model was the one that attracted them. I told him then, as I have told many others who have made similar appeals, that if support for this proposal could be clearly demonstrated and if the representiveness and depth of the support could be established beyond doubt, I would have no hesitation in lending assistance in any way that was required.

Towards the end of 1999 I received an invitation from Neil Kritz and the USIP to attend a conference in Sarajevo to consider whether or not there was sufficient local support, and, if so, to work out an agreed programme of action for establishing a commission in that deeply divided territory.

The conference was held in Sarajevo on 3 and 4 February 2000. If ever I needed a reminder that Bosnia was not South Africa, the weather on the day of my arrival in that formerly besieged city jogged my memory! I had left Cape Town the previous day in the middle of a glorious summer, and the temperature in Bosnia was below freezing. The entire area was covered with snow and at first it was impossible to land, but after flying in a holding pattern for more than a hour we landed in almost minimal visibility.

On the night of the third, a dinner was arranged by local organisations, attended by many key leaders from Bosnia as well as international guests who would be speaking at the conference. During the discussion at the dinner it was stressed that the official sanction of the Presidency was necessary if the proposed truth and reconciliation commission were to be viable, and that there must be very careful cooperation with the International War Crimes Tribunal in The Hague as well as with other relevant national and international organisations. It was emphasised that it would be extremely important to involve the inter-religious council based in Bosnia, whose members were apparently very suspicious that many of those advocating a truth commission were former communists.

It was explained to the visitors that the people attending the conference the next day were part of a broad coalition of those who felt that a truth and reconciliation commission was important for Bosnia. As one person put it, 'We have many truths but we should try to reach a consensual memory rather than to continue with contested truth.' Some suggested that the truth commission should not be confined to Bosnia and Herzegovina, but should involve the entire region: Bosnia, Croatia, and Serbia. One prominent NGO leader emphasised the need for truth and trust to go together and said there would never be real stability in Bosnia without a truth and reconciliation commission. A point that was stressed over and over again by many of the leaders who sat around the table was that the truth commission, while dealing with the past, was critical for future generations, otherwise 'we will relive our tragic past and our grandchildren will fight with each other as we have done'. A final comment came from a very old man, who said hesitantly, 'Bridges and buildings are being repaired but we are still divided... [I]nside we are in ruins.' I came away from that dinner very concerned about the formidable obstacles to the establishment of such a commission, but deeply moved by the overall commitment of those whom I had met.

The public conference was held in the Herzegovina Hall at the Holiday Inn Hotel on 4 February. This was the only hotel in Sarajevo which had remained open throughout the siege, and it was badly damaged by mortar shells – an apt setting to consider truth and reconciliation! There were approximately 150 delegates and observers at the conference. The delegates were drawn largely from Bosnia and Herzegovina, and the observers were from international organisations and foreign embassies. The embassies represented included France, the Scandinavian countries, Italy, Holland, Switzerland, the UK, Canada, and Russia. David Jacobs, the South African ambassador to Greece, also attended. He was very supportive of the proposal to establish a truth commission in Bosnia after his experience of the TRC in South Africa. The delegates represented a wide cross-section of civil society, in particular various victims' groups, missing persons' institutions, youth groups, women's groups, and ombudsmen.

The chairperson for the morning was Jakob Finci, who was very active in the small Jewish community in Sarajevo as well as in other human rights work. The first two speakers focused on 'Why do we need truth and reconciliation?' They were Vehid Sehic, who represented the Forum of

Tuzla Citizens, and Miodrag Zivanovic of the Alternative Ministry Council in Banja Luka. Sehic emphasised that Bosnia was a multi-ethnic, multi-cultural, multi-religious community but that its people lived in a straitjacket of three major ethnic groupings and that this reality had been exacerbated by the Dayton Peace Accord, which placed people permanently into three different groups. He was deeply concerned that unless there was a direct attempt to mould the three communities into one group coexisting and cooperating with each other, the former enmities would begin all over again. He further stressed that truth was necessary for reconciliation. Zivanovic, an academic by profession, emphasised that what was needed in Bosnia was a responsible society, and that the starting point for responsibility and accountability was the search for truth; for this reason alone he felt that it was imperative that a truth commission should be established in Bosnia, and possibly for the entire region.

The first international speaker was Richard Goldstone, very well known in South Africa for the work he did on the Goldstone Commission and as a judge on the Constitutional Court. In this setting, however, he was probably better known as the first prosecutor of the International War Crimes Tribunal in The Hague, and therefore could speak with authority and integrity on the need for a truth commission alongside the Tribunal. Referring to the South African model, he stressed that the proposed commission in Bosnia should never be seen to contradict the work of the Tribunal and therefore there could be no amnesty as part of the commission. Nevertheless, there should be an investigative unit in order to corroborate the stories told to the commission by victims. At all times precedence should be given to the Tribunal, and the commission should complement its work.

I followed Richard Goldstone and in my address I emphasised yet again that 'South Africa is not Bosnia and never will be'. But I did go on to say that there were some similarities:

Violence, a litany of human suffering, crimes against humanity, the loss of human and social dignity, the lies, half lies, denial and the deep longing for peace and stability are common to both Bosnia and South Africa. The South African Commission was an opportunity for ordinary people to get on with their lives and this may well help victims in Bosnia also. The approach, the strategy and the structure will be very different, but the elusive search for accountability and peace is universal and human rights are indivisible.

I outlined the starting point of South Africa's Truth and Reconciliation Commission, the problems we experienced, the resources we had, the strategies we adopted, and the unique features of the South African model. I went on to quote Albert Camus: 'Truth is as mysterious as it is inaccessible and it must be fought for eternally.' My point was that we would never succeed in South Africa or Bosnia in finding the whole truth, but if one could find a common truth accepted by the various ethnic groups as a basis for building a future, then the commission would be worthwhile. Finally, I said that if I had my way I would take all the delegates and let them attend one hearing of the South African Commission; once they had listened to the stories told by so many different people in so many different ways, they would be in no doubt about the cathartic effects and the healing possibilities of truth-telling.

Neil Kritz of the United States Institute for Peace reminded the conference of the long discussions that had taken place over the past two years and emphasised that no commission could be imposed from the outside, but that it must have the support and trust of the local people. He stressed that there was no time to waste, that myths become expanded and hardened, and that it was important, therefore, for civil society to be actively engaged in deciding whether or not to set up the necessary internal organisation to consider the preliminary work for establishing a commission. He referred to the various models that Bosnia might want to consider, such as El Salvador, which was a wholly internationally organised commission, Guatemala, which was a local process headed by an international chairperson, and the South African model, which was initiated and led by South Africans themselves. He said there was a need to consider how broad the commission's mandate should be and how long the commission should operate, but emphasised that how a country dealt with its past would strongly influence its future.

Two representatives of the Hague Tribunal, Gavin Ruxton and James Stewart, were very critical of the proposal to establish a truth commission in Bosnia and advocated extreme caution. They felt that the timing was wrong and that the Bosnians should wait until the work of the Tribunal was concluded. They argued that the necessary preconditions for a truth commission did not exist, and that they could not see support from within Bosnia for such a commission. They were sceptical about the possibility of reaching a definitive truth in a divided society. The proposal that the commission should last for only twelve months, they argued, was unrealistic. In particular they stressed that a commission should not be imposed from outside, for this would be counter-productive. Its independence would be in question because of the existence of the Hague Tribunal, there were bound to be overlaps between the two bodies, and the commission could come to be seen as an alternative to the Tribunal.

These were strong criticisms and had a considerable impact on the dynamics of the conference. It was clear from a number of the delegates' statements which followed that they saw the intervention by the Tribunal representatives as arrogant and uninformed. They were particularly critical of the suggestion that the timing was wrong and that it was too soon for a truth commission. Several pointed out that discussions about establishing a commission had been under way for more than two years. One prominent ombudsman said that the Tribunal itself was taking far too long and that ordinary people couldn't wait ten or twenty years for the truth to be known; in a divided country the need for reconciliation had to be addressed urgently. She

[395]

warned that if the Tribunal maintained its opposition to a truth commission, this would only create further divisions and tensions. Domestic courts were ineffective because of political factors, she added, and those appearing before the courts could not be certain of a fair trial. She was of the view that any overlap between a truth commission and the Tribunal could be overcome and that they owed it to their younger generation 'not to lead them toward revenge'.

The president of the Serbian Civil Council emphasised that his institution was committed to building peace and therefore strongly supported the commission. There was a need, he said, not only to reach a common truth but also to build trust and establish standards of human rights to prevent future atrocities. It was important to determine the magnitude of the suffering, to allow victims to be heard, to investigate the plight of refugees and displaced people, and to build confidence in the future. The speaker was aware that gaining consensus would be difficult, but said that the work had to start immediately if the needs of the people were to be addressed.

A particularly passionate contribution was made by Natasa Kandic, representing the Fund for Humanitarian Rights in Belgrade in the former Republic of Yugoslavia. She stressed that

> the people can't depend only on the Tribunal – we
> have to do something about the victims and the need
> for reconciliation. How many victims have appeared
> before the Tribunal? We must demonstrate care and
> compassion. We must create a space for the victims
> to tell their stories. We, the ordinary persons, must
> take action ... [W]e don't have the information that is
> necessary. There are people who are living in contra-
> diction. We must build collateral for the future ... [W]e
> must help the children who fought in the war and
> the children yet to be born ... [W]ithout this there can
> be no justice.

She also made a very strong appeal for a regional commission including Croatia and Serbia.

It became clear as the conference moved to a conclusion that the overwhelming majority of delegates were strongly committed to the establishment of a truth and reconciliation commission and that they were determined to press ahead with the next steps that had to be taken. Among the recommendations were that a working committee should be established as soon as possible, and that the draft statute which had been published in 1998 should be reviewed in the light of the criticism from the Hague Tribunal.

That draft statute contains a number of key points. It proposes that, firstly, the truth and reconciliation commission for Bosnia and Herzegovina will draw on models developed in Chile, El Salvador, South Africa, and elsewhere, and adapt them as appropriate to the context of Bosnia and Herzegovina. Secondly, while a major focus will be on victims, the commission will also acknowledge those individuals who maintained their humanity and protected neighbours of other ethnic and religious groups from abuses. Thirdly, the commission will be independent and autonomous in its work. Fourthly, all parties have agreed that the commission will comprise individuals from within Bosnia and Herzegovina of high moral standing and recognised integrity and objectivity who will be acceptable across all ethnic lines. Fifthly, the commission chairperson will be selected from the international community.

Members of the commission will be nominated by a selection board comprising the United States Institute for Peace and the OSCE Office for Democratic Institutions and Human Rights, acting in consultation with the Council of Europe and other international organisations. Members of the commission, including its international chair, will be formally appointed by the National Presidency of Bosnia and Herzegovina. Finally, the draft statute stresses that the commission will be complementary and parallel to the International War Crimes Tribunal for the Former Yugoslavia and other international and domestic processes of justice for war crimes in Bosnia and Herzegovina.

In response to the representations from the Hague Tribunal, Richard Goldstone said that in his view the arguments in favour of a truth commission in Bosnia were overwhelming. Then he made this very powerful statement: 'Insofar as South Africa is concerned, if I had to choose between criminal prosecutions and the Truth and Reconciliation Commission I would choose the TRC, which has done far more to reconcile and heal than any criminal prosecution.' These were powerful words, and they were soon backed up by further responses from the floor. A key human rights worker asked who could be harmed by the truth and gave his own answer: 'Only those who are afraid of the truth. We must proceed. It is important for the democratisation of Bosnia. We must have perseverance. We must be patient, but action is urgent.' A youth representative, Tanja Neskovic, added her own support:

> What can I do to live in this country without hatred... we are not predestined to hate. We need a comprehensive truth, not isolated from the Tribunal but part of the whole jigsaw puzzle. But the Tribunal itself is not the whole puzzle, it is only part of it. I want to listen... but I also want to be heard. There is no future without history. We need truth and reconciliation as a solid foundation to build a good house. At a recent meeting of 160 young people from all over Bosnia there was strong support for the truth and reconciliation commission.

The delegates from the Hague Tribunal were furious with Goldstone; they thought he had betrayed the club. But they acknowledged that they ought to be respectful of the suffering represented by so many who had spoken at the conference and that they would take back some very encouraging messages. James Stewart was pleased that everyone had emphasised that the commission would not be an alternative to the Tribunal but would complement it. But for him the critical question was, how could a commission come into being without putting at risk the work of the Tribunal?

In a discussion the following day with Gavin Ruxton of the Hague Tribunal, I asked him whether he would have the same objections if the people of Rwanda wanted to establish a truth and reconciliation commission. He replied that he would not, and when I asked him why, his answer was, 'I don't know.' I then asked him whether he thought that part of the problem was that the international community does not concern itself with Africa and what its people want to do and don't want to do, but because Bosnia is in Europe they take a very different stand. This was a provocative question, and I didn't mean to insult either him or the Tribunal. He answered with an emphatic no and said that the former Yugoslavia was very complicated. He denied that the Tribunal was trying to kill the proposed truth and reconciliation commission: 'There is no TRC, so how can we kill it?' My reply to him was that it was possible to kill an idea.

He then told me of his feelings of deep insecurity, about how precarious the support for the Tribunal was, and that he was concerned that the proposed truth commission would be seen as a rival with strong local support and would undermine the work of the Tribunal. I was sympathetic to his concerns, and reminded him that I appreciated the importance of the Tribunal, but said that it should not be too difficult for people of goodwill to hammer out a new draft statute which would ensure that the commission did not contradict the Tribunal's work. My final words were that no one really knew how many people had been killed in Bosnia but that figures ranged from 150 000 to 200 000. It has also been estimated that approximately 20 000 women were raped in the course of the war. There were victims and survivors who were in some kind of cold storage and needed to be brought back to life by sharing their experiences with the wider community. For the sake of the victims alone, there should be more than a Tribunal; there should also be a truth and reconciliation commission.

I cannot believe that Stewart and Ruxton, having listened to so many people at the conference speaking from their hearts, would want to stand in the way of a truth and reconciliation commission. I cannot believe that the Tribunal should be seen as the only response to the disastrous past and conflict which had the former Yugoslavia in its grip.

It is important that there is clarity about the roles of tribunals and truth commissions. In the next few years the International Criminal Court will become a reality, and it would be a tragedy if all future interventions in post-conflict societies were to take the form of trials and prosecutions only. The situation in such societies is ambiguous and traumatic, and we should leave the door open for different models to meet different situations. I am confident that a truth and reconciliation commission in Bosnia would make a tremendous contribution to the future peace and stability of that country.

On the final day of the conference, at a meeting of key NGO leaders, a working group of fourteen people was elected, with a tough and long agenda in order to take the process further. It is highly probable that the commission for Bosnia will be debated vigorously during the course of 2000 and hopefully consensus will have been reached by 2001. I have no doubt that the South African model will figure prominently in the structure and objectives of the commission.

A final point: there is one clause in the draft statute that I hope will not be changed. It concerns the need to uncover 'the existence and actions of individuals who refused to participate in the prosecution of their neighbours and who, at grave personal risk, maintained their sense of humanity and attempted to protect their neighbours of other ethnic or religious groups from abuses'. This emphasis on telling the 'good stories' is something which I think many other commissions could learn from. I am sorry that we didn't do something similar in the South African Commission. There were many people who told us stories of people from 'the other side' who assisted them in moments of great crisis, but we never sought to elicit the 'good stories', and perhaps it should still be done before we forget how much good there was as well as how much evil.

In 1999 I was invited to join a group of people from the region, including Kosovo, Serbia, Macedonia, and adjoining countries, to discuss the implications of the conflict in Kosovo and the Nato bombing. The meeting was held in Budapest under the auspices of the Open Society Institute. It was a remarkable meeting, with many disagreements about future policy and strategy. One of those who attended was Sonya Licht, president of the Soros Foundation in Belgrade. She expressed interest in the South African experience and asked me for further information. I immediately stressed the difference between South Africa and Serbia but outlined what we had attempted to do here.

Not long thereafter, Sonya Licht invited me to visit Belgrade. I was due to speak at a meeting in Cape Town on the work of the TRC, and suggested to her that she attend that conference to test whether or not there was anything that South Africa could contribute to the Serbian situation. She came to South Africa, attended the conference, and told me afterwards that she was more convinced than ever that the South African model was the one that could help people like her who were in opposition to Slobodan Milosevic and sought to move towards a democratic alternative in Serbia.

I went to Belgrade in October 1999. The journey there in itself was interesting. Serbia was under very strict embargo at the time and there were no flights in or out of Belgrade. I flew to Budapest and was driven for three hours to the Hungarian–Serbian border. I got out of the car with my suitcase, and waited in the rain for someone from the other side to meet me and assist me across the border. Being a great fan of Le Carré, I had visions of a dramatic arrest or of being refused entry to Serbia. In fact the border crossing went very smoothly. There was a delay, but it was because the computers were down. I was questioned closely by the Serbian authorities but finally allowed to proceed. We then drove for a further three hours to Belgrade.

Serbia showed all the signs of a country enduring a stringent economic boycott and political turmoil; there were black marketeers in the streets and people marching

[401]

every night in opposition to Milosevic and his policies, and a tense, brooding atmosphere overshadowed everything and everyone. I had decided that I would make no public speeches but would keep the visit private. I met with a wide range of people representing alternative academic organisations, students, NGOs, independent media, and representatives of the Orthodox Church, and I attempted to outline the procedures followed by the South African Truth and Reconciliation Commission. There was unanimous agreement that the South African model did have a contribution to make, particularly in the area of truth-telling and the need to come to terms with the truth of Serbia's involvement in Kosovo and in 'ethnic cleansing'; a truth and reconciliation commission would give people an opportunity to express their own views and ideas not only about the past but also about the future.

We agreed that a public conference would be held, at which I would give the keynote address, and that invitations would be extended to representatives from Serbia and international organisations. I intended to emphasise that while South Africa is very different and a long way from Serbia, it might offer some clues that would help the people of Serbia to enter a more normal and more democratic climate. In the letter of invitation to the conference, the organisers wrote as follows:

> After ten years of war in this region, which has claimed thousands of lives, driven tens of thousands into exile and ruined the existence of hundreds of thousands more, the political situation in Serbia has begun to change significantly. As demonstrated by the local elections at the end of 1996, and the mass three-month-long demonstrations the same winter, the ruling regime in Serbia has started to lose the support of the population... That support has further declined and the regime is now only supported by a minority of Serbian citizens. It is our belief that very soon democratic and legal elections will lead to a

change in the present government and a return to power of pro-democratic forces in Serbia.

However, a mere change in the ruling parties, even a change in the type of political system, are not enough for Serbia to take a decisive and steady step along the path towards developing into a modern democratic state. Besides political transformation and economic reconstruction, the country is also in dire need of spiritual and moral renewal. After decades of communist monism, there followed a period of wide-spread mobilisation of nationalist feeling which shaped the way of thinking of a large number of people and which forms the cultural terms of reference for a whole generation. Nationalism in Serbia was, indeed, the deliberate plan of the political elite, but actively participating in that plan were, likewise, many of the country's intellectuals, and the resulting views were accepted and upheld by most of the population.

As we have pointed out, the consequences of this plan were extremely serious and in order to start removing them, we feel that it is essential to confirm the truth about the prevailing objective circumstances (historical and structural, internal and external, collective and individual), and similarly the truth about the participants (be they members of the political elite, intellectuals and ordinary people, those who gave the orders, ideologues and those who carried the orders out) who executed this tragic plan on the political scene. Ascertaining the truth will enable us to establish the responsibility for what happened in the region, and both, we believe, will be of value not only in helping to build a new Serbia, but also in ensuring that in other circumstances certain historical events will never occur again.

We are conscious that what we strive for entails a long and complicated process. We want to start that process, learning from the experiences of others. For this reason, we intend inviting to Belgrade a number of people who have travelled similar paths in their own countries and whose positive experience may help us to form our own route towards the spiritual revival of our society.

The conference and consultation were to take place at the end of April 2000. Unfortunately, the Serbian Foreign Ministry refused me a visa and I was unable to attend. I was devastated, not only because we had spent several months planning the event but also because I felt deeply for those who were struggling to keep alive the hope of democracy in Serbia. Fortunately, two of the invited speakers, Pepe Zalaquett from Chile and Patricia Valdez from Argentina, did not require visas and were allowed in. I have since heard that the attitude of the Milosevic regime has hardened and that several opposition leaders have gone into hiding. I keep in regular touch with the brave Sonja Licht, and we are working on other ways in which I can be of help to her and her colleagues, who fight a lonely battle.

EARLY IN 1999, journalist Jacques Pauw and cameraman Rian Oberholzer visited Rwanda. The result of that visit was an astonishing video entitled 'Les Genocidales', which was broadcast on South African television on the programme *Special Assignment*. It tells the remarkable story of Enos Nsabimana.

Nsabimana was a middle-aged Hutu man who in April 1994 joined in the orgy of killing when, acting on instructions from his government to 'kill the *inyenzis*' – the Tutsi 'cockroaches' – he killed his next-door neighbour. In a bizarre act, he kept the decapitated head.

He is awaiting trial, together with approximately 125 000 of his compatriots, for the crime of genocide. When Pauw interviewed him, Nsabimana still had his neighbour's skull, and held it out, as Andrew Donaldson describes the scene in the *Sunday Times* of 11 April 1999, 'like a begging bowl'. Donaldson suggests that the man was begging 'not for forgiveness but punishment. It was as if only a trial and his subsequent sentencing could put to rest his troubled soul.'⁹ Certainly Nsabimana was haunted by his killing of his neighbour, his confinement in prison for close to five years, and his confusion and bewilderment about how he ever became involved in such ghastly behaviour.

Nsabimana was like so many other Hutus who had listened to the appeal on Radio-Télévision Libre des Mille Collines (RTLM) which urged all decent Hutus to exterminate the Tutsis. Tragically, every segment of Rwandan society participated in the massacre of between 500 000 and one million people over a period of three months. The killers included doctors, nurses, teachers, priests, nuns, business people, government officials of every rank, even children.[10] The RTLM was widely listened to by the Hutu population and was one of the major reasons for the involvement of so many in the massacres, urging 'Let whatever is smouldering erupt ... at such a time a lot of blood will be spilled.'[11]

This is not the appropriate place to deal with the history of Rwanda and the events that led to the appalling genocide. Suffice to say that massive human rights violations have characterised recent history in that country. Dr Faustin Nteziyayo, the Minister of Justice, explained at a conference in Geneva in 1998 that 'The first large-scale ethnic massacres in the history of Rwanda were incited by the authorities and occurred in the 1950s.' Other serious human rights violations followed, and people of the stature of Bertrand Russell and Jean-Paul Sartre described the massacres of the Tutsis in Rwanda in December 1963 and January 1964 as the most 'barbarous and systematic acts of genocide committed since the Jewish Holocaust under the Nazis during World War II'.[12] But previous massacres almost fade into insignificance in relation to the genocide that took place throughout the country in 1994.

The genocide not only left hundreds of thousands of people dead or injured and homes destroyed, but whatever legal structure had previously been in place in Rwanda was almost entirely destroyed. Most of the buildings, offices, and resources were burnt down or destroyed; almost all of

[405]

the judges and lawyers were killed or fled the country, and it is estimated that 'only 40 magistrates remained after the genocide'.[13] It was therefore impossible for the courts to prosecute the offenders. As a consequence, Rwanda appealed to the United Nations and requested the establishment of an international tribunal. In November 1994 the UN established the International War Crimes Tribunal for Rwanda, which was closely linked with the already established Tribunal for the former Yugoslavia.

Ironically, Rwanda was the only member of the Security Council which voted against the appointment of the very tribunal that it had asked for. There were a number of reasons for this. Firstly, the Tribunal did not provide for the death penalty. Secondly, the seat of the Tribunal was to be in Arusha, Tanzania, and not in Rwanda. Thirdly, the proposed period for consideration, from 1 January to 31 December 1994, was believed to be far too limited. Fourthly, the Rwandan government was critical of the composition and structure of the Tribunal. Finally, Rwanda was concerned that the Tribunal, based in a neighbouring country, would take precedence over and have access to better resources than the very poorly equipped courts in Rwanda.

Nevertheless, both Rwanda and the international community were concerned that those who had been involved in the massacre of the Tutsi population had to be brought to justice and prosecuted.

The appointment of a truth and reconciliation commission in Rwanda was considered as well. The South African TRC was asked by Justice Minister Nteziyayo to send a delegation to Rwanda to share the insights we had gained in our own attempts to deal with South Africa's past. In 1997 a delegation led by Hlengiwe Mkhize spent a week in the country consulting with the new government and sharing in particular the early drafts of a policy for reparation for victims. A few months later a high-level delegation from Rwanda visited South Africa at the invitation of the TRC and spent a week talking with members of the Commission as well as many people in government and relevant NGOs.

At a conference in Geneva, Nteziyayo said:

Much attention has been devoted to the question of
uncovering the truth about the genocide and other
crimes against humanity committed in Rwanda and
whether or not a truth and reconciliation commission
should be established. It is essential that the people of
Rwanda and the international community should be
aware of how such a cruel crime was conceived,
planned and carried out.[14]

He referred to an earlier conference held in Rwanda which
had urged a comprehensive documentation of the genocide,
and had recommended that a committee of distinguished
people be established to set up a memorial authority, documentation centre, or other suitable body. Although the conference did not specifically recommend the appointment of
a truth and reconciliation commission, it did recommend
'that the government of Rwanda undertake all possible
measures to ensure that those who suffered or died at the
hands of their fellow citizens are at least secured the dignity
of remembrance and truth'. Nteziyayo said that this excerpt
underscored the need for truth, 'whatever means are used to
uncover it, and the vital importance of interaction between
such a mechanism and the court system so that comple-
mentarity can exist and information [be] exchanged'.[15]

An important and interesting development is the decision by the Rwandan government to introduce participa-
tory justice in the search for truth, as well as court action.
This approach draws on customary law procedures such as
Gacaca. The word 'Gacaca' in the Kinyarwanda language
refers to the grass that village elders sat on as they
mediated the disputes of rural life in Rwanda.[16]

The main strength of this traditional approach would
be to try to resolve the impossible situation of bringing all
those incarcerated for five years, in intolerable conditions,
to trial, and the direct involvement of the population at
grass-roots level. Nevertheless there are some very real
concerns about its use as a method of seeking accountability and reconciliation.[17]

Firstly, there is no certainty that Rwanda has the personnel and resources to put such an ambitious procedure in place. The assumption underlying Gacaca is that there will be 10 000 tribunals acting concurrently within the existing system, and all members of these tribunals are to be elected. Secondly, there are bound to be strains and problems arising from the concurrent operation of an international tribunal, a national tribunal, and a local grassroots procedure such as Gacaca. It is difficult to know how the problems that will inevitably arise are going to be resolved. Thirdly, bearing in mind that Gacaca was a system instituted for the resolution of fairly basic day-to-day conflicts involving theft and the like, it is not easy to see how this system can deal with the question of genocide without trivialising it. Fourthly, traditional customary law involved old men of the village who were regarded as wise elders mediating between victim and perpetrator. But the majority of people living in Rwanda now are women; they will have to be included if the system is going to work at all, and it is likely that society will resist their role. Furthermore, as a result of the massacre, the new population consists of fewer older men and many more young people, who would have to be included in the process as well. A final concern among many within Rwanda and in the international community is that Gacaca could be seen as a short cut to amnesty without adequate acknowledgement and accountability.

It is easy to be critical of the Rwandan government, but those of us who are outside that situation should be very careful; it is one thing to be critical of a decades-old custom, but it has to be borne in mind that neither the Tribunal appointed by the United Nations nor the Rwandan courts are going to be able to bring about the criminal accountability which is their aim. Some other way must be found. It should not be beyond the wit or ability of good people in government and civil society in Rwanda to adapt the ancient custom in order to deal with an almost intractable problem. Whatever else is true, the international community must not abandon the people of Rwanda. They have endured unspeakable horror and deserve maximum assistance. If criminal prosecution is not the whole answer and if Gacaca is unworkable, then other ways must be found to resolve the current crisis. Without prescribing to the authorities in that country, I would urge that some form of limited amnesty should be given serious consideration. One can only imagine the resentment building up among those who have been incarcerated for so long, in such appalling conditions. If we are to seek justice we must do so justly. The cycle of violence must be broken, and, difficult as it is, some attempt towards forgiveness on the basis of accountability must be sought.

Several of us who were part of the South African Commission continue to receive requests to visit Rwanda and to assist in their ongoing struggle. If time and opportunity are available, we will certainly continue to do whatever we can. It is particularly important not only for Rwanda's sake but also for the sake of the wider region, because whatever happens in Rwanda will impact on Burundi and the Democratic Republic of Congo. In the final analysis, what happens there also impacts on Africa as a whole, and it is in South Africa's interests to assist a country whose people have been so savagely decimated.

THE FINAL EXAMPLE that I want to offer in terms of the role that the South African experience might play in other societies is that of Northern Ireland. A number of South Africans have spent considerable time there, at the request of political parties and officials, NGOs and churches, sharing with them not only the experience of the Truth and Reconciliation Commission but also the whole negotiation process that led to free elections in South Africa.

I have visited Northern Ireland on several occasions, meeting representatives of a wide range of organisations. In February 1999, I was there under the auspices of the Northern Ireland Association for the Care and Resettlement of Offenders (NIACRO) and Victim Support Northern Ireland.

Before leaving for Belfast, I met with United States Senator George Mitchell (through the good offices of Professor Harvey Dale, a colleague of mine at New York University). In the hour we spent together I was enormously impressed with his insights and his wisdom. Mitchell had played a key role in securing a commitment to the Good Friday Agreement, the 1998 agreement which enabled the different factions to set up a form of local government in Northern Ireland. He is held in the highest regard by all the players in the Northern Ireland drama. Even those who resented an American being appointed as chairperson of the peace talks admire his patience, impartiality, and skills. Mitchell told me then that although a political settlement was crucial, that on its own would not ensure a peaceful society. Elsewhere he has written, 'It is important to recognise that the agreement does not, by itself, provide or guarantee a durable peace, political stability or reconciliation. It makes them possible. But there will have to be a lot of effort in good faith, for a long time, to achieve these goals.'[18]

Mitchell emphasised to me that Northern Ireland is essentially a victim community. Both sides, Loyalist and Republican, see themselves as victims under siege, and have long memories. As a result, there is an absence of trust, and the need to overcome this mindset is even more important than the serious problem of decommissioning arms, of the Irish Republican Army in particular, which had proved a major stumbling block. Nevertheless, Mitchell told me that the time was not ripe for any comprehensive truth-telling process, that the situation in the country was too fragile, that there should be more visible signs of reconciliation before such a process could begin. I suggested to him that it might be impossible to reach any meaningful reconciliation without some truth-telling. This was certainly the view of many whom I was to meet.

During my visit, I met a large number of groups and individuals. The following questions were raised by the organisers of my visit:

As we in Northern Ireland observe how South Africa faces these challenges, what can we learn from their experiences? How do we begin to deal with the damage we have inflicted on each other and to ourselves in 30 years of conflict if ultimately we are to achieve personal and community healing? In particular, how do we remember our history yet find creative ways of moving on? In so doing, how do we preserve our new-found peace while building unity and reconciliation?[19]

The objectives that the organisers and a wide range of their colleagues set for themselves included the following:

(1) to conduct a comparative perspective of shared truth and healing between South Africa and Northern Ireland; (2) to explore the transitional processes evident in moving away from conflict to accommodation and compromise; (3) to conduct a critical examination and analysis of what would be appropriate for and sensitive to our needs in Northern Ireland; (4) to start a debate and develop thinking, initially within key constituencies, on approaches to truth and reconciliation, which in turn enters the public domain; (5) to explore the public discourse surrounding truth and reconciliation, in particular the use of terms such as 'victim' and 'perpetrator'; (6) to establish a working group comprising key activists to prepare reports and make recommendations to political and community leaders; and (7) to explore the issues of symbolic reparation, at a personal, community and national level.[20]

In the draft report, recognition is given to the 'significant differences between the South African and Northern Ireland experience', but in the course of discussions a number of fundamental questions were identified which relate very closely to the South African experience. The agencies underlined this by stating, 'Whilst the particular TRC mechanism may not be judged to best suit the needs of

Northern Ireland, the importance of truth-telling, the position of victims and the need for reparation and reconciliation are all themes that have significant implications for Northern Ireland.' The overwhelming majority of the individuals and groups I met during my visit stressed the importance of meeting the needs of victims and confronting perpetrators in a way that would enable that divided society to move on from conflict. Most of the people I met recognised in particular the importance of truth-telling over and above the need for a political settlement. As the draft report stated, 'If there was one factor, one truth, that emerged from the visit it is in itself the importance of establishing truth, and as far as possible an agreed truth, as a vital means of moving on from conflict.'[21]

A number of similarities between Northern Ireland and South Africa were identified by the organisers of my visit. The first is the level of suffering. While many more people were killed in the South African conflict, for a small community such as Northern Ireland the number of people killed, injured, or losing their loved ones represents a significant proportion of the population. As in South Africa, the suffering in Northern Ireland has taken place over an extended period, involving at least three generations of people.

A second similarity is that in both countries there was a conflict that neither side could win. In Northern Ireland there are two sides in the conflict, neither of which will accept defeat and neither of which can be defeated. A critical question is, is it possible to achieve a reconciled community where surrender or defeat is required by one side or the other? Stress was laid on the problems of decommissioning IRA weapons, which, of course, were later resolved in the short term by delaying the actual implementation of decommissioning. This similarity also reveals a significant difference between the two situations. In South Africa, the two warring parties were aware of their strengths and their power, while in Northern Ireland both the Unionists and the Nationalists feel under threat and perhaps subconsciously feel their minority status.

Thirdly, because of the extended period of conflict in South Africa and Northern Ireland alike, we are both damaged societies. There are many thousands of victims of violence, many thousands of people who can envisage their societies only in the context of warring cultures and conflicting political aspirations. Like South Africa, Northern Ireland has many young people and adults who have little or no experience of or contact with people of other cultures with whom they share a common country and a common destiny. There are many people in Northern Ireland, as in South Africa, who believe that acts of political violence are a potential part of the solution. In both societies healing is of primary importance and will take a very long time to achieve.

A fourth similarity is a lack of awareness of the abnormal nature of the societies. Northern Ireland has known conflict for so long that it has come to be accepted as 'normal', and many have little knowledge or vision of a society which is not at war with itself. This was certainly true in South Africa for a considerable period, and the societies could learn from each other in this regard. Abnormal societies require abnormal or unusual solutions.

Fifthly, both societies have often been dishonest and are haunted by truth. I said during my visit, 'Dishonesty has permeated the history of this lovely and tragic land. Truth haunts us all.' But I said this against the background of my own society which has sought to deny its culpability and complicity. In Northern Ireland, as in South Africa, people live in a world of different and contested realities. Whatever process is followed in Northern Ireland, one objective must be to establish a truth that the majority of both communities accept: a shared Protestant/Catholic, Unionist/Nationalist, Loyalist/Republican memory.

A final similarity is the apathy and denial experienced in both countries. In Northern Ireland, as in South Africa, most who have suffered come from the disadvantaged sections of the community. Those who have suffered least and who have benefited most from the conflict over the last thirty years reflect an apathy and lack motivation to work

[413]

hard for change. The draft report concludes, 'In the development of truth that is accepted on all sides as the truth, the apathy of the better-off must be addressed. Truth and progress require at least the acceptance, but hopefully the commitment, of all sections of society in Northern Ireland.'[22]

At the time that the draft report was issued, there was no clarity as to whether the two major groupings, the Unionists and the Nationalists, would bury their differences in order to implement the Good Friday Agreement, which called for a new joint executive and for decommissioning.

The peace process has been tortuous, with successes and setbacks, but there does seem to be a large group of people in Northern Ireland who, whatever the developments may be on the political front, feel very strongly that some form of truth-telling should take place in order to come to terms with the past, to recognise that there are victims on both sides, and to acknowledge responsibility for the previous conflict as a basis for future development towards a human rights culture. What form this truth-telling will take is still very much a decision for the future.

Clearly there is a major difference between the nature and role of the state in South Africa and in Northern Ireland. South Africa has a new democratic state with a majority party determined to deal with the past and move towards genuine reconciliation. The people of Northern Ireland have to contend with the Republic of Ireland on the one hand and the United Kingdom on the other. Nevertheless, with considerable powers granted to the Assembly, it would be preferable if that body was part of the truth-seeking process. The only alternative would be for an NGO or a collection of NGOs to organise and implement a truth commission, which of course would lack resources and authority. One thing that is clear is that any process of truth-telling would have to be accepted as legitimate by all people of Northern Ireland. It would have to be seen to be independent and have the necessary overall support to conduct its proceedings in a way that reinforced that independence.

When the draft report was issued in July 1999, under the title *All Truth is Bitter*, I was sent a copy and was asked to respond to a fairly lengthy document, which was going to be widely distributed in Northern Ireland. I wrote,

> I don't want to add very much to the report and the issues outlined for discussion by yourselves. I think you have captured all the critical points and you have certainly heard enough from me!
>
> I write this response against the depressing news that the Peace Plan has collapsed and I can understand how disturbed and depressed you are. I think very deeply of your beloved country and I remind you that the South African process to peaceful negotiations was often aborted and sidelined and the only advice I can offer is that you dare not give up and there is hope in action.
>
> To both Unionists and Nationalists I send you the words of the Polish activist and co-editor of the foremost newspaper in Eastern Europe, Adam Michnik. He spent years in prison under the Communist regime in Poland and spoke with deep feeling when he was with us in South Africa. 'The image of the enemy is a moral and political burden because you are negotiating with someone whom only yesterday you called an oppressor, a murderer or a terrorist. You promised your followers that this person would be severely punished as a reward for the oppression they had lived through. Your followers, meanwhile, are telling you justice requires punishment. They ask: "How can you negotiate and talk to a person who is responsible for all the disasters of our people?"... I am negotiating because I have chosen the logic of peace and abandoned the logic of war. This means my enemy of yesterday must become my partner and we will both live in a common state. He may still be my opponent but he is an opponent within peace, not within war.'[23]

[415]

In Northern Ireland and in South Africa we simply have to learn to live together, otherwise we will continue to kill one another. This is the stark choice. We don't have to like each other, but we have to coexist with mutual respect.

I hope that good sense will prevail and that the next steps towards a joint executive and decommissioning will take place and that peace will break out in your beautiful country.

I received an invitation to return to Northern Ireland in March 2000, where I spent a few packed days meeting with a wide range of people and groups. Once again the hosts were Victim Support Northern Ireland and the Northern Ireland Association for the Care and Resettlement of Offenders. This was a follow-up to the earlier visit of February 1999 and coincided with the launch of the publication based on that visit, *All Truth is Bitter*. Among the groups whose representatives I met were the major political parties, organisations working with victims, the two major ex-prisoner organisations, Epic and Coiste na n-Iarchimi, the Human Rights Commission, and the Protestant and Catholic churches.[24]

The mood was very different from that of a year before: because of the dispute over the decommissioning of weapons, the British Secretary of State for Northern Ireland, Peter Mandelson, had suspended the Executive and the Assembly in Northern Ireland, and the government of that territory had returned to the United Kingdom. I visited Stormont where the Parliament is housed. It is a magnificent building set upon a hill and it seemed bizarre to have such a great facility with no government. Politicians were wandering around not sure what to do in the absence of formal sessions of the Assembly.

The politicians I talked to, on both sides of the political divide, were depressed, and the consensus was that the Executive would not be reinstated before 2001 at the earliest. This seemed likely, particularly in view of the challenge to David Trimble, the leader of the Ulster Unionist Party, who was the first minister in the Executive before the suspension took place. He and many other key political leaders had visited the United States and the White House that year to mark the celebration of St Patrick's Day, and he had made a public statement there which indicated that he was willing for the Executive to come together even though there was no guarantee that the IRA would give up their arms. This brought strong criticism from his followers, and instead of being reappointed almost as a matter of form, he was challenged by the Rev. Martin Smith, who is even more to the right than Trimble. Despite announcing his challenge only four days before the conference of the Unionist Party, Smith gained 43 per cent of the vote against Trimble's 57 per cent. This was a tremendous shock, putting Trimble in a precarious position and virtually tying his hands. Furthermore, the result suggested that those Unionists who had not been happy with the Good Friday Agreement had now come out of the woodwork, were more confident, and were going to make absolutely sure that any agreement met with their preconditions.

One of those preconditions was the retention of the name of the Royal Ulster Constabulary, the official title of the police force in Northern Ireland. This has always been a matter of dissension, because most of those serving in the police force have traditionally been drawn from the Protestant community; as a result it has been viewed with great suspicion by the Catholics. The Patten Commission had recommended that the name should be scrapped and replaced with a new name which would indicate a new approach and a new spirit to policing in Northern Ireland, and certainly a much more inclusive approach. To his credit, the chief constable, Sir Ronnie Flanagan, whom I met, supported the Patten Commission's recommendation even though he was sentimentally attached to the old name and symbol. He issued a statement describing the position taken by the Unionists as counter-productive. However, the motion passed at the Unionist conference made it clear that the retention of the name was now one of their demands before the Executive could be reinstated.

[417]

Clearly, the situation had hardened and the pessimism and depression that I experienced among many of the political leaders was understandable.

The same mood of pessimism had spread beyond the political leadership into civil society, and most of the people I talked to were disappointed that just when it seemed that the elusive prize of permanent peace was within their grasp, it had once again been spurned. Even though the ceasefire seemed to be holding, there was a sense of uneasiness and uncertainty among most of the people I met.

Despite this major setback, a number of new initiatives had been taken which should not be overlooked. The Patten Commission made some very far-reaching recommendations which, if carried out, would certainly bring long-term benefits. In addition, an inquiry into Bloody Sunday was in full swing; despite the huge costs involved and the time and resources that were tied up, this was a powerful signal that accountability was important for the new society. I was also once again enormously impressed by the quality of the people I met who were caring for ex-prisoners and for victims and their families. People such as Harold Good, Oliver Wilkinson, and Dave Wall are sterling examples of so many who by word and action are building the new society. While one often wonders how it is possible for so much evil to exist in the world, it is also a wonder to me that there is so much good and so many people who are so generous with their time and energy in caring for others. This is certainly a solid foundation on which to build. I was particularly impressed this time by my discussions with the two main ex-prisoner associations, one Nationalist, the other Loyalist. Of all the people I met, the ex-prisoners seemed to be more thoughtful, more committed to peace, than anyone else. Their experience in prison had clearly sobered them and had made them rethink the situation. They expressed regret for the loss of life and a determination that they would do everything in their power to ensure that there would not be a return to violence. The ones I spoke to were all working full time in the ex-prisoner associations. They told me

[418]

something of their childhood, their involvement in the conflict, their arrest and imprisonment, and their new determination to work for peace. Many of them feel rejected by the very people who had encouraged the actions which led to their incarceration.

On my last day in Belfast the official launch of the booklet *All Truth is Bitter* was held. The booklet was a compilation of the lectures and speeches I gave in February 1999 and the responses and questions from the various organisations, groups, and individuals I had met. In summary, the compilation is a comparative report looking at the experiences of the Truth and Reconciliation Commission in South Africa and considering the lessons Northern Ireland might learn from that process to inform the search for peace and reconciliation. It was made very clear, however, that there was no intention of imposing the South African model on the vastly different situation in Northern Ireland. Speaking at the press conference I stated,

> Northern Ireland is a place where communities share
> a common space, but no common history. There is
> very little doubt that this lack of a common history
> has fueled the culture of conflict that has beset North-
> ern Ireland for generations. Political agreement of
> itself will not change this society. Unless one begins
> to discover some common truths as to what has taken
> place here – painful truths – then no sufficient
> political consensus can emerge or lasting reconcilia-
> tion can take place.

I added, 'everyone we met agreed that we need to manage the trauma of victims and to deal with victims and ex-prisoners in a way that enables all to move on from conflict'.

In this context most of the people I met accepted the need for truth-telling. However, some felt that truth-telling would be too traumatic and that it would be better to leave people in permanent denial. From my own experience in South Africa, I think 'collective amnesia' is a short-term solution and a society intent on denying the past simply will not work. Conflicts must be transformed, not simply ended. I also tried to indicate my own understanding of the difficulties which lay ahead:

> the process of truth-telling needs to be truly comprehensive if common truths and an agreed reality are to emerge. Yet I found little to suggest a compelling, political or moral authority emerging from the peace process to sanction any kind of truth commission at this time. To achieve reconciliation, first there must be an acknowledgement of what has happened and who has suffered. We must move away from a hierarchy of victims. A key indicator of success will be that victims will not be used or abused as part of some ongoing political conflict.

I concluded my remarks by saying,

> for the process to work as in South Africa, it needs to hear evidence both from victims and from ex-prisoners. It also needs to hear evidence from the state, from its political masters and from its agents. This is even more complicated in Northern Ireland where authority at different times has been exercised locally and from Westminster and when at all times that authority has been contested.

As I reflected on yet another visit to that troubled land, so deeply divided, whose violence has been so intimate, I thought again that there needs to be a common commitment which transcends the age-old divisions, a commitment which is shared and explored across the divide of Loyalist and Nationalist. Perhaps one of the best things that could emerge are small groups who would deliberately cross that divide in order to seek commonality rather than division – a kind of liberation zone which could be the precursor of a larger and wider common community. It is groups like these that can engage in a search for an ever-widening acceptance that if there is to be enduring peace, there has to be a common foundation on which to build. It is crucial to break down ancient suspicions and re-build trust. This in turn could lead to the beginnings of the fashioning of a common memory, where widely divergent groups can accept that Northern Ireland is in many ways a society of victims, that the time to condemn and to blame must come to an end, and that the time for healing must begin.

I was pushed very hard by the media to speak in favour of a truth commission. I stressed that a firm, enduring political settlement without a return to violence was the first priority, although I did add that this goal was insufficient, and that if a damaged and deeply divided society was to be healed, some form of accountability was also essential. Truth-telling could play a major role in achieving that aim. What form that truth-telling should take is up to the people of Northern Ireland.

Soon after my visit I received a further invitation from the organisers, asking me to return to Northern Ireland for a much longer period. The suggestion was that I should stay for a couple of months. I am not sure whether this will be possible, because of so many other requests that come from other countries. One thing is certain, however, and that is that those who have participated in the South African experience of negotiation politics and the quest for truth and reconciliation have a major responsibility not to intervene or to tell others what they should do, but to respond to requests as they come as far as is humanly possible.

In early May 2000, there was a remarkable turn in fortunes for the stalled peace plan. Gerry Adams, the leader of Sinn Fein, persuaded British Prime Minister Tony Blair and Peter Mandelson that, instead of the IRA surrendering their guns, they would show their caches to independent observers and prove that the guns were stowed away and would not be used. This was a novel approach to say the least. But it could and did break the deadlock. By the narrowest of margins, Trimble persuaded the Ulster Unionists to return to the Executive, and in the last week of May power was returned from the UK to the Assembly in Stormont.

Who are the observers who enjoy the trust of the IRA? They are former Finnish President, Martti Ahtisaari, who has a distinguished record in mediation, and former ANC secretary-general Cyril Ramaphosa. Ramaphosa played a central role in the successful negotiated settlement in South Africa and after a spell in Parliament has become a very successful businessman. A patient, deliberate man of very special talents and commitment, it is not surprising that the IRA felt he could be trusted. In addition, the ANC has special links with Sinn Fein and thus with the IRA. This could be a disadvantage because of Unionist suspicions about his impartiality. But knowing Ramaphosa personally, and having watched him at work in the negotiation process in South Africa, I have no doubt that he will very quickly demonstrate his commitment to peace rather than take sides.

So another chapter begins in the agonising search for peace and stability. The accord remains fragile and much remains to be done to achieve a degree of stability and the guarantee of peace. In this ongoing search, civil society will undoubtedly be called upon to play a major role in breaking down barriers and building peace.

The role of South Africans in Northern Ireland is yet another indication that our country, which received so much assistance from the international community during its years of oppression, is now in a small way able to repay that by sharing with not only the countries referred to above but many other parts of the world, some of the lessons and insights which have come about through the Truth and Reconciliation Commission.

It is clear that in the coming months and years many of us who have been directly involved in the TRC will be called upon to assist countries in transition. This in itself is an endorsement that the South African experience was worthwhile and important way beyond the country's borders.

Conclusion

WRITING ON THE documentary film 'Long Night's Journey Into Day', which features South Africa's Truth and Reconciliation Commission, *New York Times* reviewer Elvis Mitchell describes the film as 'a beautiful and often disturbing reflection on the nature of truth and forgiveness'. 'The documentary', he writes, 'captures the mandate of one of the most unusual social phenomena of the twentieth century.'[1] This is perhaps extravagant language, but it echoes the response I have heard from a wide variety of academics, activists, politicians, writers, and journalists from many parts of the world. In this book I have outlined the unique features of the Commission and I have described the remarkable interest shown by many countries in the South African model. What is the central core of South Africa's attempt to come to terms with its past?

Essentially it is the holding in balance of the political realities of a country struggling through a negotiated transition and an ancient African philosophy which seeks unity and reconciliation rather than revenge and punishment. These two poles, political and philosophical, cannot be separated from each other. The political reality of a negotiated settlement involving compromise and consensus made some form of amnesty inevitable. When South Africans began negotiating a settlement, the former regime remained in a position of strength, and therefore the options available to the incoming government were limited. We should not be surprised that political realities

[423]

influenced the choices made by South Africa in dealing with its past. This is exactly what has happened in almost every other country seeking to deal with similar problems. As explained in the last chapter, in decisions on transitional justice, moral and legal considerations are overshadowed by socio-political factors. In fact, the greater the commitment to ending violence and the more that peaceful coexistence is a declared goal of the transition, the greater the political restrictions faced by the transitional government.

The easiest response to the uneasy and uncomfortable demand facing South Africa's new dispensation would have been amnesia in the form of blanket amnesty. To the eternal credit of all involved, this did not happen, and a process was devised which on the one hand met the political demands of the time but on the other introduced a process which made acknowledgement and accountability possible. Also, this process kept the spotlight more on the victims and survivors than on the perpetrators. The challenge faced by the new government, in the words of the Interim Constitution of 1993, was to build 'a ... bridge between the past of a deeply divided society characterised by strife, conflict, untold suffering and injustice and a future founded on the recognition of human rights, democracy and peaceful coexistence'. This bridge was unity and reconciliation: unity over division, reconciliation over retribution, truth over lies and cover-ups, justice over impunity. And the hope was that the bridge of unity and reconciliation would lead towards the consolidation of democracy and a culture of human rights.

These were some of the goals that South Africa set itself, part of its vision for the future. They are summed up in the postamble to the Interim Constitution: 'The pursuit of national unity, the well-being of all South African citizens and peace require reconciliation between the people of South Africa and the reconstruction of society.' How was such reconciliation and reconstruction to be achieved? The postamble is quite explicit: 'In order to advance such reconciliation and reconstruction, amnesty shall be

granted in respect of acts and offences associated with political objectives and committed in the course of the conflicts of the past.' In order to achieve this task, the Truth
and Reconciliation Commission was appointed. Against
the background of the political realities and the needs of a
fragile emerging democracy the Commission was not a
second-best choice but was the very best approach for
South Africa.

Underlying and enhancing this political and social
pragmatism is an African view of humanity expressed in
the word *ubuntu*. The word is used quite deliberately in
the Interim Constitution: 'There is a need for understanding but not for vengeance, a need for reparation but not for
retaliation, a need for ubuntu but not for victimisation.' It
is noteworthy that the concept of *ubuntu* was not limited
to the postamble of the Interim Constitution and the
Promotion of National Unity and Reconciliation Act of
1995. In fact, the Interim Constitution and the 1996 Constitution took the unusual step of granting constitutional
status to African customary law.

As part of African custom and tradition, *ubuntu* has
therefore been granted legal significance, infusing the
country's jurisprudence with three concrete principles.
First, communitarianism and its emphasis on group solidarity enjoy primacy over individualistic tendencies in the
progress towards national unity. Second, the adjudication
process must be conciliatory in order to restore peace, as
opposed to an adversarial approach which emphasises
retribution. Third, the law promotes the individual's duty
to a larger group, rather than individual rights, demands, or
entitlement.[2]

In reflecting the *ubuntu* philosophy, the Truth and
Reconciliation Commission pointed to the need for more
community-orientated jurisprudence that acknowledges
the reality that individuals are part of a much larger social
context. This is not a unique emphasis. Gandhi repudiated
the fashion of ascribing crime to isolated individuals and
emphasised the need to focus on the character of society
that engenders depraved acts.[3] John Braithwaite reminds

[425]

us that communitarian traditions can also be found in the histories of ancient Arab, Greek, and Roman civilisations, Indian Hindus as far back as the Vedic civilisation (6000–2000 BC) for whom 'he who atones is forgiven', and ancient Buddhist, Taoist, and Confucian traditions that one can still see in the practices of Aung San Suu Kyi of Burma and the Dalai Lama.[4]

Another way of describing the choice made by South Africa is to emphasise the distinction between retributive justice and restorative justice. Restorative justice rejects the exclusive focus on punishment normally associated with retributive justice. In the words of Raul Alfonsin, Argentina's first elected President after the collapse of the military regime, 'In the final analysis punishment is one instrument but not the sole or even the most important one for forming the collective moral conscience.'[5] Restorative justice has manifested itself in the concept of a truth commission and in the South African model in particular.

Tony Marshall defines restorative justice as 'a process whereby all the parties with a stake in a particular offence come together to resolve collectively how to deal with the aftermath of the offence and its implications for the future'.[6] This definition raises the question of who is to be restored and to what they are to be restored. Braithwaite has attempted to answer these questions. In answer to the 'who' question, he says, 'Restorative justice is about restoring victims, restoring offenders and restoring communities.' To the 'what' question, he suggests, 'Whatever dimensions of restoration matter to the victims, offenders and communities affected by the crime.'[7]

These comments describe very closely the approach of South Africa's Truth and Reconciliation Commission. All the parties were involved in the negotiations and all the parties were involved in the debate leading up to the publishing of the Act which governed the TRC. It was not merely the incoming government, nor civil society, but all parties concerned who were involved in the negotiations and the commitment to dealing with the past. Furthermore, the Commission itself sought to restore not only

[426]

victims but also perpetrators and the community at large, by dealing with the past in order to move all concerned to a more stable, more decent, and more peaceful future. The Commission's stress was on the context in which offences took place: the involvement in different ways by all South Africans in the system of apartheid and the need in particular for beneficiaries of that system to acknowledge that responsibility and accept their complicity. It follows that the TRC was not only about reconciling two individuals who were on opposite sides of the apartheid struggle but the reconciliation of the whole community including structures and institutions as well as individuals.

It is precisely here that South Africa's distinctive and profound contribution is made to the debate on retroactive justice. It is not surprising that South Africa, like so many other countries, had to take seriously the political realities of the day. What is surprising and salutary is that it did not follow the retributive model of prosecutions or succumb to the strident demands from the former rulers and the military and security establishment for a blanket amnesty. The secret lay in adding to the political debate a philosophy which called into question the focus primarily on the individual and widened the focus to include the community and the whole of society. The Commission's emphasis on communitarianism is a healthy and timely counterpoint to the Western liberal emphasis on individualism.

The TRC was not 'the least unsatisfactory solution',[8] as some have argued. It should not be seen as a necessary evil, a second-best choice, when prosecution and general amnesty are politically problematic. It provided the only justice available in the context of a traumatic transition. The South African model is not an abdication of justice, it is a form of justice particularly suited to the uniqueness of the transitional context, and this is the signal contribution it makes to the ongoing debate concerning transitional justice. It is precisely here that the South African model can offer assistance to countries facing the prospect of transition. Furthermore, while broadening the concept of justice, the TRC model does not contradict retributive

[**427**]

justice. Aryeh Neier, who has consistently fought against impunity and prefers to focus on responsibility rather than reconciliation, nevertheless makes a very strong case for truth as justice:

> By knowing what happened, a nation is able to debate honestly why and how dreadful crimes came to be committed. To identify those responsible, to show what they did, is to mark them with a public stigma that is a punishment in itself and to identify the victims and recall how they were tortured and killed is a way of acknowledging their worth and dignity.[9]

Lawrence Weschler puts it even more graphically and suggests that the truth about the past serves a classic goal of justice by deterring potential human rights abusers:

> The broadcasting of truth answers and honors the scream after all, it upends the torturer's boastful claim that no-one will ever know. Prospectively, the broadcasting of truth has an effect that is at once more subtle and perhaps more momentous. For ... it is essential to the structure of torture that it takes place in secret in the dark beyond considerations of shame and account ... [T]he torturer needs to be certain that no-one will ever know; otherwise the entire premise of his own participation would quickly come into question.[10]

By the end of 2000 the TRC will have completed its work. The outstanding amnesty applications will have been heard and the codicil to the final report, incorporating the amnesty hearings which have taken place in 1999 and 2000, will have been written.

Is that the end? No, it is the end of the beginning; much more remains to be done in South Africa's pursuit of a human rights culture. But now the responsibility has shifted away from the Commission to the state and to civil society. There are, I think, several ongoing tasks at both a national and international level which will have to be undertaken if South Africa's bold initiative is to be fully exploited.

Firstly, referring specifically to South Africa, I have emphasised throughout that while reconciliation is a worthy and necessary goal, it is an endless pursuit and cannot be achieved instantly or comprehensively. The wounds on the body politic in South Africa go very deep and will take effort and time to heal. Reconciliation must be sought, encouraged, and nurtured at every level of society. I am still hopeful that President Mbeki will call for a Reconciliation Summit as recommended by the TRC. I know that he has called for a special national conference on race, which will be followed by an international conference on the same subject, to be held in South Africa. However, I have written to the President asking him to hold together race and reconciliation in the planned conferences. I have also discussed this with Barney Pityana, chairperson of the Human Rights Commission, who has been charged with the responsibility for these conferences, and he has assured me that reconciliation will figure prominently in the discussions. Of course, no number of conferences or seminars or surveys will on their own achieve reconciliation. Reconciliation must be bedded down and anchored in our political systems, our schools, our universities, and throughout society. After the American Civil War, it took generations for the wounds inflicted during that terrible conflict to be healed. Many other countries have gone through similar experiences, and it would be foolish in the extreme to imagine that South Africa will be any different. The quest for reconciliation, both structurally and individually, requires the commitment of all South Africans.

Secondly, there are many other far-reaching recommendations contained in the TRC's final report which deserve attention from government and civil society alike. While they are all important, there is one in particular that cries out for implementation. This is the critical question of reparation for victims.

Reference has already been made to the deafening silence from the government in relation to the

Commission's recommendations and the reparation policy in particular. This silence is not only lacking in compassion towards those victims who appeared before the TRC. It also ignores the judgement given by the Constitutional Court, in support of the constitutionality of the amnesty provision. A major factor in the court's findings was that reparation was to be granted in lieu of victims' right to sue in a civil court. Hopefully the matter of reparation will be pushed up the agenda. Not only so that we can fulfil our promises and meet at least some of the basic needs of the victims of the conflict, but also because I think the model proposed by the Commission can assist in the international debate concerning reparation. We have, in my view, a contribution to make, but no one is going to take us seriously unless the government responds to the Commission's recommendations. It is accepted that the heavy demands on the fiscus may make it impossible for all the recommendations to be accepted. But both in terms of individual and corporate reparations, there are many possibilities which should be open to the government. The subject of reparation is engaging and will continue to engage countries in and emerging from conflict. We should be ready to play our part.

The final area which in my view requires attention is a critical and constructive analysis of the Truth and Reconciliation Commission in South Africa as an idea as well as the outworking of that idea. A start has already been made in that a number of books have been written on the subject. But that is not enough. A survey of attitudes concerning the TRC would also be useful, but we need more than this. What would be ideal is a study group on which people from South Africa and beyond its borders could serve. It would be helpful if this study could be undertaken in dialogue with some of the commissioners and senior staff of the TRC. In that way we will be able to make an even greater contribution to the never-ending struggle for peace in South Africa and in many other countries.

A clue could be found in an initiative undertaken by the Ford Foundation, which has requested the New York

University School of Law, where I teach, to oversee a comparison of the truth commissions in Guatemala and South Africa. Several commissioners and senior staff from these two commissions have been asked to respond to what they see as the strengths and weaknesses of the respective commissions. A larger study, looking very carefully at the origins, work, and findings of the South African Commission, could prove to be invaluable to many countries that are constantly looking to South Africa for assistance in the field of transitional justice.

The South African Truth and Reconciliation Commission did not emerge and function in isolation. There were many truth commissions which went before it and many other approaches to gross human rights violations have been and continue to be made, such as the ad hoc tribunals appointed by the United Nations Security Council. It is important therefore to consider the South African model in relation to the current debate and climate as they affect transitional justice. One issue that requires consideration is the distinction between retributive and restorative justice, and the question of whether these two approaches are contradictory or complementary. It is seldom appreciated that the Western style of retributive justice is a fairly modern phenomenon. The time is long overdue that we acknowledge that the initial impulse to punish perpetrators of gross human rights violations is not enough. These acts of violence do not take place in isolation. They often have deep historical roots, sometimes accompanied by long-held grievances. They are frequently informed by deep divisions between rich and poor. If we are going to deal only with the perpetrators without seeking to restore the community in which these violations have taken place, all we will do is to make certain that the cycle of violence continues. These are serious problems and there are many different viewpoints on the two approaches. We have not been particularly successful in preventing or dealing with the acts of criminal violence and horror which continue to haunt us. We should be ready to explore every avenue to save lives and restore peace and justice. The fact that restorative justice has been central to the South African model suggests that this model could inform the current debate on crime in society.

A second issue is the possible conflict between universal jurisdiction on the one hand and national sovereignty on the other. The tendency in recent times has been to focus more on international remedies for genocide, 'ethnic cleansing', crimes against humanity, and other serious conflicts. Examples are the International War Crimes Tribunals for the Former Yugoslavia and Rwanda, and the Rome Diplomatic Conference held in 1998 which gave encouraging impetus to the formation of an international criminal court. In the final analysis, if it is possible, it would surely be better and more rewarding for national states to accept responsibility for gross violations which have taken place in their own countries. South Africa is a good example of a country which has come to terms with its past. In some circumstances the state may be so disintegrated that this is not possible, but the first attempt should always be to encourage and enable sovereign states to take the necessary legal, social, and political action. An alternative would be for neighbouring states to assume some responsibility for conflict resolution in countries adjoining their territory. An obvious example of this is the contribution made by Australia in East Timor. South Africa itself has been called upon to assist in many areas of dislocation and conflict in Africa. Nelson Mandela has been charged with particular responsibility for the troubled Burundi. There are many conflicts on our continent and it would be far better for South Africa and other African states to assume responsibility than to expect far-away countries to intervene. It does not, of course, follow that countries that are requested to assist can do so on their own. The major powers and international institutions must be ready to give maximum assistance, financial and otherwise, to those states that act, as it were, on behalf of the international community and in the name of human rights.

It is expected that the proposed International Criminal Court will regulate acts of genocide, 'ethnic cleansing', and crimes against humanity in the future. It will do so firstly by advocating norms which states are obliged to follow, and secondly by acting when states contravene international law. This will be a considerable improvement on the ad hoc tribunals which have been appointed to deal with problems of conflict. I hope, however, that when the International Criminal Court comes into being, it will not, either by definition or by approach, discourage attempts by national states to come to terms with their past. A number of unique circumstances exist in different countries, and situations of conflict have their own histories, pressures, and complexities. It would be regrettable if the only approach to gross human rights violations came in the form of trials and punishment. Every attempt should be made to assist countries to find their own solutions provided that there is no blatant disregard of fundamental human rights.

It is crucial that the cry for humanitarian intervention, however understandable, doesn't blind us to serious problems. Firstly, we have to accept that it is not possible to do everything. The United Nations, for example, simply does not have the power or the resources to engage in worldwide humanitarian assistance, and individual states are limited by the needs of their own societies. We must not promise what we can't deliver. A second problem could be that humanitarian peacekeeping could generate a reliance on military solutions, which could create more problems than it solves. Nation states will always act in their own interests, and it would be more sensible to encourage them to act humanely and positively than to impose coercive threats which could entrench the problems of dictatorship and anarchy.

A final focus which I believe is necessary is to evaluate critically the responses of the United Nations, Nato, and individual states to gross human rights violations. In his provocative and thoughtful book *Radical Evil on Trial*, Carlos S. Nino argues that such violations are so abnormal and inexplicable that they can only be termed 'radical

[433]

evil'.[11] To describe, for example, the killing of more than six million people and the unimaginable suffering of countless more in any terms less than 'radical evil' is to insult the victims of the Holocaust and contributes to the obscenity. In trying to come to terms with genocide, crimes against humanity, and other massive atrocities, not only does our moral discourse appear to reach its limit, but ordinary measures that usually apply in the field of criminal justice become inadequate. Abnormal atrocities demand abnormal measures.

A discussion on the origin and causes of evil is beyond the scope of this book, and I have discussed how the international community and individual states have attempted to deal with the fact of evil and its consequences in the last chapter. However, I think a focused and in-depth study of international interventions into areas of serious conflict is long overdue. We need to look at the credit and debit side of what has happened since the Nuremberg trials. In a recent book entitled *Deliver Us From Evil*, William Shawcross devotes an epilogue to an analysis of the situation at the end of 1999 in terms of old and new crises and interventions. His list is extremely discouraging and pessimistic. He refers to Russia's brutal assault on Chechnya, which left 200 000 refugees hopeless and helpless and many towns and villages destroyed. What is as depressing is the fact that the West hardly raised its voice against Russia's violation of basic human rights. Shawcross writes, 'Chechnya in fact showed the limits of the new humanitarianism extolled by both Bill Clinton and Tony Blair.'[12] The list of countries in turmoil is almost endless. He refers to Cambodia, Somalia, Bosnia, Kosovo, Serbia, the Great Lakes of Central Africa, Iraq, Sierra Leone, East Timor, Afghanistan, and Haiti. He could have added Angola, the growing tension between India and Pakistan, and between China and Taiwan. Humanity's capacity for evil seems to be limitless. And the response is often too little, too late, and inconsistent.

Some brave and valiant attempts have been made to try to stop the killing, the assaults, the arson, and the destruction which continue in many parts of the world. But one needs to question whether the methods used by the international community have been sufficient either to end the violence or to ensure that it doesn't recur. Rwanda teeters on the edge of further conflict. Sierra Leone remains deeply divided and the rebels have even butchered members of the United Nations peacekeeping forces. Journalists and photographers are among their latest victims. Even as I write, the situation in Zimbabwe is grim. Accounts and allegations of marauding bands of thugs who were determined that President Mugabe would stay in power continued until the election. Thankfully the election itself was relatively peaceful, but the economic situation remains bleak; with very high unemployment and with an unrepentant Mugabe, the outlook is not promising. East Timor was so badly damaged by the Indonesian army and the militia that it will take a generation at least for any significant recovery to take place. Bosnia, despite the best efforts of the Dayton Peace Accord, is a deeply divided, ethnically based society where the peace is maintained only by the presence of the Nato troops. Serbia, despite the bombing by Nato forces, continues to lurch towards greater and greater oppression.

Despite the best efforts of the International War Crimes Tribunals, little more than a handful of perpetrators have been brought to book in the former Yugoslavia or in Rwanda. To his great credit, the secretary-general of the United Nations, Kofi Anan, commissioned two investigations into quite obvious failures in Srebrenica and Rwanda. Both reports are very critical, not only of the Security Council and member states, but also of the former secretary-general, Boutros Boutros-Ghali, and of Kofi Anan himself. Several countries were singled out for particular criticism for failing to act before and during the Rwanda genocide, namely the United States, France, and Belgium. But it is not sufficient for the United Nations to sponsor investigations of its own conduct and procedures and actions. What is required is a wholly independent international commission which would try to assess both the

[435]

achievements and failures that have occurred in the human rights field over the last fifty years. We need to learn from the good news and the bad news.

In a very thoughtful and useful article entitled 'Rethinking International Human Rights: What Have We Learnt, Where Are We Going?', Richard B. Bilder attempts to outline the achievements that have taken place, and there is no doubt that these are very real achievements. He lists among others the adoption of the United Nations Charter in 1945, the Universal Declaration of Human Rights in 1948, the four Geneva Conventions on the Laws of War, and the 1968 Teheran Conference on Human Rights. He also singles out the 1975 Helsinki Final Act, which established the Conference on Security and Cooperation in Europe as an ongoing East–West dialogue dealing with human rights issues, among others.[13]

A further success is the growing number of non-governmental organisations, and there is no doubt that their involvement and influence has grown immeasurably, particularly over the last twenty years. Over the last thirty years the United Nations has become very involved in matters relating to human rights, election observation, care for refugees, and peace process monitoring. This has involved countries as far afield as Namibia, Angola, El Salvador, Nicaragua, the former Yugoslavia, South Africa, Somalia, Iraq, Haiti, Cambodia, Western Sahara, and East Timor.

Despite these achievements and many more, Bilder also quotes a large number of horrifying statistics: 'There have been some forty major conflicts during the 1990s. Some 500 000 to 800 000 people were killed in Rwanda and there are now reported to be more than 2 million dead from the war in Sudan, 100 000 dead in Algeria, 35 000 dead in Azerbaijan, 50 000 dead in Eritrea …37 000 dead in the Kurdish separatist conflict, at least 24 000 dead in the Kashmir insurgency.'[14] In his book *An Ethic for Enemies*, Donald Shriver quotes Walter Wink's estimates of people who have been killed in war:

Soldiers and civilians killed:

1500s	1 600 000
1600s	6 100 000
1700s	7 000 000
1800s	19 400 000

This gives a total of 34 million people, but, according to Wink, three times that number, 107 800 000 people, were killed in the twentieth century alone.[15] Those who towards the end of the century imagined that humankind was on an ever-upward escalator to greater and nobler things were doomed to disappointment. Tragically, more people were killed in the twentieth century than in the combined 5000 preceding years.

In a very interesting article entitled 'The Writing Life', Adam Hochschild states, 'The most interesting journey of exploration in my writing life began with a footnote.' He explains, 'A book I was reading quoted something by Mark Twain. At the bottom of the page a note said that Twain had written the passage when he was active at the turn of the century in the worldwide movement against atrocities in the Congo – events that had taken 5–8 million lives.' Hochschild couldn't believe the figures. After all, he had visited Africa half a dozen times as a journalist, once even to the Congo. A little later he took from his shelf a copy of Hannah Arendt's *The Origins of Totalitarianism*, in which there was a passing reference to the conquest of the Congo by King Leopold II of Belgium. According to Hochschild, Arendt cited an even higher death toll of 12 million, and described it as 'the blackest pages in the history of Africa'. But the astonishing point is that Arendt also mentioned this astounding number only in a footnote.[16]

The point that I am making, and others have made, is that while the credit balance is long and encouraging, the debit balance is depressing and discouraging. This surely points to the need to stand back and make a fresh evaluation of the attempts that have been made over the last fifty years to counter the evil acts of men and women in so many parts of the world. This is not to suggest that if we do an accounting we will be able to solve all the problems, extinguish all the fires, repair all the damage. Not at all. But we would be in a better position to learn from our mistakes and build on our successes. In any organisation, institution, or household, there comes a time to take stock, and I think it is now appropriate for such stock-taking to take place.

It is particularly important to take into account the objectives, the methods, and the unintended consequences of the actions of international agencies, individual states, or combinations of states which act to halt human rights violations which have taken place in a particular area. We also need to consider the possibility of anticipating areas of conflict. Are there early warning signals that we are simply ignoring or misinterpreting? Would it be possible to devise a set of guidelines with the emphasis on prevention rather than cure? At the moment, action always follows a disaster which has already taken place. In one sense this is almost impossible to avoid. It is difficult to get support from the Security Council or from individual states if there is only a threat of disintegration and massive violence. A response, tragically, is usually triggered by reports on CNN and other television services. By the time action is taken, and East Timor is a good example of this, the damage has been done. I can understand that there will be considerable cynicism about the possibility of early warning systems, of prevention, of anticipation, but no one can be pleased with the present approaches and their results. Despite the very best efforts of so many, evil continues to flourish. While it would be impossible to do away with this evil, we need to discover new ways, new approaches, to manage and to prevent at least some of the genocide and 'ethnic cleansing' which has haunted us in the past few years, and continues to haunt us as we begin the new century.

Some people will agree that such an inquiry is possible but will warn against the costs involved. I think there is a very short and powerful reply to that. How much did it cost to bomb Serbia? What does a single bomber cost? It is estimated that the United States has thus far spent some $5.5 trillion in 1996 terms on its nuclear forces; a single US B2 bomber costs $2 billion; and it has spent $60 billion in the last few years and will spend billions more in the next few years on its 'Star Wars' defence programme against missiles which many experts believe will never work and will not in any case protect against other simpler and more likely methods of nuclear, chemical or bacteriological attack.[17]

The point is that if a very small portion of the money expended on military hardware, or simply the cost incurred by the United States and other Nato countries in bombing Serbia and then having to find additional funds to repair the damage incurred in Kosovo itself, could be made available to fund such a study, it would provide very rich dividends. It is in the self-interest of the major powers and the international agencies to engage in an independent evaluation involving a range of experts in diplomacy and the formation of state policy, as well as NGOs, journalists, and scholars.

Finally, I want to return to the words of that remarkable political philosopher, Hannah Arendt. She argues that societies can be assisted to overcome the evils in their past and can be helped to change for the better through forgiveness on the one hand and promise on the other: 'The possible redemption from the predicament of irreversibility – of being unable to undo what one has done though one did not and could not have known what he was doing – is the faculty of forgiving.'[18] This concept of forgiveness as a means of assisting individuals and societies to overcome the evil of their past is not a popular concept. Nevertheless, it is an approach without which there can be very little hope in the world. Forgiveness is not something that can be demanded from the victims, but conditions can be created whereby forgiveness becomes at least a possibility. It would be simplistic to argue from the particular to the general but it nevertheless deserves stating that very few relationships or marriages or partnerships would survive without the quality of forgiveness. We understandably spend a great deal of time remembering. But this too can be a powerful tool for the continuation of violence. There comes a time when forgiveness needs to take place in order to deal with the past. Donald Shriver makes the case for forgiveness in politics in a way that collapses the dichotomies of remembering/forgetting, morality/pragmatism, ends/means:

> Forgiveness in a political context ... is an act that joins moral truth, forbearance, empathy, and commitment to repair a fractured human relation. Such a combination calls for a collective turning from the past that neither ignores past evil nor excuses it, that neither overlooks justice nor reduces justice to revenge, that insists on the humanity of enemies even in their commission of dehumanising deeds, and that values the justice that restores political community above the justice that destroys it.[19]

The second proposal Arendt offers, which must be held together with the first, relates to the future: 'The remedy for unpredictability, for the chaotic uncertainty of the future, is contained in the faculty to make and keep promises.'[20] Here, too, some would argue that you cannot accept the promises made by dictators and tyrants whose history contradicts what they say. But we do not live in a perfect world, and if one can gain agreement on a new constitution for a society emerging from the horrors of the past, this is the contract, this is the promise, to which all parties can give their consent. This is the foundation on which the new society can be built. South Africa is a living example of this faculty to make and keep promises as enshrined in its new Constitution and carried forward by the Truth and Reconciliation Commission.

I believe that Hannah Arendt points to the direction in which the current debate concerning transitional justice needs to go. On the one hand there is the recognition that full justice is impossible and that, unless there is something beyond punishment, there is very little hope for the restoration and healing of societies which have been deeply divided and deeply wounded by the conflicts of the past. On the other, there is the emphasis on the need for a new contract, a new commitment: a promise that the past will not be repeated, that the future will bring democracy, stability, and a culture of human rights based on a commitment to the rule of law. Dealing with the past is not dwelling in the past – it is part of the promise of a new future. South Africa, in the view of many international commentators, academics, and politicians, has struck new ground and has given a new dimension to responses to human rights violations. It is hoped that its approach in dealing with the past, and its emphasis on the promise of a new future, will inspire new and creative thinking and action in many parts of the world. Maya Angelou captures the essence of the South African approach:

> History, despite its wrenching pain,
> Cannot be unlived, and if faced
> With courage, need not be lived again.[21]

South Africa has indeed lived through its history. As I look back on the life and work of the Truth and Reconciliation Commission I have three major recollections. The first is the mixture of agony and joy which characterised so many of the public hearings. The second is the missed opportunities for reconciliation because of the ambiguous apologies offered by F.W. de Klerk and the National Party leadership. My experience was that victims and survivors were in the main more than ready to forgive but waited in vain for the apartheid leaders to say sorry.

Thirdly, despite the suspicion, distrust, and racism experienced within the Commission itself and among members of its staff, it did not succumb to these negative forces. Instead, it finally rose above them and completed its mandate. Some will argue that if the Commission itself found it difficult to be reconciled, how could it promote reconciliation in South Africa? This is to miss the point. South Africans, despite our differences and distrust of each other, despite incipient racism, can and often do rise above these problems in order to work together in our common pursuit for a new vision and a new society. The Commission was a microcosm of the country and in large measure achieved its goals. This surely is a pointer to the new South Africa. Despite the legacy of the past and the real divisions which still prevail, we can make it. It is therefore with a sense of hope rather than despair that I view the future of our country.

Endnotes

INTRODUCTION

1 'The Anatomy of Hate', 28 August 1990.
2 *Time*, 31 December 1999.
3 Timothy Garton Ash, *The File: A Personal History* (New York: Vintage, 1997).
4 Ibid.
5 Cathleen E. Smith, *Remembering Stalin's Victims* (Ithaca and London: Cornell University Press, 1996).
6 Timothy Garton Ash, *The File: A Personal History*.
7 Bruce Ackerman, *We The People: Transformations* (Cambridge, Mass.: Harvard University Press, 1991).
8 Quoted in Alex Boraine, Janet Levy, and Ronel Scheffer (eds.), *Dealing With The Past* (Cape Town: IDASA, 1994), p. 122.
9 Uri Savir, *The Process: 1100 Days That Changed the Middle East* (New York: Random House, 1998), quoted in Shari Motro, 'Behind Tinted Glass: The Oslo peace team's decision to negotiate a "peace without history"; cynical charade or political pragmatism?' (unpublished essay, New York University School of Law, December 1999).
10 Ibid.

CHAPTER I

1 The Commission was chaired by Dr Sam Motsuenyane and included two jurists from Zimbabwe and the United States, Advocate D.M. Zamchiva and the Hon. Margaret Burham respectively.
2 Kader Asmal, 'After Motsuenyane',

Mayibuye, October 1993, p. 14.
3 Kader Asmal, 'Coping With the Past', *Mayibuye*, February 1994, p. 27.
4 African National Congress, 'National Executive Committee's Response to the Motsuenyane Commission's Report', August 1993. In the end, 1960 was adopted as the cut-off date, because it was then that the massacre at Sharpeville took place and major political parties were banned.
5 Kader Asmal, Louise Asmal, and Ronald Suresh Roberts, *Reconciliation Through Truth: A Reckoning with Apartheid's Criminal Governance* (Cape Town: David Philip, 1996), p. 3.
6 Alex Boraine et al. (eds.), *Dealing with the Past*, p. 34.
7 Ibid.
8 Ibid.
9 Kader Asmal, 'Victims, Survivors and Citizens – Human Rights, Reparations and Reconciliation' (inaugural lecture at the University of the Western Cape, 25 May 1992).
10 Interview in the *Cape Times*, 24 February 1997.
11 The South Africans in the group included Pieter le Roux from the University of the Western Cape; Bill and Elsie Nair, trade unionists and members of the ANC; John de Gruchy from the University of Cape Town; Wiseman Nkuhlu from the University of Transkei; Sarah Pienaar from the University of South Africa; Sipho Radebe from the National Union of Public Service

Workers; Charlene Smith, a journalist; Gerhard Erasmus from the University of Stellenbosch; Neo Moikangoa from the ANC; and Jasper Walsh, Democratic Party member of Parliament.

12 Alex Boraine et al. (eds.), *Dealing with the Past*, pp. ix–x.
13 Lawrence Weschler, *A Miracle, A Universe: Settling Accounts with Torturers* (New York: Penguin, 1990).
14 Alex Boraine et al. (eds.), *Dealing with the Past*, p. 8.
15 Hansard, 21 June 1977, cols 10954–55.
16 Ibid.
17 Ibid.
18 *Democracy in Action*, August 1987, p. 2.
19 *Democracy in Action*, October 1987, p. 1.
20 *Democracy in Action*, February 1988, p. 4.
21 Ibid.
22 *Democracy in Action*, May 1989, p. 1.
23 Ibid, p. 2.
24 Alex Boraine et al. (eds.), *Dealing with the Past*, p. 109.
25 Hansard, 27 May 1994, col. 187.
26 Alex Boraine and Janet Levy (eds.). *The Healing of a Nation?* (Cape Town: Justice in Transition, 1995), p. xiv.
27 Ibid.
28 Ibid., p. xviii.
29 Ibid., p. 30.

CHAPTER 2

1 The following organisations were represented at the workshop: the South African Council of Churches; the Legal Resources Centre; the Trauma Centre for Victims of Violence and Torture; the Black Sash; Lawyers for Human Rights; the Department of Justice; the Institute for Democracy in South Africa (IDASA); the Black Lawyers' Association; the Centre for Socio-Legal Studies, University of Natal; the Mayibuye Centre; the Department of Psychology, University of the Western Cape; the Law Faculty, University of the Witwatersrand; the Department of Public Law, University of Natal; the Department of Religious Studies, University of Cape Town; the Department of Political Studies, University of Cape Town; the National Association of Democratic Lawyers; the Centre for the Study of Violence and Reconciliation; the World Conference on Religion and Peace; and the Independent Board of Inquiry. Several people attended the workshop in their personal capacities, including Mohsina Chenia, Muhammed Haron, Zubeida Jaffer, and Essa Moosa.
2 Letter from Dullah Omar to author, dated 7 February 1995.
3 Hansard, 17 May 1995, col. 1339.

CHAPTER 3

1 *Sowetan*, 22 January 1997.
2 *Citizen*, 23 January 1997.
3 Malan's minority report and the Commission's response are included in the TRC report, Vol. 5, pp. 436–60.

CHAPTER 4

1 The other three were Matthew Goniwe, Sparrow Mkonto, and Sicelo Mhlauli.
2 Antjie Krog, *Country of My Skull* (Johannesburg: Random House, 1998), p. 42.
3 Alex Boraine et al. (eds.), *Dealing With The Past*, p. 31.
4 Four people died in the attack. Beth had open heart surgery, half her large intestine was removed, and she had permanent bowel dysfunction.
5 Cosas is an acronym for the Congress of South African Students.
6 Judgement in Case CCT17/96, p. 35.
7 TRC report, Vol. 1, p. 176.
8 Ibid., Vol. 5, Chapter 7, pp. 259ff.
9 Eugene de Kock, *A Long Night's Damage: Working for the Apartheid State* (Saxonwold: Contra Press, 1998), p. 227.
10 Koevoet was a notoriously brutal military unit active against South West African People's Organisation guerrillas in Namibia.
11 TRC report, Vol. 3, p. 38.
12 Ibid., Vol. 5, p. 306.

CHAPTER 5

1 TRC report, Vol. 4, p. 1.
2 Ibid., p. 5.
3 Ibid., Vol. 5, pp. 233–4.
4 Sapa. 14.5.1997.

Endnotes

5 Piet Meiring, *Chronicle of the Truth Commission* (Vanderbijlpark: Carpe Diem, 1999), p. 139.
6 Piet Koornhof was former Minister of National Education, Sport, and Recreation and later Minister of Cooperation and Development.
7 Notice of Motion in High Court of South Africa, Case 8034/97, p. 21.
8 Ibid p. 22; Alex Boraine and Janet Levy (eds.), *The Healing of a Nation?*, pp.xvi–xvii.
9 *Star*, 22 October 1996.
10 *Cape Argus*, 17 May 1996.
11 F.W. de Klerk, *The Last Trek: A New Beginning* (London: Macmillan, 1998), p. 370–71.
12 State Security Council hearing, October 1997.
13 Ibid.
14 Ingrid Jonker, *Selected Poems* (London: Jonathan Cape, 1968), translated from the Afrikaans by Jack Cope and William Plomer.
15 *Twenty South African Photographs*, edited by Omar Badsha, introduction and text by Francis Wilson (Cape Town: University of Cape Town, 1986).
16 Speech by Cecil John Rhodes, 1887.
17 Hansard, 1953.
18 The institutional hearings are recorded in the TRC report, Vol. 4, pp. 8–219, and the special hearings on pp. 220–316.
19 TRC report, Vol. 4, p. 32 .
20 Ibid., p. 52.
21 Ibid., p. 22.
22 Ibid., pp. 22–3.
23 Ibid., p. 24.
24 Ibid., Vol. 5, p. 308.
25 Ibid., p. 319.
26 Dietrich Bonhoeffer, *The Cost of Discipleship*, trans. R.H. Fuller (New York: Macmillan, 1963), Chapter 1.
27 TRC report, Vol. 5, p. 316.
28 Ibid.
29 David Dyzenhaus, 'With the Benefit of Hindsight' (University of Toronto, 1998).
30 TRC report, Vol. 4, p. 107.
31 Ibid., p. 108.

CHAPTER 6
1 Biographical information taken in part from Shelagh Gastrow, *Who's Who in South African Politics* (Johannesburg: Ravan Press, 1995).

2 F.W. de Klerk, *The Last Trek*, p. 146.
3 Hansard, Vol. 50, col. 802.
4 Hansard, 26 Aug. 1974, col. 1481. 'Wits' is the University of the Witwatersrand.
5 F.W. de Klerk, *The Last Trek*, pp. 125–6. *Leierstryd* was published by Tafelberg, Cape Town, in 1990.
6 Ibid., p. 130.
7 Ibid., p. 146.
8 Victor Lugagu was born in the Eastern Cape and worked as a court interpreter, prosecutor, and Regional Court magistrate in Umtata. He was a lecturer in law at the University of the Transkei and has an MA degree from the University of South Africa.
9 *Star*, 12 February 1998.
10 *Rapport*, 5 April 1998.
11 Ibid.
12 Ibid.
13 Quoted in Piet Meiring, *Chronicle of the Truth Commission*, pp. 337–8.
14 *Cape Times*, 4 June 1998.
15 *Mail & Guardian*, 5–11 June 1998.
16 *Cape Argus*, 5 June 1998.
17 Ibid.
18 *Star*, 5 June 1998.
19 *Cape Argus*, 15 June 1998.
20 Appeal Court's notes for judgement, in respect of P.W. Botha v The State, 1 June 1999.
21 TRC report, Vol. 5, pp. 223–5.

CHAPTER 7
1 *Cape Times*, 6 January 1998.
2 Quotations in this chapter are drawn from the transcript of the Human Rights Violations hearing into the Mandela United Football Club, Johannesburg, 24 November 1997 and 28 January 1998.
3 Biographical information taken in part from Shelagh Gastrow, *Who's Who in South African Politics*.
4 Fatima Meer, *Higher than Hope* (London: H. Hamilton, 1990).
5 *Sunday Times*, 26 October 1997.
6 Oscar Wilde, *The Importance of Being Ernest*, Act I, Scene I.
7 *Sechaba*, 18 February 1989.
8 The statement declared, inter alia, 'In recent years, Mrs Mandela's actions have increasingly led her into conflict with various sections of the oppressed people and with the Mass Democratic Movement as a whole. The recent conflict in the

community has centred largely around the conduct of her so-called Football Club which has been widely condemned by the community. In particular, we are outraged by the reign of terror that the team has been associated with. Not only is Mrs Mandela associated with the team, in fact, the team is her own creation.

'We are of the view that Mrs Mandela has abused the trust and confidence which she has enjoyed over the years. She has not been a member of any of the democratic structures of the UDF and Cosatu, and she has often acted without consulting the democratic movement. Often, her practices have violated the spirit and ethos of the democratic movement.

'Numerous efforts have been made to reconcile the conflict between Mrs Mandela and the community. The last of these efforts was the formation of a crisis committee comprising some of our most able and respected members. On every occasion Mrs Mandela has refused to co-operate and has chosen to disregard the sentiments of the community.

'The Democratic Movement has uncompromisingly fought against violations of human rights from whatever quarter. We are not prepared to remain silent where those who are violating human rights claim to be doing so in the name of the struggle against apartheid.

'We are outraged at Mrs Mandela's complicity in the recent abductions and assault of Stompie. Had Stompie and his three colleagues not been abducted by Mrs Mandela's 'Football Team', he would have been alive today.

'The Mass Democratic Movement hereby distances itself from Mrs Mandela and her actions.'

9 *Daily News*, 12 December 1997.
10 W.H. Auden, 'September 1, 1939', in *Selected Poems*, ed. Edward Mendelson (London: Faber and Faber, 1979), p. 86.
11 TRC report, Vol. 4, p. 251.
12 *Star*, 11 December 1997. Kole Omotoso comments, 'The question

that all victims must answer is this, at which point do we become what we are fighting against?', *Cape Times*, 16 February 1999.
13 Max Frankel, *The Times of My Life and My Life With The Times* (New York: Random House, 1999).
14 TRC report, Vol. 5, pp. 243–4.

CHAPTER 8
1 Albie Sachs, 'Fourth D.T. Lakdawala Memorial Lecture', New Delhi, 18 December 1998.
2 Ibid.
3 Ibid.
4 Statement by the president of the African National Congress, Thabo Mbeki, on the report of the TRC: Joint Sitting of the Houses of Parliament, Cape Town, 25 February 1999.
5 Albie Sachs, 'Fourth D.T. Lakdawala Memorial Lecture'.
6 Ibid.
7 Antjie Krog, *Country of My Skull*, p. 152.
8 Albie Sachs, 'Fourth D.T. Lakdawala Memorial Lecture'.
9 Ibid.
10 F.W. de Klerk is very interesting in his comments on the postamble, which provides for a limited form of amnesty. 'However, the question of amnesty was not resolved. In the end, the best that our negotiating team could do was to reach agreement on the inclusion of a paragraph at the end of the interim constitution that stipulated that "amnesty shall be granted in respect of acts and omissions and offences associated with political objectives and committed in the course of the conflicts of the past." Amnesty was to be dealt with "in a spirit of reconciliation, on the basis that there is a need for understanding but not for vengeance, a need for reparation but not for retaliation, a need for *ubuntu* (traditional African humanism) but not for victimisation." This wording – although guaranteeing that amnesty would be granted for politically motivated acts – provided little or no indication of how the process would be managed in practice. It soon became clear that the ANC was determined to delay the clarification

of this question until after the election, when it would be able to enforce its will through its majority in Parliament. They later did exactly this through the adoption of the Promotion of National Unity and Reconciliation Act of 1995, which led to the establishment of the Truth and Reconciliation Commission. By that time, all that the National Party could do was to fight a rearguard action and reach agreement on the best deal that was then possible. The manner in which we dealt with the question of amnesty was probably our greatest failure during the negotiating process.' *The Last Trek*, p. 289.

11 Ronald C. Slye, 'Amnesty, Truth, and Reconciliation: Reflections on the South African Amnesty Process' (unpublished paper, May 1998).

12 100 Yale LJ 2537, 2542–44 (1991).

13 Carlos Santiago Nino, *Radical Evil on Trial* (New Haven: Yale University Press, 1996), p. 188.

14 In 1946 the General Assembly adopted Resolution 95(1) which ratified the principles of international law recognised by the Charter and judgement of the Nuremberg trials. The International War Crimes Tribunals were governed by the United Nations Charter, Chapter VII, Article 41.

15 Tina Rosenberg, *The Haunted Land: Facing Europe's Ghosts After Communism* (New York: Vintage, 1995), p. 312.

16 See Priscilla B. Hayner, 'Fifteen Truth Commissions 1974–1994: A Comparative Study', *Human Rights Quarterly* 597, 614 (1994); 'Commissioning the Truth: Further Research Questions', 17, *Third World Quarterly* 19, 20 (1996).

17 Marvin Frankel, *Out of the Shadows of the Night: The Struggle for International Human Rights* (New York: Delacorte Press, 1989), pp. 103–4.

18 Azapo judgement, para. 17.

19 Antjie Krog, *Country of My Skull*, p. 36.

20 *Remaking the Past* (Department of Adult Education and Extramural Studies, University of Cape Town, 1968).

21 Michael Ignatieff, 'Articles of Faith',

Index on Censorship 5 (1996), p. 113.

22 Alex Boraine and Janet Levy (eds.), *The Healing of a Nation?*

23 Ibid., p. 105.

24 *Africa News*, January 1998.

25 Ibid.

26 TRC report, Vol. 5, pp. 170–95.

27 Aryeh Neier, Review of Truth Commission of South Africa report, New York, January 1999.

28 Cherry Annette Hill, 'Transitional Justice in South Africa: The Truth and Reconciliation Commission is the Most Appropriate Policy to Deal with Human Rights Violations in South Africa' (unpublished MA thesis, University of Otago, Dunedin, New Zealand, April 1997).

29 TRC report, Vol. 5, p. 309.

CHAPTER 9

1 Many of us who served on the Commission are among its sternest critics. I believe very deeply that the process was right, has served a purpose and will influence many other countries and institutions. I am acutely aware, however, of many of its shortcomings. In Volume 5 of its report, the Commission places on record its recognition of some of these shortcomings (pp. 206–8).

2 *Bookseller*, February 1999.

3 TRC report, Vol. 5, p. 212.

4 Ibid., pp. 240–41.

5 Ibid., pp. 241–2.

6 Ibid., pp. 242–3.

7 Ibid., pp. 245–7.

8 *Saturday Argus*, 31 October 1998.

9 *Sunday Times*, 1 November 1998.

10 Ibid.

11 Ibid.

12 Ibid.

13 Ibid.

14 Ibid.

15 Hansard, 5 February to 26 March 1999, col. 33.

16 Ibid., cols 33–6.

17 Ibid., cols 47–9.

18 TRC report, Vol. 1, p. 68.

19 Ibid., pp. 67, 69.

20 André du Toit, 'Perpetrator Findings as Artificial Even-Handedness' (unpublished paper), p. 7.

21 Ibid., p. 8 .

22 Ibid., pp. 12–13.

23 Ibid., p. 13. Du Toit, in developing his paper, also comes to the

conclusion that the TRC ought not to have made findings, not on the basis of moral equation or otherwise, but because the Commission was not qualified to make those findings and they should have been left to the courts. I do not agree with this conclusion. The Act which governed the work of the TRC, particularly Sections 3 and 4, set out very clearly the objectives of the Commission. One of the major tasks given to the TRC was 'Analysing and describing the causes, nature and extent of gross violations of human rights that occurred between 1 March 1960 and 10 May 1994, including the identification of the individuals and organisations responsible for such violations.' It is my considered view that the TRC would have been derelict in its duty if it had not made perpetrator findings.

24 Hansard, 5 February to 26 March 1999, cols 146–7.

25 Address by Barney Pityana to the 29th Provincial Synod of the Church of the Province of Southern Africa, Durban, 16 July 1999.

26 Ibid. Dot Cleminshaw, a human rights activist and member of the ANC, takes Pityana to task for siding with the ANC in an unpublished paper which is an excellent corrective to Pityana's argument.

27 TRC report, Vol. 5, p. 240.

28 Ibid., pp. 175–6. A full explanation of the reparation and rehabilitation policy as recommended to government is set out in Vol. 5, pp. 170–95.

29 Ibid., pp. 312–13.

30 Robert Burns, 'Man Was Made to Mourn'.

CHAPTER 10

1 Hugo van der Merwe, Polly Dewhirst, and Brandon Hamber, 'The Relationship between Peace/Conflict Resolution Organisations and the Truth and Reconciliation Commission: An Impact Assessment' (paper prepared for the International Study of Peace Organisations – SA, funded by the Aspen Institute, April 1998).

2 *Baltimore Sun*, 30 July 1998.

3 *New York Times*, 3 November 1998.

4 *New York Times*, 5 November 1998. Johnson, revealing remarkable bias, includes a number of factual errors in his article, but the worst aspect was his claim that F.W. de Klerk was 'harangued in the witness box for six straight hours without a recess (a chain smoker, he was denied even a cigarette break)'. In my response to the editor of the *New York Times* I responded, 'The complaint that de Klerk was denied a "cigarette break" when he appeared before the Commission is not only frivolous, it is obscene. Even if it were true, which it is not, it pales into insignificance when one considers the thousands of South Africans who were hounded, detained without trial, tortured and killed by agents of the State of which Mr de Klerk was minister and then State President!'

5 *The Times*, 31 October 1998.

6 *New York Times*, 1 November 1998.

7 *Washington Post*, 13 September 1998.

8 Richard Penwill, in *Track Two* 6, 3–4 (Centre for Conflict Resolution, University of Cape Town, December 1997), p. 27.

9 This demonstration occurred at the amnesty hearing of Captain Jeffrey Benzien in Cape Town, on 14 July 1997.

10 Richard Penwill, in *Track Two* 6, 3–4, p. 47.

11 'National Reconciliation: Holy Grail or Secular Pact?', in Charles Villa-Vicencio and Wilhelm Verwoerd (eds.), *Looking Back Reaching Forward: Reflections on the Truth and Reconciliation Commission of South Africa* (Cape Town: Juta and University of Cape Town Press, 1999)

12 National Assembly, 29 May 1998.

13 Inaugural address, 16 June 1999.

14 TRC report, Vol. 5, p. 352.

15 Ibid., p. 353.

16 Ibid., p. 354.

17 Guguletu is a township outside Cape Town.

18 TRC report, Vol. 5, p. 366.

19 Ibid., p. 374.

20 Ibid., p. 377.

21 Ibid., p. 378.

22 Ibid., p. 382.

23 Ibid., p. 392.

24 Ibid., p. 308.

25 Ibid.

26 Ibid., p. 309.

27 Ibid.

28 J. Cabazares in Walter Wink, *Healing a Nation's Wounds* (Uppsala, Sweden: Life & Peace Institute: 1996), p. 23.

29 Yvonne Mokgoro *Ubuntu and the Law in South Africa*, 4 Buff.Hum.Rts.L.Rev.15 (1998)

30 Yvonne Mokgoro, *The Protection of Cultural Identity in the Constitution and the Creation of National Unity in South Africa: A Contradiction in Terms?*, 52 SMU l.Rev.1549, 1557 (1999). The phrase is cited in Xhosa and Setswana.

31 Anton Lembede, quoted in Peter Dreyer, *Martyrs and Fanatics, South African and Human Destiny* (New York; Simon and Schuster, 1980), 154.

32 Pepe Zalaquett, 'Balancing Ethical Imperatives and Political Constraints: the Dilemma of New Democracies Confronting Past Human Rights Violations', in Neil Kritz (ed.), *Transitional Justice* (Washington DC: US Institute for Peace, 1995), Vol. 2, p. 495–96.

33 Hannah Arendt, *The Human Condition: A Study of the Central Conditions Facing Modern Man* (Garden City, NY: Doubleday Anchor Books), p. 214. I think Hannah Arendt exaggerates. It is more exact to say that Jesus gave centrality to the concept of forgiveness in an individual and community sense. Certainly there are a number of references in the Old Testament which refer to forgiveness, both individual and in the community.

34 Donald Shriver, *An Ethic For Enemies: Forgiveness in Politics* (New York: Oxford University Press, 1995), p. 34.

35 Karl Jaspers, *The Question of German Guilt* (New York: The Dial Press, 1947), p. 31.

36 Ibid., p. 112.

37 Walter Niemoller, *Neuenfang 1945: Zur Biographie Martin Niemoller* (Frankfurt: Guttersloh, 1976).

38 Walter Niemoller, 'Letter of the Council of the Evangelical Churches in Germany to the Allied Control Council and the German State Governments', 2 May 1946, published in *Wort zur Verantwortung der Kirche fur das Offentliche Leben*, ed. Friedrich Sohlmann (Lunenberg Heliand Verlag, 1945–46).

39 Geoffrey Hartmann (ed.) appendix *Bitburg*, pp. 262–73.

40 Ibid.

41 Ibid.

42 *New York Times*, 22 April 1985. It is important to bear in mind that this speech was made at the liberation of Bergen-Belsen, where more than 50 000 Russian prisoners were killed by the Germans.

43 Quoted by Donald W Shriver, in *An Ethic for Enemies*, as reproduced in *Redress!* Japanese American Citizens League, n.d. (c. 1983), p. 2. Shriver reminds us that it was only in the Civil Liberties Act of 1988 that a formal Congressional apology for the internments was made which authorised a fund of $1.2 billion for payments of $20 000 each to the 60 000 or more internees still alive in 1988. The Act also established a foundation of $50 million for the promotion of the cultural and historical concerns of Japanese-Americans.

44 Ibid.

45 *Bringing Them Home: Report of the National Inquiry into the Separation of Aboriginal and Torres Strait Islander Children from their Families*, Human Rights and Equal Opportunities Commission, Australia, 1997.

46 Michael Ignatieff, *Index on Censorship: Wounded Nations, Broken Lives* 25 (1996), p. 122. The massacre took place at Jasenovac during the Second World War.

47 Ibid., p. 121.

48 Desmond Tutu, media statement issued on 8 May 1997.

49 Alex Boraine and Janet Levy (eds.), *The Healing of a Nation?*, p. 113.

50 Antjie Krog, in Alex Boraine and Janet Levy (eds.), *The Healing of a Nation?*, pp. 113–15.

51 Constitutional Court Case CCT 17/96.

52 Adam Michnik, in Alex Boraine et al. (eds.), *Dealing With the Past*,

p. 16. Michnik is co-editor of *Gazetta*, the Warsaw-based successor to Solidarity's underground journal which is now the foremost newspaper in Eastern Europe. He is recognised internationally as a key philosopher and theorist of Poland's Solidarity movement.

53 *Siyaya*, Spring 1998, p. 60.
54 *Index on Censorship: Wounded Nations, Broken Lives* 25 (1996), p. 122.

CHAPTER 11

1 Aryeh Neier, Review of Truth Commission of South Africa report.
2 *New York Review of Books*, 18 November 1999, p. 18.
3 Timothy W. Ryback, 'Violence Therapy for a Country in Denial', *New York Times Magazine*, 30 November 1997.
4 *Time*, 27 September 1999.
5 Organisation for Security and Cooperation in Europe.
6 Neil J Kritz, 'Is a Truth Commission Appropriate in the Former Yugoslavia', International Conference on War Crimes Trials, Belgrade, 7–8 November 1998.
7 Ibid.
8 'Appeal to the Presidency to Establish A Truth And Reconciliation Commission', Tuzla, August 27 1998.
9 *Sunday Times*, 11 April 1999.
10 Lawyers' Committee for Human Rights, Washington DC, July 1997, p. 4.
11 Gourevitch, Philip. *We Wish to Inform You that Tomorrow We Will Be Killed With Our Families: Stories from Rwanda* (New York: Farrar Straus and Giroux, 1998).
12 From an unpublished paper delivered by the then Minister of Justice, Dr Faustin Nteziyayo at a conference held in Geneva in December 1998, organised by me at the request of the Swiss government.
13 Madeleine Morris, 'The Trials of Concurrent Jurisdiction: The Case of Rwanda', *Duke Journal of Comparative and International Law* (Spring 1997), p. 353.
14 Faustin Nteziyayo, unpublished paper at conference in Geneva in December 1998.

15 Ibid.
16 *International Herald Tribune*, 25 April 1999.
17 Stef Vandeginste of the University of Antwerp (Belgium) delivered an excellent paper on this subject at the All Africa Conference on African Principles of Conflict Resolution and Reconciliation, November 1999. The paper is entitled 'Justice, Reconciliation and Reparation After Genocide and Crimes Against Humanity: The Proposed Establishment of Popular Gacaca Tribunals in Rwanda'.
18 George Mitchell, 'Towards Peace in Northern Ireland', 22 Fordham Intl, LJ 1136, 1138.
19 *All Truth is Bitter: A Report of the Visit of Dr Alex Boraine, Deputy Chairman of the South African Truth and Reconciliation Commission, to Northern Ireland* (Belfast: NIACRO and Victim Support Northern Ireland 1999).
20 Ibid.
21 Ibid.
22 Ibid.
23 Alex Boraine et al. (eds.), *Dealing with the Past*, p. 16.
24 The organisations working with victims included the Victim Liaison Unit, the Social Services Omagh, North Belfast Survivors of Trauma, Cost of the Troubles, and Wave.

CONCLUSION

1 *New York Times*, 29 March, 2000, p. E5.
2 Yvonne Mokgoro, *The Protection of Cultural Identity in the Constitution and the Creation of National Unity in South Africa: A Contradiction in Terms?*
3 *The Moral and Political Writings of Mahatma Gandhi*, 624 (Raghava Iyer ed, 1986).
4 John Braithwaite, *Restorative Justice: Assessing Optimistic and Pessimistic Accounts*, 25 Crime and Justice 1, 2 (1999).
5 Luc Huyse, 'Justice After Transition: On the Choices Successor Elites Make in Dealing with the Past', in Neil Kritz (ed.), *Transitional Justice*, p. 342.
6 In an unpublished paper entitled 'Institutions for Restorative Justice:

The South African Truth and Reconciliation Commission', Jennifer J. Llewellyn and Robert Howse offer a very important and valuable defence of the South African model as an exercise in restorative justice. They are both in the Faculty of Law at the University of Toronto. Jennifer Llewellyn worked for the Research Department of the TRC at the national office in Cape Town. Robert Howse served on a panel in 1994 advising the South African government on the legal framework for the TRC.

7   Ibid.
8   Luc Huyse, 'Justice After Transition'.
9   Aryeh Neier, 'What Should Be Done About The Guilty?', *New York Review of Books*, 1 February 1990, p. 34.
10 Lawrence Weschler, *A Miracle, A Universe*, pp. 245–6.
11 Carlos Nino, *Radical Evil on Trial*, p. 7.
12 William Shawcross, *Deliver Us From Evil* (New York: Simon & Schuster, 2000), p. 399.
13 Richard B. Bilder, 'Rethinking

International Human Rights: What Have We Learnt, Where Are We Going?' (paper presented at the European University Institute, Academy of European Law, 10th Anniversary Session on Human Rights, 21 June–2 July 1999).
14 Ibid., p. 13.
15 Donald W. Shriver, *An Ethic for Enemies*, p. 65.
16 Adam Hothschild, 'The Writing Life', *Book World*, 19 December 1999, p. 9.
17 Surveys published in the *New York Times*, 9 October 1996, 12 June 1999, and 15 July 1999, quoted in Richard B. Bilder, 'Rethinking International Human Rights'.
18 Hannah Arendt, *The Human Condition*, pp. 212–13.
19 Quoted By Shari Motro in a short essay prepared for my class at the School of Law, New York University, October 1999.
20 Hannah Arendt, *The Human Condition*.
21 Maya Angelou, Inaugural Poem, *The Complete Collected Poems of Maya Angelou*, (New York: Random House, 1994).

Select bibliography

ACKERMAN, BRUCE. *The Future of Liberal Revolution.* New Haven: Yale University Press, 1992.

ALOMES, ANNA. *Power in Philosophy: Two Arguments for Nonviolence Today.* Unpublished PhD Thesis, University of Tasmania, Australia, 1998.

ARENDT, HANNAH. *The Human Condition: A Study of the Central Conditions Facing Modern Man.* Garden City, NY: Doubleday Anchor Books, 1959.

———. *Eichmann in Jerusalem: A Report on the Banality of Evil.* New York: Penguin, 1977.

ASMAL, KADER. *Victims, Survivors and Citizens – Human Rights, Reparations and Reconciliation.* Inaugural Lecture at the University of the Western Cape Town, 25 May 1992.

ASMAL, KADER, LOUISE ASMAL, and ROBERT SURESH ROBERTS. *Reconciliation Through Truth: A Reckoning of Apartheid's Criminal Governance.* Cape Town: David Philip, 1996.

BALDWIN, PETER. *Reworking the Past: Hitler, the Holocaust, and the Historians' Debate.* Boston: Beacon, 1990.

BASSIOUNI, M. CHERIF. *Crimes Against Humanity in International Criminal Law.* Norwell, Mass.: Nijhoff, 1992.

———. *The Statute of the International Criminal Court: A Documentary History.* New York: Transnational Publishers Inc., 1998.

BONHOEFFER, DIETRICH. *The Cost of Discipleship.* Norwich: Fletcher & Son, 1948.

BORAINE, ALEX, JANET LEVY, and RONEL SCHEFFER (eds.). *Dealing With the Past.* Cape Town: IDASA, 1994.

BORAINE, ALEX, and JANET LEVY (eds.). *The Healing of a Nation?* Cape Town: Justice in Transition, 1994.

Bringing Them Home: Report of the National Inquiry into the Separation of Aboriginal and Torres Strait Islander Children From Their Families, Human Rights and Equal Opportunities Council, Australia, 1997.

BROOKS, ROY L. (ed.). *When Sorry Isn't Enough: The Controversy over Apologies and Reparations for Human Injustice.* New York

[453]

and London: New York University Press, 1999.

DE KLERK, F.W. *The Last Trek: A New Beginning.* London: Macmillan, 1998.

DYZENHAUS, DAVID. *Judging the Judges, Judging Ourselves: Truth, Reconciliation and the Apartheid Legal Order.* Oxford: Hart Publishing, 1997.

FRANKEL, MARVIN. *Out of the Shadows of the Night: The Struggle for International Human Rights.* New York: Delacorte Press, 1989.

FRIEDMAN, LEON, and SUSAN TIEFENBRUN (eds.). *War Crimes and War Crimes Tribunals: Past, Present and Future*, Vol. 3. Hofstra University School of Law, 1999.

FUKUYAMA, FRANCIS. *The End of History and the Last Man.* London: Penguin, 1992.

GALAWAY, BURT, and JOE HUDSON (eds.). *Restorative Justice: International Perspectives.* New York: Criminal Justice Press (USA), Kugler Publications, 1996.

GARTON ASH, TIMOTHY. *The Magic Lantern: The Revolution of '89 Witnessed in Warsaw, Budapest, Berlin and Prague.* New York: Random House, 1990.

——. *The File: A Personal History.* New York: Vintage Books, 1997.

GASTROW, SHELAGH. *Who's Who in South African Politics.* Johannesburg: Ravan Press, 1995.

GERWEL, GERT JOHANNES. 'Reconciliation: Holy Grail or Secular Pact?', in Charles Villa-Vicencio and Wilhelm Verwoerd (eds.), *Looking Back/Reaching Forward: Reflections on the South African Truth and Reconciliation Commission.* Cape Town: Juta and University of Cape Town Press, 1999.

GLENNY, MISHA. *The Fall of Yugoslavia: The Third Balkan War*, third revised edition. New York: Penguin Books, 1996.

GOLDHAGEN, D. *Hitler's Willing Executioners.* New York: Knopf, 1996.

GOUREVITCH, PHILIP. *We Wish to Inform You that Tomorrow We Will Be Killed With Our Families: Stories from Rwanda.* New York: Farrar Straus and Giroux, 1998.

HAYNER, PRISCILLA B. 'Fifteen Truth Commissions, 1974–1994: A Comparative Study', in *Human Rights Quarterly* 16 (4). November 1994.

HILL, CHERRY ANNETTE. *Transitional Justice in South Africa: The Truth and Reconciliation Commission is the Most Appropriate Policy to Deal with Human Rights Violations in South Africa.* Unpublished MA dissertation, University of Otago, Dunedin, New Zealand, 1997.

HOLBROOK, RICHARD. *To End a War*, revised edition. New York: Modern Library, 1999.

IGNATIEFF, MICHAEL. 'Articles of Faith', in *Index on Censorship* 5, 1996.

——. *The Warrior's Honor: Ethnic War and the Modern Conscience.* New York: Owl Books, 1997.

Index on Censorship, Volumes 5 and 25, Writers & Scholars
  International Ltd., London, 1996.
JASPERS, KARL. *The Question of German Guilt*. New York: The Dial
  Press, 1947.
JONKER, INGRID. *Selected Poems*. Cape Town: Human & Rousseau,
  1988.
JOYNER, CHRISTOPHER C. (ed.). *Reining in Impunity for
  International Crimes and Serious Violations of Fundamental
  Human Rights: Proceedings of the Siracusa Conference 17–21
  September 1998*, Association Internationale de Droit Penal, 1998.
KRITZ, NEIL J. (ed.). *Transitional Justice: How Emerging
  Democracies Reckon With Former Regimes*, Volumes I, II, and III.
  Washington DC: United States Institute for Peace, 1995.
KROG, ANTJIE. *Country of My Skull*. Johannesburg: Random
  House, 1998.
LEVINSON, SANFORD. *Written in Stone: Public Monuments in
  Changing Societies*. Durham and London: Duke University Press,
  1998.
MAIER, CHARLES. *The Unmasterable Past: History, Holocaust and
  German National Identity*. Cambridge, Mass.: Harvard University
  Press, 1988.
MALAMUD-GOTI, JAIME. *Game Without End*. Norman and
  London: University of Oklahoma Press, 1996.
MCADAMS, A. JAMES. *Transitional Justice and the Rule of Law in
  New Democracies*. Notre Dame: University of Notre Dame Press,
  1997.
MEIRING, PIET. *Chronicle of the Truth Commission*.
  Vanderbijlpark: Carpe Diem Books, 1999.
MEREDITH, MARTIN, and TINA ROSENBERG. *Coming to Terms:
  South Africa's Search for Truth*. New York: Public Affairs, 1999.
MICHNIK, ADAM. *Letters from Prison and Other Essays*. Berkeley:
  University of California Press, 1990.
MIGNONE, EMILIO F. *Witness to the Truth: The Complicity of
  Church and Dictatorship in Argentina*. New York: Orbis Books,
  1988.
MINOW, MARTHA. *Between Vengeance and Forgiveness*. Boston:
  Beacon Press, 1998.
NEIER, ARYEH. *War Crimes: Brutality, Genocide, Terror, and the
  Struggle for Justice*. New York: Times Books, 1999.
NINO, CARLOS SANTIAGO. *Radical Evil on Trial*. New Haven and
  London: Yale University Press, 1996.
ORENTLICHER, DIANE F. 'Addressing Gross Human Rights
  Abuses: Punishment and Victim Compensation', in Louis Henkin
  and John L. Hargrove (eds.), *Human Rights: An Agenda for the
  Next Century*. Washington DC: American Society of International
  Law, 1994.
ORR, WENDY. *From Biko to Basson*. Saxonwold: Contra Press, 2000.
OSIEL, MARK. *Mass Atrocity, Collective Memory, and the Law*.
  New Brunswick, NJ: Transaction Publishers, 1997.
OTTAWAY, DAVID. *Chained Together: Mandela, de Klerk, and the*

Struggle to Remake South Africa. New York: Times Books, 1993.

PROSS, CHRISTIAN. *Paying for the Past: The Struggle Over Reparations for Surviving Victims of the Nazi Terror.* Baltimore: Johns Hopkins University Press, 1998.

RATNER, STEVEN R., and JASON S. ABRAMS. *Accountability for Human Rights Atrocities in International Law: Beyond the Nuremberg Legacy.* Oxford: Oxford University Press, 1997.

ROSENBERG, TINA. *Children of Cain: Violence and the Violent in Latin America.* New York: Penguin, 1992.

————. *The Haunted Land: Facing Europe's Ghosts After Communism.* New York: Vintage Books, 1995.

SHAWCROSS, WILLIAM. *Deliver Us From Evil: Peacekeepers, Warlords and a World of Endless Conflict.* New York: Simon & Schuster, 2000.

SHRIVER, DONALD W., JR. *An Ethic for Enemies: Forgiveness in Politics.* New York: Oxford University Press, 1995.

SMITH, KATHLEEN E. *Remembering Stalin's Victims.* Ithaca and London: Cornell University Press, 1996.

TAYLOR, TELFORD. *The Anatomy of the Nuremberg Trials.* New York: Knopf, 1992.

TIMMERMAN, JACOBO. *Prisoner Without a Name, Cell Without a Number.* New York: Alfred Knopf, 1981.

TRUTH AND RECONCILIATION COMMISSION. *Report of the Truth and Reconciliation Commission*, Volumes 1–5. Cape Town: Juta, 1998.

TUTU, DESMOND. *No Future Without Forgiveness.* London: Rider Books, 1999.

VILLA-VICENCIO, CHARLES, and WILHELM VERWOERD (eds.). *Looking Back/Reaching Forward: Reflections on the South African Truth and Reconciliation Commission.* Cape Town: Juta and University of Cape Town Press, 1999.

VOLF, MIROSLAV. *Exclusion and Embrace: A Theological Exploration of Identity, Otherness and Reconciliation.* Nashville: Abingdon Press, 1996.

WESCHLER, LAWRENCE. *A Miracle, A Universe: Settling Accounts with Torturers.* New York: Penguin, 1990.

WIESENTHAL, SIMON, *The Sunflower: On the Possibilities and Limits of Forgiveness.* New York: Schocken Books, 1998.

WINK, WALTER. *Healing a Nation's Wounds.* Uppsala, Sweden: Life and Peace Institute, 1997.

ZALAQUETT, JOSÉ. 'Balancing Ethical Imperatives and Political Constraints: The Dilemma of New Democracies Confronting Past Human Rights Violations', in Neil J. Kritz (ed.), *Transitional Justice*, Washington DC: US Institute for Peace, 1995.

Index